Scalable Data Management for Future Hardware

Kai-Uwe Sattler • Alfons Kemper •
Thomas Neumann • Jens Teubner
Editors

Scalable Data Management for Future Hardware

Springer

Editors

Kai-Uwe Sattler
Databases and Information Systems Group
TU Ilmenau
Ilmenau, Germany

Thomas Neumann
Chair of Data Science and Engineering
TU München
Garching, Germany

Alfons Kemper
Chair of Database Systems
TU München
Garching, Germany

Jens Teubner
Databases and Information Systems Group
TU Dortmund
Dortmund, Germany

ISBN 978-3-031-74099-2 ISBN 978-3-031-74097-8 (eBook)
https://doi.org/10.1007/978-3-031-74097-8

This work was founded by the German Research Foundation (DFG) as part of the priority programs “Scalable Data Management for Future Hardware” (SPP 2037).

This Springer imprint is published by the registered company Springer Nature Switzerland AG
The registered company address is: Gewerbestrasse 11, 6330 Cham, Switzerland

Foreword

Computer science and the IT industry are currently undergoing significant and fundamental changes at many levels. On the one hand, the business model has evolved from a manufacturing industry (software and hardware) to a service industry based on cloud providers offering hardware and software as a service. This alone has enormous implications for the technology as the economies of scale and the highly shared infrastructure of the cloud create opportunities for optimization and specialization not available before. On the other hand, the relevant applications, use cases, and workloads have become mainly data driven, involving extraordinary amounts of data and very tight performance as well as efficiency requirements. These changes are happening at a time where limitations at the physical and economic level prevent us from producing faster general-purpose processors (CPUs), a drawback that is being addressed through hardware specialization where use-case-specific hardware is developed to be able to meet the requirements of common applications.

The Scalable Data Management for Future Hardware of the DFG priority program has tackled these challenges from the perspective of data processing, a cornerstone of data science and the machine learning revolution we are experiencing. Data management systems, and especially relational databases, are still one of the largest software industries. Neither the cloud nor machine learning has changed that. However, their role and how they are used have changed and are quickly evolving. For instance, on the software side, now all major database machines support vector search and large-scale vectors, something that would have been difficult to imagine just 5 years ago given the characteristics of vector data and the operations performed over it. On the hardware side, there is a growing amount of examples from both industry and academia of tailoring database engines to new hardware (networking, new memory models, new processors, accelerators, etc.). The researchers in the program have pioneered and led many of these efforts, their work having now become a major reference for anybody exploring the area. The program has also been a great, and much needed, source of talent covering both the data management and the hardware specialization side, creating the basis for future research and education programs.

The chapters in this book provide a glimpse of the highly innovative work done as part of the program, covering topics that encompass from new memory models and new memory technologies to heterogeneous computing, tackling research questions related to high-scale parallelism, consistency, bottlenecks caused by interconnects, reconfigurable computing, modern networking, and non-volatile memory in the context of various applications (query processing, graph databases, event processing, etc.). The work reported provides a comprehensive coverage of the topics and provides excellent examples of the opportunities new hardware has to offer. It is important to note that the topics explored do so in great detail, not only in terms of describing a design but also exploring the practical implications for data management systems and database engines in terms of how their architecture needs to evolve. It is also interesting that the book covers a very insightful spectrum between ideas that can be applied to existing engines without having to do major changes to radically new designs that open up intriguing opportunities for future systems.

Data management is and remains a key component of the data science revolution, maybe attracting less attention than machine learning and large language models but still acting as a key enabler and a source of ideas to improve the performance and efficiency of what are now the largest data processing engines ever built. But data management systems need to evolve with the times, and that requires to adapt and adopt new hardware. This book summarizes an impressive amount of work done in the priority program in this direction, with many valuable insights that will serve as inspiration for future work and also having trained the first generation of researchers equipped to address the challenges ahead of us.

Zurich
June 2024

Gustavo Alonso

Preface

Data management is one of the central tasks in many applications and an indispensable component in modern IT stacks. The spectrum of applications ranges from managing structured business data in ERP or ordering systems, over answering queries in decision-support systems, backends on cloud applications, or embedded systems, to managing data and models in AI applications. The requirements have continued to evolve in recent years: While initially the management transactional data with consistency (ACID) guarantees was the main tasks of database systems, modern data management solutions now also support complex analyses on very differently structured data (from tables, graphs, and semi-structured data to texts, images, and videos) through to highly dynamic data streams. Data management systems typically provide abstractions for the application layers above them: data structures and models for representing data, query languages for accessing and processing data, and system abstractions for transparently leveraging storage hierarchies or parallel or distributed architectures. However, the efficient implementation of data management requires leveraging the underlying layers down to the hardware, with the boundaries constantly shifting. While disk-based external storage used to be the bottleneck in the past, main memory accesses or concurrency control in multi-core systems are now performance critical. At the same time, hardware developments in recent years offer a wide range of possibilities for efficient use in data management tasks. Examples are:

- Multi-core CPUs: Modern CPUs offer up to 100 cores at the commodity level, and next-generation CPUs are expected to offer several hundred cores. To enable high levels of parallelism, some architectures already provide hardware support for the necessary synchronization, such as transactional memory. Leveraging this parallelism for database processing is still an open question.
- Co-processors such as GPUs and FPGAs: Special-purpose computing devices such as GPUs and FPGAs allow for much higher levels of parallelism, significantly accelerating compute-intensive tasks, including database tasks. In addition, heterogeneous hardware designs such as coupled CPU-FPGA and CPU-GPU architectures, as well as fast interconnects between the CPU and

co-processing units, represent a trend toward tighter integration that makes expensive data transfers cheaper or even unnecessary.
- Novel memory and storage technologies like NVRAM and SSD: Modern in-memory database system solutions still rely mostly on block-based media for ensuring persistence of data. In recent years, memory technologies such as non-volatile or persistent memory (PMem) have promised byte-addressable persistence with latencies close to DRAM. Though commercial PMem products are discontinued, emerging technologies such as CXL offer new opportunities for architectures with remote, shared, or disaggregated memory. These memory technologies together with advances in SSD performance require to revisit memory and storage hierarchies in data management systems.
- High-speed networks: Both in scale-up and scale-out scenarios, efficient interconnects play a crucial role. Network technologies like RDMA (Remote DMA), e.g., based on Gbit Ethernet or InfiniBand, provide direct access to memory of remote nodes. Furthermore, smart network interface cards (NIC) can act as accelerators for in-network processing. Utilizing these technologies in database systems requires new concepts.

Based on these observations, we derived the thesis that data management architectures need to undergo a radical shift to meet current and future requirements. Since 2017, we have been tackling this challenge within the framework of the DFG-funded priority program SPP 2037 "Scalable Data Management for Future Hardware." The goal of the priority program was to bring together researchers from the fields of database systems, operating systems, and distributed systems to investigate the possibilities and consequences of modern and future hardware in system architectures for data management.

In two 3-year phases, a total of 12 projects from 22 PIs investigated a wide range of data management architectures in conjunction with current hardware developments. The program was accompanied by two Dagstuhl seminars (Seminar 18251, "Database Architectures for Modern Hardware," 2018, and Seminar 21283, "Data Structures for Modern Memory and Storage Hierarchies," 2021) as well as regular internal workshops. The results of this priority are summarized in this book. In nine chapters, the authors present results primarily from the second phase of the program.

In Chap. 1, "ADAMANT: Hardware-Accelerated Query Processing Made Easy," an approach for the integration of co-processing units such as FPGA and GPUs is presented that supports cross-device parallelization of SQL queries. Furthermore, techniques for FPGA-based query-specific hardware acceleration as well as approximate query processing are introduced.

Heterogeneous hardware environments are also addressed in Chap. 2, "Query Processing on Heterogeneous Hardware," by exploring methodologies for executing database queries on any processor without manual adjustments. For this purpose, a compilation of database and stream processing queries into optimized code is discussed considering the use of GPUs, workload distribution, and data transfer bottlenecks, e.g., by examining NVLink 2.0 technology.

Next, in Chap. 3, “Efficient Event Processing on Modern Hardware,” the domain of complex event processing with both continuous queries and analytical ad hoc queries is considered. Multi-core CPUs and GPUs are explored for efficient processing of pattern-matching operators, while modern storage technologies are used for ingestion and ad hoc queries.

In Chap. 4, “Hybrid Transactional/Analytical Graph Processing in Modern Memory Hierarchies,” the authors exploit modern memory hierarchies including persistent memory for graph database systems supporting hybrid transactional/analytical (HTAP) workloads. In addition, graph analysis in GPU-based accelerators with dedicated memory is enabled by efficient mechanisms for data transfer and consistency.

Chapter 5, “MxKernel: A Bare-Metal Runtime System for Database Operations on Heterogeneous Many-Core Hardware,” presents a runtime environment that provides control flow primitives called MxTasks that can be annotated with application-specific hints. Using such hints, the runtime system provides automatic synchronization, prefetching, and dynamic resource partitioning.

The authors of Chap. 6 “Scaling beyond DRAM without Compromising Performance” present approaches for scaling database systems beyond the main memory capacity of a single server. This includes system approaches for a storage engine and PMem-optimized storage for transactional workloads, a programming model for disaggregated systems, and a just-in-time query compilation framework for ARM processors.

The topic of Chap. 7, “ReProVide: Query Optimization and Near-Data Processing on Reconfigurable SoCs for Big Data Analysis,” is near-data processing using FPGA accelerators. Based on a SoC architecture, a reconfigurable approach for flexible loading and execution of query operators on relational and streaming data is presented.

The work presented in Chap. 8, “Scalable Data Management on Next-Generation Data Center Networks,” examines how modern network infrastructure such as RDMA affects the design of disaggregated databases. In addition to RDMA, programmable networks are considered for database processing by presenting in-network OLTP processing and a network-driven data shuffling approach.

Finally, the authors of Chap. 9, “Managing Very Large Data Sets on Directly-Attached NVMe Arrays,” discuss the impact of modern fast storage devices such as NVMe arrays on the architecture and implementation of storage engines for database systems. Based on an evaluation of the performance tradeoffs, they show that the aggregated bandwidth of ten or more NVMe SSDs can approach main memory.

We hope that this book will not only give readers an insight into the results of the program but also provide inspiration for future work beyond the database area.

Especially a comprehensive system view as a combination of data management, operating systems, distributed systems, and computer architecture is on the one hand necessary to address the requirements from practice and on the other hand offers great potential for innovative ideas and exciting research questions.

Ilmenau, Germany — Kai-Uwe Sattler
Garching, Germany — Alfons Kemper
Garching, Germany — Thomas Neumann
Dortmund, Germany — Jens Teubner
June 2024

Acknowledgements

The work presented in this book was funded by the German Research Foundation (DFG) in the context of the priority program SPP 2037 "Scalable Data Management for Future Hardware."

We would like to thank the DFG for the funding, without which this research work would not have been possible.

We also thank the members of our advisory board, Goetz Graefe, Peter Boncz, Theo Härder, and Franz Färber, who accompanied us, especially at the beginning of the program.

Finally, we thank all reviewers of the program, the projects, and our research papers for their valuable feedback.

Contents

Contributors

David Broneske German Center for Higher Education Research and Science Studies, Hannover, Germany

Vitalii Burtsev Hardware-Oriented Technical Computer Science, Faculty of Electrical Engineering and Information Technology, University of Magdeburg, Magdeburg, Germany

Anna Drewes Hardware-Oriented Technical Computer Science, Faculty of Electrical Engineering and Information Technology, University of Magdeburg, Magdeburg, Germany

Thilo Pionteck Hardware-Oriented Technical Computer Science, Faculty of Electrical Engineering and Information Technology, University of Magdeburg, Magdeburg, Germany

Bala Gurumurthy Databases and Software Engineering, Faculty of Computer Science, University of Magdeburg, Magdeburg, Germany

Gunter Saake Databases and Software Engineering, Faculty of Computer Science, University of Magdeburg, Magdeburg, Germany

Anastasiia Kozar Technische Universität Berlin, Berlin, Germany

Janis von Bleichert vB Internet GmbH, Berlin, Germany

Sebastian Breß Snowflake, Inc., Berlin, Germany

Philipp M. Grulich Technische Universität Berlin, Berlin, Germany

Clemens Lutz NVIDIA, Santa Clara, CA, USA

Tilmann Rabl HPI, University of Potsdam, Potsdam, Germany

Viktor Rosenfeld Technische Universität Berlin, Berlin, Germany

Jonas Traub Technische Universität Berlin, Berlin, Germany

Steffen Zeuch Technische Universität Berlin, Berlin, Germany

Volker Markl Technische Universität Berlin, DFKI GmbH, Berlin, Germany

Marius Kuhrt University of Marburg, Marburg, Germany

Nikolaus Glombiewski University of Marburg, Marburg, Germany

Michael Körber University of Marburg, Marburg, Germany

Andreas Morgen University of Marburg, Marburg, Germany

Dominik Brandenstein University of Marburg, Marburg, Germany

Bernhard Seeger University of Marburg, Marburg, Germany

Alexander Baumstark Database & Information Systems Group, TU Ilmenau, Ilmenau, Germany

Muhammad Attahir Jibril Database & Information Systems Group, TU Ilmenau, Ilmenau, Germany

Kai-Uwe Sattler Database & Information Systems Group, TU Ilmenau, Ilmenau, Germany

Marcel Lütke Dreimann Osnabrück University, Osnabrück, Germany

Michael Müller Osnabrück University, Osnabrück, Germany

Olaf Spinczyk Osnabrück University, Osnabrück, Germany

Jan Mühlig TU Dortmund University, Dortmund, Germany

Jens Teubner TU Dortmund University, Dortmund, Germany

Lukas Vogel Technische Universität München, München, Germany

Christoph Anneser Technische Universität München, München, Germany

Ferdinand Gruber Technische Universität München, München, Germany

Thomas Neumann Technische Universität München, München, Germany

Jana Giceva Technische Universität München, München, Germany

Alfons Kemper Technische Universität München, München, Germany

Tobias Hah Friedrich-Alexander-Universität Erlangen-Nürnberg (FAU), Erlangen, Germany

Maximilian Langohr Friedrich-Alexander-Universität Erlangen-Nürnberg (FAU), Erlangen, Germany

Andreas Becher TU Ilmenau, Erlangen, Germany

Lekshmi Beena Gopalakrishnan Nair Friedrich-Alexander-Universität Erlangen-Nürnberg (FAU), Erlangen, Germany

Klaus Meyer-Wegener Friedrich-Alexander-Universität Erlangen-Nürnberg (FAU), Erlangen, Germany

Jürgen Teich Friedrich-Alexander-Universität Erlangen-Nürnberg (FAU), Erlangen, Germany

Stefan Wildermann Friedrich-Alexander-Universität Erlangen-Nürnberg (FAU), Erlangen, Germany

Matthias Jasny Technische Universität Darmstadt, Darmstadt, Germany

Tobias Ziegler Technische Universität Darmstadt, Darmstadt, Germany

Carsten Binnig Technische Universität Darmstadt, Darmstadt, Germany

Gabriel Haas Technische Universität München, Darmstadt, Germany

Adnan Alhomssi RelationalAI, Erlangen, Germany

Viktor Leis Technische Universität München, München, Germany

Chapter 1
ADAMANT: Hardware-Accelerated Query Processing Made Easy

David Broneske, Vitalii Burtsev, Anna Drewes, Bala Gurumurthy, Thilo Pionteck, and Gunter Saake

Abstract We present ADAMANT, an adaptive data management architecture for evolving heterogeneous hardware/software systems. The ADAMANT system enables plug'n'play integration of co-processors such as GPUs and FPGAs, provides a unified runtime that supports cross-device parallelization of SQL query execution on arbitrary co-processors at runtime, and supports multi-query processing. We discuss the concepts behind and performance of ADAMANT following an example query (TPC-H Q6), present different execution models for cross-device execution, and provide an FPGA hardware architecture that allows the implementation of query-specific hardware accelerators at runtime. In addition, we introduce a new approach for approximate query processing for FPGAs. Our performance analysis concludes that the use of hardware accelerators and device-specific implementations of query operators as part of a common system can provide significant speedups over state-of-the-art query execution engines.

1.1 Introduction

The database community faces the extreme challenge that the volume of data to be processed has increased exponentially in recent years. While the amount of data created, captured, copied, and consumed in 2020 was approximately 64.2 zettabytes,

D. Broneske (✉)
German Center for Higher Education Research and Science Studies, Hannover, Germany
e-mail: broneske@dzhw.eu

V. Burtsev · A. Drewes · T. Pionteck
Hardware-Oriented Technical Computer Science, Faculty of Electrical Engineering and Information Technology, University of Magdeburg, Magdeburg, Germany
e-mail: vitalii.burtsev@ovgu.de; anna.drewes@ovgu.de; thilo.pionteck@ovgu.de

B. Gurumurthy · G. Saake
Databases and Software Engineering, Faculty of Computer Science, University of Magdeburg, Magdeburg, Germany
e-mail: bala.gurumurthy@ovgu.de; gunter.saake@ovgu.de

K.-U. Sattler et al. (eds.), *Scalable Data Management for Future Hardware*,
https://doi.org/10.1007/978-3-031-74097-8_1

it is predicted that it will grow to more than 180 zettabytes by 2025 [42]. CPU-based database systems reach their performance and scalability limits with this amount of data, especially with regard to the memory wall, power consumption, and fast response times. This requires new approaches at the hardware and algorithm level, such as integrating co-processors into database systems or approximating query processing to lower response times.

The traditional approach to data analytics has been to process data in batches, often taking minutes or hours to yield results. This offline processing contrasts sharply with the goals of interactive analytics, which aims to deliver query responses within seconds, thereby enabling rapid hypothesis testing. Approximate query processing (AQP) has emerged as a solution, allowing database systems to provide aggregated responses to queries on large datasets in a timely way, thereby bringing us closer to the ideal of interactive analytics.

In order to speed up the exact response to database queries, the use of heterogeneous hardware architectures appears to be promising. In heterogeneous systems, CPUs are supported by specialized co-processors such as Graphical Processing Units (GPUs) or Field Programmable Gate Arrays (FPGAs). The advantage of heterogeneous hardware systems is that multiple operations can be performed in parallel on different devices. Query operators can be mapped to the hardware device for which the most efficient implementation of an operator is available. However, these benefits are countered by significant challenges. First, a mechanism must be provided to integrate co-processors with their supported set of query operators into the database management system (DBMS), and second, all co-processors require custom operator implementations to process the queries. In particular, the provision of operator implementations for a specific hardware device can be very time-consuming and requires domain knowledge.

To address these challenges, we developed ADAMANT, an adaptive data management solution for evolving heterogeneous hardware/software systems. ADAMANT allows new co-processors to be integrated without reworking other components of the query engine. This is supported by pluggable interfaces that encapsulate all interactions with co-processors and a unified runtime that handles execution on arbitrary co-processors, with a chunked execution model for scalable query processing.

We show the features, flexibility, and benefits of ADAMANT through Query 6 of the TPC-H benchmark [45] throughout this chapter. In particular, we will discuss the execution model of ADAMANT, which is based on (device-specific) primitives, the influence of the underlying hardware on an appropriate primitive realization, and how primitive fusion can increase efficiency. We will present an approach to produce hardware accelerators for arbitrary queries on an FPGA at runtime and discuss different execution models for cross-device execution of queries on CPUs and GPUs. In addition, we will present approaches for multi-query processing. For approximate query processing, an approach based on the concept of Bag of Little Bootstraps (BLP) will be discussed.

The rest of the chapter is organized as follows: Sect. 1.2 presents the overall structure of ADAMANT and discusses the specific challenges for realizing plug'n'play capabilities in DBMSs. Section 1.3 presents a novel approach to an FPGA-based approximate query-processing accelerator. The concept of device-specific primitives is introduced in Sect. 1.4, which is used to discuss the FPGA overlay architecture in Sect. 1.5 and the cross-device execution models in Sect. 1.6. Optimization possibilities for multi-query processing are presented in Sect. 1.7. The chapter ends with a conclusion in Sect. 1.8.

1.2 Challenges for ADAMANT's Plug'n'Play Architecture

For an effective integration of modern heterogeneous processors into the query-processing pipeline, there are several adaptations necessary, each posing a specific challenge. The challenges are (C1) the tuning for device-specific processing capabilities, (C2) the exploitation of the full processing power, and (C3) the effective simultaneous execution of multiple queries at once. We exemplify necessary changes to the database system in Fig. 1.1 by using the standard database processing workflow split into query translation and query execution [39]. In query translation, the SQL query is parsed and standardized, after which optimization takes place, which usually transforms the logical query graph into a physical optimized execu-

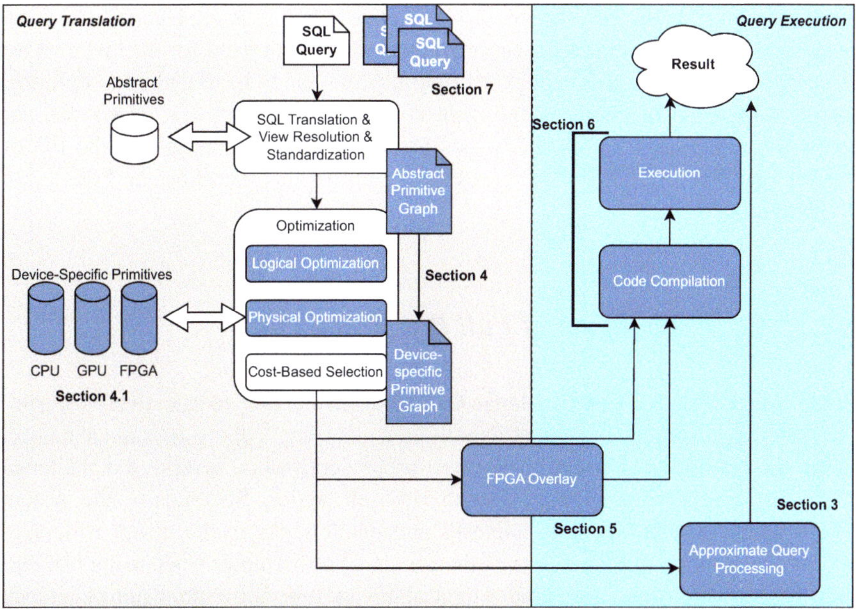

Fig. 1.1 Adapted query-processing workflow when incorporating heterogeneous co-processors in a plug'n'play fashion. White components represent unchanged steps, while blue components represent adaptations to the standard process

tion plan. This plan is then prospectively compiled and executed. In the following, we outline the necessary changes to this query-processing workflow in order to overcome the challenges.

1.2.1 C1: Device-Specific Processing Capabilities

Due to their task-based specialization, processors and co-processors provide different processing capabilities [6, 37, 38]. For instance, CPUs provide out-of-order execution and branch prediction, which is why they are best suited for latency-critical tasks. In contrast, GPUs offer massive data-parallel processing capabilities in a SIMT-fashion (single instruction, multiple threads), which is why they are optimized for throughput. FPGAs, on the other hand, can be programmed for any number of operations and sequences of operations. However, due to their limited space and lower clock-frequency, data parallelism is limited, and small pipelines cannot exploit the FPGA's advantages compared to CPUs or GPUs. As a result, the query plan (e.g., operator-at-a-time processing on GPUs vs. pipelining on the FPGA) and also implementations of operators (branching on CPU vs. branch-free processing on GPU) differ per involved device.

Hence, we adapted the standard query-processing workflow by adding primitive definitions (suboperations of database operators introduced in Sect. 1.4) and respective code bases per device in our ADAMANT system. Hence, when co-processors are plugged in, also respective primitives optimized for the device have to be provided. Furthermore, physical optimization has to be extended to optimize for the dimension of choosing the right device-specific primitive. Moreover, our adapted query-processing workflow has a special step for configuring the FPGA overlay (see Sect. 1.5), which is a necessary step for incorporating the FPGA into the workflow.

1.2.2 C2: Exploitation of Full Processing Power

When overcoming the first Challenge C1, the system is able to effectively incorporate different co-processors and efficiently execute a single query on a single device. Given the possibility to use arbitrary (co)-processors from a system, the challenge arises to put all (co)-processors concurrently into action. Specifically, the system would enable a distribution of subtasks and data chunks to the different devices and mind the memory restrictions of the devices. Furthermore, when using FPGAs, their configuration time may hinder their application because the resulting latency overshadows their performance benefits compared to other devices, which keeps this processing power unused.

In order to overcome this challenge, we extend the query execution capabilities of the ADAMANT system by allowing to start executing the query processing in an interpreted fashion. This effectively hides any compilation or configuration time (see Sect. 1.6). Furthermore, we provide a chunking approach that allows for cross-device query execution and even executing larger-than-memory workloads.

1.2.3 C3: Effective Parallel Execution of Multiple Queries

Due to our contributions for C1 and C2, we are now capable of executing a single query across different devices. However, the usual use case is to serve several user requests in parallel, leading to multiple queries being processed concurrently. The question is whether concurrently running queries with enough similarity can be optimized by sharing intermediate results when executing. This is a feature that would influence the final query plan and is, thus, impacting logical query optimization. Furthermore, since many users are on an exploratory search for data, their results do not always need to be 100 % exact. Hence, this is an additional optimization that could decrease the load on the system and lead to a better throughput when running multiple queries.

To this end, we investigate mechanisms to share and reuse results of concurrently running queries (see Sect. 1.7), where the impact of query similarity on the resulting performance needs to be regarded. Moreover, we propose an alternative approximate query execution for exploratory queries that do not need the exact query result (see Sect. 1.3).

1.3 Approximate Query Processing

Approximate query processing (AQP) is essential for rapidly analyzing large datasets where traditional methods are inefficient due to high computational costs and long processing times. AQP strategies balance accuracy and performance by providing fast, though approximate, insight into the data. The following are the main AQP methodologies, each offering solutions to specific data analysis problems that we considered as a basis for developing our own solution.

1.3.1 Approximation Approaches

The online aggregation method by Hellerstein et al. [25] introduces a technique that incrementally refines query results, enabling users to halt the process when results fall within an acceptable error range. This method facilitates interactive data analysis by offering initial rough estimates that progressively become more accurate, thereby considerably shortening the time to reach preliminary insights.

The Stratified Sampling approach, as showcased in BlinkDB [1] and VerdictDB [32], enhances AQP effectiveness by smartly dividing the dataset. This technique segments the dataset into uniform groups, from which samples are independently drawn, boosting sample representativeness, particularly in diverse datasets. The LAQy framework [40] improves stratified sampling by enabling efficient and adaptive sample reuse. It allows for partial reuse of samples by dynamically adjusting them based on the changing predicates of query workloads.

Machine Learning Models for AQP, illustrated by DBEst [30] and DeepDB [26], utilize past query behaviors and data features to anticipate query results. This sophisticated strategy employs machine learning's predictive capabilities to estimate query responses, notably lowering the computational demand by avoiding conventional exhaustive query evaluations.

The AQP++ framework, as developed by Peng et al. [33], introduces a transformative approach by synergizing sampling-based techniques with aggregate precomputation (AggPre) for enhanced interactive analytics. This integration not only speeds up query answering by utilizing precomputed aggregates to refine estimates but also maintains unbiasedness and balances between speed, accuracy, and preprocessing costs. Key to its innovation is the inclusion of Bootstrap Methods for Error Estimation, which utilizes resampling to offer a robust framework for assessing the precision of AQP outcomes.

Bootstrapping [15] is a widely used statistical algorithm for the evaluation of data distributions in datasets. This technique creates a series of resamples from smaller subsets of the original dataset by repeated sampling with replacement. Because of its statistical foundation, bootstrapping is widely used in machine learning. However, bootstrap-based algorithms typically face a significant computational burden due to the resampling process. The size of the resamples in bootstrapping is comparable to the size of the original sample, contributing to the procedure's computational intensity.

1.3.2 Bag of Little Bootstraps

The concept of bootstrapping in statistics involves generating numerous subsamples from the original dataset by resampling with replacement, to form an empirical distribution. This method allows for the estimation of the population distribution based on these subsamples. However, traditional bootstrapping requires processing a large number of data, resulting in significant computational demands, which limits its applicability in various fields.

To address the computational challenges of traditional bootstrapping, Kleiner et al. introduced the Bag of Little Bootstraps (BLB) algorithm [27]. This approach minimizes computational load by utilizing smaller subsamples for resampling and then scaling the results to match the size of the original dataset. This method significantly reduces the amount of data that needs to be processed, making the bootstrapping process more efficient with negligible compromising on accuracy.

When applying the BLB algorithm, a database query is executed on each resampled subset to obtain bootstrap estimates. These individual estimates are then averaged to derive an approximate answer to the original query. The BLB algorithm has demonstrated that to achieve a 95% confidence level in query answers, it is sufficient to use subsamples sized according to a specific formula, where the subsample size b is proportional to the original data size n as $b = n^{\gamma}$ raised to a power γ between 0.6 and 0.9.

This scaling of subsample size, as recommended by the BLB algorithm, means that for a large dataset, the amount of data to be processed can be dramatically reduced, by orders of magnitude. For example, for a dataset of one million values, only twenty to thirty subsamples of approximately four to sixteen thousand values would need to be processed to obtain reliable results, demonstrating the efficiency of the BLB algorithm in reducing computational requirements.

The BLB algorithm's approach to optimizing the balance between accuracy and computational burden by strategically selecting subsample sizes represents a significant advance in the field of statistics. By enabling efficient processing of large datasets while maintaining a high level of confidence in the results, the BLB algorithm offers a practical solution for a wide range of applications and has the potential to transform the way statistical analysis is conducted in large data environments.

1.3.3 Streaming BLB

In order to address the computational demands of traditional bootstrapping and to bring bootstrapping to aggregate approximate query answering, we have developed our approach from standard BLB to allow streamed and pipelined data processing. Several important elements of the algorithm have been revised and replaced. In particular, Poisson bootstrapping [3, 35] allows stream data processing and reduces data transfer, using a method where a subset of distinct values is resampled, each multiplied by a Poisson-distributed coefficient as an estimate of the frequency of occurrence for that particular point in the resample. By crossing the BLB algorithm with Poisson-distributed resampling coefficients, the n-fold resampling of BLB is effectively transformed into a b-fold computation.

Figure 1.2 illustrates the Streaming BLB approach versus the traditional BLB method. In the naive BLB, an entry is selected randomly n times from a subsample of size b, requiring n memory accesses per resample. Each entry's representation in the resample, indicated by a numerical value next to each group, shows the resampling coefficient, which varies across resamples. The right side shows the Streaming BLB method, where resampling coefficients k_i are derived from a distribution, often approximated by a Poisson distribution with $\lambda = n/b$, facilitating the generation of b random numbers. For large λ, the Poisson can be approximated with a normal distribution ($\mu = \lambda$, $\sigma = \sqrt{\mu}$). Data normalization ensures total resampling coefficients match the original data size n.

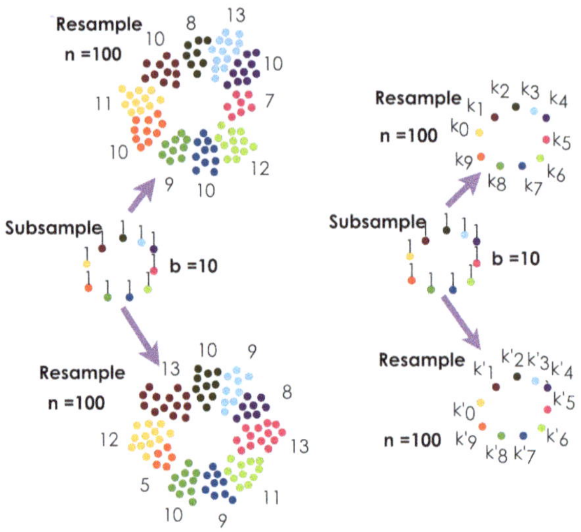

Fig. 1.2 Naive bootstrapping (left) vs. Streaming BLB (right) [8]

The original BLB algorithm lacks data streaming capabilities. Streaming BLB overcomes this by allowing data streaming through its coefficient-based bootstrapping method, enabling parallel processing and hardware acceleration. Yet, this method demands a high-performance generation of random variables with specific probability distributions.

1.3.4 FPGA-Based Bag of Little Bootstraps

Taking into account all the advantages of BLB described above and our modifications to make this algorithm more applicable to accelerators, we chose FPGAs as the test platform. On the one hand, FPGAs offer pipelining and parallelization capabilities that are unmatched by other systems. On the other hand, they are very efficient in terms of power consumption.

1.3.4.1 Gaussian Random Number Generation (GRNG) on FPGAs

The efficient generation of random numbers with a given distribution is critical to the overall performance of the BLB streaming approach. Several strategies [2, 28, 44] balance performance with resource demands, with the Multihat [31] algorithm standing out for its efficiency in streaming resampling, producing a random number each clock cycle. It alters the probability density of uniformly distributed random numbers using additional bits and multiplexers, closely approximating a Gaussian distribution with an 8σ tail accuracy. The Streaming BLB method reduces the

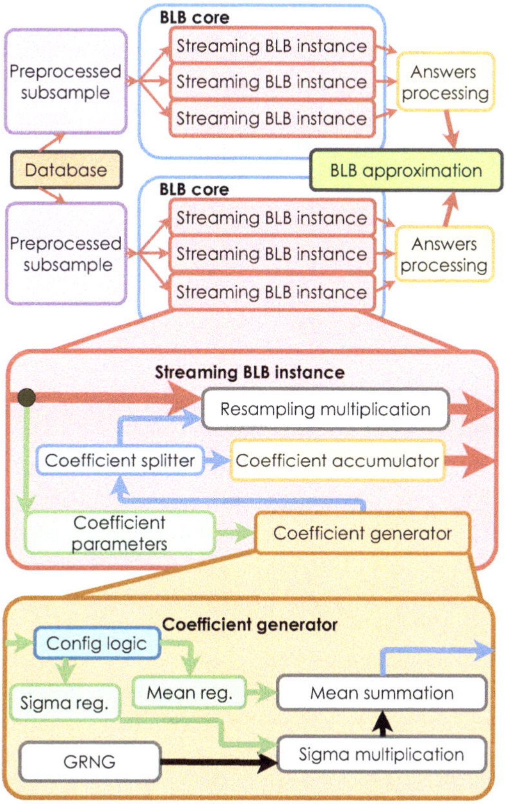

Fig. 1.3 Structure of the BLB Block Design [8]

need for true random numbers by aligning the resampling rate with the expected probability distribution.

1.3.4.2 BLB Block Design

The overall structure of the BLB hardware accelerator is shown in the top part of Fig. 1.3. Each BLB core processes one subsample per time step, while the number of resamples per time step is determined by the number of streaming BLB instances. For each subsample, the individual query response is determined outside the BLB core in a preprocessing step that produces row-wise subsample results, either on CPU or on FPGA. In a post-processing step, the CPU aggregates the results of the individual BLB cores derived from a combination of resamples and subsample counts.

The middle part of Fig. 1.3 shows the structure of a BLB streaming instance, which is responsible for resampling the data. A coefficient generator produces a random value every clock cycle, split for query multiplication and output normalization, ensuring coefficient sums align with the original dataset size. Parameters for the coefficient generator are obtained from the same stream as data for resampling.

The bottom part of Fig. 1.3 shows details of the coefficient generator, with Gaussian values x set to $x' = \sigma x + \mu$. The Multihat GRNG provides a random number for each cycle, supporting a flexible design for alternative generators. Configuration values define resampling coefficient distribution parameters for processing in Streaming BLB.

1.3.5 Test Setup

For evaluation, we tested the performance of the BLB streaming approach for TPC-H Q6 [45] with subsamples on different scale factors (1–100) as an example of a data-intensive query with a heavy aggregation load. The testing was done on a Xilinx ZC706 board with a Zynq-7000 SoC FPGA, running at 125 MHz. For performance evaluation, the FPGA solution is tested against an Intel Core i7-6850K (12 threads, 4 GHz) CPU and an AMD Ryzen 7 5800X (16 threads, 3.6 GHz) CPU. Data storage is facilitated by a Patriot Burst SATA III 2.5" SSD.

The FPGA test system is shown in Fig. 1.4. Subsamples are created on the host CPU and then transferred to the FPGA where the query result for each subsample is computed. The results are then passed to the BLB unit. Here, subsample entries are multiplied by resampling coefficients, and data is aggregated at the output stage. When subsample processing is complete, the system prepares output data and sends it to the host.

The Xilinx DMA/Bridge Subsystem for PCI Express facilitates data transfers via the PCIe interface on the ZC706 accelerator board, which supports two AXI4-Stream channels. Consequently, it can host up to two BLB cores, while the number of resampling threads can scale with the FPGA's capacity, reaching 64 in our setup. For processing TPC-H Q6, the FPGA handles extra arithmetic operations, including comparisons, additions, and multiplications, utilizing 32-bit floating-point arithmetic for enhanced precision and optimization opportunities. This implementation leverages the LOGIcore Floating Point v7.1 [46] IP core for streamlined data processing across the AXI4-Stream interface.

The system's result-processing logic comprises a multiplexer that compiles data packets from the resampling streams, answer accumulators, and normalization

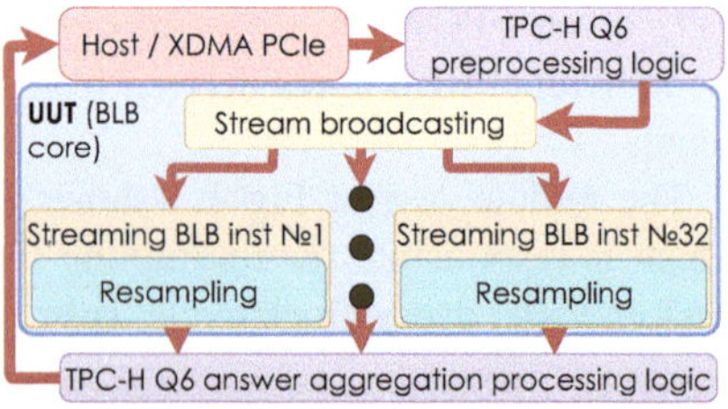

Fig. 1.4 Test system structure [8]

Table 1.1 Zynq XC7Z045 SoC resource utilization

Resource	2 BLB cores Utilization %	One resampling BLB instance
LUT	78.19	2977
LUTRAM	23.92	357
FF	57.83	3587
BRAM	6.69	0
DSP	64.44	9

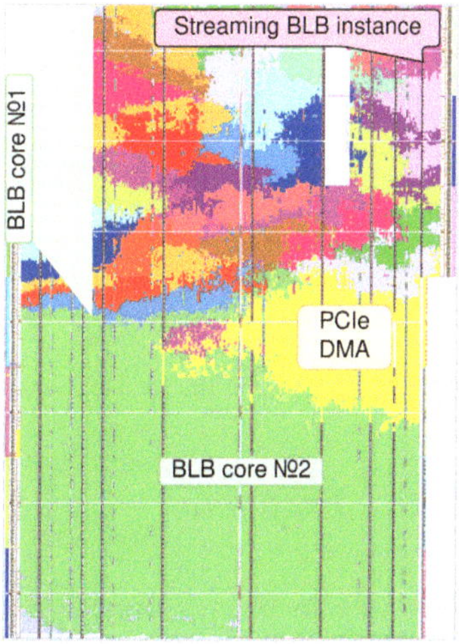

Fig. 1.5 Logic placement on Zynq XC7Z045 SoC [8]

coefficients. These packets are then dispatched to the host via PCI Express XDMA for final processing and answer generation (Table 1.1).

Figure 1.5 illustrates the layout of Streaming BLB instances within the BLB core. Each core consists of 32 Streaming BLB instances. The diagram highlights a full BLB core in green on the bottom. At the same time, the upper side displays another core, segmented into 32 individual Streaming BLB instances, each represented by a different color, such as the pink section in the upper right. The logic for processing TPC-H Q6 is positioned left from the yellow PCIe DMA block. Due to FPGA resource constraints, the system supports a maximum of 32 Streaming BLB instances per core.

The CPU-based reference algorithm is developed in C++ using GCC v11.3.0 on Ubuntu 22.04. Its performance significantly depends on the choice of Gaussian random number generator. We explore this by comparing the standard C++ library's GRNG and the Ziggurat algorithm from the GNU Scientific Library [17]. For parallel execution, we employ OpenMP v4.5 [9].

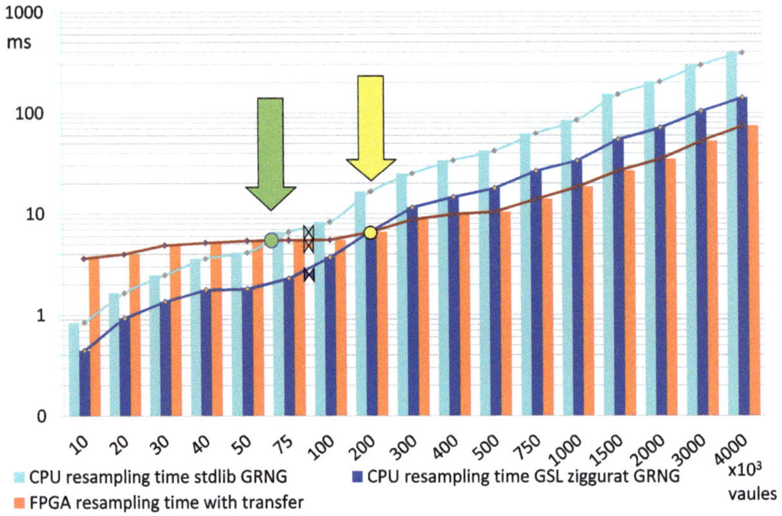

Fig. 1.6 Execution time for TPC-H Q6 varying data size in log scale [8]

1.3.6 Evaluation

We evaluate the performance of the streaming BLB algorithm for the TPC-H Q6 query on both FPGA and i7-6850K CPU platforms, as shown in Fig. 1.6. As discussed in Sect. 1.3.2, the subsample size depends on two values. The first is the number of values in the dataset (scale factor, SF) and γ. We choose the TPC-H dataset with SF1 and $\gamma = 0.6$, resulting in $10 \cdot 10^3$ values as the leftmost point on the graph. The rightmost point corresponds to a set of subsamples created from a dataset with SF100 and $\gamma = 0.75$, resulting in ($\sim 4000 \cdot 10^3$) values.

The CPU's setup includes a single BLB core with eight Streaming BLB instances across CPU cores. Similarly, the FPGA setup consists of one BLB core and eight Streaming BLB instances. The FPGA, however, could support more cores and instances with negligible overhead. FPGA time measurements account for PCIe data transfer delays.

Our results indicate that the CPU performs better for smaller datasets, but FPGAs excel as data size increases, surpassing CPU around 60,000 entries (see green arrow), showcasing FPGA's resampling efficiency. The CPU performance, which relies heavily on generating normal distributions, improves with the Ziggurat generator from the GSL library but still lags behind FPGA performance at about 200,000 entries, as shown by the yellow arrow.

The analysis underscores the superior efficiency of the FPGA even with modest data volumes, with CPU limitations primarily due to random number generation. Initially, FPGA's performance is hampered by PCIe setup times, which diminishes with larger datasets. Eventually, the FPGA's constraint shifts to its interface

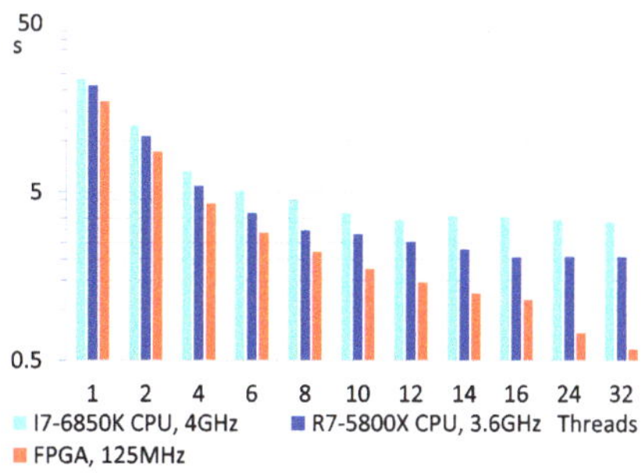

Fig. 1.7 Execution time over threads [8]

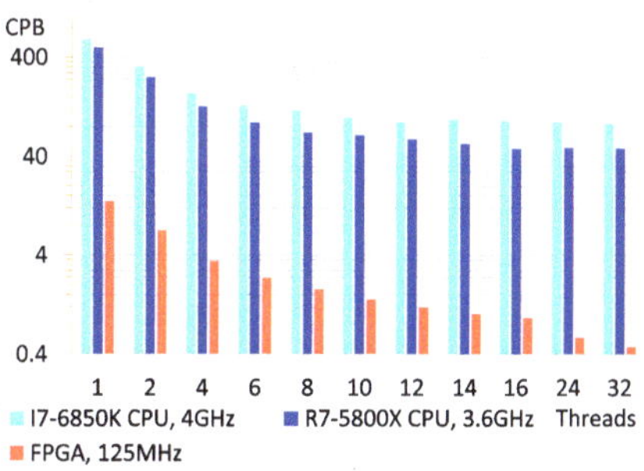

Fig. 1.8 Clock Cycles per Byte [8]

bandwidth, achieving twice the speed of the best CPU setup at 40 million entries, as evidenced by the logarithmic scale comparison.

Figure 1.7 displays the Streaming BLB algorithm's execution time for TPC-H Q6, analyzing a 6 billion entry dataset, roughly 1 TB. With $s = 10$ subsamples and $r = 100$ resampling iterations per subsample, as recommended by Kleiner et al. [27] for 95% accuracy, the subsample size is around one million entries (15.3 MB). The FPGA consistently outperforms the CPU in single-threaded operations, maintaining this advantage against the newer R7-5800X CPU.

Figure 1.8 illustrates the Clocks Per Byte (CPB) efficiency with varying Streaming BLB instances under the same setup as prior measurements. This comparison helps evaluate how the number of instances affects the efficiency of the algorithm. Despite its high clock speed, the CPU requires many cycles for random number generation, a challenge solved by the FPGA in one clock cycle. The Ryzen CPU reaches its peak efficiency at 16 threads with a CPB of approximately 48, showcasing the algorithm's scalability with increased parallelism. In contrast, the FPGA's efficiency, constrained only by resource availability, is significantly higher, achieving about 50 times more efficiency than the CPU, even considering the logarithmic scale. Given the 32-bit data processing, the ideal FPGA efficiency would be CPB $= 0.25$. However, due to PCIe XDMA transfer overheads, the achieved efficiency is CPB $= 0.58$.

1.3.7 Conclusion

We presented an FPGA-based architecture for approximate query-processing acceleration. It relies on a Streaming BLB algorithm for efficient resampling. This approach significantly reduces data transfer, addressing the common bottleneck of data transfer rates in processing accelerators. The FPGA implementation shows a higher performance (from 2 times) compared to CPUs at moderate to large sample sizes, including data transfer times. Compared to CPUs, FPGAs are more efficient at generating random numbers based on multihat algorithm.

1.4 Device-Specific Primitive Graphs

The usual execution unit in traditional database systems is on the granularity of operators. However, given the Challenge C1 of exploiting device-specific computing capabilities, the operator level is too complex and broad to give a device-specific implementation per new device. This is why we introduce the concept of primitives and their tuning in the following sections.

1.4.1 Primitives

1.4.1.1 Motivation

One of the key motivations for tuning algorithms for different modern processors is the diversity in their processing capabilities. Specifically, modern devices support different paradigms of parallelism and have dedicated hardware units for efficient parallel execution. For example, a GPU supports massive data-parallel execution via multiple lightweight cores. On the other hand, FPGAs support the execution of deep processing pipelines. Hence, with devices supporting different levels of parallelism, we must also investigate ways to exploit their capabilities for faster database operations [19].

In order to minimize the implementation efforts as well as to explore the different device capabilities, database operators are split into granular functions that can be reused across multiple database operators, known as `primitives` [24]. Many researchers have proposed as well as investigated primitives of database operators for co-processors [5, 34]. In our ADAMANT project, we have surveyed these existing primitives and used them for creating a primitive-based query execution plan.

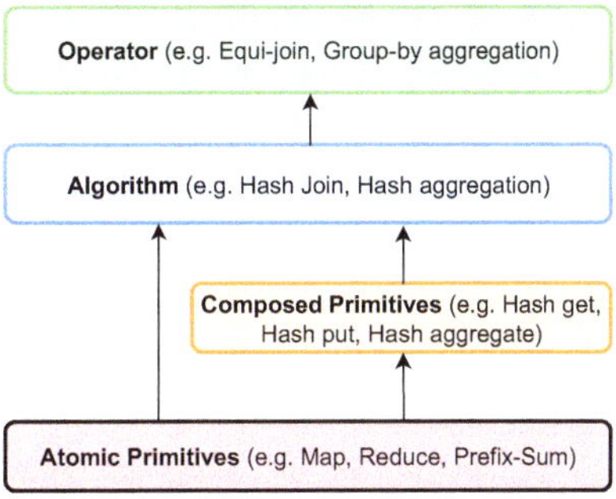

Fig. 1.9 DBMS primitives in hierarchy based on [19]

1.4.1.2 Survey of primitives

Based on our survey, we identify various granularities of primitives, which we show in Fig. 1.9: atomic, composed, algorithms, and finally the database operators.

Atomic primitives, such as map, reduce, and prefix sum, consist of a single processing loop with internal functional statements that cannot be split further. A composed primitive uses one or more atomic primitive or extends a primitive with custom implementations. Hash-build or hash-probe are examples of a composed primitive. A hash build, for example, can be built with a map primitive for the hash function to compute the target location and custom hashing technique implementation (like linear probing, cuckoo hashing) for placing the input in the hash table. Finally, these atomic and composed primitives can be used to run a complete database operator. A detailed list of these primitives is given in [19].

On the example of Q6, we can use the abovementioned primitives to define its query execution plan as given in Fig. 1.10. This plan is flexible w.r.t. execution, such that the selection primitives can be executed on the CPU with the materialize primitive executed on the GPU. This allows for tandem execution across different co-processors.

In summary, due to the divide-and-conquer implementation style of primitives, these granular primitives minimize the implementation efforts as well as allow for exploring optimization opportunities. Using these definitions, we can freely plug in any device-specific implementation of a primitive without reworking the database operators. In upcoming sections, we show the ways to realize implementation of these primitives.

1.4.2 Grouped Aggregation as Device-Specific Primitive

1.4.2.1 Motivation

Though primitives allow re-usability of functionalities, we still need expertise about the underlying co-processor architecture to realize an optimal primitive implemen-

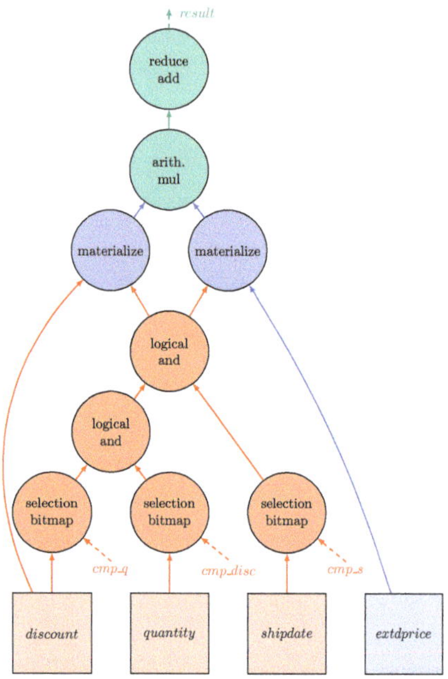

Fig. 1.10 A primitive-based query execution plan for TPC-H Query 6

tation. Depending on the capability of the device, a particular implementation and its relevant parameter set might lead to optimal performance [38]. In this section, we take one such case of optimizing a device-specific primitive for processing a group-by aggregation using GPUs.

Group-by is most commonly implemented using hashing techniques, which group the input into buckets including an on-the-fly aggregation. The hashing techniques, however, incur a lot of random memory access due to the nature of the hash function when grouping the values. Though such random accesses have minimal effects on CPUs and can be handled by the cache hierarchy [36], they will have severe effects for GPUs. Hence, we explore the alternative of using a sorting-based technique for group-by aggregation in GPUs.

Sorting has been a ubiquitous operation in query execution. Once sorted, the groups in the input are already arranged in a continuous sequence. In such sequences, resultant aggregation is computed in a single pass. However, such a sequential pass over an array of data needs to be efficiently partitioned among threads in a GPU, with all threads aggregating their respective value.

1.4.2.2 Method

To aggregate values from concurrent threads, various software-based synchronization mechanisms are used. Modern GPUs (like NVIDIA GTX 1050) offer direct hardware support via `atomic` instructions to simplify such synchronization. These instructions serialize aggregation on a particular target, ensuring the correctness of results. Still, using atomics reduces execution performance as it increases the concurrency of the threads (see [22] for related experiments). Hence, we must implement an atomics-based aggregation technique that uses minimal atomics to get better performance. To this end, we propose two main techniques: (1) private aggregate variable and (2) private aggregate array.

1.4.2.3 Minimizing Atomics Using Private Space

Since the input is sorted, we can exploit their sequence to reduce the overall atomics instructions executed. We achieve this by chunking the input such that all values of a single group are assigned to a single thread. In case multiple groups are present in a chunk, atomics are issued to store their partial aggregates. We store these partial aggregates using thread-private variables or arrays so that aggregated via an atomic instruction only when necessary. Both versions are shown in Fig. 1.11, where two threads aggregate their own chunk of three values.

The execution flow of both variants is roughly the same. In both, a thread sequentially reads its chunk of the prefix-sum and aggregates the corresponding input values within its private space until it encounters a group boundary. However, the variants differ in handling their partial aggregates and thus in the number of required atomics.

1.4.2.4 Evaluation

We compare the performance of the best-performing chunk and thread-size combination of the two private aggregate variants with the naive atomic variants with an optimal thread size on the two consumer GPUs GTX 1050Ti and RTX 2080Ti (see [21] for the choice of best-performing variants). The results are shown in Fig. 1.12.

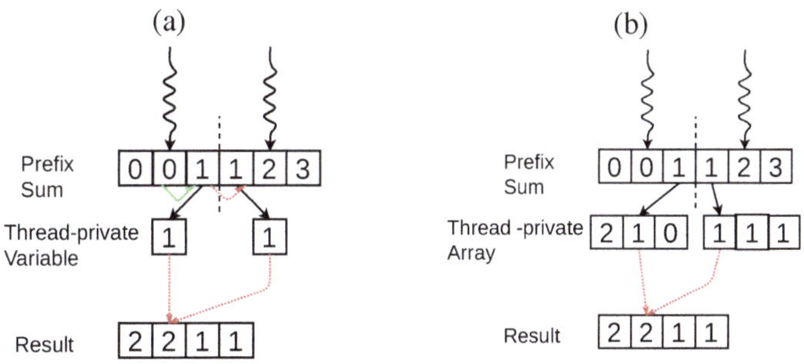

Fig. 1.11 Using private address space in GPU for storing partial aggregates. (**a**) Private aggregate variable. (**b**) Private aggregate array

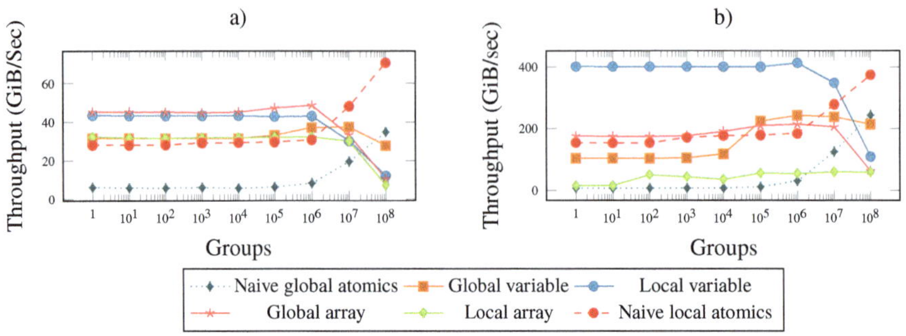

Fig. 1.12 Performance profile for hardware-aware aggregation variants. (**a**) GTX 1050Ti. (**b**) RTX 2080Ti

The variants in Fig. 1.12 are named as Naive representing the simple atomic aggregation without the variants, global/local represent the target memory, and variable/array represent the data structure for intermediate storage.

Our results indicate that the global array and local variable have higher throughput than the naive atomic variants for almost all numbers of groups (i.e., except a larger number of groups). This limitation of our variants is expected, as a larger number of groups leads to multiple groups within a chunk. In this case, a thread has to repeatedly insert the final result into global memory, degrading its performance. We also see only a small improvement in using local memory for our variants on the GTX 1050Ti, which in contrast is a considerable improvement on the RTX 2080Ti. Finally, for very high amounts of groups, the overhead of internal synchronization for the private aggregate variants does not pay off. Hence, naive local atomics performs best in this case.

1.4.2.5 Conclusion

Our variants reach a speedup of 6x–12x to the naive atomics and 1.5–2.6x to the naive local memory atomics. For GTX 1050Ti, the variant using a private array in global memory is optimal with a speedup of 6x the naive atomics and 1.6x the naive local memory atomics. For RTX 2080Ti, the variant using a local variable is clearly superior with a speedup of about 12x the naive atomics and up to 2x the local memory atomics.

1.4.3 Primitive Libraries

A handwritten primitive can be optimized based on the underlying device for best performance. However, as shown in the previous section, we need extensive evaluation as well as expertise of the underlying device to come up with such an implementation. Alternatively, we can also use pre-written libraries from device experts that circumvent such extensive implementation and evaluation setups.

1.4.3.1 Motivation and Method

These device-specific libraries are general-purpose and support multiple generations of a co-processor out of the box. Additionally, these libraries add wrappers to device-specific implementations that hide the internal details from the end user. Thus, the user does not need to be an expert on the underlying device. In this context, we are looking into the support of such GPU-based libraries for database workloads. Based on our findings, we identify three libraries (ArrayFire, boost.compute, Thrust) that have partial support for database operations. These libraries and their implementation options for different database operators are given in Table 1.2. Overall, the most common database operators and primitives are supported by different libraries. However, especially joins are not yet supported. More information about the library support in GPUs and their extensive evaluation with TPC-H queries can be found in [43].

1.4.3.2 Evaluation

Using the three libraries, we can now execute TPC-H Q6 as per the query plan in Fig. 1.10. The performance of Q6 with TPC-H scale factor (SF) 1 using these libraries is plotted in Fig. 1.13. Our microbenchmark shows a poor performance from ArrayFire compared to boost.compute and Thrust [43]. Hence, we consider these for a complete query execution. Furthermore, due to its small runtime, the arithmetic step is not visible in the execution of Q6. Our results show that selection takes a considerable time compared to aggregation in the overall query execution. Even with the fast-performing library for the individual operators, we only get poor performance from using libraries. Additionally, we see a performance jump from using A100, but even in this case, the relative performance of selection is higher than aggregation. Overall, the results show that the libraries are not tuned for database workload and must be code-optimized for better execution.

1.4.3.3 Conclusion

Though these libraries support easy integration of alternative primitive implementations, they still lack complete support for databases. We summarize our findings for the library support for database operations in three dimensions:

- **Usefulness**: The usefulness of libraries for DBMS is fairly restrictive. Not all database operations are supported out-of-the-box through these libraries.

Table 1.2 Mapping of library functions to database operators

Database operators	ArrayFire		boost.compute		Thrust	
	Support	Function	Support	Function	Support	Function
Selection	+	where(operator())	~	transform() & exclusive_scan() & gather()	~	transform() & exclusive_scan() & gather()
Nested-Loops Join	–	–	+	for_each_n()	+	for_each_n()
Merge Join	–	–	–	–	–	–
Hash Join	–	–	–	–	–	–
Grouped aggregation	+	sumByKey(), countByKey(),	+	reduce_by_key()	+	reduce_by_key()
Conjunction & disjunction	+	setIntersect(), setUnion()	+	bit_and<T>(), bit_or<T>()	+	bit_and<T>(), bit_or<T>()
Reduction	+	sum<T>()	+	reduce()	+	reduce()
Sort by key	+	sort()	+	sort_by_key()	+	sort_by_key()
Sort	+	sort()	+	sort()	+	sort()
Prefix sum	–	–	+	exclusive_scan()	+	exclusive_scan()
Scatter & gather	–	–	+	scatter(), gather()	+	scatter(), gather()
Product	+	operator*()	+	transform() & multiplies<T>()	+	transform() & multiplies<T>()

+ *full support*, ~ *partial support*, – *no support*

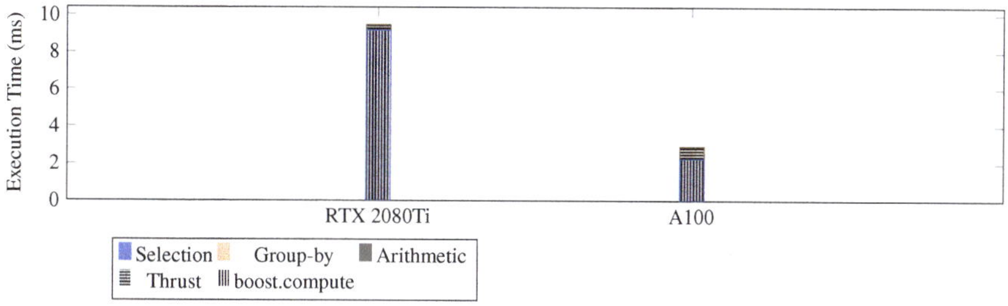

Fig. 1.13 Performance of TPC-H Q6 using GPU libraries

- **Usability**: Not all library functions are performance efficient. For optimal performance, a developer must test different libraries and combine their operators based on the query.
- **Portability**: Libraries can be executed across various devices out-of-the-box with fewer rework.

1.4.4 Primitive Fusion

1.4.4.1 Motivation

When executing tasks in a primitive-based system, common combinations of primitives might occur. These are of special interest for optimization, since planning with and scheduling and execution of a multitude of primitives allows dispatch overheads to accumulate drastically. Using code fusion to automatically implement Composed Primitives allows the system to take advantage of this potential and to better adapt to evolving circumstances without requiring humans in the loop. In addition to directly reducing the system overhead during execution, fused primitives offer also more optimization potential to the underlying (compiler or synthesis) tool chain. Finally, if the system has available Composed Primitives for commonly occurring subgraphs of query graphs, higher-level optimization and planning functions are simplified, as query graphs are reduced in size.

The per-primitive optimization potential is especially interesting for FPGAs, since during implementation of a circuit, the tool chain has access to every element, which allows for much more thorough optimizations across component boundaries than for software [4]. Also, each primitive must contain the logic required to interface with the rest of the accelerator system.

1.4.4.2 Method

For successful adoption of primitive fusion into a primitive-based system, two abstract problems need to be solved: First, from a set of query plans, common subgraphs need to be identified. Second, during runtime, incoming queries need to be analyzed and instances of Composed Primitives need to be identified. As both of these problems are NP-hard, we propose a non-optimal but best-effort approach [12].

For the first problem, we propose a constructive greedy approach guided by a heuristic. Iteratively, the pair of primitives that is estimated to be most commonly replaced by the resulting Composed Primitive in the input set of queries by the heuristic is selected for fusion. The set of query graphs induced by this replacement is then taken as input for the next iteration. The advantage of this approach over taking the most commonly occurring combination is that due to the often treelike interconnections in the input graphs, not all instances can be replaced.

For the matching process at runtime, we propose another greedy approach, namely, iteratively matching the largest possible Composed Primitive in the topologically sorted query graph. This process should be fuzzy, since it can make sense to replace a subgraph of a query with a Composed Primitive doing additional work if the estimated runtime is lower.

1.4.4.3 Results

Evaluating the proposed algorithms for a set of TPC-H query graphs and a library of streaming primitives for FPGA resulted on average in a reduction of 47% in terms of FPGA resource use without any change in throughput [12]. TPC-H Query 6, for example, is reduced to only three Composed Primitives and one filter primitive implementing materialization. Due to the reductions in resource use, additional computations could be mapped to the FPGA. In the set of queries considered, the proposed heuristic chose the optimal candidates in 86% of the 21 iterations, more than three times more accurate than the naive approach [12].

1.5 FPGA Overlay Template

In this section, we describe the FPGA component of the ADAMANT system. After discussing the advantages and challenges of integrating FPGAs into a heterogeneous, runtime-adaptive data processing system, we present an overview of our research into flexible and scalable FPGA accelerators in the form of our template for creating reconfigurable FPGA overlay architectures.

1.5.1 Motivation

The standard approach to creating FPGA designs is to use a hardware description language (HDL) and describe the design at the register transfer level (RTL). While this level of abstraction is sufficient for defining data paths and associated control logic, it is not suitable for creating complex system designs. High-level synthesis (HLS) has emerged as an alternative to HDL designs, raising the level of abstraction to a more software-like approach. HLS is the technique of writing hardware designs (kernels) in software languages such as C++ or OpenCL and automatically generating the RTL design that implements those kernel functions. Yet, there is the disadvantage that HLS creates RTL sources that still need to pass through the entire FPGA tool flow before they can be run, which can require hours. Other approaches to increasing the level of abstraction for FPGA designs and speeding implementation can be summarized under the term overlay architectures, which describes the process of bundling the raw FPGA resources into higher-level components that themselves provide some sort of programming interface. These systems are usually not fully programmable and feature specialized compute units tailored explicitly to the application domain. Coarse-grained reconfigurable architectures (CGRAs) are a more generalized and more structured class of accelerators that can be implemented on FPGAs. Instead of on the level of single-bit resources, reconfiguration happens at a higher level: The accelerator contains word-sized interconnects and implements common arithmetic and logic operations on that level as well. The compute units are usually structured in a 2D-tiled grid with local connections between neighboring cells because that maps well onto existing (FPGA) technology. This allows programmers without FPGA knowledge to assemble deep pipelines at runtime, but existing designs are usually both closely coupled to a specific FPGA in order to fully exploit its resources and are tailored to the needs of a specific application. An extension of this concept is possible with dynamic partial reconfiguration (DPR), which allows exchanging parts of the FPGA at runtime. This can be used to increase flexibility and area efficiency by not having to ship every required function in one FPGA bit stream, but DPR also incurs some overhead over static designs.

Before introducing the FPGA approach taken for the ADAMANT architecture, the next paragraphs present some key findings from related work about accelerating database query processing with FPGAs. According to a 2020 survey, the programmability gap and difficulties in achieving desired performance levels have impeded widespread adoption of FPGAs in this domain [16].

Lu and Fang [29] present research on running TPC-H queries on a system with a CPU and two FPGAs running static database accelerators with limited configurability. Without the specialized query plan optimization passes they propose, half of all TPC-H queries either cannot make use of any acceleration or run slower than on CPU.

The runtime-reconfigurable accelerator for analytical query processing proposed by Ziener et al. [47] consists of four separate areas for loading pipelines of operators via DPR combined with static, non-reconfigurable compute units for sot and join. Each area has the form of 16 small adjacent reconfigurable partitions, through which data moves strictly sequentially. Reorder units are used to adapt row-oriented data to compute units.

Schmid et al. [41] proposed a tool for automatically building FPGA images for accelerating database query processing. The tool uses a standardized interface to integrate several HLS kernels into one bit stream. Kernels can exchange data through a single global streaming interconnect, and the tool connects a memory-mapped bus to all kernels for setting configuration parameters at runtime. Both approaches are limited in terms of scalability.

1.5.2 Investigation of OpenCL-Based HLS

Ideally, a primitive-based DBMS for heterogeneous hardware could be extended to FPGAs by synthesizing available portable kernels from a common pool with a HLS tool and creating an FPGA image capable of executing them. While this is possible using OpenCL with some limitations, such as non-standard behaviour of some platforms, this approach has some serious drawbacks [14].

We show that the lack of flexible on-chip data flow routing in existing HLS tool flows essentially negates the main benefit of FPGAs. Figure 1.14 shows four OpenCL kernels integrated into one FPGA bit stream. Two communication techniques supported by the HLS tool are shown: The red arrows show how kernels can exchange data through buffers in memory, while the blue arrow shows two kernels passing data between them on-chip through a FIFO, or pipe.

A sequence of operations involving kernels zero and one requires intermediate data to be stored into DRAM and for kernel one to wait until kernel zero is finished. Processing data with kernels two and three requires no storage for intermediate data and no coordination from software, since the transfer between the kernels happens on the fly through hardware handshaking signals and entirely within the FPGA. Performance of the first example can be improved by executing the kernels on chunks of the whole dataset, but even with chunked execution, the first option

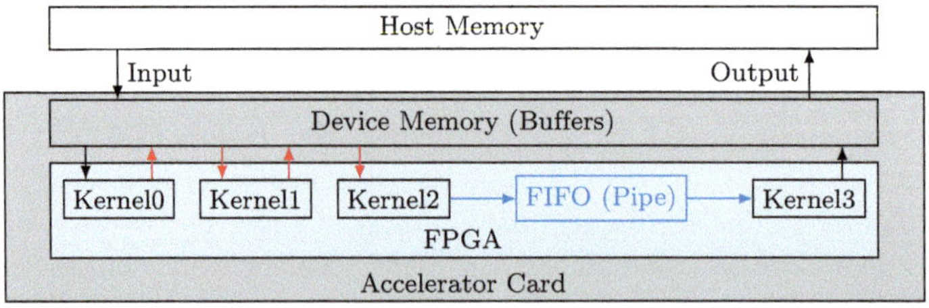

Fig. 1.14 Communication between OpenCL kernels implemented on FPGAs (Reprinted with permission from [14])

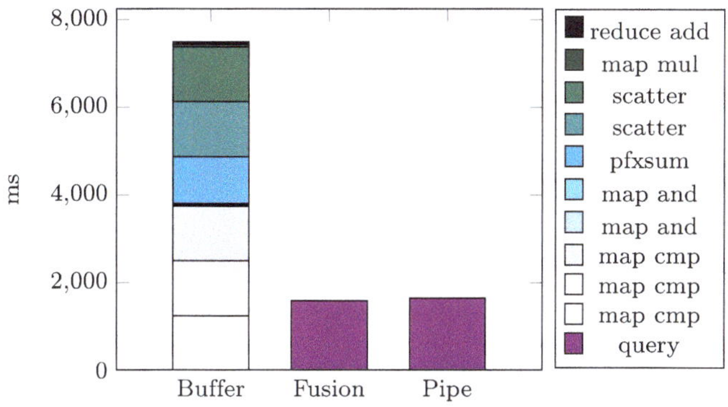

Fig. 1.15 Stacked bar plot of execution time for TPC-H Query 6 for Buffer- and Pipe-based kernel communication, as well as single-kernel/fused primitives. Reprinted with permission from [14]

consumes double the necessary memory bandwidth. For deeper pipelines, such as encountered with primitive-based systems, this penalty worsens drastically. The second example also is unsuitable for such a system, as Pipes between kernels have to be exactly one to one and known at design time.

Figure 1.15 shows the execution time of TPC-H Query 6 for the different communication techniques on an OpenCL-based FPGA accelerator On the left-hand side, independent kernels are exchanging data through the DRAM on the FPGA accelerator card. The right-hand bar shows the execution time for a set of kernels assembled into a hardware pipeline through on-chip FIFO buffers. For comparison, the bar in the middle shows the performance of a custom kernel implementing Query 6.

These results show that with an operator-at-a-time execution model, it is impossible to build deep pipelines that take advantage of the inherent spatial parallelism and essentially infinite internal bandwidth of FPGAs. The low clock rates and simpler memory controllers compared to CPU and GPU will in that case limit performance severely. We also show that intermediate data exchange through DRAM also requires the most FPGA resources [14].

1.5.3 FPGA Overlay Template

Existing research and the findings from the first system lead to the conclusion that an FPGA-based accelerator for the ADAMANT systems requires a proper reconfigurable overlay architecture in order to efficiently provide the infrastructure desired for executing queries at runtime. Query execution plans are represented as data flow graphs, where nodes are functions that are implemented in compute units, which are then loaded into reconfigurable partitions in the FPGA. The edges, which represent data dependencies, are mapped to on-chip paths between compute units. Our approach thus targets streaming applications in general, of which the aforementioned query execution plans are a subset. After uncovering hardware limitations present in some FPGA devices that impede the implementation of an overlay with high performance and a flexible, user-centric compute unit interface at the same time [10, 13], the need to broaden the scope beyond an ADAMANT FPGA accelerator system became apparent.

In order to provide portability and scalability, we designed a parametrizable template that is used to instantiate domain-specific overlay architecture instances at specified performance levels and resource footprints [11]. The template consists of a 2D grid of tiles with local streaming connections between neighbors. Each tile contains a reconfigurable partition, into which compute units are loaded at runtime via DPR. In addition to the local streaming links, the template provides a novel lightweight on-chip network, which is used for small data transfers such as scalar arguments or results instead of reserving dedicated data flow connections. The template builds on existing standards in order to support a wide range of implementation techniques for compute units and defines consistent interfaces between components.

Figure 1.16 shows a high-level block diagram of the overlay architecture template. The area shaded in dark gray is the 2D-grid of tiles, each of which contains a configurable partition for a compute unit. Through local streaming links between neighboring tiles, compute units can exchange data. The area shaded in light gray shows the infrastructure that enables memory access through DMA blocks. From the edge of the tile, grid data is fed into pipelines assembled using multiple compute units/tiles, and from the edges, output data is stored back into arrays in memory. The light-weight on-chip network is shown with dashed arrows. It connects every programmable component of the overlay template to the host software via the PCIe block (top left) more efficiently and with higher throughput than a memory-mapped bus system. The PCIe block is also used for transferring data between host and device memory. At deployment time, the topology and bit width of the local streaming connections can be configured, trading off base resource use with SIMD capabilities and in order to adapt to different expected shapes and densities of data flow graphs.

Figure 1.17 shows a high-level architecture of a single tile. The reconfigurable partition, into which compute units can be loaded at runtime, is surrounded by data flow routing resources, supporting logic and a router for the on-chip network. The data flow routing resources are placed in the tile instead of integrating them into compute units in order to generalize and simplify the latter. The streaming connections between tile and compute unit contain FIFO buffers in order to improve performance. Since data streaming can only deal with known, fixed-access patterns, the template provides a configuration flag to instantiate some tiles with full bus master ports for random memory access to the device memory. This option is especially costly in terms of resources and therefore, some consideration into the required number of memory access-enables tiles is necessary.

In order to deploy any reconfigurable overlay architecture, a floor plan of the reconfigurable partitions is required. For traditional overlays, a significant amount

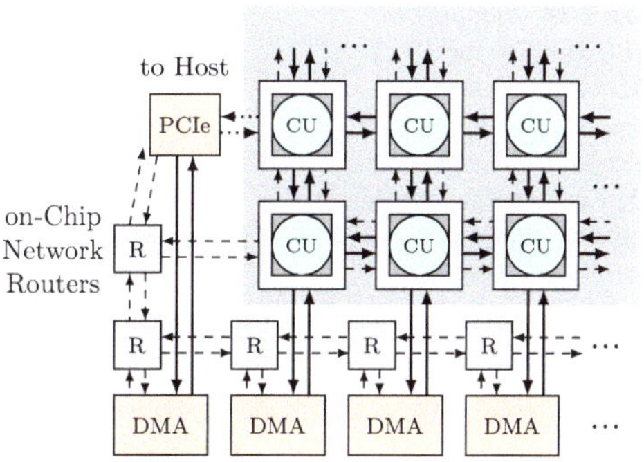

Fig. 1.16 Block diagram of the FPGA overlay architecture template (Reprinted with permission from [11])

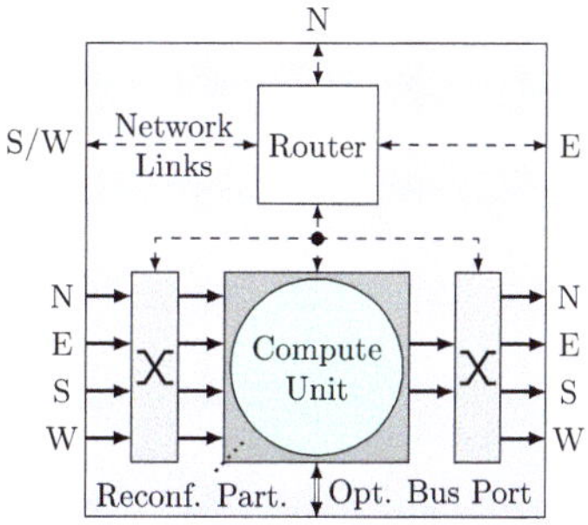

Fig. 1.17 Overlay template tile with compute unit in reconfigurable partition (Reprinted with permission from [11])

of thought and design space exploration is invested in order to come up with a suitable layout. The template character of our work aims to address this step in the design process as well with a user-guided floor planning tool based on open source device information [11].

1.5.4 Results

For the ADAMANT system for analytical database query processing, a 4 × 10 FPGA overlay with 11 DMA engines is instantiated from the template on an AMD U280 data center FPGA accelerator card [11]. Based on expected performance and resource impact of the primitives from the ADAMANT library, a configuration with four-way SIMD-style data parallel processing of 32 bit words was selected.

Thus, the system was configured with 128 bit streaming links and connections to neighboring tiles in a 4-neighborhood. The tiles were set up for compute units with up to two output streams. Resource estimations lead to a partition size of 1440 LUTs/2880 FFs for streaming compute units and double that amount for a subset of four tiles for compute units with the optional memory bus connection. The system runs at 250 MHz, and the external memory bandwidth is sufficient for 9 DMA operations in parallel.

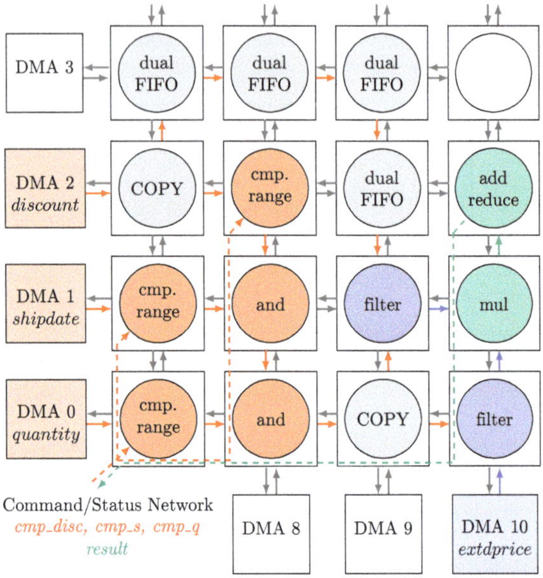

Fig. 1.18 Mapping of TPC-H Q6 to the 10×4 ADAMANT overlay instance [7, 11]. Shaded tiles/DMAs are occupied. Data columns are written in cursive. Reprinted with permission from [11]

The compute units based on database primitives require between 175 and 662 LUTs and 342 and 1689 FFs [11] each. In total, the system occupies 33% of the available FPGA resources, the overlay grid accounting for approximately half of that. In this form, the system is not just used to take performance measurements but also serves as a basis for further experiments, since more resources are free.

Figure 1.18 shows TPC-H Query 6 mapped to the ADAMANT overlay instance. In total, 15 tiles are occupied, 9 for compute units and 6 for data flow routing between non-adjacent compute units. The different parts of the query execution plan are color-coded similar to Fig. 1.10. Executing this query on the ADAMANT overlay instance takes 11.27 ms for 10 million rows, 2.7× faster than an AMD Vega 56 GPU (30.67 ms) and reaching near-parity with an AMD Epyc 7351P 16-core CPU (11.07 ms). While both the OpenMP primitives for the CPU and OpenCL primitives for the GPU are optimized well already, the U280 contains enough resources to fit an overlay large enough to execute Q6 several times in parallel, improving performance further [11].

1.6 Cross-Device Query Execution Methods

With the introduction of an FPGA overlay and device-specific primitives, it is now possible to execute a whole query on a single device. However, to use the maximum available compute power, it is necessary to be able to distribute work among all co-processors. Hence, for overcoming Challenge C2, we (1) now need to incorporate different co-processors for executing a single query and (2), especially considering the FPGA, hide the delay in FPGA configuration. The former is resolved by using our 4-phase chunked execution, and the latter is achieved by using a combined execution of compiled and interpreted execution.

1.6.1 4-Phase Chunked Execution for Cross-Device Execution

1.6.1.1 Motivation

One of the key components for data processing using a co-processor is using an appropriate execution model. Traditional execution models like operator-at-a-time (or volcano executor) or compiled execution that are optimal for a CPU might not work the same for a GPU. Execution models directly define the process and data flow during query execution. For co-processor acceleration, an execution model defines the amount of memory to be used in a co-processor and the execution flow within a co-processor and between the co-processor and its host. Defining a suitable execution model for co-processor acceleration in turn characterizes the execution flow of our runtime engine. To overcome the limitation, we introduce an abstract chunk-based execution model that can support any arbitrary co-processor.

1.6.1.2 Method

In order to have an optimal execution flow, we create two identical memory spaces to alternate execution and transfer. The transfer and execution threads alternate between these memories that access the chunks. Additionally, the intermediate results of any pipeline breaker are also transferred back to the host using host-addressable memory. All other intermediate results are stored in the device memory to limit data transfers. Once the execution is complete, we deallocate these memory locations.

An overview of these different methods of query execution is given in Fig. 1.19. The naive chunked execution—Fig. 1.19a—has inherent delays with execution due to transfer and execute loop, which can be improved by concurrent transfer and execution as shown in Fig. 1.19b. Additionally, as explained above, we can reuse memory spaces thereby reducing allocation and de-allocation overheads. In this final variant, the execution starts by creating pinned memory spaces (stage phase) over which the chunks are copied (copy phase). Once a chunk is copied, the compute phase processes these data. Once all the chunks are processed, the deletion phase deallocates the memories for the next queries.

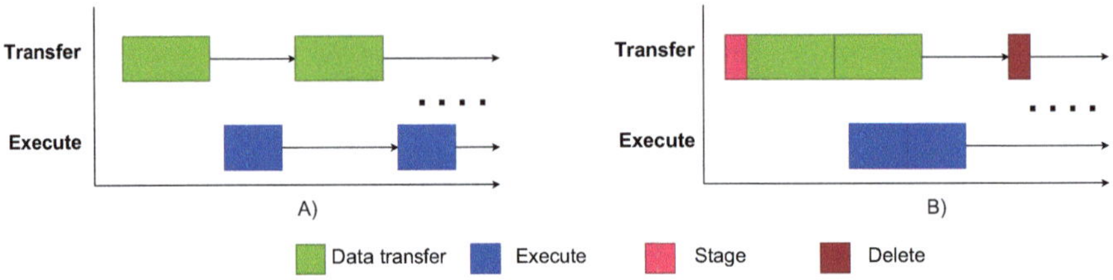

Fig. 1.19 Execution model alternatives for co-processor acceleration. (a) Chunked execution. (b) 4-phase pipelined execution

1.6.1.3 Evaluation

For evaluation, we test the performance of these execution models with CUDA implementations of our primitives on GPUs. To test the scalability of our execution models, we consider TPC-H Q6 with scale factors 100 and 140, and we compare the performance with HeavyDB, which uses a compiled execution model. From our results, we see a clear improvement in performance when using 4-phase model in NVIDIA RTX 2080Ti. This is mainly due to the poor transfer time, which leads to considerable wait time before execution. Our pipelined execution reduces this wait time leading to an improvement in overall performance. However, we see that A100 does not reflect the same. This is due to the faster transfers from NVlink. We also see a considerable performance difference from HeavyDB. This shows that the interpretation-based approach is faster than the compiled execution mainly due to the improvement in data transfers. A more detailed evaluation of various primitives as well as other implementations is given in [20] (Fig. 1.20).

Overall, our execution models can support any arbitrary co-processor without a complete rework of the query execution engine.

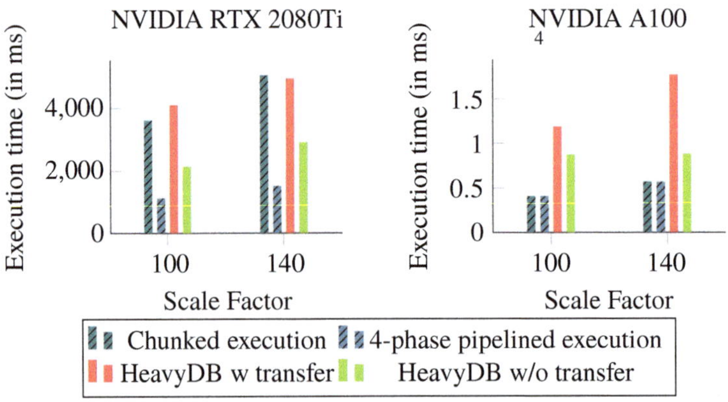

Fig. 1.20 Performance of the execution models and HeavyDB execution with larger-scale factors

Though the execution models support any abstract co-processors, they require the primitives to be pre-compiled. Many co-processors also support runtime compilation, which might not be a viable option for our query engine. For such cases, we designed an alternative hybrid query engine, Tether [23], which is described in the next section.

1.6.2 Combining Compiled and Interpreted Execution

1.6.2.1 Motivation

In the above execution models, the co-processors execute queries without compilation overhead or configuration time for the FPGA overlay. However, adding runtime compilation or FPGA configuration incurs a considerable delay in query execution. To hide this delay, we consider a hybrid execution model that combines interpreted execution with compiled execution. Specifically, we hide the compilation and configuration overhead by concurrently processing a query in the interpreted mode. Once the query is compiled and configured, the remaining execution is completed using the compiled query and configured device.

1.6.2.2 Method

Since the compilation and configuration can be completed at any arbitrary point during interpreted execution, it is not feasible to identify this switchover point in advance. Therefore we split a query into multiple pipelines and use them to switch between the execution models. A pipeline consists of a sequence of primitives that ends with a pipeline breaker primitive (like an aggregate primitive). An example of our hybrid execution plan is like the one given Fig. 1.21. In this case, the pipeline P1 will be executed in the interpreted mode while others are compiled or configured. The pipeline breaker—join—is used to switch from P1 to other pipelines to be executed in compiled mode.

Let us consider the case of processing TPC-H Q6 with our hybrid execution model. Unlike others, Q6 has only one pipeline that ends with an aggregate operator. Hence, we use this operator as the switching point for the execution models. During execution, the interpreted execution processes the query and generates partial aggregate results (cf. Fig. 1.22). Once compiled execution takes over, the partial aggregates are updated to get the final result.

1.6.2.3 Evaluation

To test the performance gain from this execution, we test our hybrid execution on an Intel Xeon Gold 6130 CPU with varying scale factors.

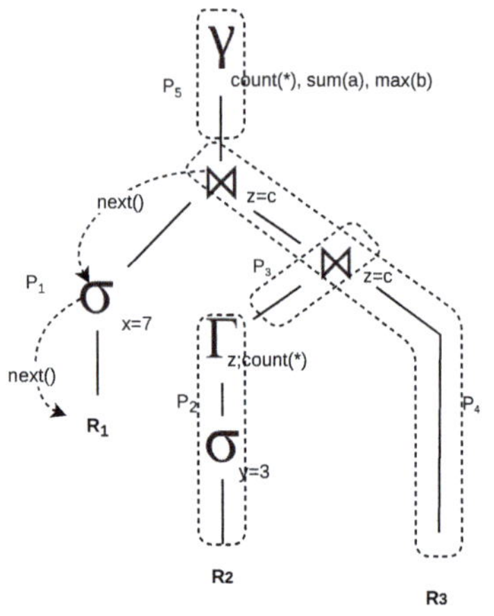

Fig. 1.21 A sample hybrid query plan

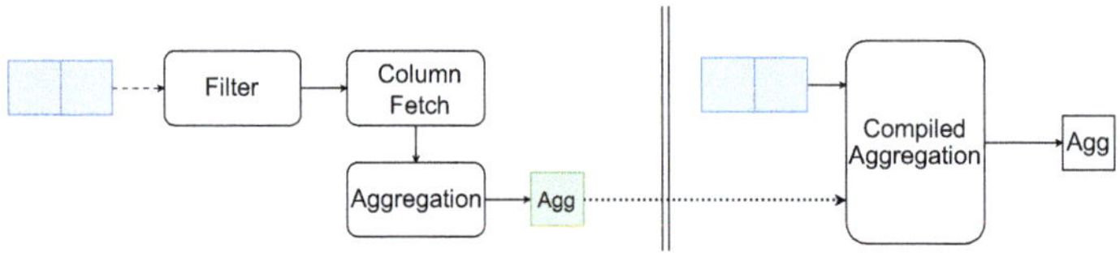

Fig. 1.22 Processing TPC-H Q6 with the hybrid execution model

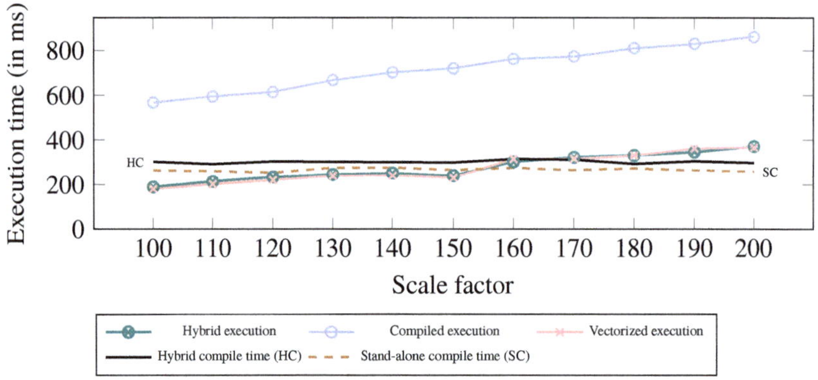

Fig. 1.23 Hybrid vs. traditional query execution of TPC-H Q6

The chart in Fig. 1.23 shows the performance benefit from our hybrid execution for Q6. The execution is clearly faster than naive compiled execution as the overhead of compilation is so large. In case of SF 100 until SF 150, we see that our hybrid execution completes query execution even before the compilation can finish. Therefore in these data ranges, our hybrid execution and vectorized execution have nearly identical execution time. Once this threshold is crossed, we see that our hybrid execution can slightly benefit from both the compiled and vectorized execution, thereby improving the performance further. Due to a single pipeline and only one final pipeline breaker, Q6 is not the optimal case for the proposed approach. For other TPC-H queries (e.g., Q1 and Q3), we achieve speedups of up to 3x, which can be found in the corresponding paper [23].

1.7 Multi-query Processing

With the introduction of the ADAMANT query execution engine, device-specific primitives, and FPGA overlay, we are now able to execute a single query. Since usually multiple queries are executed concurrently, the final Challenge C3 is to improve the system's performance by exploiting the results of multiple queries at any given instant.

1.7.1 Motivation

Our idea to counter C3 is to exploit the potential of reusing results. Current multi-query optimizers (MQOs) devise a shared execution strategy across multiple queries based on their commonalities, generally using any of the two strategies: *batched* or *cached*. In this contribution, we investigate how to combine these two approaches. Therefore, we propose a hybrid-MQO optimizer that can enhance the performance of HW-aware query execution with processing multiple queries at a time, thereby improving the overall query throughput of a DBMS. Our hybrid-MQO system merges batched query results as well as caches the intermediate results, thereby any new query is given a path within the previous plan as well as reusing the results. A detailed description of this hybrid optimizer is given in our article [18].

1.7.2 Method

To explain the optimization flow of our hybrid optimizer, let us consider the set of queries in Fig. 1.24. Out of these, Q_N and Q_6 share the table lineitem as well as the columns quantity and discount. So, our hybrid optimizer creates a common plan for

Q_N: **SELECT** l_quantity, **AVG**(l_tax)
FROM lineitem
WHERE l_quantity < 25
AND l_discount < 0.03
GROUP BY l_quantity

Q_6: **SELECT** **sum**(l_extendedprice $*$ l_discount)
FROM lineitem
where l_shipdate >= '1994− 01− 01'
and l_shipdate < '1995− 01− 01'
and l_discount **between** 0.05 **and** 0.07
and l_quantity < 24

Fig. 1.24 Exemplary queries to be optimized in the MQO approach these queries forming a common filter clause to fetch the desired rows. Afterward, the execution is split for the group-by aggregation and simple aggregation for Q_N and Q_6, respectively. In addition to this batched query plan, we also store the intermediate results to be reused with future queries.

Since storing intermediate results incurs considerable memory space, we only cache the results for a window of queries. In case the cache is full, we use traditional caching techniques to evict some of the existing results. Such execution of a common query plan as well as reusing pre-computed results drastically improves query execution.

1.7.3 Evaluation

We measure the overall gain of executing aggregate queries using our hybrid approach. We use a Google Cloud—E2-Highmem—instance (with Intel Skylake) with 32GB of memory for our evaluation. The results are given in Fig. 1.25. Here, we compare the performance of randomly generated aggregate query execution (i.e., different modifications of Q6) using our hybrid execution in comparison with a simple sequential execution, using Materialized View Reuse (MVR), and using the Shared Sub-Expression (SSE) optimization technique. As the results show, the hybrid technique can achieve around 1.5x times faster query execution than other techniques, but in some cases, we also see a considerable slowdown. The slowdown is mainly due to the additional caching and query batching being done before execution. The speedup is from the time saved from reusing the processed results. The extensive description of these results and the impact of caching are discussed in [18].

1.7.4 Conclusion

With this contribution, we studied the exploitation of synergies across queries (which is the core for developing a shared execution plan). Apart from these limited experiments using a simple query like Q6, we contributed extensive experiments in [18]. For instance, we studied the impact of the `derivability` factor, represent-

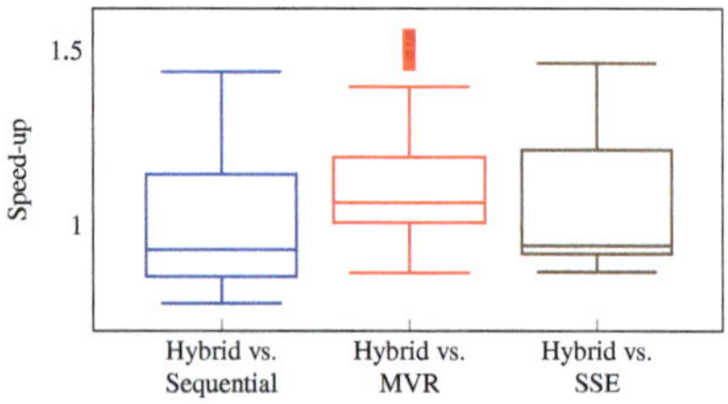

Fig. 1.25 Speedup of our hybrid optimization for aggregation queries against sequential, MVR, and SSE techniques. A speedup above 1 means that the hybrid execution is better than the competitor

ing the similarity of the results within a query batch, and varying the cache sizes to study the influence of caching. Moreover, we also study the role of different database operators in the performance of our hybrid system. The results of our MQO suggest that, depending on the individual operators, our hybrid method gains a speedup of up to 4x from using MQO techniques in isolation. Furthermore, our results show that workloads with a generously sized cache that contain similar queries benefit from using our hybrid method, with an observed speedup of 2x over sequential execution in the best case.

1.8 Conclusion

In this chapter, we presented ADAMANT's core concepts that enable the integration of heterogeneous co-processors into a common query-processing engine. These core concepts range across the whole execution workflow of database systems and solve the main challenges when incorporating heterogeneous co-processors in a database system on the single-device level (C1), the multi-device level (C2), and the multi-device multi-query level (C3). We solved these challenges as follows.

In order to integrate heterogeneous co-processors and exploit their capabilities (C1), we classified existing device-specific primitives and exemplarily tuned the sorted grouped aggregation primitive for GPUs and applied primitive fusion. Furthermore, to integrate the FPGA into the processing, we proposed an overlay for flexible query processing.

With the possibility of using best-performing co-processor implementations, we moved toward concepts to incorporate multiple (co-)processors into the query execution (C2). These concepts solve the problem of different compilation and configuration times (e.g., for the FPGA overlay) by hiding them using interpreted execution. Furthermore, to enable a chunked execution for larger-than-memory workloads, ADAMANT offers a flexible device-specific execution model.

On the level of processing multiple queries simultaneously (C3), we devised concepts for two alternative execution strategies: exact multi-query processing and approximate query processing, which can run simultaneously in ADAMANT. While the former uses batched processing and materialized views to lower execution costs per query, the latter lowers the accuracy for exploratory queries to effectively improve query runtimes and system load.

In summary, the proposed concepts of ADAMANT push database systems research toward exploiting the whole capabilities of the diverse landscape of processing platforms. They enable a system that can dispatch processing tasks flexibly to heterogeneous processing devices depending on load factor, data locality, and estimated performance.

Acknowledgments Funded by the Deutsche Forschungsgemeinschaft (DFG, German Research Foundation) within the SPP 2037 on Scalable Data Management for Future Hardware—361499466.

References

1. Agarwal, S., Mozafari, B., Panda, A., Milner, H., Madden, S., & Stoica, I. (2013). BlinkDB: Queries with bounded errors and bounded response times on very large data. *EuroSys, 03.*
2. Alimohammad, A., Fard, S. F., Cockburn, B. F., & Schlegel, C. (2008). A compact and accurate gaussian variate generator. *VLSI, 16*(5), 517–527.
3. Babu, G. J., Pathak, P. K., & Rao, C. R. (1999). Second-order correctness of the Poisson bootstrap. *The Annals of Statistics, 27*(5), 1666–1683.
4. Becher, A., Lekshmi, B. G., Broneske, D., Drewes, T., Gurumurthy, B., Meyer-Wegener, K., Pionteck, T., Saake, G., Teich, J., & Wildermann, S. (2018). Integration of FPGAs in database management systems: Challenges and opportunities. *Datenbank-Spektrum, 18*(3), 145–156.
5. Boncz, P. A., & Kersten, M. L. (1999). MIL primitives for querying a fragmented world. *The VLDB Journal, 8*, 101–119.
6. Broneske, D., Breß, S., Heimel, M., & Saake, G. (2014). Toward hardware-sensitive database operations. In *EDBT* (pp. 229–234).
7. Broneske, D., Drewes, A., Gurumurthy, B., Hajjar, I., Pionteck, T., & Saake, G. (2021). In-depth analysis of OLAP query performance on heterogeneous hardware. *Datenbank-Spektrum, 21*(2), 133–143.
8. Burtsev, V., Wilhelm, M., Drewes, A., Gurumurthy, B., Broneske, D., Pionteck, T., & Saake, G. (2023). FPGA-integrated bag of little bootstraps accelerator for approximate database query processing. In *Applied reconfigurable computing. architectures, tools, and applications* (pp. 115–130).
9. Dagum, L., & Menon, R. (1998). OpenMP: An industry-standard API for shared-memory programming. *Computing in Science & Engineering, 5*(1), 46–55.
10. Drewes, A., Burtsev, V., Gurumurthy, B., Wilhelm, M., Broneske, D., Saake, G., & Pionteck, T. (2023). A flexible and scalable reconfigurable FPGA overlay architecture for data-flow processing. In *FCCM* (p. 212). IEEE.
11. Drewes, A., Burtsev, V., Gurumurthy, B., Wilhelm, M., Broneske, D., Saake, G., & Pionteck, T. (2024). An architectural template for FPGA overlays targeting data flow applications. In *IPDPSW*. IEEE.
12. Drewes, A., Joseph, J. M., Gurumurthy, B., Broneske, D., Saake, G., & Pionteck, T. (2020). Optimising operator sets for analytical database processing on FPGAs. In *ARC* (Vol. 12083, pp. 30–44). Springer.
13. Drewes, A., Koppehel, M., & Pionteck, T. (2021). Dead-ends in FPGAs for database acceleration. In *SAMOS* (Vol. 13227, pp. 493–504). Springer.
14. Drewes, T., Joseph, J. M., Gurumurthy, B., Broneske, D., Saake, G., & Pionteck, T. (2018). Efficient inter-kernel communication for OpenCL database operators on FPGAs. In *FPT* (pp. 266–269). IEEE.
15. Efron, B. (1979). Bootstrap methods: Another look at the jackknife. *The Annals of Statistics, 7*(1), 1 – 26.
16. Fang, J., Mulder, Y. T. B., Hidders, J., Lee, J., & Hofstee, H. P. (2020). In-memory database acceleration on FPGAs: a survey. In *The VLDB Journal, 29*, 33–59.
17. Gough, B. (2009). *GNU scientific library reference manual*. Network Theory Ltd.
18. Gurumurthy, B., Bidarkar, V. R., Broneske, D., Pionteck, T., & Saake, G. (2023). What happens when two multi-query optimization paradigms combine? A hybrid shared sub-expression (SSE) and materialized view reuse (MVR) study. In *ADBIS* (pp. 74–87). Springer.
19. Gurumurthy, B., Broneske, D., Drewes, T., Pionteck, T., & Saake, G. (2018). Cooking DBMS operations using granular primitives: An overview on a primitive-based RDBMS query evaluation. *Datenbank-Spektrum, 18*, 183–193.
20. Gurumurthy, B., Broneske, D., Durand, G. C., Pionteck, T., & Saake, G. (2023). ADAMANT: A query executor with plug-in interfaces for easy co-processor integration. In *ICDE* (pp. 1153–1166). IEEE.

21. Gurumurthy, B., Broneske, D., Schäler, M., Pionteck, T., & Saake, G. (2021). An investigation of atomic synchronization for sort-based group-by aggregation on GPUs. In *HardBD* (pp. 48–53).
22. Gurumurthy, B., Broneske, D., Schäler, M., Pionteck, T., & Saake, G. (2023). Novel insights on atomic synchronization for sort-based group-by on GPUs. *Distributed and Parallel Databases, 41*(3), 387–409.
23. Gurumurthy, B., Hajjar, I., Broneske, D., Pionteck, T., & Saake, G. (2020). When vectorwise meets hyper, pipeline breakers become the moderator. In *ADMS@VLDB* (pp. 1–10).
24. He, B., Lu, M., Yang, K., Fang, R., Govindaraju, N. K., Luo, Q., & Sander, P. V. (2009). Relational query coprocessing on graphics processors. *TODS, 34*(4), 1–39.
25. Hellerstein, J. M., Haas, P. J., & Wang, H. J. (1997). Online aggregation. *SIGMOD Record, 26*(2), 171–182.
26. Hilprecht, B., Binnig, C., & Röhm, U. (2020) DeepDB: Learn from data, not from queries! *Proceedings of the VLDB Endowment, 13*(7), 992–1005.
27. Kleiner, A., Talwalkar, A., Sarkar, P., & Jordan, M. I. (2014). A scalable bootstrap for massive data. *Journal of the Royal Statistical Society Series B (Statistical Methodology), 76*(4), 795–816.
28. Li, Y., Chow, P., Jiang, J., Zhang, M., & Wei, S. (2012). Software/hardware framework for generating parallel Gaussian random numbers based on the Monty Python method. In *FPT* (pp. 190–197).
29. Lu, A., & Fang, Z. (2024). SQL2FPGA: Automatic acceleration of SQL query processing on modern CPU-FPGA platforms. In *FCCM* (pp. 184–194).
30. Ma, Q., & Triantafillou, P. (2019). DBEst: Revisiting approximate query processing engines with machine learning models. In *SIGMOD* (pp. 1553–1570).
31. Malik, J. S., & Hemani, A. (2016). Gaussian random number generation: A survey on hardware architectures. *ACM Computing Surveys, 49*(3), 1–37.
32. Park, Y., et al. (2018). Verdictdb: Universalizing approximate query processing. In *SIGMOD* (pp. 1461–1476).
33. Peng, J., Zhang, D., Wang, J., & Pei, J. (2018). AQP++: Connecting approximate query processing with aggregate precomputation for interactive analytics. In *SIGMOD* (pp. 1477–1492).
34. Pirk, H., Moll, O., Zaharia, M., & Madden, S. (2016). Voodoo-a vector algebra for portable database performance on modern hardware. *Proceedings of the VLDB Endowment, 9*(14), 1707–1718.
35. Radhakrishna Rao, C., Pathak, P. K., & Koltchinskii, V. I. (1997). Bootstrap by sequential resampling. *Journal of Statistical Planning and Inference, 64*(2), 257–281.
36. Richter, S., Alvarez, V., & Dittrich, J. (2015). A seven-dimensional analysis of hashing methods and its implications on query processing. *PVLDB, 9*(3), 96–107.
37. Rosenfeld, V., Heimel, M., Viebig, C., & Markl, V. (2015). The operator variant selection problem on heterogeneous hardware. In *ADMS* (pp. 1–12).
38. Rosenfeld, V., Heimel, M., Viebig, C., & Markl, V. (2015). The operator variant selection problem on heterogeneous hardware. In *ADMS@ VLDB* (pp. 1–12).
39. Saake, G., Sattler, K.-U., & Heuer, A. (2019). *Datenbanken. Implementierungstechniken.* MITP-Verlags GmbH & Co. KG.
40. Sanca, V., Chrysogelos, P., & Ailamaki, A. (2024). Efficient and reusable lazy sampling. *SIGMOD Record, 53*(1), 33–42.
41. Schmid, R., Plauth, M., Wenzel, L., Eberhardt, F., & Polze, A. (2020). Accessible near-storage computing with FPGAs. In *EuroSys*. ACM.
42. ICD & Statista. (2024). Volume of data/information created, captured, copied, and consumed worldwide from 2010 to 2020, with forecasts from 2021 to 2025. https://www.statista.com/statistics/871513/worldwide-data-created. Accessed 20 March 2024.
43. Subramanian, H. K. H., Gurumurthy, B., Durand, G. C., Broneske, D., & Saake, G. (2023). Out-of-the-box library support for DBMS operations on GPUs. *DAPD, 41*(3), 489–509.

44. Thomas, D. B. (2015). The table-hadamard GRNG: An area-efficient FPGA gaussian random number generator. *ACM Transactions on Reconfigurable Technology and Systems, 8*(4), 1–22.
45. Transaction Processing Performance Council. TPC: TPC-H Decision Support Benchmark. https://www.tpc.org/tpch. Accessed 20 March 2024.
46. Xilinx. (2020). LogiCORE IP product guide. https://docs.xilinx.com/v/u/en-US/pg060-floating-point
47. Ziener, D., Bauer, F., Becher, A., Dennl, C., Meyer-Wegener, K., Schürfeld, U., Teich, J., Vogt, J. S., & Weber, H. (2016). FPGA-based dynamically reconfigurable SQL query processing. *ACM Transactions on Reconfigurable Technology and Systems, 9*(4), 1–24.

Chapter 2
Query Processing on Heterogeneous Hardware

Anastasiia Kozar, Janis von Bleichert, Sebastian Breß, Philipp M. Grulich, Clemens Lutz, Tilmann Rabl, Viktor Rosenfeld, Jonas Traub, Steffen Zeuch, and Volker Markl

Abstract In modern processor design, power efficiency has become the primary constraint, prompting manufacturers to develop processors that balance energy consumption with the growing demand for speed. This shift has initiated an era of heterogeneous multi-core computing, characterized by machines utilizing various processors such as GPUs, MICs, and FPGAs. These processors significantly enhance performance due to their computational capabilities and memory bandwidth, essential for optimizing query processing performance. However, executing database queries efficiently across diverse processors presents challenges due to architectural differences, leading to varied performance outcomes for different operator implementations. This chapter explores methodologies for executing database queries on any processor with maximum efficiency without manual adjustments. We propose compiling database queries into optimized code that can adapt continuously

A. Kozar (✉) · P. M. Grulich · V. Rosenfeld · J. Traub · S. Zeuch
Technische Universität Berlin, Berlin, Germany
e-mail: anastasiia.kozar@tu-berlin.de; grulich@tu-berlin.de; jonas.traub@tu-berlin.de; steffen.zeuch@tu-berlin.de

J. von Bleichert
vB Internet GmbH, Berlin, Germany
Work done while the author was employed at Technische Universität Berlin, Berlin, Germany

S. Breß
Snowflake, Inc., Berlin, Germany
Work done while the author was employed at Technische Universität Berlin, Berlin, Germany

C. Lutz
NVIDIA, Santa Clara, CA, USA
Work done while the author was employed at Technische Universität Berlin, Berlin, Germany

T. Rabl
HPI, University of Potsdam, Potsdam, Germany
e-mail: Tilmann.Rabl@hpi.de

V. Markl
Technische Universität Berlin, DFKI GmbH, Berlin, Germany
e-mail: volker.markl@tu-berlin.de

K.-U. Sattler et al. (eds.), *Scalable Data Management for Future Hardware*,
https://doi.org/10.1007/978-3-031-74097-8_2

to achieve optimal performance across a wide array of processors. Key areas of focus include the use of GPUs in database systems, addressing challenges such as workload distribution and data transfer bottlenecks, and introducing a classification scheme for strategies developed to tackle these issues. Additionally, we examine NVLink 2.0 technology's potential to improve data transfer efficiency between GPUs and CPUs, enhancing GPU-accelerated query processing. Furthermore, we present a novel adaptive query compilation-based stream processing engine (SPE) that surpasses traditional interpretation-based SPEs by incorporating runtime optimizations and task-based parallelization. This approach allows for dynamic adjustments to data characteristics, significantly improving query execution efficiency and throughput. Through these explorations, we aim to provide insights into current systems and highlight areas for future research, ultimately contributing to the advancement of heterogeneous query processing systems.

2.1 Introduction

In the realm of modern processor design, the primary constraint is power efficiency. This limitation compels manufacturers to tailor their processors, ensuring they remain within energy budgets while meeting the increasing demands for speed from applications. This trend has led to the emergence of machines equipped with a variety of heterogeneous processors such as GPUs, MICs, or FPGAs. These processors offer significant performance enhancements due to their additional computational capabilities and memory bandwidth. They represent a crucial strategy for boosting query processing performance as the era of homogeneous multi-core computing draws to a close [1–3].

The advent of the heterogeneous multi-core era necessitates efficient execution of database queries across various processors. Although parallel programming APIs like OpenCL facilitate the operation of single operators across a broad spectrum of processors, they fall short of ensuring consistent performance across different architectures. This discrepancy arises from the architectural variances among processors, which lead to divergent performances for different operator implementations. For instance, CPUs favor sequential memory access patterns, whereas GPUs benefit from coalesced memory access. Achieving optimal performance typically requires processor-specific data structures and code optimizations.

Past approaches have either concentrated on generating highly efficient code tailored to a single processor [4, 5] or on enabling database operators to function across multiple processors using a unified codebase [6, 7]. Code generation strategies often face challenges such as lengthy compilation times or limitations to a single processor type due to the generation of low-level machine code (e.g., LLVM, CUDA, OpenCL, or HSA). On the other hand, hardware-agnostic methods struggle with achieving performance portability [8].

This chapter, a part of the SPP project's broader initiative, aims to explore methodologies for executing database queries on any processor at maximum efficiency without manual adjustments. To this end, we propose the concept of compiling database queries into efficient code capable of running across a wide array of processors. By fine-tuning the generated code, the database system can continuously adapt until it achieves optimal performance on the specified processors. The efforts documented here specifically aim to shed light on several key areas, demonstrating the SPP project's commitment to overcoming the contemporary challenges of heterogeneous computing environments and setting new standards for query processing performance. Specifically, the chapter aims to shed light on several key areas:

- Overview of the significant interest in leveraging GPUs within the database systems research community, attributed to their high computational power and memory bandwidth. We discuss the intricacies of creating heterogeneous query processing systems that utilize both CPUs and GPUs, outlining the challenges of workload distribution, data transfer bottlenecks, and multi-processor support, and introduce a classification scheme to organize the strategies developed to tackle these issues, offering insights into current systems and highlighting areas for future research (Sect. 2.3).
- Exploration of the potential of GPUs as accelerators for database query processing, highlighting their limitations due to small onboard memory and inadequate CPU interconnect bandwidth, which lead to scalability issues for large datasets. We explore how NVLink 2.0, a new interconnect technology, can alleviate these bottlenecks by enabling efficient data transfer between GPUs and CPUs, thereby enhancing the processing of large datasets on GPUs. Through an analysis of NVLink 2.0, we demonstrate significant performance improvements in a no-partitioning hash join operation, achieving speedups over traditional connections and optimized CPU implementations, suggesting that fast GPU interconnects could revolutionize GPU-accelerated query processing (Sect. 2.4).
- Development of a novel adaptive query compilation-based stream processing engine (SPE) that overcomes the limitations of traditional interpretation-based SPEs, which do not utilize runtime optimizations and therefore cannot fully leverage modern hardware or accommodate changing data characteristics. By incorporating query compilation and task-based parallelization specifically designed for stream processing, alongside adaptive compilation techniques for runtime re-optimizations, we allow for dynamic adjustments to fluctuating data characteristics, significantly enhancing query execution efficiency and markedly improving throughput compared to current state-of-the-art SPEs (Sect. 2.5).

2.2 Background

We now discuss the state of the art of query optimizations on modern processors in a database context. We focus on query compilation, related work from the compiler community on translating programs to processors with different architectures, and query processing on heterogeneous processors.

2.2.1 Query Compilation

The concept of query compilation traces its roots back to the pioneering System R project [9], gaining initial attention in the field of database management systems. Throughout the 1980s [10] and with the rise of main memory databases, the focus on query compilation intensified, driven by the need to minimize main memory traffic and CPU instruction execution. The advent of just-in-time compilation capabilities, exemplified by Rao et al.'s work [11], allowed for the generation of query-specific code, marking a significant advancement in the field. The approach of template-based code generation for compiling queries into C code, as explored by Krikellas et al., further contributed to this evolution, leading to efficient machine code production via C compilers [12].

Neumann's introduction of the produce-consume model revolutionized the way code could be generated for data-centric query processing, emphasizing the fusion of operators in an operator pipeline for streamlined execution [4]. This model also highlighted the efficiency of generating LLVM IR code over C code to reduce compilation times significantly. Further developments, such as the morsel framework proposed by Leis et al., introduced NUMA-aware parallelization techniques for compiled operator pipelines, enhancing performance and scalability [13].

Comparative studies, like those conducted by Sompolski et al., critically evaluated the merits of compiled execution against interpreted vector-at-a-time processing, suggesting a hybrid approach that incorporates blockwise query processing for optimal performance [14]. This period also saw the manual compilation of TPC-H queries by Dees and Sanders, revealing the substantial performance potential of query compilation [15]. The exploration of query compilation in various contexts, including language-integrated queries and high-level language database systems, underscored the versatility and potential of this approach [16]. Notably, the DBToaster platform emerged as a pioneering solution for compiling view maintenance queries into efficient machine code, demonstrating the practical applicability and benefits of query compilation in commercial products like Hekaton and Impala [17–19].

Innovative compiler frameworks, such as Kernel Weaver proposed by Wu et al. [5], have shown the ability to automatically fuse relational operator kernels with those from other domains, broadening the applicability of query compilation. Similarly, the compute/accumulate model introduced by Rauhe et al. for GPU code compilation represents a notable advancement, structuring query operations into distinct phases for enhanced efficiency [20]. The trend toward high-level language utilization for database system development, illustrated by projects like LegoBase and DBLAB, emphasizes the move toward generative programming and domain-specific languages for generating low-level code, showcasing the continuous evolution and refinement of query compilation techniques [21, 22].

2.2.2 Compilers

The development of frameworks like Delight by Brown et al. has facilitated the creation, compilation, and execution of domain-specific languages (DSLs), promoting ease of programmability at high abstraction levels while ensuring high performance through generic and DSL-specific compiler optimizations [23]. Dandelion, a versatile compiler that leverages .NET LINQ for compiling data-parallel programs to various heterogeneous processors, exemplifies the advancements in compiler technology, enabling efficient data processing across different computing environments, including CPUs, GPUs, and FPGAs [24].

2.2.3 Databases on Heterogeneous Hardware

The exploration of database operations on heterogeneous hardware has led to significant research into optimizing relational operators for multi-core CPUs and GPUs, as demonstrated by studies on efficient hash and sort-merge joins [25–27]. The development of GPU-accelerated database engines, such as GPUQP, and investigations into the performance of hash joins on coupled CPU/GPU architectures have highlighted the potential of heterogeneous processing environments for enhancing query execution efficiency [28]. Projects like OmniDB and the approximate and refine technique propose innovative approaches to database engine design and query processing, emphasizing the importance of hardware obliviousness and lossy data compression techniques for efficient co-processing [7].

This growing body of research underscores the diverse strategies employed to harness the capabilities of heterogeneous hardware for database query processing, reflecting a broader trend toward leveraging specialized processors for improved performance and efficiency in data management systems.

2.3 Query Processing on Heterogeneous CPU/GPU Systems

Due to the high computational power and internal memory bandwidth, graphic processing units (GPUs) have been extensively studied by the database systems research community. A heterogeneous query processing system that employs CPUs and GPUs simultaneously faces several challenges, including how to effectively distribute the workload on processors with different capabilities, how to overcome the data transfer bottleneck, and how to support efficient implementations for multiple processors. In this section, we introduce a classification scheme, a first contribution to the SPP project, designed to categorize techniques developed to address these challenges. This scheme helps in structuring existing approaches and guides the development of new strategies, thereby facilitating the broader project's goals of enhancing computational efficiency and scalability in heterogeneous systems.

2.3.1 Processor Architectures

In this section, we describe the architectures of CPUs and GPUs as well as different strategies for integrating GPUs in a heterogeneous system. We also briefly introduce the traditional GPU programming model and describe differences to CPU programming. GPUs are typically characterized by high computational power and memory bandwidth, especially compared to CPUs. These performance advantages of GPUs over CPUs are often cited as a major motivation to use GPUs for query processing in database research [29–35].

Yet it is too simplistic to reduce GPUs to these performance advantages. In fact, when we focus on other metrics, CPUs outperform GPUs. Instead, the different performance characteristics of CPUs and GPUs indicate that they are optimized for different usage scenarios. Both processor types are constrained by the power wall, i.e., the requirement to keep their power consumption, and the resulting heat dissipation, inside a manageable level [36]. To achieve high performance under these constraints, the architectures of CPUs and GPUs are based on different design trade-offs, which are driven by concrete application requirements. This specialization implies that the choice of the best processor depends on the type of the problem. In the following, we describe the design considerations that motivate the architecture of CPUs and GPUs in more detail. In Table 2.1, we contrast a number of processor properties of the EPYC 7702P and the Ampere A100 for reference.

Table 2.1 Comparison of processor properties of the AMD EPYC 7702P and the NVIDIA Ampere A100

	EPYC 7702P	Ampere A100
Release year	2019	2020
Transistors	38.7 billion	54.2 billion
Thermal design power	200 W	400 W
Independent cores/SMs	64 cores	108 SMs
Concurrent threads	2/core	128/SM
Maximum frequency	3.35 GHz	1.41 GHz
Register file size	6.4 KiB/core	256 KiB/SM
L1 data cache	32 KiB/core	192 KiB/SM
L2 cache	512 KiB/core	–
Last-level cache	16x 16 MiB	40 MiB
Memory interface	8x 64-bit DDR4-3200	10x 512 bit HBM2
Memory clock	1.6 GHz	1.215 GHz

2.3.2 Conventional CPUs

The primary optimization goal of conventional CPUs is their serial performance [36]. Historically, manufacturers relied on Dennard scaling [4] to increase processor frequency and thus processing speed. Dennard scaling relates the size of transistors with their operating frequency and voltage. As transistors shrink, more of them can be integrated on a die, and their operating frequency increases. To keep power consumption constant, the operating voltage has to be reduced. This effect alone has led to a 100× performance increase of recent CPUs compared to early CPUs [36].

Processor vendors have also implemented microarchitecture advances that extract implicit instruction level parallelism (ILP) from the instruction stream, to improve serial performance. The core technique of these advances is the processor pipeline that overlaps the execution stages of different instructions. Ideally, the pipeline is always full, and the processor can issue and complete one instruction per cycle per functional unit. However, the pipeline stalls when instructions are dependent on each other or when the processor has to wait on memory access.

Modern CPUs implement a number of techniques to keep the pipeline from stalling and increase ILP [37]. For example, branch prediction continues to fetch and decode instructions of the predicted branch in the instruction stream, which keeps the early stages of the pipeline full. Speculative execution also executes the instructions of predicted branches and only discards their results if the prediction later proves to be incorrect. Out-of-order execution reorders the instruction stream to reduce the impact of dependent instructions and memory stalls. Together with Dennard scaling, these microarchitecture advances have increased scalar performance significantly over the years.

The exploitation of ILP is limited by the performance of the memory system. Data references stall the processor pipeline if the processor cannot find independent instructions to execute. The length of the stall depends on the memory latency and the number of concurrent memory accesses that can be satisfied by the available memory bandwidth. Unfortunately, the rate of improvement of memory performance has lagged processor performance over time, both for latency and bandwidth. Whereas early CPUs could access memory in a single clock cycle, they now have to wait hundreds of cycles. In typical programs, especially in those that depend on integer performance, there is not enough instruction-level parallelism available to overcome this access latency. To reduce memory access latency, modern CPUs feature large caches, which allow CPUs to exploit temporal and spatial data access locality. However, even with perfect caches, the performance of data-intensive applications is limited by memory access due to compulsory cache misses when loading previously unseen data.

The processes that drove performance increases in the past no longer work. Due to physical limitations, manufacturers cannot further reduce operating voltages without compromising reliability. Thus, they cannot increase the operating frequency without excessive power consumption and heat dissipation. On the other hand, the microarchitecture advances to increase ILP are not energy-efficient because their implementation requires an increasing amount of the processor's transistor budget. Consequently, scalar performance has slowed significantly in recent years.

Since scalar performance is no longer increasing, manufacturers have turned to increase throughput, by exploiting explicit data parallelism. Multi-core CPUs integrate multiple processor cores on a single die. Simultaneous multi-threading (SMT) enables independent threads to utilize different execution units of a core, which explicitly increases ILP. SIMD instructions work on multiple data items in a single cycle. These developments mean that multi-core CPUs are becoming more similar to GPUs.

2.3.3 Dedicated GPUs

GPUs were originally developed as special-purpose processors to accelerate graphics rendering in 3D games. The generic computing capabilities of GPUs are an artifact of making the graphics rendering pipeline more flexible to better support a greater variety of 3D games [35]. Consequently, GPUs are optimized for throughput applications of which graphics rendering is a prime example. Throughput applications are characterized by a high degree of data parallelism, latency tolerance, and high demands on memory bandwidth.

Instead of extracting the implicit ILP from an instruction stream, GPUs rely on explicit data parallelism to keep processing cores busy. Consequently, GPUs contain many simple processing cores instead of implementing fewer complex processing cores, as CPUs do. As a result, the processing performance of GPUs scales (almost) linearly with the transistor budget, whereas the microarchitectural enhancements of CPUs scale only proportional to the square root of the transistor budget.

Since GPUs are optimized for aggregate throughput instead of serial performance, the latency of processing an individual data item is less important. This latency tolerance has two important effects on the hardware design. First, it allows us to reduce the processing frequency and use more transistors to implement processing cores within a given power budget. Second, instead of reducing the latency of an individual data item through caches and microarchitectural advances, the latency is hidden by processing other data items. To support latency hiding, the GPU hardware allows for a massive oversubscription of threads. For example, each streaming multiprocessor (SM) of an Ampere A100 GPU can execute four independent warps at a time. At the same time, each SM can manage 64 different warps that await execution. At each cycle, the SM can switch between active and inactive warps without overhead. To support these many threads, GPUs contain very large register files that are orders of magnitude larger than the register files of CPUs. Compared to CPUs, the GPU cache hierarchy also places more emphasis on large L1 caches, which are close to the processing cores. In contrast, the shared last-level cache is smaller on GPUs than on CPUs. The streaming data access pattern of GPU graphics workloads exhibits relatively little data reuse, and therefore caches are less useful.

The memory subsystem of GPUs is optimized for high memory bandwidth, in order to feed input data to the large number of processing cores. GPUs typically use more independent memory controllers than CPUs and therefore have a wider memory data bus. The memory bus is also clocked faster, up to 7 GHz for GDDR6 memory. High-performance GPUs use three-dimensional stacked memory, which is packaged together with the GPU processor die in a single package. Stacked memory is addressed through an ultrawide data bus. For example, the Ampere A100 uses ten 512-bit memory controllers, which results in an overall bus width of 5120 bits. This is an order of magnitude wider than the 8x 64-bit bus width of the EPYC 7702P.

2.3.4 GPU Integration

Traditionally, GPUs are dedicated processors that are accessed over a system bus. In a typical system, the CPU and the GPU are connected by a PCI express (PCIe) 3.0 bus [52], which offers up to 14.9 GiB/s in theoretical bandwidth. This connection is an order of magnitude slower than the main memory bandwidth of the CPU and two orders of magnitude slower than GPU memory. It therefore represents a significant performance bottleneck [36, 55, 83]. Furthermore, the separate CPU and GPU memory spaces are not coherent. Consequently, shared data structures have to be synchronized manually, which increases implementation complexity [83]. Recent GPU architectures reduce this problem somewhat. For example, AMD GPUs use PCIe atomics [52] to synchronize execution between CPUs and GPUs [84]. NVIDIA GPU support software-assisted memory coherence and system-wide atomics through page faults and automatic page migrations, but this mechanism causes runtime overheads [85]. On IBM Power9 systems, NVIDIA GPUs can be connected to the CPU over NVLink 2.0 [86], which supports cache coherence and atomic operations between CPU and GPU memory in hardware and eliminates these overheads [83]. NVLink 2.0 is also $5\times$ faster than PCIe 3.0, which reduces the effects of data transfer bottleneck [83].

2.3.5 GPU Programming Model

GPUs are programmed in a specialized programming model that allows programmers to formulate a parallel program in a scalable way [37]. The programming model represents GPU hardware as an abstract parallel processor. It defines how a parallel program is executed on the processor and how the workload is partitioned to achieve scalable parallelism. As a result, GPU programming differs from CPU programming in a number of important ways. Two popular implementations of this programming model are CUDA [37, 87] and OpenCL [88, 89]. In the following, we primarily use OpenCL terminology to describe the programming model but also state equivalent CUDA terms.

2.3.5.1 Abstract Parallel Programming Model

OpenCL represents parallel processors, e.g., multi-core CPUs or GPUs, as computational devices consisting of compute units (CUs). On NVIDIA GPUs, each compute unit maps to a SM, and on multi-core CPUs, a compute unit represents a logical CPU core. An OpenCL program is divided into host code and device code. The host code executes in a single thread on the host CPU. It is responsible for coordinating operations on the device, e.g., initiating the execution of device code and transferring data between separate memory spaces. The device code executes in parallel on the OpenCL device. It consists of kernels that are scalar functions, expressing the operations on a single datum of a data-parallel task. When launching a kernel, the programmer specifies a hierarchy of independent kernel instances that execute on the device. Each kernel instance is called a work item (or a thread in CUDA). Individual work items are arranged into work groups (called thread block in CUDA). All work items of a kernel invocation make up the nd-range of the kernel (called grid in CUDA). The work items of a single work group can cooperate with each other through special instructions, fast barrier synchronizations, and a very fast shared memory space called local memory. The last two hardware features enable the work items of a work group to process a datum, store the result in a shared cache, and wait until the other work items have finished their computations before accessing their results. In contrast, work items from different work groups execute completely independently.

2.3.5.2 Scalable Parallelism

It is through this two-tiered hierarchy of work items and work groups that the OpenCL and CUDA programming models support scalable parallelism [37]. Using the programming model, a programmer must partition a problem into two levels. The first level, i.e., the individual work groups, works on coarse-grained subproblems that can be solved independently in parallel. Each work group executes on a dedicated compute unit. Multiple work groups can execute on different compute units in parallel or on the same compute unit sequentially. The second level, i.e., the work items within a single work group, work on fine-grained subproblems, which can be solved cooperatively in parallel. The GPU hardware supports this fine-grained thread and data parallelism through fast barrier synchronization, access to shared local memory, lightweight thread creation, and zero-overhead scheduling.

Additionally, independent nd-ranges can execute concurrently given sufficient hardware resources. This concurrent execution allows for coarse-grained task parallelism.

2.3.5.3 Differences to CPU Programming

A major difference between programming on GPUs and CPUs is the number of running threads and how these threads work together. In general, on CPUs, comparatively few threads operate independently on coarse-grained subproblems. Specifically, on multi-core CPUs, each CPU core typically executes a single hardware thread that consumes an independent partition of the data [13]. Although threads running on different CPU cores can communicate with each other, they must avoid performance pitfalls caused by accessing shared or nearby data, e.g., false sharing. In contrast, GPUs execute many thousands of hardware threads to hide the latency of individual operations. Moreover, individual threads have to cooperate with each other to achieve peak performance. A classic example of a data-processing task that showcases this cooperation to achieve high throughput is parallel reduction on GPUs [40].

A second important difference between GPU and CPU programming is the Single Instruction, Multiple Thread (SIMT) [35] execution model. In the SIMT execution model, a number of work items share the instruction pointer and execute a common instruction. For example, on NVIDIA GPUs, 32 threads make up a warp and execute the same instruction at the same time. The SIMT execution model is similar to the Single Instruction, Multiple Data (SIMD) execution model supported by CPU vector instructions. However, a crucial difference is that GPU kernels are written as scalar functions, independent of the SIMD instruction width of the processor. The GPU hardware also takes care of masking results when different work items follow separate branches in the kernel code. Nevertheless, to maximize performance, programmers still have to take hardware details, such as the warp size, into account. Programmers should avoid diverging code paths for the threads inside a warp [41, 42]; utilize warp-level primitives [43], e.g., warp-level reductions [44] or ballot and shuffle instructions [41, 45, 46]; and let the threads of a warp access adjacent global memory locations, so that the GPU can coalesce these accesses into as few memory transactions as possible [44, 47].

In conclusion, the content presented in this section serves as the first contribution to the SPP project, effectively outlining query processing challenges and solutions within heterogeneous CPU/GPU systems. Through the introduction of a comprehensive classification scheme, this work categorizes and clarifies various techniques that address workload distribution, data transfer bottlenecks, and efficient processor utilization. Further exploration into the architectures of CPUs and GPUs, integration strategies, and programming models underlines the foundational work delivered by this project. These insights significantly enhance the project's impact on developing advanced database systems capable of leveraging the unique strengths of heterogeneous processing environments.

2.4 Processing Large Data on GPUs with Fast Interconnects

Despite GPUs' potential to accelerate database query processing owing to their high processing power and memory bandwidth, their effectiveness is limited by challenges such as low onboard memory and insufficient interconnect bandwidth. This chapter investigates how emerging interconnect technologies, notably NVLink 2.0, address these limitations by facilitating more efficient data transfer and enabling the processing of large datasets on GPUs. We demonstrate that NVLink 2.0 offers substantial improvements in speed compared to traditional interconnects like PCI-e 3.0 and optimized CPU implementations, marking a second major contribution to the SPP project (Fig. 2.1).

Over recent years, GPUs, alongside other co-processors like FPGAs and ASICs, have gained traction in fields ranging from high-performance computing to deep learning [39, 48–51]. However, in the database domain, their adoption has been slower, primarily due to a significant data transfer bottleneck [52]. This bottleneck, arising from the constraints of current GPU interconnects, hinders effective data processing at the speed required by modern databases. Our analysis breaks down the GPU data-processing bottleneck into three critical challenges.

L1: Low Interconnect Bandwidth When the database decides to use the GPU for query processing, it must transfer data ad hoc from CPU memory to the GPU. With current interconnects, this transfer is slower than processing the data on the CPU [53–55]. Consequently, we can only speed up data processing on GPUs by increasing the interconnect bandwidth [5, 34, 56–58]. Although data compression [59] and approximation [60] can reduce transfer volume, their effectiveness varies with the data and query.

L2: Small GPU Memory Capacity To avoid transferring data, GPU-enabled databases cache data in GPU memory [50, 53, 61, 62]. However, GPUs have limited on-board GPU memory capacity (up to 32 GiB). In general, large datasets cannot be stored in GPU memory. The capacity limitation is intensified by database operators that need additional space for intermediate state, e.g., hash tables or sorted arrays. In sum, GPU co-processing does not scale to large data volumes.

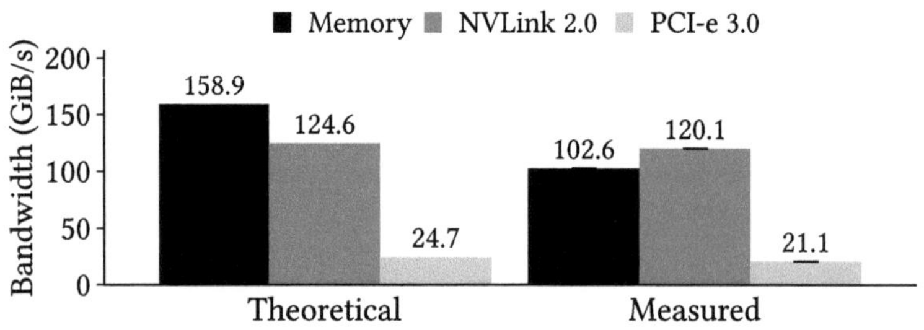

Fig. 2.1 NVLink 2.0 eliminates the GPU's main-memory access disadvantage compared to the CPU

L3: Coarse-Grained Cooperation of CPU and GPU Using only a single processor for query execution leaves available resources unused [56]. However, co-processing on multiple, heterogeneous processors inherently leads to execution skew [63, 64] and can even cause slower execution than on a single processor [53]. Thus, CPU and GPU must cooperate to ensure that the CPU's execution time is the lower bound. Cooperation requires efficient synchronization between processors on shared data structures such as hash tables or B-trees, which is not possible with current interconnects [65].

In addressing these challenges, we explore the capabilities of fast new interconnects, such as NVLink, Infinity Fabric, and CXL, which provide high bandwidth and low latency, enabling nearly full memory bandwidth access from GPU to CPU memory. This analysis leads to the proposal of an innovative co-processing strategy that utilizes cache-coherence offered by these fast interconnects to enable fine-grained CPU-GPU cooperation. Such advancements not only enhance the scalability of GPU co-processing but also integrate GPUs more tightly with CPUs, significantly alleviating the data transfer bottleneck.

This exploration and the subsequent technological advancements form a core part of the SPP project's contributions, setting a new standard in the integration of GPUs into database systems and potentially transforming their applicability in real-world scenarios.

2.4.1 Analysis of Fast Interconnect

In this section, we analyze the class of fast interconnects by example of NVLink 2.0 to understand their performance and new functionality in the context of data management. The main improvements of fast interconnects compared to PCI-e 3.0 are higher bandwidth, lower latency, and cache-coherence. We investigate these properties and examine the benefits and challenges for scaling co-processing. Bandwidth & Latency. We start by quantifying how much NVLink 2.0 improves the GPU's interconnect performance. We compare NVLink 2.0's performance to GPU (PCI-e 3.0) and CPU interconnects (Intel Xeon Ultra Path Interconnect (UPI), IBM POWER9 X-Bus), CPU memory (Intel Xeon, IBM POWER9), and GPU memory (Nvidia V100).

We first compare NVLink 2.0 to the other GPU and CPU interconnects in Fig. 2.2a. Our measurements show that NVLink 2.0 has 5x more sequential bandwidth than PCI-e 3.0 and twice as much as UPI and X-Bus. Random access patterns are 14x faster than PCI-e 3.0 and 35% faster than UPI. However, while the latency of NVLink 2.0 is 45% lower than PCI-e 3.0, it is 3.6x higher than UPI and 2x higher than X-Bus. Overall, NVLink 2.0 is significantly faster than PCI-e 3.0 and more bandwidth-oriented than the CPU interconnects. Next, we show the NVLink 2.0 vs. CPU memory in Fig. 2.2b. We note that the IBM CPU has eight DDR4-2666 memory channels, while the Intel Xeon only has six channels of the same memory type. We see that for sequential accesses, the Intel Xeon and IBM POWER9 have

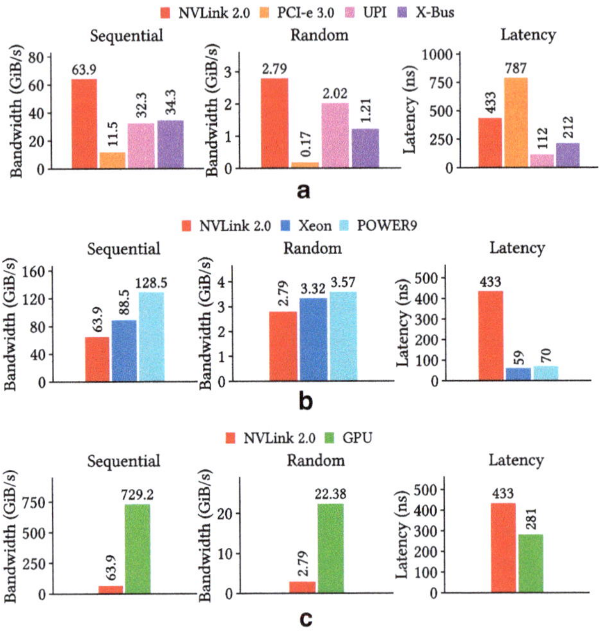

Fig. 2.2 Bandwidth and latency of memory reads on IBM and Intel systems with Nvidia GPUs. (**a**) NVLink 2.0 vs. CPU & GPU interconnects. (**b**) NVLink 2.0 vs. CPU memory. (**c**) NVLink 2.0 vs. GPU memory

28% and 65% higher bandwidth than NVLink 2.0, respectively. For random access, NVLink 2.0 is on par with the Intel Xeon, but 30% slower than the IBM POWER9. The latency of NVLink 2.0 is 6x higher than the latency of CPU memory. We take away that although NVLink 2.0 puts the GPU within a factor of two of the CPUs' bandwidth, it adds significant latency.

Finally, in Fig. 2.2c, we compare GPU accesses to CPU memory over NVLink 2.0 with GPU memory. We observe that both access patterns have an order-of-magnitude higher bandwidth in GPU memory, but that latency over NVLink 2.0 is only 54% higher. As GPUs are designed to handle such high-latency memory accesses [38], they are well equipped to cope with the additional latency of NVLink 2.0. Cache-coherence. Cache-coherence simplifies the practical use of NVLink 2.0 for data processing. The advantages are threefold. First, the GPU can directly access any location in CPU memory, therefore pinning memory becomes unnecessary. Second, allocating pageable memory is faster than allocating pinned memory [66–68]. Third, the operating system and database are able to perform background tasks that are important for long-running processes, such as memory defragmentation [69] and optimizing NUMA locality through page migration [38].

In contrast, the non-cache-coherence of PCI-e has two main drawbacks. First, data consistency must be managed in software instead of in hardware. The programmer either manually flushes the caches [70] or the OS migrates pages [71]. Second, system-wide atomics are unsupported. Instead, a work-around is provided by first migrating Unified Memory pages to GPU memory and then performing the atomic operation in GPU memory [72]. Research shows that adding fine-grained cache-coherence to PCI-e is not feasible due to its high latency [73]. However, NVLink 2.0 removes these limitations [74] and thus is better suited for data processing.

Benefits We demonstrate three benefits of NVLink 2.0 for data processing with a no-partitioning hash join. First, we are able to scale the probe-side relation to arbitrary data volumes due to NVLink 2.0's high sequential bandwidth. With the hash table stored in GPU memory, we retain the GPU's performance advantage compared to a CPU join. Second, we provide build-side scalability to arbitrary data volumes using NVLink 2.0's low latency and high-random-access bandwidth. Thus, we are able to spill the hash table from GPU to CPU memory. Third, we employ the cache-coherence and system-wide atomics of NVLink 2.0 to share the hash table between a CPU and a GPU and scale-up data processing.

Challenges Despite the benefits of NVLink 2.0 for data processing, translating high interconnect performance into high-performance query processing will require addressing the following challenges. First, an out-of-core GPU join operator must perform both data access and computation efficiently. Early GPU join approaches cannot saturate the interconnect [49, 75]. More recent algorithms saturate the interconnect and are optimized to access data over a low-bandwidth interconnect [58, 76]. This can involve additional partitioning steps on the CPU [58]. We investigate how a GPU join operator can take full advantage of the higher interconnect performance. Second, scaling the build-side volume beyond the capacity of GPU memory in a NP-HJ requires spilling the hash table to CPU memory. However, spilling to CPU memory implies that the GPU performs irregular accesses to CPU memory, as, by design, hash functions map keys to uniformly distributed memory locations. Such irregular accesses are inefficient over high-latency interconnects. For this reason, previous approaches either cannot scale beyond GPU memory [75, 76] or are restricted to partitioning-based joins [58]. Higher interconnect performance requires us to reconsider how well a NP-HJ that spills to CPU memory performs on GPUs. Third, fully exploiting a heterogeneous system consisting of CPUs and GPUs requires them to cooperatively process the join. We must take into account data locality, synchronization costs, and differences in hardware architectures to achieve efficiency.

Conclusions Overall, this chapter has thoroughly explored the role of advanced interconnect technologies such as NVLink 2.0 in overcoming traditional barriers to GPU utilization in database systems. By addressing key issues such as low interconnect bandwidth, limited GPU memory capacity, and the need for more refined CPU-GPU cooperation, these technologies represent a significant leap forward in database query processing capabilities. The introduction of high-speed, low-latency interconnects has not only mitigated the data transfer bottleneck but also enhanced the feasibility of GPUs for handling larger datasets more efficiently.

Our findings indicate that with improved interconnects, GPUs can achieve performance parity with CPUs, even in data-intensive scenarios that were previously impractical. This breakthrough in technology enables a more seamless and dynamic integration of heterogeneous processing units, offering a scalable solution that aligns with the evolving demands of modern databases. Furthermore, the strategies developed for fine-grained synchronization and data sharing between CPUs and GPUs pave the way for more sophisticated query processing techniques that can exploit the full potential of both architectures.

The advancements discussed in this chapter are a direct result of the SPP project's commitment to pushing the boundaries of technological innovation in database systems. These contributions not only enhance the performance and scalability of database systems but also set new benchmarks for future research in this area. As we continue to refine these interconnect technologies and co-processing strategies, the implications for the database systems research community and related industries are profound, underscoring the foundational shift in how data-processing tasks are approached and executed in heterogeneous computing environments.

2.5 Efficient Stream Processing Through Adaptive Query Compilation

Following the exploration of advanced computational architectures in previous chapters, this section introduces Grizzly [77], a groundbreaking stream processing engine (SPE) that represents the final contribution of the SPP project. While previous discussions have highlighted the challenges and innovations in handling large-scale data processing on heterogeneous systems, Grizzly specifically addresses the unique demands of stream processing in real-time analytics environments.

SPEs traditionally suffer from limitations such as inefficient hardware utilization and a lack of adaptability to changing data characteristics [78, 79], due to their reliance on interpretation-based processing models. These challenges often lead to suboptimal performance, especially as the volume and velocity of data continue to increase. Grizzly emerges as a solution specifically designed to overcome these hurdles by employing adaptive query compilation, which significantly enhances the efficiency of query execution within SPEs.

Grizzly's innovative approach combines specialized query compilation with task-based parallelism, tailored to the needs of streaming data. This allows for dynamic adaptation to data changes through an integration of lightweight statistics collection and on-the-fly compilation techniques. As a result, Grizzly achieves an order-of-magnitude improvement in throughput compared to existing SPEs, marking a significant advancement in stream processing technology.

By focusing on adaptive query compilation, Grizzly addresses a gap in the current landscape of SPEs, where most systems do not fully exploit the capabilities of modern hardware. This SPE not only enhances the execution of long-running queries over unbounded, continuously changing data streams but also sets new benchmarks for performance and scalability within the field.

As we detail Grizzly's architecture and operational dynamics, it becomes clear that this SPE not only aligns with the objectives of the SPP project but also pushes the boundaries of what is possible in real-time data processing. This section will explore how Grizzly tackles fundamental challenges in stream processing, such as managing diverse windowing semantics and optimizing long-term query performance amidst fluctuating data conditions, thereby demonstrating its pivotal role in advancing stream processing technologies.

2.5.1 *Query Compilation*

Over the last decade, query compilation for data-at-rest processing has been extensively studied [11, 80, 81] and implemented in several systems [81, 82]. To generate code for a query, many of these systems apply the produce/consume [81] model. In this approach, a query compiler segments a query plan into pipelines whenever a materialization of intermediate results is required (e.g., for Aggregation or Join operators). All operations inside a pipeline are fused to one combined operator that performs a single pass over the data such that data stays in CPU registers [81]. To implement the produce/consume model, the compiler requires each operator to implement two functions. First, the produce function is called on the root operator, which navigates the query plan from the root to the leaves and segments the query in pipelines. Second, the consume function is called from the leaf nodes, navigates to the root node, and generates the code for each pipeline. This results in a very compact code fragment that combines the processing of all pipeline operators.

2.5.2 *Grizzly*

In this section, we introduce Grizzly, our novel adaptive, compilation-based SPE. Grizzly's primary goal is to provide a high-level query interface for end users while at the same time achieving the performance of hand-optimized code.

2.5.2.1 Challenges for Compilation-Based SPEs

Similar to query compilation for data-at-rest, a compilation-based SPE segments queries into multiple pipelines and fuses operators within pipelines. However, stream processing workloads introduce several new challenges.

Challenge 1 Stream processing semantics. To the best of our knowledge, there is no SPE that is able to fuse stream processing queries involving windowing. The main challenges are threefold. First, the window triggering depends on the window assignment and is order sensitive. Second, the window function needs to be performed after the windowing but defines the state that needs to be stored in windows. Third, triggering involves a final aggregation step (e.g., to compute the average). The cyclic control flow between these three tasks makes it hard to apply state-of-the-art query compilation techniques to an SPE because they assume only linear compile-time dependencies between operators.

Challenge 2 Order-preserving semantics. In contrast to relational algebra, the outcome of stream processing operators depends on the order of records in the data stream. Thus, data-parallel execution requires coordination among processing threads before the next pipeline can process window results. A compilation-based SPE has to take this requirement into account during code generation. As a result, a compilation-based SPE has to adjust the coordination among threads depending on the query to ensure correct processing results while enabling efficient processing.

Challenge 3 Changing data characteristics. Stream processing queries are deployed once and executed for a long time, while the input stream may change. In particular, they may face unpredictable changes in the data characteristics at runtime, e.g., a changing number of distinct values or a changing data distribution of keys. As a consequence, the efficiency of generated code may change over time. Thus, a compilation-based SPE has to re-evaluate the applied optimizations and, if required, generate new code during runtime.

2.5.2.2 Core Principles of Grizzly

Grizzly addresses the challenges by applying query compilation, enabling task-based parallelization, and adaptively optimizing the generated code with regard to hardware and data characteristics.

Query Compilation. Grizzly introduces query compilation for stream processing and handles the complexity of windowing. Within pipelines, Grizzly fuses operations to compact code fragments and performs all pipeline operations in one single pass over a chunk of input records without invoking functions. Thus, data remains in CPU registers as long as possible without loading records repeatedly. To improve data locality in contrast to managed runtimes, Grizzly avoids serialization and accesses all data via raw memory pointer. As a result, query compilation in Grizzly increases code and data locality significantly.

Order-preserving task-based parallelization. To exploit multi-core CPUs efficiently, Grizzly executes pipelines concurrently in a task-based fashion on a global state. This eliminates the overhead of data pre-partitioning and state merging. However, it requires coordination between threads to fulfill the order requirements of stream processing. Grizzly addresses these by introducing a lightweight, lock-free window-processing approach based on atomics.

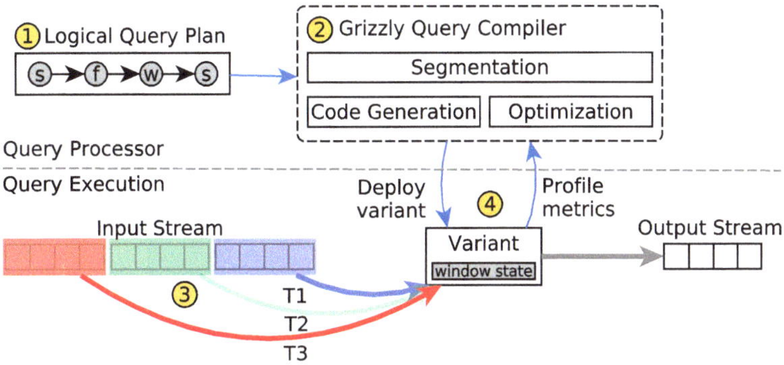

Fig. 2.3 Query Execution Workflow in Grizzly [77]

Adaptive optimizations. Grizzly introduces a feedback loop between code generation and query execution to exploit dynamic workload characteristics. Grizzly continuously monitors performance characteristics, detects changes, and generates new code variants. As a result, Grizzly performs speculative optimizations and assumptions about the incoming data. If an assumption is invalidated, Grizzly re-optimizes a code variant. To reduce the performance overhead, Grizzly combines lightweight but coarse-grained performance counters with fine-grained code instrumentalization.

2.5.2.3 Compilation-Based Query Execution

In Fig. 2.3, we present the architecture of Grizzly's compilation-based query execution model, which consists of four phases. From the logical query plan (1) to the continuous adaption to changing data characteristics (4).

5.2.1 Logical Query Plan In the first phase, Grizzly offers a high-level Flink-like API and translates each query to a logical query plan. This plan contains a chain of operators that consumes a stream with a static source schema. Grizzly supports traditional relational operators, e.g., selection and map, and stream-processing-specific operators for windowing. Window definitions consist of a window type, a window measure, and a window function. Furthermore, Grizzly supports global windows that create one aggregate over the whole stream and keyed windows that created partitioned aggregations per key. Based on these operators, Grizzly supports common stream processing queries.

5.2.2 Query Compiler In the second phase, Grizzly segments the logical query plan into pipelines, performs optimizations, and generates code for each pipeline.

Segmentation Query compilers for data-at-rest fuse operations until they reach a pipeline-breaker, which requires a full materialization of intermediate results (e.g., joins or aggregations). However, the unbounded nature of data streams prevents the full materialization of intermediate results. To this end, Grizzly separates pipelines at operators that require partial materialization, similar to soft-pipeline-breakers [78]. In particular, non-blocking operators (e.g., map or filter) are fused. In contrast, all blocking operations in-stream processing are computed over windows (e.g., aggregations or joins) and terminate pipelines. Thus, the support of windowed operations is crucial for a compilation-based SPE.

Optimization After query segmentation, Grizzly optimizes the individual pipelines. To this end, Grizzly exploits static information, e.g., the hardware configuration, as well as dynamic data characteristics. To collect data characteristics, Grizzly introduces fine-grained instrumentation into the generated code. This enables Grizzly to derive assumptions about the workload, e.g., predicate selectivity and the distributions of field values. Based on these assumptions, Grizzly chooses particular physical operators.

Code Generation In the last step, Grizzly translates each physical pipeline to C++ code and compiles it to an executable code variant. Note that all variants of the same pipeline are semantically equivalent but execute different instructions and access different data structures. For code generation, Grizzly follows the produce/consume model and extends it with support for rich stream processing semantics. In particular, we consider code generation and operator fusion for the window operator.

5.2.3 Execution In the third phase, Grizzly executes the generated pipeline variant. Each variant defines an open and close function to manage the state of the variant. Depending on the physical operators, state is completely pre-allocated or dynamically allocate during execution. For the input stream, Grizzly exploits the fact that input records physically arrive in batches over the network and schedules each batch as a task for an individual thread to utilize multi-core CPUs. Thus, pipelines and their associated state are accessed concurrently by multiple threads. This introduces challenges for window processing, as all threads have to pass the window-end before one thread outputs the result. To this end, Grizzly introduces a lock-free data structure, such that multiple threads can concurrently process a window without starvation.

5.2.4 Profiling & Adaptive Optimization In the final phase, Grizzly continuously collects profiling information and reoptimizes the query in two steps. During query execution, Grizzly collects hardware performance counters, e.g., number of cache misses, to detect changing data characteristics. Hardware performance counters have a negligible performance impact but give a coarse-grained intuition about the evolution of data characteristics. If the collected counters indicate a change, Grizzly collects more fine-grained profiling information, via code instrumentation. Based on this information, Grizzly re-optimizes the query and generates a new code variant.

In our paper [77], we have demonstrated that Grizzly and a handwritten C++ implementation are the only solutions that fully utilize the available hardware to its maximum potential in the context of stream processing engines. Our comparative analysis shows that Grizzly not only matches but significantly outperforms state-of-the-art SPEs by up to an order of magnitude. Importantly, this superior performance does not come at the expense of generality. Grizzly maintains a versatile and adaptable framework suitable for a wide range of streaming applications. These findings underscore Grizzly's advanced architectural design and optimization capabilities, positioning it as a leading solution in the field of high-performance stream processing.

The successes demonstrated by Grizzly reflect the overarching objectives of the SPP project to push the frontiers of processing technologies and adapt them for real-world applications. Through collaborative research and development, the SPP project has made substantial strides in enhancing the capabilities of SPEs. These achievements not only highlight the project's impact but also set a benchmark for future endeavors in the field.

2.6 Conclusion

This chapter has presented key findings from the SPP project's exploration of query processing on modern hardware. We have specifically analyzed the utilization of GPUs to enhance query performance in heterogeneous systems. Our study has acknowledged the substantial benefits of leveraging GPUs while also identifying a significant research gap: a predominant focus on dedicated GPUs, often neglecting integrated GPUs. This oversight limits the broader applicability of our findings, as optimizations tailored for dedicated GPUs do not necessarily apply to integrated ones, given their distinct performance characteristics.

Furthermore, the analysis has highlighted a prevalent CPU-centric approach in the implementation of relational heterogeneous query processors, where the processing model of the GPU was often dictated by that of the CPU. This realization underscores the necessity for further research to establish the most effective processing models for GPUs and to explore potential synergies between CPU- and GPU-processing models.

The advent of innovative GPU technology, particularly fast interconnects like NVLink 2.0, opens new research avenues and practical applications in database processing and the integration of machine learning with relational query processing. However, the adoption of such cutting-edge technologies in commodity hardware remains limited, suggesting that their full potential is yet to be realized in mainstream applications.

Additionally, this chapter introduces Grizzly, an adaptive, compilation-based SPE designed within the framework of the SPP project. Grizzly stands out by supporting various window types, measures, and functions and employs adaptive optimizations to accommodate dynamic data characteristics. It leverages profiling techniques and task-based parallelization to maximize the utilization of modern multi-core CPUs, ensuring that stream processing's ordering requirements are met effectively.

In summary, this chapter not only underscores the promise of heterogeneous hardware in enhancing query processing but also highlights the challenges and opportunities that lie ahead. It calls for a broader research focus that includes integrated GPUs and fast interconnects and showcases Grizzly as a pioneering effort in adaptive, compilation-based stream processing. This effort represents a substantial contribution of the SPP project to the field, pushing the boundaries of what is possible in modern data-processing environments.

Acknowledgments This work has been supported by the German Research Foundation (DFG) under grant nos. 447268056 and 361497736.

References

1. Esmaeilzadeh, H., et al. (2011). Dark silicon and the end of multicore scaling. In *ISCA* (pp. 365–376). ACM.
2. Borkar, S., & Chien, A. A. (2011). The future of microprocessors. *Communications of the ACM, 54*(5), 67–77.
3. Zeuch, S., Chaudhary, A., Del Monte, B., Gavriilidis, H., Giouroukis, D., Grulich, P. M., Breß, S., Traub, J., & Markl, V. (2019). The nebulastream platform: Data and application management for the Internet of Things. arXiv preprint arXiv:1910.07867.s
4. Neumann, T. (2011). Efficiently compiling efficient query plans for modern hardware. *PVLDB, 4*(9), 539–550.
5. Wu, H., Diamos, G., Cadambi, S., & Yalamanchili, S. (2012). Kernel Weaver: Automatically fusing database primitives for efficient GPU computation. In *MICRO* (pp. 107–118). IEEE.
6. Heimel, M., Saecker, M., Pirk, H., Manegold, S., & Markl, V. (2013). Hardware-oblivious parallelism for in-memory column-stores. *PVLDB, 6*(9), 709–720.
7. Zhang, S., et al. (2013). OmniDB: Towards portable and efficient query processing on parallel CPU/GPU architectures. *PVLDB, 6*(12), 1374–1377.
8. Rosenfeld, V., Heimel, M., Viebig, C., & Markl, V. (2015). The operator variant selection problem on heterogeneous hardware. In *ADMS@VLDB. VLDB Endowment.*
9. Chamberlin, D., et al. (1981). A history and evaluation of System R. *Communications of the ACM, 24*(10), 632–646.
10. Freytag, J. C., & Goodman, N. (1989). On the translation of relational queries into iterative programs. *ACM Transactions on Database Systems, 14*(1), 1–27.
11. Rao, J., Pirahesh, H., Mohan, C., & Lohman, G. (2006). Compiled query execution engine using JVM. In *ICDE* (p. 23). IEEE.
12. Krikellas, K., Viglas, S. D., & Cintra, M. (2010). Generating code for holistic query evaluation. In *ICDE* (pp. 613–624). IEEE.
13. Leis, V., Boncz, P., Kemper, A., & Neumann, T. (2014). Morsel-driven parallelism: A NUMA-aware query evaluation framework for the many-core age. In *SIGMOD* (pp. 743–754). ACM. https://doi.org/10.1145/2588555.2610507
14. Sompolski, J., Zukowski, M., & Boncz, P. (2011). Vectorization vs. compilation in query execution. In *DaMoN* (pp. 33–40). ACM.
15. Dees, J., & Sanders, P. (2013). Efficient many-core query execution in main memory column-stores. In *ICDE* (pp. 350–361). IEEE.
16. Nagel, F., Bierman, G. M., & Viglas, S. D. (2014). Code generation for efficient query processing in managed runtimes. *PVLDB, 7*(12), 1095–1106.
17. Ahmad, Y., & Koch, C. (2009). DBToaster: A sql compiler for high-performance delta processing in main-memory databases. *PVLDB, 2*(2), 1566–1569.

18. Freedman, C., Ismert, E., & Larson, P. Å. (2014). Compilation in the Microsoft SQL server hekaton engine. *IEEE Data Engineering Bulletin, 37*(1), 22–30.
19. Wanderman-Milne, S., & Li, N. (2014). Runtime code generation in cloudera impala. *IEEE Data Engineering Bulletin, 37*(1), 31–37.
20. Rauhe, H., Dees, J., Sattler, K.-U., & Faerber, F. (2013). Multi-level parallel query execution framework for cpu and GPU. In *Advances in Databases and Information Systems: 17th East European Conference, ADBIS 2013*, Genoa, Italy, September 1–4, 2013. Proceedings 17 (pp. 330–343). Springer.
21. Klonatos, I., Koch, C., Rompf, T., & Chafi, H. (2014). Building efficient query engines in a high-level language. *Proceedings of the VLDB Endowment, 7*(10), 853–864.
22. Shaikhha, A., Klonatos, Y., Parreaux, L., Brown, L., Dashti, M., & Koch, C. (2016). How to architect a query compiler. In *Proceedings of the 2016 International Conference on Management of Data* (pp. 1907–1922).
23. Brown, K. J., Sujeeth, A. K., Lee, H. J., Rompf, T., Chafi, H., Odersky, M., & Olukotun, K. (2011). A heterogeneous parallel framework for domain-specific languages. In *PACT* (pp. 89–100). IEEE.
24. Rossbach, C. J., Yu, Y., Currey, J., Martin, J. P., & Fetterly, D. (2013). Dandelion: A compiler and runtime for heterogeneous systems. In *SOSP* (pp. 49–68). ACM.
25. Balkesen, C., Teubner, J., Alonso, G., & Özsu, M. T. (2013). Main-memory hash joins on multi-core CPUs: Tuning to the underlying hardware. In *ICDE* (pp. 362–373).
26. He, B., Yang, K., Fang, R., Lu, M., Govindaraju, N., Luo, Q., & Sander, P. (2008). Relational joins on graphics processors. In *SIGMOD* (pp. 511–524). ACM.
27. He, J., Lu, M., & He, B. (2013). Revisiting co-processing for hash joins on the coupled CPU-GPU architecture. *Proceedings of the VLDB Endowment, 6*(10), 889–900.
28. He, B., Lu, M., Yang, K., Fang, R., Govindaraju, N. K., Luo, Q., & Sander, P. V. (2009). Relational query co-processing on graphics processors. *ACM Transactions on Database Systems, 34*, 1–39.
29. Breß, S., Köcher, B., Funke, H., Zeuch, S., Rabl, T., & Markl, V. (2018). Generating custom code for efficient query execution on heterogeneous processors. *The VLDB Journal, 27*(6), 797–822.
30. Fang, W., He, B., & Luo, Q. (2010). Database compression on graphics processors. *Proceedings of the VLDB Endowment, 3*(1–2), 670–680.
31. Govindaraju, N., Gray, J., Kumar, R., & Manocha, D. (2006). GPUTeraSort: High performance graphics co-processor sorting for large database management. In *Proceedings of the ACM SIGMOD International Conference on Management of Data* (pp. 325–336).
32. He, B., Lu, M., Yang, K., Fang, R., Govindaraju, N. K., Luo, Q., & Sander, P. V. (2009). Relational query coprocessing on graphics processors. *ACM Transactions on Database Systems, 34*(4), 21.
33. He, J., Lu, M., & He, B. (2013). Revisiting co-processing for hash joins on the coupled CPU-GPU architecture. *Proceedings of the VLDB Endowment, 6*(10), 889–900.
34. Karnagel, T., Müller, R., & Lohman, G. M. (2015). Optimizing GPU-accelerated group-by and aggregation. In *Proceedings of the ADMS@VLDB* (pp. 13–24).
35. Lindholm, E., Nickolls, J., Oberman, S., & Montrym, J. (2008). NVIDIA Tesla: A unified graphics and computing architecture. *IEEE Micro, 28*(2), 39–55.
36. Gregg, C., & Hazelwood, K. (2011). Where is the data? Why you cannot debate CPU vs. GPU performance without the answer. In *Proceedings of the IEEE International Symposium on Performance Analysis of Systems and Software (ISPASS)* (pp. 134–144).
37. Nickolls, J., Buck, I., Garland, M., & Skadron, K. (2008). Scalable parallel programming with CUDA. *Queue, 6*(2), 40–53.
38. Li, Y., Pandis, I., Müller, R., Raman, V., & Lohman, G. M. (2013). NUMA-aware algorithms: The case of data shuffling. In *CIDR*.
39. Shimoni, A. (2017). Which GPU database is right for me? Retrieved October 1, 2019 from https://hackernoon.com/which-gpu-database-is-right-for-me-6ceef6a17505

40. Luitjens, J. (2014). Faster Parallel Reductions on Kepler. https://developer.nvidia.com/blog/faster-parallelreductions-kepler/
41. Funke, H., & Teubner, J. (2020). Data-parallel query processing on non-uniform data. *Proceedings of VLDB Endow, 13*(6), 884–897. https://doi.org/10.14778/3380750.3380758
42. He, B., & Yu, J. X. (2011). High-throughput transaction executions on graphics processors. *Proceedings of the VLDB Endowment, 4*(5), 314–325. https://doi.org/10.14778/1952376.1952381
43. Lin, Y., Grover, V. (2018). Using CUDA warp-level primitives. https://developer.nvidia.com/blog/usingcuda-warp-level-primitives/
44. NVIDIA Corporation. (2020). NVIDIA A100 tensor core GPU architecture.
45. Li, C., Gu, Y., Qi, J., He, J., Deng, Q., & Yu, G. (2018). A GPU accelerated update efficient index for kNN queries in road networks. In *Proceedings of IEEE ICDE'18* (pp. 881–892). https://doi.org/10.1109/ICDE.2018.00084
46. Sioulas, P., Chrysogelos, P., Karpathiotakis, M., Appuswamy, R., & Ailamaki, A. (2019). Hardware-conscious hash-joins on GPUs. In *Proceedings of IEEE ICDE'19* (pp. 698–709). https://doi.org/10.1109/ICDE.2019.00068
47. Appuswamy, R., Karpathiotakis, M., Porobic, D., & Ailamaki, A. (2017). The case for heterogeneous HTAP. In *Proceedings of the CIDR'17*. http://infoscience.epfl.ch/record/224447
48. Chrysogelos, P., Sioulas, P., & Ailamaki, A. (2019). Hardware-conscious query processing in GPU-accelerated analytical engines. In *Proceedings of the Conference on Innovative Data Systems Research (CIDR)*.
49. He, B., Yang, K., Fang, R., Lu, M., Govindaraju, N., Luo, Q., & Sander, P. (2008). Relational joins on graphics processors. In *SIGMOD* (pp. 511–524). ACM.
50. Heimel, M., et al. (2013). Hardware-oblivious parallelism for in-memory column stores. *PVLDB 6*(9), 709–720.
51. Koliousis, A., Weidlich, M., Castro Fernandez, R., Wolf, A. L., Costa, P., & Pietzuch, P. (2016). SABER: Window-based hybrid stream processing for heterogeneous architectures. In *SIGMOD* (pp. 555–569). ACM.
52. Ajanovic, J. (2009). PCI express 3.0 overview. In *HCS* (Vol. 69). IEEE.
53. Breß, S., Funke, H., & Teubner, J. (2016). Robust query processing in co-processor-accelerated databases. In *Proceedings of the SIGMOD* (pp. 1891–1906). ACM.
54. Gregg, C., & Hazelwood, K. (2011). Where is the data? Why you cannot debate CPU vs. GPU performance without the answer. In *ISPASS* (pp. 134–144). IEEE.
55. Yuan, Y., Lee, R., & Zhang, X. (2013). The Yin and Yang of processing data warehousing queries on GPU devices. *PVLDB, 6*(10), 817–828.
56. Chrysogelos, P., Karpathiotakis, M., Appuswamy, R., & Ailamaki, A. (2019). HetExchange: Encapsulating heterogeneous CPU–GPU parallelism in JIT compiled engines. *Proceedings of the PVLDB, 12*(5), 544–556.
57. Funke, H., Breß, S., Noll, S., Markl, V., & Teubner, J. (2018). Pipelined query processing in coprocessor environments. In *SIGMOD* (pp. 1603–1618). ACM.
58. Sioulas, P., Chrysogelos, P., Karpathiotakis, M., Appuswamy, R., & Ailamaki, A. (2019). Hardware-conscious Hash-Joins on GPUs. In *ICDE*. IEEE
59. Rozenberg, E., & Boncz, P. (2017). Faster across the PCIe bus: A GPU library for lightweight decompression: Including support for patched compression schemes. In *DaMoN* (pp. 8:1–8:5). ACM.
60. Pirk, H., Manegold, S., & Kersten, M. (2014). Waste not. Efficient co-processing of relational data. In *ICDE* (pp. 508–519). IEEE.
61. Karnagel, T., Habich, D., & Lehner, W. (2017). Adaptive work placement for query processing on heterogeneous computing resources. *PVLDB 10*(7), 733–744.
62. Root, C., & Mostak, T. (2016). MapD: A GPU-powered big data analytics and visualization platform. In *SIGGRAPH* (pp. 73:1–73:2). ACM.
63. Dursun, K., Binnig, C., Çetintemel, U., Swart, G., & Gong, W. (2019). A morsel-driven query execution engine for heterogeneous multi-cores. *PVLDB 12*(12), 2218–2229.

64. Gubner, T., Tomé, D., Lang, H., & Boncz, P. (2019). Fluid co-processing: GPU bloom-filters for CPU joins. In *DaMoN* (pp. 9:1–9:10). ACM.
65. Appuswamy, R., Karpathiotakis, M., Porobic, D., & Ailamaki, A. (2017). The case for heterogeneous HTAP. In *CIDR*.
66. Frey, P. W., & Alonso, G. (2009). Minimizing the hidden cost of RDMA. In *ICDCS* (pp. 553–560). https://doi.org/10.1109/ICDCS.2009.32
67. Mietke, F., Rex, R., Baumgartl, R., Mehlan, T., Hoefler, T., & Rehm, W. (2006). Analysis of the memory registration process in the Mellanox InfiniBand Software Stack. In *Euro-PAR* (pp. 124–133).
68. Trivedi, A., Stuedi, P., Metzler, B., Lutz, C., Schmatz, M., & Gross, T. R. (2015). RStore: A direct-access DRAM-based data store. In *ICDCS* (pp. 674–685). https://doi.org/10.1109/ICDCS.2015.74
69. Corbet, J. (2015). Making kernel pages movable. LWN.net. July 2015. https://lwn.net/Articles/650917/
70. Nvidia. (2018). CUDA C programming guide. Nvidia. http://docs.nvidia.com/pdf/CUDA_C_Programming_Guide.pdf. PG-02829-001_v10.0.
71. Nvidia. (2016). Nvidia Tesla P100. Nvidia. https://images.nvidia.com/content/pdf/tesla/whitepaper/pascal-architecture-whitepaper.pdf. WP-08019-001_v01.1.
72. Nvidia. (2019). Tuning CUDA applications for Pascal. Nvidia. https://docs.nvidia.com/cuda/pdf/Pascal_Tuning_Guide.pdf. DA-08134-001_- v10.1.
73. Garcia-Flores, V., Ayguadé, E., & Peña, A. J. (2017). Efficient data sharing on heterogeneous systems. In *ICPP* (pp. 121–130).
74. IBM POWER9 NPU Team. (2018). Functionality and performance of NVLink with IBM POWER9 processors. *IBM Journal of Research and Development 62*(4/5), 9.
75. He, B., et al. (2009). Relational query coprocessing on graphics processors. *TODS 34*, 4.
76. Kaldewey, T., Lohman, G. M., Müller, R., & Volk, P. B. (2012). GPU join processing revisited. In *DaMoN* (pp. 55–62). ACM.
77. Grulich, P. M., Breß, S., Zeuch, S., Traub, J., von Bleichert, J., Chen, Z., Rabl, T., Markl, V. (2020). Grizzly: Efficient stream processing through adaptive query compilation. In *Proceedings of the 2020 ACM SIGMOD International Conference on Management of Data (SIGMOD '20)* (pp. 2487–2503). Association for Computing Machinery. https://doi.org/10.1145/3318464.3389739
78. Zeuch, S., Del Monte, B., Karimov, J., Lutz, C., Renz, M., Traub, J., Breß, S., Rabl, T., & Markl, V. (2019). Analyzing efficient stream processing on modern hardware. In *PVLDB* (Vol. 12). VLDB Endowment (pp. 516–530).
79. Zhang, S., He, B., Dahlmeier, D., Zhou, A. C., & Heinze, T. (2017). Revisiting the design of data stream processing systems on multi-core processors. In *ICDE* (pp. 659–670).
80. Kohn, A., Leis, V., & Neumann, T. (2018). Adaptive execution of compiled queries. In *ICDE* (pp. 197–208). IEEE.
81. Carbone, P., Katsifodimos, A., Ewen, S., Markl, V., Haridi, S., & Tzoumas, K. (2015). Apache flink: Stream and batch processing in a single engine. *IEEE Data Engineering Bulletin, 36*(4).
82. Toshniwal, A., Taneja, S., Shukla, A., Ramasamy, K., Patel, J. M., Kulkarni, S., Jackson, J., Gade, K., Fu, M., Donham, J., Bhagat, N., Mittal, S., Ryaboy, D. (2014). Storm @Twitter. In *Proceedings of the ACM SIGMOD International Conference on Management of Data* (pp. 147–156). Association for Computing Machinery. https://doi.org/10.1145/2588555.2595641
83. Lutz, C., Breß, S., Zeuch, S., Rabl, T., & Markl, V. (2020). Pump up the volume: Processing large data on GPUs with fast interconnects. In *Proceedings of the 2020 ACM SIGMOD International Conference on Management of Data* (pp. 1633–1649). Association for Computing Machinery. https://doi.org/10.1145/2588555.2595641.
84. Advanced Micro Devices, Inc. (2023). How ROCm uses PCIe Atomics. https://rocm.docs.amd.com/en/docs-5.5.1/understand/More-about-how-ROCm-uses-PCIe-Atomics.html. Accessed 09 Dec 2024.
85. Sakharnykh, N. (2018). Everything you need to know about unified memory. *In GPU Technology Conference (GTC).*

86. NVIDIA Corporation. (2017). NVIDIA Tesla V100 GPU Architecture, Technical whitepaper.
87. NVIDIA Corporation. (n.d.). CUDA Toolkit Documentation. https://docs.nvidia.com/cuda/index.html. Accessed 09 Dec 2024.
88. Stone, J. E., Gohara, D., & Shi, G.. (2010). OpenCL: A parallel programming standard for heterogeneous computing systems. *Computing in Science & Engineering, 12*(3), 66–73. https://doi.org/10.1109/MCSE.2010.69.
89. The Khronos Group. (n.d.). The open standard for parallel programming of heterogeneous systems. https://www.khronos.org/opencl/. Accessed 09 Dec 2024.

Chapter 3
Efficient Event Processing on Modern Hardware

Marius Kuhrt, Nikolaus Glombiewski, Michael Körber, Andreas Morgen, Dominik Brandenstein, and Bernhard Seeger

Abstract Complex event processing (CEP) is an essential technology for analyzing streams of events. A key feature of a modern CEP architecture is the ability to process both continuous queries and analytical ad hoc queries on high-volume streams. Both query types support common operations (filter, aggregation, joins) known in event stream and database systems. Additionally, a crucial and unique operation in CEP is pattern matching, which matches user-defined predicates to subsequences of events.

We present our solution for a system supporting continuous queries, fast ingestion, and efficient analytical ad hoc queries. The system follows the principles of a Lambda Architecture and is specialized for a large variety of pattern-matching queries, including sequential, situation, and group patterns.

To offer efficient processing, we use modern hardware in each of the components. For continuous queries, we explore multi-core CPUs and GPUs. For ingestion and ad hoc queries, we analyze SSDs and persistent memory as ways to provide a robust system. Furthermore, we explore unique characteristics of the hardware and event processing applications such as temporal data, energy efficiency, and compression. We give an overview of the overall systems, highlight the research accomplishments, and describe common application scenarios that benefit from our architecture.

3.1 Introduction

In many applications, it is of utmost importance to monitor processes, business objects, and infrastructures continuously. Examples of such applications are fraud detection of (credit card) transactions, replenishment of a warehouse, and life-maintenance of complex systems like aircraft and production plants. The primary

M. Kuhrt (✉) · N. Glombiewski · M. Körber · A. Morgen · D. Brandenstein · B. Seeger
University of Marburg, Marburg, Germany
e-mail: kuhrt@mathematik.uni-marburg.de; glombien@mathematik.uni-marburg.de; koerberm@mathematik.uni-marburg.de; morgen@mathematik.uni-marburg.de; seeger@mathematik.uni-marburg.de; dominik.brandenstein@uni-marburg.de

K.-U. Sattler et al. (eds.), *Scalable Data Management for Future Hardware*,
https://doi.org/10.1007/978-3-031-74097-8_3

goal is to react to unusual situations and state changes quickly, e.g., block user transactions, reorder items in a warehouse, and trigger an emergency alarm. These data-driven applications have led to new requirements for data processing systems like supporting the ingestion of potentially infinite data streams and delivering answers with low latency. While stream processing systems offer general-purpose functionality for data-driven applications, complex event processing (CEP) additionally provides a temporal data model and dedicated operators like Match-Recognize (MR) for processing temporal data streams, also known as event streams. The first designs of CEP systems were limited to processing event streams in main memory without considering the persistence of streams. Such a traditional CEP-based approach comes with certain limitations. First, many applications require persistence and reproducibility to make real-time CEP decisions legally secure. Second, a postmortem analysis of alert situations often leads to a better situational understanding and supports improving the reactive actions if such situations are observed again.

This chapter introduces the two layers of a stream architecture similar to the Lambda Architecture [1]. The first layer offers the CEP system JEPC [2] for in-memory processing, while the second layer consists of a novel event store called ChronicleDB [3] for making event streams persistent. The CEP system JEPC is unique in the sense that it serves as a bridge to various implementations of operators running on modern hardware like iGPUs. ChronicleDB is a new type of database system that offers high ingestion rates and supports the typical operators known from CEP systems. Both systems are semantically equivalent, i.e., queries running at the same snapshots on one of these systems return the same results.

The chapter is structured in the following way. After a few preliminaries, Sect. 3.4 introduces the Lambda Architecture with emphasis on the design of ChronicleDB. Then, Sect. 3.5 first introduces the probably most important CEP operator Match-Recognize (MR) and presents a novel index-accelerated implementation offered in ChronicleDB. Furthermore, we go beyond event streams to so-called situation streams. Finally, emphasis is given to so-called group patterns in spatial applications. Section 3.6 examines the problem of making the stream processing algorithms energy-efficient by using iGPUs as hardware accelerators. Section 3.7 studies offset-value codes, a special compression technique for saving expensive comparisons in composed keys. Section 3.8 provides examples of applications built on the technologies previously introduced. Finally, Sect. 3.9 provides a brief conclusion and an outlook to future work.

3.2 Preliminaries

This section addresses problems related to events, event streams, situations, and situation streams. First, we provide a formal introduction to these concepts. All of them are related to a time domain $\mathcal{T}$ that is discrete and ordered. Furthermore, a payload p is assumed to be from a given domain $\mathcal{D}$.

3.2.1 Data Model

Definition 3.1 (Event) An event e is a pair (p, t) consisting of a payload $p \in \mathcal{D}$ and an event timestamp $t \in \mathcal{T}$. The validity of e is the instant t.

Definition 3.2 (Situation) A situation s is a triple (p, ts, te) consisting of a payload $p \in \mathcal{D}$ and two timestamps ts (start timestamp) and te (end timestamp) where $ts, te \in \mathcal{T}$ and $ts < te$. The validity of s is the half-open time interval $[ts, te)$.

The notion of an event and a situation are the basis for defining event streams and situation streams, respectively. For the sake of limited space, we do not make the general distinction between system time and application and refer the interested reader to [4] for a detailed discussion. We first introduce a formal definition of an event stream and a situation stream.

Definition 3.3 (Event Stream, Situation Stream) An event stream E is a potentially unbounded sequence of events $\langle e_1, e_2, \ldots\rangle$ with $e_i \in \mathcal{D} \times \mathcal{T}$ ordered by their event timestamp t.
A situation stream is a potentially unbounded sequence of situations $\langle s_1, s_2, \ldots\rangle$ with $s_i \in \mathcal{D} \times \mathcal{T}$ ordered by their event timestamp te.

Without loss of generality, we assume a stream is totally ordered, i.e., there are no two stream elements with the same order timestamp.

3.2.2 Operations

The following section gives a brief overview of the underlying operations that need to be supported for event streams and situation streams. While most of the snapshot-based operations are known from the early days of event processing, we focus on those operations that are very unique for event processing.

The first proposals for event processing systems by the database community like [5] strived to introduce (sliding) window operators and to limit the processing to these finite windows rather than on the entire, potentially infinite stream. In general, a window consists of two parameters: size and slide. The first parameter cuts out the maximum subsequences (the window) out of the stream such that the time difference among the stream elements is at most size. The second parameter slide denotes the length of the jumps until the next subsequence has to be considered. Here, we assumed a temporal window, but as shown in [4], count windows can also be modelled as special cases of temporal windows.

The concept of windows is used to define the classical stateful operators of the relational algebra like joins and aggregates on event streams. In addition, stateless operations like filters are directly applicable to streams without further modifications.

However, the focus of our work is on more advanced pattern queries supporting the search for specific subsequences within the stream. As an example, consider the pattern query in Listing 3.1 expressing a landing maneuver of an airplane assuming that the stream FLIGHT continuously delivers the values of a plane. The pattern query is expressed by Match-Recognize (MR), which is part of the SQL standard since 2016 [6]. MR consists of a PATTERN clause where a regular expression of symbols is given and a DEFINE clause for the specification of the symbols, each of them representing a Boolean expression. For example, symbol A is a range condition on the variables VEL and BA, and the condition of B uses the function PREV to refer to the previous values of VEL and BA. For the lack of space, we refer the interested reader to [6] for the details of MR. While almost all proposals for pattern queries assume event streams as input, our work presented in [7] supports pattern queries with more powerful predicates on situation streams. In addition, MR is not only of relevance for in-memory event stream systems, but it also has become an important operation in conventional database systems. These two extensions of pattern matching have largely motivated our work, and we will present our approaches later in more detail.

Listing 3.1 Analytical pattern matching query for landing maneuvers

```
SELECT COUNT(*) FROM FLIGHT MATCH_RECOGNIZE(
  ORDER BY T
  MEASURES A.T AS TS, C.T AS TE
  PATTERN ( A B+ C ) WITHIN 15 MINUTES
  DEFINE
    A AS VEL >= 150 AND BA > 500,
    B AS PREV(VEL) > VEL AND BA <= PREV(BA) - 20,
    C AS VEL < 80 AND GA < 200
)
```

3.3 Related Work

Since the beginning of the current century, there has been a plethora of early work [8–10] addressing the challenging problems of event processing. Our work has been largely inspired by PIPES [11] and its extension JEPC [2], one of the early approaches for event processing to support implementations of operators using hardware accelerators. Since the first seminal works addressing event pattern matching [12, 13], there has been a continuation of work (see [14] for a recent survey). Patterns are not only known from event processing but also in other domains like moving objects [15].

While most work on event processing focuses on in-memory processing, there have been a few system approaches addressing the problem of persistent event streams. These systems have to support high ingestion rate [16], pattern queries [17, 18], and ad hoc analytics [19]. For that, novel approaches employ hardware accelerators like GPUs [20], SSDs [21], and persistent memory technology [22]

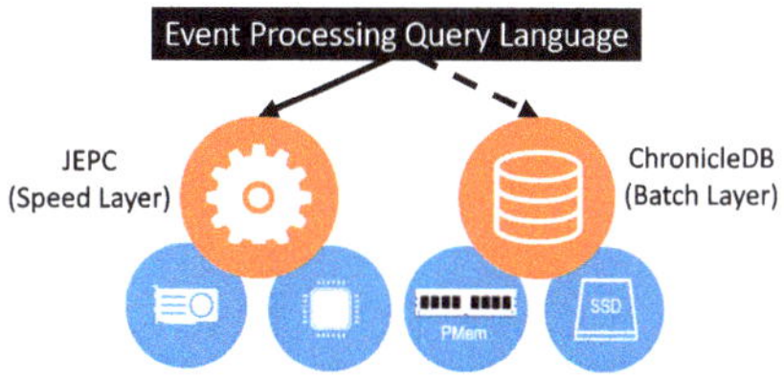

Fig. 3.1 Overall system architecture

in combination with advanced algorithms for compression [23] and indexing [3]. While these approaches aim at improving latency and throughput, there have been only very few works, e.g., [24], on improving the energy footprint of event processing.

3.4 System and Hardware Overview

The overall system design follows the principles of the well-known Lambda Architecture [1]. Figure 3.1 shows an overview of the components[1] as well as hardware used in each component. Each component can be addressed via a shared event processing query language, i.e., the same queries can be processed on a database on historical data (batch layer) as well as in real time (speed layer). ChronicleDB is the long-term data storage component and the core of the batch layer. It is optimized for storing and querying event data, with optimizations for SSDs and persistent memory. JEPC represents processing at the speed layer. Originally conceived as a middle layer for event processing with various bridges to different event processing systems, new bridges address event processing with GPUs. Even though JEPC is optimized for low latency, windows in common event processing operations result in a natural batching of events that fits GPU processing. Furthermore, some types of pattern matching in JEPC have been optimized for multi-core and distributed processing.

3.4.1 ChronicleDB

ChronicleDB is a database system specialized for storing and querying multi-variate event stream data. Event application scenarios usually involve a high amount of continuously arriving data in a short period of time. To support these scenarios, ChronicleDB is designed around three requirements:

($R1$) Ingestion of high input rate streams
($R2$) Fast stream replay and time travel operations

[1] Source code for our research projects is available at https://github.com/umr-dbs.

(*R*3) Fast processing of point, range, and aggregation queries on secondary attributes

While R1 is required to avoid load shedding in cases of high-volume input streams, R2 and R3 allow excellent query response times in a variety of use cases like postmortem analysis of event stream queries and continuous batch processing for dashboard applications as well as to some degree serving traditional OLAP demands. Since ChronicleDB stores the entire event stream as is, R1 focuses on ingestion of events, and we only support deletes of time ranges for space reclamation. The following three sections will overview ChronicleDB's three core components and briefly describe their interaction in the system. Then, we will briefly discuss novel optimizations for ChronicleDB.

3.4.1.1 Index and Storage Design

Primary Index ChronicleDB's target data model are multivariate event streams, i.e., data consisting of multiple measurements per timestamps, with a fixed schema. Thus, a single primary index in ChronicleDB stores events in a *Temporal Aggregated* B^+*-tree* (TAB$^+$-tree) index. The overall index layout is presented in Fig. 3.2a. At its core, the index is an augmented B$^+$-tree with the event's timestamp as its key domain and doubly linked nodes on every level. This index design is important for temporal access (R2). To support fast ingestion (R1), ChronicleDB primarily adopts an append-only model, where the data log is also the database. This is reflected in the index design. As the default behavior, insertions are treated as a continuous bulk loading operation in a traditional B$^+$-tree index. Under the assumption that the event stream is in temporal order, a new event can be appended to the leaf node containing the most recent data. This leaf node and its predecessors are referred to as the *right flank* of the TAB$^+$-tree. To speed up ingestion in temporal order, the right flank is kept in DRAM at all times. Thus, without an additional log [25], the last leaf can be lost in a crash.

Secondary Index Besides the primary index, ChronicleDB allows adaptive and ad-hoc creation of two types of secondary indexes, which are referred to as *heavyweight* and *lightweight* indexes. Heavyweight indexes are traditional secondary index struc-

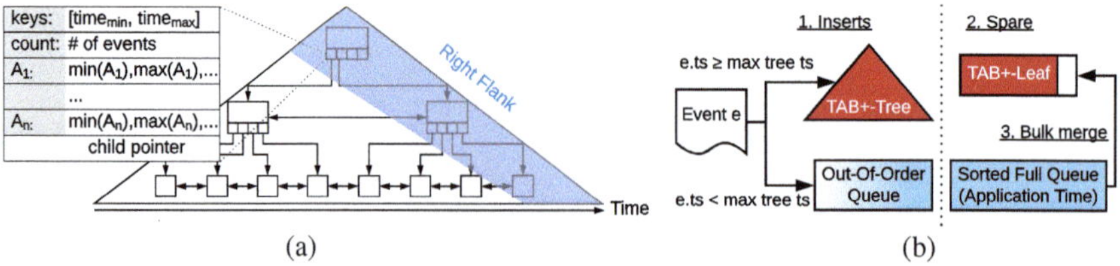

Fig. 3.2 ChronicleDB layout [22]. (**a**) Primary index (TAB$^+$-tree). (**b**) Out-of-order (OOO) handling

tures such as LSM [26] built for one or more attributes of the stream. Leaf pages of heavyweight indexes refer to primary index pages with a record offset. Lightweight indexes are an adaptation of small materialized aggregates (SMAs) [27], which can be arbitrary aggregate functions on the event's data domain. In contrast to [27], those aggregates are stored within the primary index nodes of the TAB$^+$-tree. Each child reference is associated with aggregated information of their respective nodes. In Fig. 3.2a, an index entry consists of an overall event count aggregate and the minimum and maximum values for each attribute. The interleaved aggregates boost the query performance (R3) of event processing queries.

Storage Layout Efficient data compression is of utmost importance in reducing the high storage cost of event streams. Especially continuous sensor values, such as temperature and humidity measurements, feature a lot of similar values that can be easily compressed to reduce space requirements. Thus, ChronicleDB compresses each TAB+-node with a configurable compression algorithm. However, the sizes of the compressed nodes are not constant anymore, requiring an explicit mapping to fixed-size block addresses. An address translation layer optimized for sequential access patterns maps logical node IDs to physical storage locations, which solves this issue with minimal impact on insertion and query performance.

Out-of-Order Data When data does not arrive in temporal order, it cannot be appended to the TAB$^+$-tree as part of the continuous bulk loading process. This type of data is known as *out-of-order (OOO) data*. Inserting OOO data into existing tree nodes can lead to cascading node splits and result in sub-optimal fill levels, negatively affecting insert and query performance. ChronicleDB uses a three-step strategy depicted in Fig. 3.2b to offset performance degradation from OOO data. First, OOO data is put into a dedicated OOO queue to preserve the append-only nature. Second, nodes in the TAB$^+$-tree can leave spare space to absorb OOO insertions without cascading node splits. For cheap spinning disks used to store large amounts of data, this has the additional benefit of preserving a sequential node layout. Third, whenever the OOO queue reaches a given size, it is merged into the primary index. This merge stabilizes query performance by adjusting lightweight indexes to more accurate values and merging logical temporal regions into physically near ones.

3.4.1.2 Optimizations

Various research [3, 22, 28, 29] optimized ChronicleDB for three different performance dimensions: ingestion, query, and robustness. Novel algorithms for each dimension focus on extending the core design principles described above and leveraging characteristics of event data.

Ingestion Even with fast random access of modern SSDs, sequential I/Os are still faster [22]. For better ingestion performance, load scheduling in ChronicleDB can turn off secondary indexes. Removing random access required for maintaining heavyweight secondary indexes trades query performance for ingestion performance. Since ChronicleDB maintains application time order in the primary index, the amount of OOO data also determines the ingestion performance, because maintaining a persistent OOO queue requires random access. In case of heavy load, the temporal dimension of the primary index can be switched to system time [3] while still maintaining lightweight indexing information on the application time dimension. This strategy guarantees a sequential access pattern for ingestion. A query recognizes different temporal dimensions within the primary index and introduces an optional sorting step for regions in system time. The lightweight index on application time can be used to speed up sorting [29], offsetting some of the query performance penalties.

Query Since ChronicleDB supports event processing queries, it has a query pipeline that uses the primary index for fast access to temporal regions that can be fed into JEPC [3]. This results in the same semantics as the event processing component. This pipeline has an optimization layer to speed up common event processing queries. Given a temporal region, a core mechanism is scanning a tree level above the leaves for lightweight index information. If a lightweight index on a query predicate exists, some temporal regions can be excluded for replay. This is a straightforward way to speed up filter or join queries. For aggregation queries, ChronicleDB also supports arbitrary aggregates within lightweight indexes. If a lightweight index aggregate matches the query aggregate and the result aggregate for a temporal window can be composed from partial aggregates, a query mechanism can use the lightweight index aggregate to save computation time as well as explore favorable access IO patterns [3, 28]. Similar optimizations exist for sequential pattern-matching queries, which will be discussed in more detail in Sect. 3.5.1.

Robustness An essential requirement for an event processing database is robust ingestion performance. If the characteristics of the stream (i.e., arrival rate, out-of-order data, etc.) vary over time, the system might support varying ingestion rates over time. However, if a user requires hard guarantees for data ingestion to avoid any data loss, this behavior is unacceptable. To support robust performance, the load scheduler observes stream characteristics to change the ingestion scheme (i.e., a switch from application time indexing to system time) to support a robust ingestion rate. For secondary indexes, waves of node splits in B-trees or waves of merge activity in LSM trees also impact query and ingestion performance. De-amortization techniques can reduce or eliminate these waves [29, 30]. Furthermore, using persistent memory in ChronicleDB improves the overall robustness of the system. A study [22] analyzed moving different components of ChronicleDB (the right flank, lightweight indexing information, address translation, and the OOO queue) to persistent memory. Through new hardware configurations, it is possible to achieve a new type of balance between ingestion, query, and recovery performance. By using fast random access on a persistent medium, it is possible to reduce performance fluctuations, resulting in a robust system [29].

3.4.2 Java Event Processing Connectivity (JEPC)

Java Event Processing Connectivity (JEPC) is a middle layer for event processing systems [2]. Initially, JEPC offered bridges for complex event processing platforms to obey a standardized semantics [31] based on a multi-set algebra [32]. Besides these bridges, JEPC has a bridge to mobile devices for energy-efficient pre-processing [33]. Most core research contributions in our system are implemented in the *native bridge* that consists of operators that match the algebra and semantics of our event processing language.

Although JEPC supports the standard event processing operators, it focuses on pattern matching with specialized operators for sequential, situation, and group patterns, not all of which are supported in state-of-the-art CEP software such as Apache Flink [34]. For event processing on modern hardware, we use the same semantics for implementations on multi-core CPUs, dedicated GPUs, and integrated GPUs. The following sections focus on our results for various pattern-matching implementations as well as algorithms for GPU processing.

3.5 Event Pattern Matching

Pattern matching is probably the most essential operator for the analysis of event streams. The core pattern-matching operator corresponds to the Match-Recognize (MR) clause that first occurred in the area of complex event processing (CEP). However, MR is now part of the current SQL standard [6] and first implementations exist for database systems [35] as well as stream processing engines [34]. An example of the semantics was discussed in Sect. 3.2.2. In this section, we will first discuss index acceleration techniques for pattern matching as defined in MR and used in ChronicleDB. Then, we will discuss a second type of pattern-matching query to support so-called situation patterns. We will briefly describe processing techniques for multi-core CPUs and distributed systems based on JEPC. Finally, we will describe a third type of pattern query for matching evolving groups of moving spatial objects in JEPC.

3.5.1 Index Acceleration

The basic approach for index acceleration in pattern-matching queries is to use an index on a condition to find regions of a stream where all possible matches for a given query exist. We term those regions *replay intervals* in the following. For each replay interval, a standard pattern-matching algorithm provides a correct result for a query.

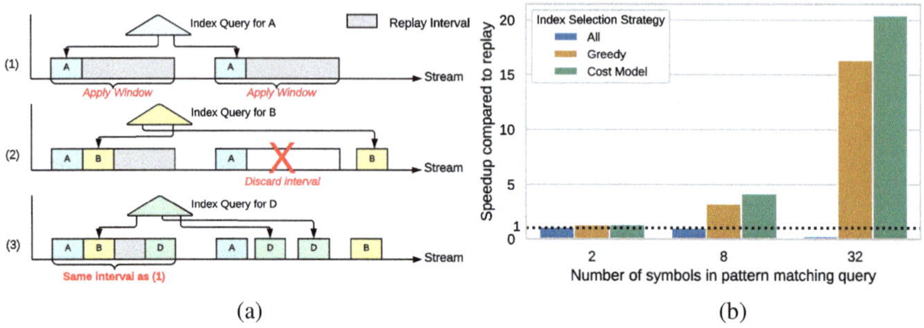

Fig. 3.3 Index-based pattern-matching evaluation [17]. (**a**) Evaluation strategy. (**b**) Experimental results

The example query in Listing 3.1 contains two types of predicates. A *range predicate* (e.g., VEL $\geq$ 150) checks if an attribute falls into an attribute range. A *delta predicate* (e.g., PREV(VEL) $>$ VEL) checks if the value of an event stream changed in comparison to a previous event in the stream. We will focus our discussion on the handling of range predicates [17] and will then briefly mention a method for handling delta predicates [29].

As a baseline, we assume that there exist (some) index structures that can answer a range predicate efficiently, e.g., a B-tree on the attribute.

Figure 3.3a shows the core idea of the approach for a pattern ABC*D such that the symbols A, B, and D are range predicates on attributes with index support and C is some predicate without index support. In the first step, an index query for A reveals two possible matches in the stream, resulting in two replay intervals. In the second step, an index query for B can exclude one of those replay intervals due to a temporal constraint (i.e., B happens too late after A). An additional query for D shows no improvements when constructing replay intervals.

The baseline approach shows the key challenge for index-accelerated pattern matching: There are diminishing returns when using multiple index structures for the query. Therefore, the system has to select a suitable set of indexes for efficient query processing. We developed a novel cost model to choose the best set of indexes. Given the selectivity of a range condition, we assume the events fulfilling the condition occur uniformly over the data streams. In particular, the cost model considers the sequential nature of pattern matching—combining subsequent symbols such as *A* directly followed by *B* has a higher combined selectivity than symbols with arbitrary gaps in between them. For details, we refer to the full publications [17]. In Fig. 3.3b, we compare a replay of the entire stream into a pattern-matching operator, using all index structures and our cost-model-based approach for pattern-matching queries with various complexities, i.e., the number of range conditions in the query. Our cost-model-based approach outperforms other methods. To overcome the assumption of equally distributed symbols, ChronicleDB introduces an additional preprocessing step to identify temporal regions where a symbol can occur with a certain frequency.

The given approach works well for range conditions but fails if the range conditions are not very selective or do not occur in a pattern-matching query. In addition, we developed a new indexing strategy for ChronicleDB [29] to handle delta predicates. Since delta predicates compare two values within a stream with each other, the underlying idea is to add index capabilities for the corresponding difference. Moreover, lightweight indexing contains information about minimum and maximum attribute values, and thus, ChronicleDB already offers coarse-grained filtering by computing the difference between those two values. In combination with an efficient scan and a highly compressed storage strategy for events (with some similarities to Column Sketches [36]), ChronicleDB supports delta predicates in its current index-accelerated implementation of pattern matching.

3.5.2 Situation Pattern Matching

The sequential nature of regular expression-based patterns as in MR has two major deficiencies. First, the expressible temporal relationships are limited to before/after/at the same time relationships. Conditions lasting for periods of time and their temporal relationships (e.g., A happens during B) cannot or only hardly be expressed in this approach. Second, due to the sequential nature of this process, efficient parallel execution strategies are scarce. Nevertheless, efficient parallel and distributed execution is a crucial aspect of dealing with ever-increasing data rates.

As a solution to both issues, we developed *TPStream* [37], an operator for pattern matching on situation streams. Unlike previous approaches that require situations as input, *TPStream* derives situations on the fly from point-based events before matching them. By closely coupling deriving situations and pattern matching, *TPStream* improves the detection latency because matches can be detected before the situations are completed. Figure 3.4 shows an example of the basic concept. A traffic monitoring system is continuously receiving sensor data from connected cars (i.e., position, speed, acceleration). The stream of raw sensor readings is transformed into three situation streams (acceleration, speeding, deceleration), one for each component of the pattern. A pattern match occurs when an acceleration is followed by a deceleration situation and a speeding situation overlaps with both. A traditional situation-based matching approach would detect matches after each

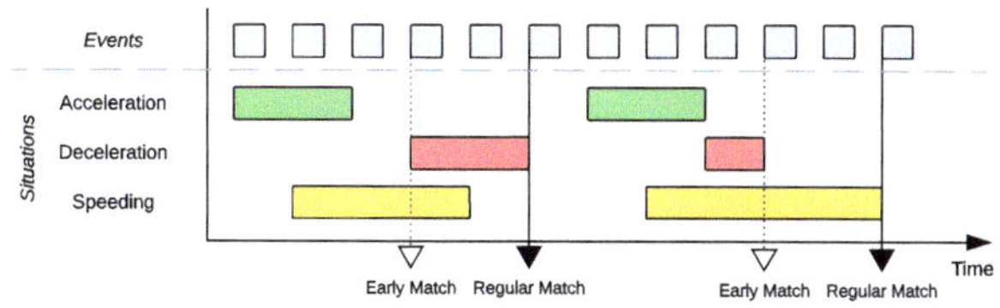

Fig. 3.4 Detecting aggressive driving with situation-based pattern matching [7]

Listing 3.2 TPStream—aggressive drivers query

```
FROM    CarStream PARTITION BY id
DEFINE  A AS acceleration >  7m/s^2 AT LEAST 3s,
        D AS acceleration < -8m/s^2 AT LEAST 1s,
        S AS speed > 88 mph
PATTERN A overlaps;during S
    AND D overlaps;during S
    AND A before;meets D
WITHIN  6 minutes
RETURN  FIRST(A.id) AS id;
```

situation concluded. In the above example, *TPStream* allows finding a match earlier while a situation is still ongoing. Listing 3.2 shows the example in the *TPStream* query language, which is similar to the Match-Recognize syntax. Note that, in the `PATTERN` clause, there are multiple valid alternatives for the relation between situations, e.g., `D` (deceleration) and `S` (speeding) might *overlap*, but `D` might also happen *during* `S`. This is also the case in the example in Fig. 3.4.

For multi-core processing, *TPStream* supports processing events in parallel [7]. If the query has a `PARTITION BY` clause, threads process each partition in parallel before a final merge step sorts results into temporal order. If there is no meaningful way to partition data, *TPStream* batches consequent events and processes batches in parallel. The same principles apply to distributed processing. Experiments confirmed the benefits of early result detection as well as the effectiveness of parallelization on both multi-core CPUs and distributed processing via an implementation in Apache Kafka.

3.5.3 Group Pattern Matching

The detection of groups of moving objects is a challenging task in moving object databases [38]. While a few tailor-made algorithms exist, an important challenge is the translation of group pattern detection from moving object databases to event streams. As an underlying data model, we consider a spatial event, where each event contains an identifier and a spatial position to reference a moving object and its location.

The cross-pattern operator [38] allows the definition of a wide range of different patterns for groups of moving objects. The operator has three parameters: a predicate p, a minimum duration m_d, and membership constraint m_c. The predicate p is essential for determining which moving objects are in the same group, e.g., objects within a certain radius. The minimum duration m_d specifies how long each object has to be in the group. The membership constraint indicates the minimum number of objects m_c in a matching group at any given time.

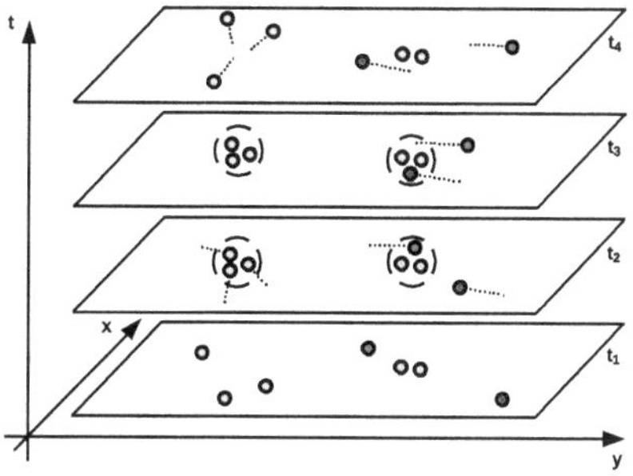

Fig. 3.5 Pattern matching on evolving groups of moving objects

Figure 3.5 shows an example of a cross-pattern operator and the life cycle of a match. The pattern is defined such that the objects need to fulfill a range constraint p, moving objects need to be members for at least $m_d = 2$ timestamps, and the group has to consist of at least $m_c = 3$ moving objects. At time t_2, the green objects form a group as they are located within the specified range. This group moves together for some time and dissolves at time t_4. As all constraints are met, the group is a valid match. In contrast, the moving objects on the right do not form a match, as the red and blue objects are only part of the group for a single timestamp. This is typically the case when objects only cross the path of a group or move along for a short time.

Originally introduced for spatiotemporal databases [38], the translation to continuous queries in event streams causes challenges, which makes a new processing method necessary. Hence, we have developed the cross-pattern operator for spatial event streams. This includes the incremental processing of continuous event streams, as well as parallelization and suitable index structures, to achieve low latency and high throughput required in this context.

Our method for processing spatial event streams is structured in three phases. First, the predicate is applied at each timestamp to identify members of potential matching groups, utilizing a parallel index-based approach. The intermediate result is a predicate graph, where the nodes of the graph refer to moving objects and edges exist between objects that fulfill the predicate. Second, the predicate graph is analyzed to identify connected groups regarding the specified pattern and a sufficiently high number of moving objects. Third, as the incoming event stream progresses, it is checked whether all the conditions outlined above are satisfied for the required duration.

Besides efficient processing, our approach allows the tracking of changes in compositions of groups over several points in time, such that splitting or merging of groups can be tracked precisely. This goes beyond previous research. The first experimental results confirm that the processing of our approach is effective and more efficient than its competitors due to its index-based predicate evaluation.

3.6 Energy Efficiency and iGPUs

One of the most challenging aspects when dealing with data streams is the ability to continuously process large amounts of incoming data while meeting tight latency constraints. In order to offer both, high throughput and low latency, stream processing engines can benefit from parallelization techniques. Unrelated data streams can be handled independently by multiple computing units in parallel. Among the most promising developments for *scaling up* a single node is the vast variety of graphics processing units (GPU). However, when dealing with latency-sensitive stream applications, the transfer time from main memory to the GPU via PCIe is an ever-prominent limiting factor. Modern hardware using recent advancements in the Heterogeneous System Architecture (HSA), a platform specification for heterogeneous computing, makes masking these limitations more feasible. In particular, integrated GPUs (iGPU) that reside on the same die as the CPU and can natively access the main memory seem like a natural fit for accelerating low-latency stream processing applications. The reason is that data does not have to be shipped to a very size-limited memory on the GPU. In addition, the advent of so-called signals, which reduce start-up time for GPU kernels, further increases the potential for low-latency processing in HSA. We developed an event stream processing system prototype featuring the most common operations such as filter, aggregation, and joins [39] as well as solutions for pattern matching [40]. This system showcases the potential of using shared-memory CPU-GPUs in a data stream environment.

3.6.1 HSA Facilities

The following features of HSA are essential to building our prototype.

Memory Management In contrast to traditional programming models, HSA supports fine-grained shared virtual memory (SVM), allowing all compute devices to share a unified address space. This feature is especially useful in combination with iGPUs. Due to a physically unified memory hierarchy, no memory copy operations are required to ship data to the GPU. In comparison with traditional work patterns on dedicated GPUs, iGPUs in combination with SVM reduce both, latency introduced by copying data back and forth, and interaction with the CPU when new data is available.

Signals HSA provides a signaling mechanism, enabling lightweight communication between CPUs and GPUs. A signal is a signed integer value that can be manipulated via runtime functions available on all processing units, allowing them to atomically manipulate the signal value (e.g., via compare-and-swap, exchange, etc.). The most interesting feature of signals is that processing units can wait for value updates, which can be used to implement *persistent kernels* [41]. Unlike with

Unit	Consists of	Memory for Exchange
Grid	$\lceil \frac{N}{wgs} \rceil$ Work Groups	Global Memory
Work Group	$\lceil \frac{wgs}{64} \rceil$ Wavefronts	Group Memory
Wavefront	64 Threads	Register

(a)

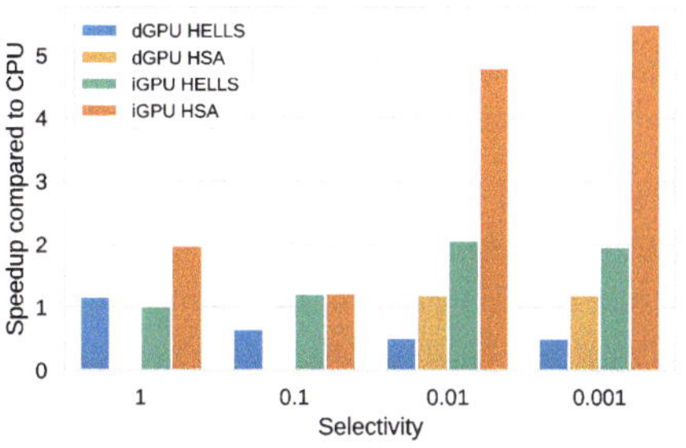

(b)

Fig. 3.6 Event processing on HSA [39]. (**a**) HSA thread-group hierarchy. (**b**) Performance of stream joins on integrated and dedicated GPUs

dispatch-based execution, a persistent kernel is launched once and stays active for the rest of the application's lifetime. This HSA feature reduces the overhead of a kernel launch and, for iGPUs, fully eliminates the need for CPU interaction upon the arrival of new data.

Communication and Data Exchange Threads in HSA are organized in a hierarchy of thread groups similar to traditional GPU programming languages. Figure 3.6a contains a visualization of this hierarchy. At the lowest level, within a *wavefront* consisting of 64 threads, data can be exchanged by swapping register values. Special primitives provided by HSA, sometimes called *vote operations*, are used at the wavefront level, e.g., to reserve slots in an output buffer without serializing the operation. At the next level, *work groups* consist of several wavefronts. Data is exchanged between wavefronts via the size-limited group memory. At the highest *grid* level, data is exchanged between work groups via the larger, albeit slower, global memory.

3.6.2 Operators

Consecutive operators in the system are coupled via specialized lock-free queues. These queues are implemented as ring buffers backed by contiguous arrays. Because of SVM, the queues are easily accessible by every compute device. Read/write indexes are implemented as HSA signals so that updates are properly propagated across devices. Additionally, producers and consumers can wait for space/data by waiting for updates on the respective signals.

Filter A filter consumes a single input stream, applies a predicate to every event, and forwards all qualifying events to the output stream. Since every event is processed exactly once, parallelism is achieved through batching at the cost of additional latency. Special care has to be taken to preserve the temporal order of output events. Two kernels, a *driver-kernel* and an *eval-kernel*, work in tandem, communicating via signals and shared buffers, to ensure that data is written to the output queue correctly and efficiently.

Windowed Aggregation The aggregation operator manages a count window of fixed size over a single input stream. Every time the window is updated (i.e., after the arrival of one or more events), an aggregation function is applied to the window. The result is an event with the aggregated value and the timestamp of the most recent event within the window. The operator is again composed of a driver-kernel that waits for and then reads data from the input and updates the window with the new events, triggering re-evaluation of the aggregate if necessary. The eval-kernel then performs this evaluation via a reduction and propagates the resulting event to the output queue.

Windowed Joins The join operator consumes two input streams and manages a count window for each of them. Incoming events on one input are added to the respective window and probed against the other, using a user-defined predicate. If two events satisfy the condition, a single output event is created by combining the payloads and attaching the timestamp of the event that arrived later. A driver-kernel again waits for data on the two input streams, updates windows, and triggers the evaluation of the join predicate. The eval-kernel then evaluates the predicate on the new event and each event in the window of the other input in parallel, writing events directly to the output queue's buffer. Eventually, the state of the queue is updated, making the new events available to the consumer.

Pattern Matching Sequential pattern-matching implementations typically adapt NFA-based evaluation approaches. For every symbol, there is a state in the automaton holding a list of *partial matches*. If a new event, possibly together with a partial match, fulfills a symbol's condition, the event is added to the partial match, and the corresponding transitions are triggered, moving the partial match to the next state. Our approach [40] performs pattern matching using the CPU and GPU cooperatively. Partial matches reside in dense arrays in shared memory, and condition/transition functions are implemented via GPU-kernels. Upon arrival of a new event, the CPU launches these kernels which then evaluate the conditions on the new event and all partial matches of each state in parallel. Additionally, the kernels extend and propagate partial matches to the next state by reserving slots in the target array using a signal as synchronization. Finally, the CPU materializes output events for matches that have reached a final state of the automaton and also performs compaction of the dense arrays to purge them of partial matches that have not reached a final state within the defined time window.

Our experimental analysis shows that our HSA-enabled implementations using persistent kernels achieve a reasonable speedup compared to traditional dispatch-based GPU variants. As an example, Fig. 3.6b shows the speedup of join operation with varying selectivities on different compute devices. HELLS [42] is a dispatch-based join, and the baseline is a single-threaded algorithm on the CPU.

In general, iGPUs are well suited for relieving workload from CPU cores, and the corresponding implementations outperform even multi-threaded CPU implementations in many cases. However, it also shows that dedicated GPUs are not suitable for a tuple-at-time or micro-batch processing scheme, due to the additional cost of shipping data to the device over PCIe.

3.6.3 Energy Efficiency

The rising importance of energy consumption due to environmental and cost-efficiency reasons [43] has significantly increased awareness of energy efficiency. A vision paper in 2008 [44] laid out multiple challenges for database servers, including energy-aware query optimization, buffer techniques, physical design, and hardware.

3.6.3.1 iGPUs

Integrated GPUs, due to being designed for the low energy constraints of mobile devices, are obvious candidates for such optimizations. Our experimental analysis showed that, for many operations, stream operations on iGPUs not only process data faster (i.e., provide a higher throughput) than, e.g., multithreaded algorithms on the CPU, but also consume less energy. If, however, input rates are slow, single-threaded algorithms on the CPU are generally more efficient, in particular, if dynamic voltage frequency scaling is used to throttle down the CPU. This indicates that there are ample opportunities for optimization. An energy-aware scheduler should, based on user-defined latency constraints and a given energy budget, assign processing tasks to the best-suited processing unit. However, our goal of building this scheduler using our HSA-based iGPU algorithms could not be achieved. This was because ROCr/ROCm, the HSA runtime provided by AMD, does not officially support integrated GPUs and general instability made continuing development of this project impossible. We considered processors with integrated GPUs from Intel and Apple as alternatives; however, both options require a complete rewrite of our system as neither supports HSA.

3.6.3.2 Mobile Devices

We also developed a multi-modal CEP framework for mobile devices [33]. A key idea is to use Berkeley Packet Filters (BPF) to perform some filter operations in an energy-efficient manner. The framework allows query executions in user space (user mode), in the operating system (kernel mode), on the Wi-Fi chip (Wi-Fi mode), and/or on a sensor hub (hub mode). The framework was included as a bridge to JEPC framework (without the support for pattern matching) such that different operators may be executed using our native processing algorithms while others can

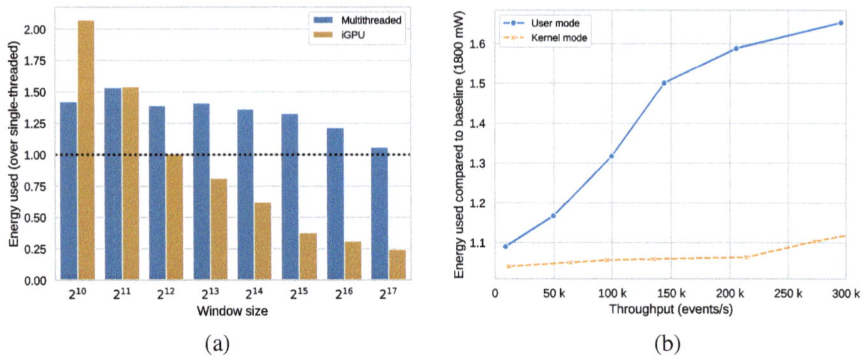

Fig. 3.7 Evaluation of energy consumption in CEP. (**a**) Energy consumption of a pattern-matching operation with the single-threaded CPU variant as a baseline. (**b**) Power consumption of filter and aggregation queries in mobile devices using user and kernel mode while processing events

leverage the mobile device frameworks. Our approach allows aggressively placing operators within the overall query graph onto lower-powered chips or into kernel mode, leaving a smaller number of operators for the more energy-hungry user-mode execution. Such a placement strategy results in significant improvements in terms of energy consumption and throughput.

3.6.3.3 Evaluation

Figure 3.7 shows the experimental evaluation of both approaches. Figure 3.7a shows the evaluation of a pattern matching operation using three different implementations, two on a CPU and one on the integrated GPU. The pattern is of the form `AB`, where `A` is *true* and `B` is very unlikely, resulting in an extremely large number of partial matches. As the window size increases, the operation on the integrated GPU can increasingly exploit parallelity and consumes only a fraction of the energy of the CPU variants over the full operation. Figure 3.7b shows an excerpt from the evaluation of our multi-modal CEP framework for mobile devices. The experiments were performed on the Dragonboard 410c SoC. We vary the throughput of events and measure the power consumption of different strategies. The benchmark to determine a baseline is obtained from a one-byte write to an in-memory character device (`/dev/null`), which basically is a single system call and an in-memory write. We compare kernel mode and user mode execution of filter operators. Clearly, executing in kernel mode shows significant improvements in terms of energy consumption. Details on the experimental setup and other experiments for the multi-modal CEP framework can be found in the full publication [33].

3.7 Compression

The input data model for our system offers event streams with a schema to support multiple different measurements per timestamp. For efficient storage, data has to be compressed, and due to temporal correlation, event database systems such as ChronicleDB already use various compression techniques to reduce storage requirements. However, compression can also be leveraged for query processing. Sort-based query methods are prominent in most operations in almost every system. For example, ChronicleDB applies sorting to restore the temporal order in case of out-of-order data. In addition, range predicate evaluation for pattern matching requires a sorted index on a multi-columnar key that considers the attribute, the timestamp, and the sequence number within the event stream. Similar sort requirements exist for situation and group predicates. For this reason, we evaluated a solution for compression strategies that enable sort-based operations and found the integration of *offset-value coding* into our system as a promising solution.

Offset-value coding [45] is a technique closely related to prefix truncation on multi-columnar keys in database rows or strings. In a sorted stream of data, the index of the column within the key, at which a row differs from its preceding row, is folded with the value in this column into the *ascending offset-value code* using the formula $(arity - index) \times domain + value$. Here, $arity$ is the number of key columns, and $domain$ is a number higher than each domain of each key column, assuming integer values. Two rows with offset-value codes with respect to the *same*, smaller base row can now be compared efficiently: a smaller offset-value code indicates that the row shares a longer prefix with the base row, or both rows share the same prefix, but one has a smaller value at the next column. In both cases, the row with the smaller code sorts earlier than the other row. If the offset-value codes coincide, additional column comparisons are performed, beginning at the key column following the encoded offset. Duplicate rows are encoded with the special offset-value code 0, which arises by inserting $arity$ for the index and a $value$ of 0 into the formula, thereby making duplicate detection trivial.

The comparison logic shows the two main benefits of offset-value coding. First, they function as surrogate keys similar to hash values, reducing many would-be column comparisons when comparing two rows into a single, fast integer comparison. Second, offset-value codes are a means of caching previous comparisons. If a comparison is not immediately decided by offset-value codes, the known shared prefix of two rows is not compared again. Additionally, the offset-value code of the larger row can be adjusted during the actual comparison so that the lower row becomes the new base row. This is essential for all merge-based sort operations using offset-value codes. Reducing the number of column comparisons performed is particularly valuable if, as is the case in many database systems, these comparisons are interpreted and thus substantially more expensive than simple integer comparisons.

Offset-value coding can vastly improve the performance of sort-based operations in database systems such as aggregation and duplicate removal but also joins [46].

Utilizing and maintaining offset-value codes across operator pipelines is invaluable for sort-based query execution [47]. An operator should not only use existing offset-value codes in sorted input but also produce sorted output with offset-value codes. Moreover, storage engines should provide facilities to either store sorted data together with offset-value codes, e.g., in B-trees with prefix truncation, or make deriving them possible, as is the case with run-length encoding in column stores.

3.8 Applications

The overall architecture works well in any event processing scenario but can showcase its particular strengths in applications that require live event stream processing, long-term storage, pattern matching, and a large amount of data. We successfully used the system in multiple application scenarios with varying degrees of complexity, such as part of a data pipeline for analysis of cryogenics data, movement data, and flight data.

The most challenging use cases are usually spatiotemporal applications featuring multiple sensors. While our event processing system has both spatial and temporal processing capabilities, the application scenarios usually have a visual component and require a combination of data types (such as combining vector and raster data) that are not natively supported in event processing systems. For this purpose, we built a processing pipeline [48, 49] that connects our architecture with the Visualization, Analysis and Transformation (VAT) System [50, 51]. VAT is an interactive spatiotemporal processing platform consisting of a processing backend and a Web-based frontend. We will briefly highlight challenges and opportunities faced in application scenarios with this pipeline in a flight data use case.

Flight data as provided by the OpenSky Network [52] feature a lot of the characteristics described above. Due to the large number and variety of airplanes as well as high-frequency updates, there is a plethora of movement (landing, starting, evasion) and group patterns (airplanes closing in on each other) that can be continuously monitored with CEP to avoid potential catastrophes like collisions. However, tuning the parameters of a CEP query to deliver the desired results is challenging and typically requires a combination of domain expertise and historical data analysis. Furthermore, in many cases, pure CEP queries need to be combined with additional data sources (e.g., remote sensing images) and processing technologies (e.g., machine learning models). To alleviate some of those challenges, our pipeline utilizes an often-overlooked key characteristic for data analysis that flight data exhibits: It can be visualized in a system like VAT.

Figure 3.8 shows multiple flight trajectories approaching the Frankfurt airport. Black lines show all flight trajectories. We used pattern-matching queries similar to Listing 3.1 to identify starting (green) and landing (red) trajectories. Parameter tuning for these queries is not straightforward, as finding good thresholds for both range and delta predicates requires some work on data in long-term storage. The combination of VAT and ChronicleDB simplifies this process as ChronicleDB

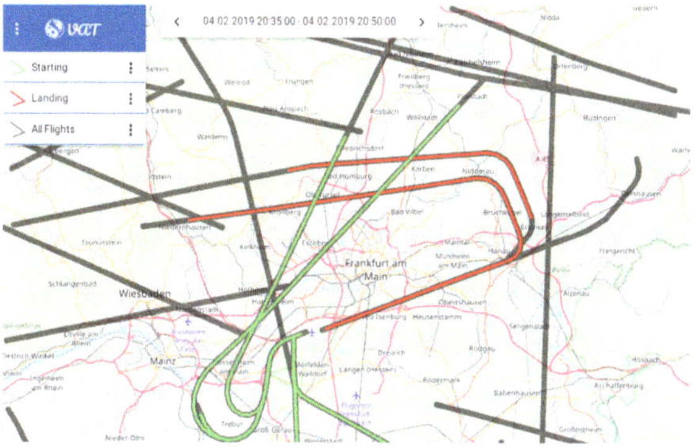

Fig. 3.8 Visual pattern-matching queries for flight starting and landing patterns [48]

features efficient access and processing capabilities for CEP queries that allow for fast, interactive feedback through VAT.

In this context, we also analyzed opportunities for detecting flights in severe weather conditions by combining data from ChronicleDB with raster data and the analysis of group pattern queries [48]. Furthermore, we introduced a component for performing multi-query optimizations and introduced an extrapolation operator for JEPC to enrich events [49]. All these queries can leverage some of the overall research contributions mentioned before.

3.9 Conclusion and Outlook

Event processing systems evaluate continuous queries over an endless stream of events. A modern holistic event processing architecture requires an approach that combines continuous queries with a long-term event storage system that allows for fast ingestion and efficient analytical ad hoc queries. We presented our system that combines an event processing solution (JEPC) and an efficient event store (ChronicleDB) with the same query semantics. We used modern hardware in each component to speed up both types of queries. In particular, we proposed solutions for iGPU-based processing using JEPC semantics that can accelerate continuous queries in an energy-efficient manner. Furthermore, we used novel indexing techniques and query strategies in ChronicleDB. For each component, we developed new strategies to process queries like sequential, situation, and group pattern queries.

There are many new research directions within such a holistic approach. For pattern matching, our solutions can be further enhanced with a comprehensive cost model for various strategies. Our research on group pattern queries can further be extended with hardware-acceleration strategies such as iGPUs. Since large amounts of event data usually showcase correlation and are compressed in event stores such as ChronicleDB, we will further explore the use of offset-value codes within event stream applications. In particular, the use of hardware accelerators for offset-value codes is a promising direction for new research.

Acknowledgments This work has been supported by the German Research Foundation (DFG) under grant no. 361498127. This work was partially funded by the LOEWE initiative (Hesse, Germany) within the emergenCITY center, by the German Research Foundation DFG under the grant agreement number 442032008 (NFDI4Biodiversity), and by the BMBF project FAIR Data Spaces (FAIRDS10).

References

1. Marz, N., & Warren, J. (2015). *Big Data: Principles and best practices of scalable realtime data systems* (1st ed.). Manning Publications.
2. Hoßbach, B., Glombiewski, N., Morgen, A., Ritter, F., & Seeger, B. (2013). JEPC: The java event processing connectivity. *Datenbank-Spektrum, 13*(3), 167–178.
3. Seidemann, M., Glombiewski, N., Körber, M., & Seeger, B. (2019). Chronicledb: A high-performance event store. *ACM Transactions on Database Systems, 44*(4), 13:1–13:45.
4. Krämer, J., Seeger, B. (2009). Semantics and implementation of continuous sliding window queries over data streams. *ACM Transactions on Database Systems, 34*(1), 4:1–4:49.
5. Babu, S., & Widom, J. (2001). Continuous queries over data streams. *SIGMOD Record, 30*(3), 109–120.
6. ISO/IEC TR 19075-5:2016. (2016). Information technology—Database languages—SQL Technical Reports—Part 5: Row Pattern Recognition in SQL. http://standards.iso.org/ittf/PubliclyAvailableStandards/. Accessed 13 March 2019
7. Körber, M., Glombiewski, N., Morgen, A., & Seeger, B. (2021). Tpstream: Low-latency and high-throughput temporal pattern matching on event streams. *Distributed Parallel Databases, 39*(2), 361–412.
8. Arasu, A., Babu, S., & Widom, J. (2006). The CQL continuous query language: semantic foundations and query execution. *The VLDB Journal, 15*(2), 121–142.
9. Chandrasekaran, S., Cooper, O., Deshpande, A., Franklin, M. J., Hellerstein, J. M., Hong, W., Krishnamurthy, S., Madden, S. R., Reiss, F., & Shah, M. A. (2003). Telegraphcq: Continuous dataflow processing. In A. Y. Halevy, Z. G. Ives & A. Doan (Eds.), *Proceedings of the 2003 ACM SIGMOD International Conference on Management of Data, San Diego, California, USA, June 9–12, 2003* (p. 668). ACM.
10. Abadi, D.J., Carney, D., Çetintemel, U., Cherniack, M., Convey, C., Lee, S., Stonebraker, M., Tatbul, N., & Zdonik, S. B. (2003). Aurora: A new model and architecture for data stream management. *The VLDB Journal, 12*(2), 120–139.
11. Krämer, J., Seeger, B. (2005). A temporal foundation for continuous queries over data streams. In J. R. Haritsa & T. M. Vijayaraman (Eds.), *Advances in Data Management 2005, Proceedings of the Eleventh International Conference on Management of Data, January 6, 7, and 8, 2005, Goa, India* (pp. 70–82). Computer Society of India.
12. Wu, E., Diao, Y., & Rizvi, S. (2006). High-performance complex event processing over streams. In S. Chaudhuri, V. Hristidis & N. Polyzotis (Eds.), *Proceedings of the ACM SIGMOD International Conference on Management of Data, Chicago, Illinois, USA, June 27–29, 2006* (pp. 407–418). ACM.
13. Agrawal, J., Diao, Y., Gyllstrom, D., & Immerman, N. (2008). Efficient pattern matching over event streams. In J. Tsong-Li Wang (Ed.), *Proceedings of the ACM SIGMOD International Conference on Management of Data, SIGMOD 2008, Vancouver, BC, Canada, June 10–12, 2008* (pp. 147–160). ACM.

14. Giatrakos, N., Alevizos, E., Artikis, A., Deligiannakis, A., & Garofalakis, M. (2020). Complex event recognition in the big data era: A survey. *The VLDB Journal, 29*(1), 313–352.
15. Sakr, M. A., & Güting, R. H. (2011). Spatiotemporal pattern queries. *GeoInformatica, 15*(3), 497–540.
16. Dong, S., Kryczka, A., Jin, Y., & Stumm, M. (2021). Rocksdb: Evolution of development priorities in a key-value store serving large-scale applications. *ACM Transactions on Storage, 17*(4), 26:1–26:32.
17. Körber, M., Glombiewski, N., & Seeger, B. (2021). Index-accelerated pattern matching in event stores. In G. Li, Z. Li, S. Idreos & D. Srivastava (Eds.), *SIGMOD '21: International Conference on Management of Data, Virtual Event, China, June 20–25, 2021* (pp. 1023–1036). ACM.
18. Zhu, E., Huang, S., & Chaudhuri, S. (2023). High-performance row pattern recognition using joins. *Proceedings of the VLDB Endowment, 16*(5), 1181–1194.
19. Gomes, H. M., Read, J., Bifet, A., Barddal, J. P., & Gama, J. (2019). Machine learning for streaming data: state of the art, challenges, and opportunities. *SIGKDD Explorations, 21*(2), 6–22.
20. Cugola, G., & Margara, A. (2012). Low latency complex event processing on parallel hardware. *Journal of Parallel and Distributed Computing, 72*(2), 205–218.
21. Lee, G., Eo, J., Seo, J., Um, T., & Chun, B.-G. (2018). High-performance stateful stream processing on solid-state drives. In *Proceedings of the 9th Asia-Pacific Workshop on Systems, APSys 2018, Jeju Island, Republic of Korea, August 27–28, 2018* (pp. 9:1–9:7). ACM.
22. Glombiewski, N., Götze, P., Körber, M., Morgen, A., & Seeger, B. (2020). Designing an event store for a modern three-layer storage hierarchy. *Datenbank-Spektrum, 20*(3), 211–222.
23. Blalock, D. W., Madden, S., & Guttag, J. V. (2018). Sprintz: Time series compression for the Internet of Things. *Proceedings of the ACM on Interactive, Mobile, Wearable and Ubiquitous Technologies, 2*(3), 93:1–93:23.
24. Michalke, A., Grulich, P. M., Lutz, C., Zeuch, S., & Markl, V. (2021) An energy-efficient stream join for the Internet of Things. In D. Porobic & S. Blanas (Eds.), *Proceedings of the 17th International Workshop on Data Management on New Hardware, DaMoN 2021, 21 June 2021, Virtual Event, China* (pp. 8:1–8:6). ACM.
25. Seidemann, M., & Seeger, B. (2017). Chronicledb: A high-performance event store. In V. Markl, S. Orlando, B. Mitschang, P. Andritsos, K.-U. Sattler & S. Breß (Eds.), *Proceedings of the 20th International Conference on Extending Database Technology, EDBT 2017, Venice, Italy, March 21–24, 2017* (pp. 144–155). OpenProceedings.org.
26. O'Neil, P., Cheng, E., Gawlick, D., & O'Neil, E. (1996). The log-structured merge-tree (LSM-tree). *Acta Informatica, 33*(4), 351–385.
27. Moerkotte, G. (1998). Small materialized aggregates: A light weight index structure for data warehousing. In A. Gupta, O. Shmueli & J. Widom (Eds.), *VLDB'98, Proceedings of 24rd International Conference on Very Large Data Bases, August 24–27, 1998, New York City, New York, USA* (pp. 476–487). Morgan Kaufmann.
28. Körber, M. (2022). *Accelerating event stream processing in on- and offline systems*. Ph.D. Thesis, University of Marburg.
29. Glombiewski, N. (2023). *Robust stream indexing*. Ph.D. Thesis, University of Marburg.
30. Glombiewski, N., Seeger, B., & Graefe, G. (2019). Waves of misery after index creation. In T. Grust, F. Naumann, A. Böhm, W. Lehner, T. Härder, E. Rahm, A. Heuer, M. Klettke & H. Meyer (Eds.), *Datenbanksysteme für Business, Technologie und Web (BTW 2019), 18. Fachtagung des GI-Fachbereichs, Datenbanken und Informationssysteme" (DBIS), 4.–8. März 2019, Rostock, Germany, Proceedings*, volume P-289 of *LNI* (pp. 77–96). Gesellschaft für Informatik.
31. Hoßbach, B. (2015). *Design and implementation of a middleware for uniform, federated and dynamic event processing*. Ph.D. Thesis, University of Marburg.
32. Krämer, J. (2007). *Continuous queries over data stream—semantics and implementation*. Ph.D. Thesis, University of Marburg.
33. Graubner, P., Thelen, C., Körber, M., Sterz, A., Salvaneschi, G., Mezini, M., Seeger, B., & Freisleben, B., (2018). Multimodal complex event processing on mobile devices. In A. Hinze,

D. M. Eyers, M. Hirzel, M. Weidlich & S. Bhowmik (Eds.), *Proceedings of the 12th ACM International Conference on Distributed and Event-based Systems, DEBS 2018, Hamilton, New Zealand, June 25–29, 2018* (pp. 112–123). ACM.
34. Carbone, P., Katsifodimos, A., Ewen, S., Markl, V., Haridi, S., & Tzoumas, K. (2015). Apache flink™: Stream and batch processing in a single engine. *IEEE Data Engineering Bulletin, 38*(4), 28–38.
35. Pattern matching (match_recognize) in oracle database 12c release 1 (12.1), 2021.
36. Hentschel, B., Kester, M. S., & Idreos, S. (2018). Column sketches: A scan accelerator for rapid and robust predicate evaluation. In G. Das, C. M. Jermaine & P. A. Bernstein (Eds.), *Proceedings of the 2018 International Conference on Management of Data, SIGMOD Conference 2018, Houston, TX, USA, June 10–15, 2018* (pp. 857–872). ACM.
37. Körber, M., Glombiewski, N., & Seeger, B. (2018). Tpstream: Low-latency temporal pattern matching on event streams. In M. H. Böhlen, R. Pichler, N. May, E. Rahm, S.-H. Wu & K. Hose (Eds.), *Proceedings of the 21st International Conference on Extending Database Technology, EDBT 2018, Vienna, Austria, March 26–29, 2018* (pp. 313–324). OpenProceedings.org.
38. Sakr, M. A., & Güting, R. H. (2014). Group spatiotemporal pattern queries. *GeoInformatica, 18*(4), 699–746.
39. Körber, M., Eckstein, J., Glombiewski, N., & Seeger, B. (2019). Event stream processing on heterogeneous system architecture. In T. Neumann & K. Salem (Eds.), *Proceedings of the 15th International Workshop on Data Management on New Hardware, DaMoN 2019, Amsterdam, The Netherlands, 1 July 2019* (pp. 3:1–3:10). ACM.
40. Kuhrt, M., Körber, M., & Seeger, B. (2022). iGPU-accelerated pattern matching on event streams. In S. Blanas & N. May (Eds.), *International Conference on Management of Data, DaMoN 2022, Philadelphia, PA, USA, 13 June 2022* (pp. 6:1–6:7). ACM.
41. Mukherjee, S., Sun, Y., Blinzer, P., Ziabari, A. K., & Kaeli, D. (2016). A comprehensive performance analysis of HSA and opencl 2.0. In *2016 IEEE International Symposium on Performance Analysis of Systems and Software, ISPASS 2016, Uppsala, Sweden, April 17–19, 2016* (pp. 183–193). IEEE Computer Society.
42. Karnagel, T., Habich, D., Schlegel, B., & Lehner, W. (2013). The hells-join: A heterogeneous stream join for extremely large windows. In R. Johnson & A. Kemper (Eds.), *Proceedings of the Ninth International Workshop on Data Management on New Hardware, DaMoN 2013, New York, NY, USA, June 24, 2013* (p. 2). ACM.
43. Jones, N., et al. (2018). How to stop data centres from gobbling up the world's electricity. *Nature, 561*(7722), 163–166.
44. Graefe, G. (2008). Database servers tailored to improve energy efficiency. In S. Apel, M. Rosenmüller, G. Saake & O. Spinczyk (Eds.), *EDBT'08 Workshop on Software Engineering for Tailor-made Data Management, Proceedings, Nantes, France, March 29, 2008* (pp. 24–28). ACM.
45. Conner, W. M. (1977). Offset-value coding. *IBM Technical Disclosure Bulletin* 2832–2837.
46. Do, T., Graefe, G., & Naughton, J. (2023). Efficient sorting, duplicate removal, grouping, and aggregation. *ACM Transactions on Database Systems, 47*(4), 16:1–16:35.
47. Graefe, G, & Do, T. (2023). Offset-value coding in database query processing. In J. Stoyanovich, J. Teubner, N. Mamoulis, E. Pitoura, J. Mühlig, K. Hose, S. S. Bhowmick & M. Lissandrini (Eds.), *Proceedings 26th International Conference on Extending Database Technology, EDBT 2023, Ioannina, Greece, March 28–31, 2023* (pp. 464–470). OpenProceedings.org.
48. Beilschmidt, C., Drönner, J., Glombiewski, N., Heigele, C., Holznigenkemper, J., Isenberg, A., Körber, M., Mattig, M., Morgen, A., & Seeger, B. (2019). Pretty fly for a VAT GUI: Visualizing event patterns for flight data. In *Proceedings of the 13th ACM International Conference on Distributed and Event-based Systems, DEBS 2019, Darmstadt, Germany, June 24–28, 2019*, (pp. 224–227). ACM.
49. Beilschmidt, C., Drönner, J., Glombiewski, N., Körber, M., Mattig, M., Morgen, A., & Seeger, B. (2019). VAT to the future: Extrapolating visual complex event processing. In C. Pöpper & M. Strohmeier (Eds.), *Proceedings of the 7th OpenSky Workshop 2019, Zurich, Switzerland, November 21–22, 2019*, volume 67 of *EPiC Series in Computing* (pp. 25–36). EasyChair.

50. Beilschmidt, C., Drönner, J., Mattig, M., & Seeger, B. (2017). VAT: A system for data-driven biodiversity research. In V. Markl, S. Orlando, B. Mitschang, P. Andritsos, K.-U. Sattler & S. Breß (Eds.), *Proceedings of the 20th International Conference on Extending Database Technology, EDBT 2017, Venice, Italy, March 21–24, 2017* (pp. 546–549). OpenProceedings.org.
51. Beilschmidt, C., Drönner, J., Mattig, M., Schmidt, M., Authmann, C., Niamir, A., Hickler, T., & Seeger, B. (2017). VAT: A scientific toolbox for interactive geodata exploration. *Datenbank-Spektrum, 17*(3), 233–243.
52. Schäfer, M., Strohmeier, M., Lenders, V., Martinovic, I., & Wilhelm, M. (2014). Bringing up opensky: A large-scale ADS-B sensor network for research. In *IPSN'14* (pp. 83–94).

Chapter 4
Hybrid Transactional/Analytical Graph Processing in Modern Memory Hierarchies

Alexander Baumstark, Muhammad Attahir Jibril, and Kai-Uwe Sattler

Abstract Today's enterprise computing architectures are characterized by a complex memory hierarchy: different application requirements in terms of latency, bandwidth, persistence, and access pattern, as well as characteristics of available memory and storage technology require combining different technologies. Building highly efficient data management and analytics solutions that meet the challenges of modern applications requires to utilize this memory hierarchy, i.e., taking the specific characteristics of a given technology into account and keeping data objects in the optimal level. In this paper, we present results of our project on exploiting modern memory hierarchies in support of hybrid transactional/analytical processing (HTAP) on graph data. First, we discuss the design and evaluation of data structures and query operations for graph data in persistent memory. Second, we present an approach to support the analysis of graph data on GPU-based accelerators with dedicated memory by efficient data transfer and consistency mechanisms. Finally, we propose a storage and processing strategy for (bi-)temporal graphs using temporal materialized views while exploiting the memory hierarchy.

4.1 Introduction

Today's enterprise computing architectures are characterized by a complex memory hierarchy: the different application requirements in terms of latency, bandwidth, persistence, and access pattern, as well as the characteristics of available memory and storage technology required to combine different technologies. In the past, such hierarchies could be classified into a few levels with one technology at each level (e.g., CPU cache, DRAM as primary storage, magnetic disks as secondary storage, tapes); the hardware development of the last years has broadened the memory and

A. Baumstark · M. A. Jibril · K.-U. Sattler (✉)
Database & Information Systems Group, TU Ilmenau, Ilmenau, Germany
e-mail: alexander.baumstark@tu-ilmenau.de; muhammad-attahir.jibril@tu-ilmenau.de; kus@tu-ilmenau.de

K.-U. Sattler et al. (eds.), *Scalable Data Management for Future Hardware*,
https://doi.org/10.1007/978-3-031-74097-8_4

storage landscape. Modern multi-core CPUs provide at least three cache levels (L1–L3); with the advent of persistent memory, primary storage is not restricted to volatile DRAM anymore, and solid-state disks (SSD) connected via PCIe (NVMe) outperform traditional hard disks by an order of magnitude. Furthermore, some architectures such as GPUs or even CPUs provide in addition to standard DRAM so-called High Bandwidth Memory (HBM). In addition, co-processing units like GPUs introduce their device memory to the overall hierarchy.

Building highly efficient data management and analytics solutions that meet the challenges of modern applications requires the utilization of the memory hierarchy, e.g., by using inclusive and exclusive caching strategies, taking the specific characteristics of a given memory technology into account for designing data structures or algorithms, or by keeping data objects in the optimal level, in the optimal memory region, and in the optimal data structure. Particularly, trends such as HTAP—Hybrid transactional/analytical processing—aiming at a combination of OLTP (transaction processing) and OLAP (analytics) in a common architecture to be efficient both for operational and analytical workloads pose a great challenge in exploiting the memory hierarchy.

An interesting addition to the traditional memory hierarchy is non-volatile memory or persistent memory (PMem), which—ideally—combines the best of two worlds: persistency of block devices with byte-level access granularity and low latency of DRAM. Based on the 3D XPoint technology, Intel started to ship Optane DC persistent memory modules (DCPMM) as the first non-volatile memory DIMMs in 2019 but discontinued the product in 2022. Despite this fact and the lack of a commercially available product, PMem poses some interesting aspects that affect the design of future data management solutions.

In this work, we investigate how we can effectively exploit the modern memory hierarchy and particularly the opportunities of persistent memory. Based on an analysis of the characteristics of Optane DCPMM and approaches to integrating PMem into the memory hierarchy, we discuss design decisions for PMem-based data structures and storage engines.

Our work is centered around Poseidon, a hybrid transactional/analytical processing (HTAP) graph database system that enables transactional graph processing based on the property graph model. Graph databases represent an important class of NoSQL systems. They come in a broad range of usage cases and approaches, ranging from systems for analyzing large graphs over systems for querying knowledge bases to transactional systems with support for navigational queries. Depending on the primary use case, the underlying data model is either based on a property graph model, represents a graph by RDF triples, or maps the graph to relational tables. Also, the processing models range from standard database query processing to dedicated parallel programming models such as the bulk synchronous parallel (BSP) model. Most available systems follow the typical architectures of database systems like traditional disk-based architecture, in-memory architecture, or scalable, distributed solutions. Thus, graph data are either stored in disk-based data structures or loaded into memory for processing. However, the nature of graph processing, e.g., traversals along relationships between nodes, makes it a promising use case for byte-addressable storage eliminating the need for transferring data between external block storage and memory.

Our work has the following main contributions:

1. We provide a system beyond the scope of standard relational or record-based data models by supporting graph data, both in the form of transactional updates and graph analytics to realize HTAP for graph data. Primarily, we focus on utilizing PMem for storing graph data and the interplay with volatile memory for transaction processing.
2. In addition to PMem, we consider further elements of the memory hierarchy such as device memory and high bandwidth memory as part of GPU devices for specific analytical tasks.
3. Due to the nature of evolving graphs in topology and properties, we extend the standard data model to capture time-varying information for future processing. However, this leads to higher storage and processing requirements due to more data. Exploiting the modern memory and storage hierarchy can significantly improve the overall processing.

4.2 Background

In the following we provide an overview of the main characteristics of persistent memory technology as well as of the fundamental assumptions regarding the data model underlying our work.

4.2.1 Persistent Memory Characteristics

In our work, we rely on Intel's Optane DCPMM as the only commercially available DIMM-packaged persistent memory. Though the basic principles of our work can be applied to other potential PMem technologies, we have designed our approach around the special characteristics of Optane DCPMM. What makes persistent memory in general interesting is the byte-addressability and direct persistence at DRAM speed. On modern CPU architectures, byte-addressability corresponds to cache-line granularity (typically 64 bytes). Further interesting features are a higher density and better economic characteristics than DRAM (both in monetary and energy terms) as well as direct load and store semantics. Another important fact is that the Optane devices internally work with cache lines, but a write-combining buffer aggregate writes to 256-byte blocks (cf. [66]). This is mainly to avoid write-amplification, although we could not notice a significant performance difference when switching from 64-byte to 256-byte aligned data structures.

Table 4.1 summarizes some of the characteristics and compares them with those of DRAM and SLC NAND flash. We remeasured the latencies using Intel's

Table 4.1 Main characteristics of different memory/storage technologies (cf. [24])

	DRAM	Optane DC	NAND Flash
Idle read latency	80 ns	175 ns	15 μs
Loaded random latency	90 ns	325 ns	200 μs
Read bandwidth	85 GB/s	32 GB/s	3 GB/s
Write bandwidth	46 GB/s	13 GB/s	0.6 GB/s
Write endurance	$>10^{15}$	N/A	10^4–10^5
Density	1×	2–4×	4–8×

Memory Latency Checker [31] and Flexible I/O tester [20]. Since we focus on single-threaded experiments, total bandwidth numbers are not relevant for us here. Similar to flash, PMem exhibits a read-write asymmetry and lower write endurance than DRAM. However, we could not find any actual endurance data of the DCPMMs. When designing new data structures, these properties mean that writes should be minimized using more computing power instead. DCPMMs provide two possible operating modes: Memory and App Direct mode. The Memory mode allows applications to use DCPMMs as an extension to volatile memory, where DRAM acts like a kind of L4 cache. For that, no rewrite of in-memory software is necessary. However, to fully utilize PMem and its persistence, the App Direct mode must be used. Therefore, developers have to take care of persistence, failure-atomicity, performance, and others themselves. On the software level, we used the de facto standard Persistent Memory Development Kit (PMDK) [32] that provides functionality to manage PMem including allocations, transactions, object management, etc.

From our experiments and the work of other researchers, we can derive the following main characteristics of PMem (cf. also [34]):

- **(C1)** PMem has a higher latency and lower bandwidth than DRAM (3x read latency).
- **(C2)** Reads and writes on PMem behave asymmetrically.
- **(C3)** DCPMMs internally work on 256-byte blocks, which means read operations benefit when a multiple of the block size is used [66, 70].
- **(C4)** Failure atomicity is only guaranteed for 8-byte aligned writes; anything larger has to be implemented in software.
- **(C5)** PMem allocations are expensive [24, 25, 45].
- **(C6)** Dereferencing persistent pointers (a 16-byte structure consisting of a pool identifier and an offset in this pool) can prevent optimizations.

Considering these characteristics, a system using PMem has to be designed in a way that negative impacts of the hardware are minimized.

4.2.2 Property Graph Model

In the following, we assume a property graph model as the data model where a graph $G = (N, R)$ consists of nodes N and directed relationships $R \subseteq N \times N$. Each node $n \in N$ is identified by a unique identifier $id : N \rightarrow ID$. Furthermore, a label (used, e.g., as a type descriptor) is assigned to each node and each relationship via a labeling function $l : \{N \cup R\} \rightarrow L$ where L is the set of labels.

To each node and relationship, a set of properties can be associated via $p : \{N \cup R\} \rightarrow \mathcal{P}(P)$ where $\mathcal{P}(P)$ denotes the power set of P. Such properties are represented as key-value pairs $(k, v) \in P$ with $P = K \times D$ where K denotes the set of property keys and D is the set of possible values including numbers, strings, etc.

Property graphs are supported by several graph database systems, and even RDF data can be mapped to property graphs [3]. Furthermore, the new SQL standard SQL:2023 (ISO standard ISO/IEC 9075-16) adds also support for property graphs.

4.2.3 Temporal Graphs

In transactional graph databases, the managed graphs change, leading to a structural transformation of the graph over time with various states. Each of such update operations creates a new state of the underlying graph. Analyzing these different states over time can be valuable for analysis, facilitating future business decisions through the identification of patterns or the training of models. The time dimension is an already known feature in modern DBMSs, which are referred to as temporal DBMS. While a traditional DBMS does not preserve the old state of the data before updates, a temporal DBMS invalidates the old data and creates new valid data. The support for temporal features in SQL was introduced with the SQL:2011 standard, enabling the processing of evolving data through temporal query operators [42]. However, current graph database systems lack efficient support for the storage and processing of temporal data.

For our purpose, we extend the above-introduced property graph model with additional time information as properties on the nodes and relationships. Storing additional time information describes historical changes in the graph structure itself and the changes in the corresponding properties. This time dimension is often referred to as the real-world or *valid time interval* of a record, which indicates the start and end time point when the object was available. A user can define these periods, by adding them directly to the records. However, considering a transactional database reveals a discrepancy between the valid time defined by the user and the actual time when the changes are committed and are visible by the system. Therefore, an additional time dimension is necessary to retrieve the transactional time of the tuples. Furthermore, we extend the model by the *transaction time interval*, which is the interval when a transaction started processing the record and the time when the transaction committed the changes to the DBMS. Storing two different time dimensions allows processing the historical changes in a graph at a certain time point concerning the state when the changes take place. Providing these two dimensions of times in a system enables the processing of bi-temporal queries in a graph database.

Let T_{tx} be the transaction-time domain and T_v the valid time domain. An event in one of the domains $t_i \in T_{tx} \cup T_v$ is an interval (t_{begin}, t_{end}) where t_{begin} marks the beginning time of the event and t_{end} the end time of the event. Events in the time domains T_{tx} and T_v are linearly ordered so that $t_i < t_{i+1}$ where $t_i \in T_{tx} \cup T_v$.

Then, we extend a node $n \in N$ to be a tuple (id, t_{tx}, t_v), where id is a unique identifier to identify a node using $id : N \to ID$ and t_{tx} and t_v are time intervals denoting the validity of the node considering the time domains T_{tx} and T_v. A relationship $r \in R$ is a tuple (id, t_{tx}, t_v), where id is a unique identifier to identify a relationship using $id : R \to ID$ and t_{tx} and t_v are time intervals denoting the validity of the relationship wrt. the time domains T_{tx} and T_v.

Considering the structure of a graph, it should be noted that the graph is only valid in a certain time interval when all nodes and relationships are also valid. A relationship is only valid when both the source and destination node are valid in the appropriate time domain. In contrast to the model used in other systems, this model restricts multiple nodes with the same identifier in the same graph. Dropping this constraint relaxes the model definition and has the advantage of improving the query processing, as the storage of a graph contains only valid nodes and relationships.

4.3 Data Structures for Transactional Graph Data in PMem

The characteristics of PMem and the performance consequences require a careful design of data structures for persistent data. Based on the main goals, we describe in the following our design decisions for graph structures.

4.3.1 Design Goals

Based on the observations of PMem characteristics listed in Sect. 4.2.1, we can derive several goals when designing data structures for PMem [34]:

(DG1) **Algorithmically save writes** (C1 & C2). The idea is to reduce the number of writes by trading them off for more reads.

(DG2) **Opt for a DRAM/PMem hybrid storage design** (C1 & C2). It has been shown that a pure PMem-only architecture causes too much performance degradation compared to its DRAM counterpart [24, 25].

(DG3) **Optimize the access granularity to 256 bytes** (C3). The data structures should be aligned to cache lines.

(DG4) Prefer failure-atomic writes over logging or shadowing (C4). For this purpose, flushing of cache lines via the `clwb` (cache line write back) instruction and barriers such as `sfence` (store fence) have to be used.

(DG5) Use group allocations and reuse blocks of memory instead of deallocating (C5). Not every new record in a system should be associated with an allocation.

(DG6) Avoid dereferencing of persistent pointers (C6). Persistent pointers should preferably only be used during application (re)start for initialization. In addition, pointer chasing should be avoided as well, as shown in [24, 25].

Based on the idea of a periodic table of data structures [30], we worked already on the evaluation of the design space [24] where we presented a set of design primitives and micro-operations for PMem-based data structures. A design primitive is a layout for a data structure. This helps identify bottlenecks and optimization potential of micro-operations. Examples are data node layouts in index trees and the actual search for a key within a tree node.

4.3.2 Data Structures for Graphs

Sticking to the outlined design objectives for update-optimized property graph management led to crucial design choices. Fundamentally, nodes and relationships are kept in distinct tables. Given the absence of fixed schemas for nodes and relationships and the variability in property sets, all nodes and relationships are each consolidated into their respective single tables. Figure 4.1 gives an overview of Poseidon's storage architecture. Poseidon is based on the following design decisions:

- Tables are managed as **linked lists of chunks**. A chunk is a fixed-sized array (cache-line aligned and a multiple of 256 bytes) of records.
- Records in a chunk are of the same type (nodes, relationships, properties) and **equally sized**. Access to individual records is **addressed via their offsets**. Further, a sparse index is used as a persistent lookup table for efficient access to chunks based on record offsets (DG1, DG6).
- **Properties are outsourced** to a separate table to fulfill equally sized records. Further, all variable-length values (e.g., strings) are **dictionary encoded**. This leads to a reduced number of write operations (DG1).
- The **connections** between nodes and their relationships and between nodes and relationships and their properties are represented via **offsets**.
- **Storage model** is designed **hybrid** for secondary indexes and for transaction management (DG2).

The data structure and algorithms are implemented using Intel's PMDK library for persistent memory [32].

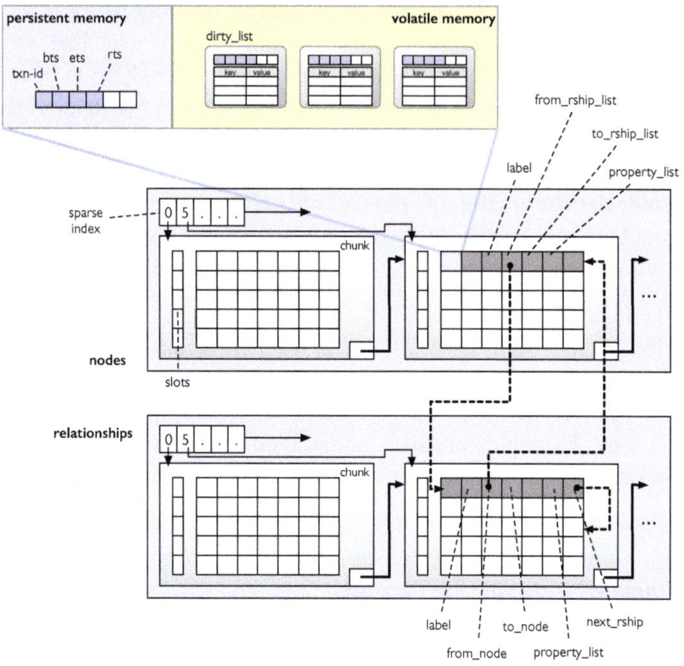

Fig. 4.1 Graph data structures

For HTAP workload support, a high-performance concurrency control protocol is required. Based on related work [58, 68], we decided to implement a multi-version concurrency control (MVCC) as it exhibits higher concurrency than their single-version counterparts. With this protocol, transactions can be concurrently executed on different versions of the same object increasing the overall throughput, especially for long-running transactions and high contention [43]. With this, modern multiple CPUs can be effectively leveraged.

We adopted and implemented the Multi-version Timestamp Ordering (MVTO) protocol to the specifics of PMem. The main idea, as described in [34], is to extend node and relationship records by additional *persistent* fields—`txn-id`, begin timestamp `bts`, end timestamp `ets`, and read timestamp `rts`—and a volatile field, pointer. The `txn-id` field is used for write locking using a CaS instruction [43]. Validity for objects is marked with the begin and end timestamps for access by a read transaction. The read timestamp indicates the latest read by a transaction. The pointer field stores a *volatile* pointer to a list of dirty objects in DRAM to address (DG1) and (DG2). Thus, all updates are performed on the DRAM record version until the commit. Keeping uncommitted data in volatile memory minimized the number of weird to PMem, whose access is more costly than on DRAM. Only the final version needs to be written on PMem during the commit. Volatile versions can be dropped effectively.

To manage variable-length labels, property keys, and values efficiently, a dictionary compresses strings, reducing space and writing overhead while maintaining offset-addressable records. This also accelerates operations like filters by comparing codes instead of strings. The dictionary has a persistent string pool in a large array for storing strings successively, using string offsets as dictionary codes. A volatile memory hash table, rebuilt at startup, maps strings to codes, enabling quick bi-directional translation. The dictionary is separate from the storage structures, optimizing performance and storage.

Lookup queries can benefit from secondary indexes since full table scans are too expensive. To accelerate these queries, we additionally provide B^+-Tree indexes. Indexes can be constructed for record labels or properties. The values of these properties are used as keys in the index. Secondary indexes can be constructed at DBMS startup or rebuilt in the event of a failure. Therefore, there is no complete persistence required. We adopted a hybrid DRAM/PMem approach to provide a good compromise between recovery and query performance, similar to [37, 55, 69]. Leaf nodes are stored in PMem while inner nodes in DRAM. Inner nodes of the tree can be rebuilt from the persistently stored leaf nodes in PMem. Further, this results in only one PMem-resident node needing to be read per lookup, which reduces recovery time. Following DG3, all nodes on PMem are cache-line-aligned and have a multiple of 256 bytes.

4.4 Graph Query Processing

The higher latency and lower bandwidth of PMem impact query processing directly. However, the advantage of PMem is the byte-addressable access allowing in-memory-like access to storage, which is especially useful for graph DBMSs. Still, the characteristics require careful consideration for designing the query engine.

4.4.1 Push-Based Approach

We address the PMem characteristics by providing a push-based query engine that leverages multithreaded processing. First, we provide a set of graph-specific operators, which we adapt from a graph algebra [27]. This algebra extends the relational algebra by navigational operators for graphs such as `NodeScan` or `Expand`. We split the `Expand` operator to also address relationship directly into a further `ForeachRelationship` operator [34]. An index to access particular nodes and relationships can be used with the `IndexScan` operator.

We design the query engine as a push-based engine as shown in Fig. 4.2, where tuples are passed from one operator to another until a *pipeline breaker* is reached. A pipeline-breaker is an operator that materializes the tuples for further calculation or

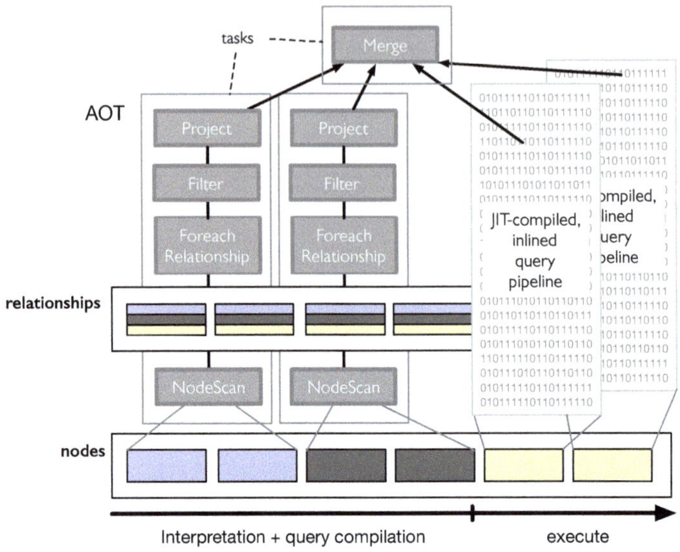

Fig. 4.2 Query execution plan

printing. Further, we leverage a Morsel-driven approach [44]. We execute a query plan on individual chunks (the Morsels) on different threads and merge results at pipeline breakers. For this, we implement a task-based approach, where chunks are assigned to a task and pushed into a task pool where they will be pulled from threads and executed. Every operator is implemented as an ahead-of-time (AOT)-compiled query engine, which we use as an interpreter. When a query arrives, the individual operators are linked into a cascade of operator functions and executed.

For convenience, Poseidon also supports the `Match` operator from the Cypher query language, which is rewritten in a sequence of `NodeScan` or `IndexScan` and `ForeachRelationship` operators. Query 4.1 shows an example of Poseidon's query language using query 10 of the GTPC benchmark [36].

```

Sort([$5:double ASC],
  GroupBy([$0.id:uint64, $0.last:string, $0.city:string, $0.phone
      :string, $6.name:string], [sum($4.amount:double)],
    Expand(OUT, 'Nation',
      ForeachRelationship(FROM, 'isLocatedIn', $0,
        Filter($2.entry_d:datetime >= pb::to_datetime('2007-01-02
            00:00:00.000000')
            $2.entry_d:datetime <= $4.delivery_d:datetime,
          Match((c:Customer)-[:hasPlaced]->(o:Order)-[:contains]->(
              ol:OrderLine))
)))))
```

Query 4.1 Query 10 of GTPC in Poseidon notation

4.4.2 Just-in-Time Query Compilation

We use query compilation to mitigate the higher access latencies of PMem. Graph queries can be perfectly optimized since the emitted (unoptimized) code contains similar patterns and the same function calls, which usually increase the execution overhead. For short-running queries, the problem is the compilation time itself since it can be longer than the actual query execution time. For this, we use an adaptive approach, similar to [41]. The query engine starts every query in an interpretation mode, which uses an interpreter for query execution and compiles the query in the background. As soon as the compilation is complete, the engine switches to the optimized code. Access latencies for underlying memory are effectively hidden since more data can be executed using the optimized code [9].

We use the LLVM framework as the just-in-time (JIT) compiler to generate code on runtime. Using this framework allows to generate an intermediate representation (IR) from given queries and executing hardware-independent code optimization.

We transfer every algebra operator into an IR code to compile it into a single function. Internally, this is achieved by using the visitor code pattern. Every algebra operator in IR starts with a basic block that contains the first initialization and branching to the next operator-specific code. Further, each operator ends with a basic block that contains the link to the next operator, since the operators are push-based. In between these two blocks is the operator-specific code. Ultimately, this forms a chain of operators. The IR code can then be optimized and compiled JIT.

4.4.3 Adaptive Query Compilation

For the adaptive approach, we start executing the interpreter on the given graph query in graph algebra. For this, every chunk will be assigned to a task, which will be pushed into a task pool. A task contains a chunk and the query function that points to the interpreter initially. Participating threads work on the task pool by polling tasks from it and executing the function on the chunks given in the task. The query interpreter uses ahead-of-time compiled code, which uses a function cascade of the operators in the given query to interpret the code. In the meanwhile, the query compilation process starts. As soon as the compilation is complete, a thread switches the code of the tasks in the task pool. When the next task is pulled from a thread, it will execute the freshly optimized and compiled code.

When comparing interpretation and the adaptive approach, the adaptive approach can hide the PMem latencies more effectively. Since more tasks are executed with the optimized machine code, the runtimes can be decreased, which hides the latencies of PMem.

4.4.4 *Query Recovery*

PMem offers opportunities for efficient, near-instant query recovery. The challenge remains to manage intermediate results and query states in PMem without incurring significant latency and slowing down processing when tracking states. We utilize a chunked vector for holding temporary data and query checkpoints. Tuple elements are separated and stored in a specialized structure, focusing only on node and relationship identifiers to minimize memory usage. Property elements are stored by their record ID. This structure encapsulates element details, such as identifiers or property keys, and aligns with design choices at 256-byte multiples. Elements are interconnected through offsets within the chunked vector, facilitating element association. We leverage the push-based query engine of Poseidon. By persisting the last processed chunk vector position in a map, we can restart from these checkpoints. We initiate iterator objects for incomplete chunks from the last saved position, enabling the continuation and recovery of the failed query for further processing. Because of the rebuilding costs of intermediate results, we use a cost model that calculates the costs for rebuilding the intermediate results to continue or restart the query from the beginning [8].

4.5 Graph Analytics on Transactional Data

Support for HTAP workload means, in addition to transactional updates and queries, also supporting complex graph analytics tasks (e.g., pathfinding, centrality analysis, etc.) on the same dataset and, at the same time, ensuring the freshness of the results. Experiments have shown that hardware accelerators such as GPUs deliver significant performance benefits when processing analytical tasks on graphs.

This has led to the development of several GPU-based graph analytics frameworks that facilitate the leveraging of GPUs' parallelization potential for executing operations on graphs. However, these graph analytics frameworks rely on dedicated data structures and graph representations (e.g., based on adjacency lists or matrices), which are not well suited for efficient transactional updates on parts of the graph. Consequently, one is left with two options. The first option is to not utilize GPU for performance benefits in the analytical part of the workload, thereby accepting performance losses. The second option is to store the graph in two different representations, which ultimately raises the problem of *update propagation*.

4.5.1 *Data Structures for Graph Analytics*

To address this task, we have extended Poseidon to a hybrid architecture. For this purpose, we use the Compressed Sparse Row (CSR) format, which is the most

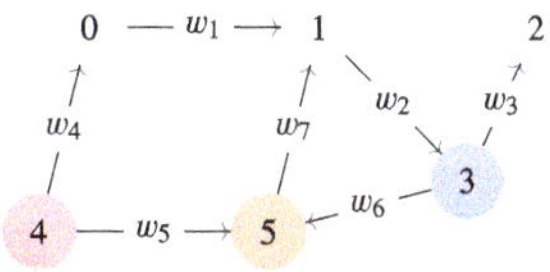

Fig. 4.3 Sample graph

Fig. 4.4 CSR Representation of sample graph

Edge Values	w_1	w_2	w_3	w_6	w_4	w_5	w_7

Column Indices	1	3	2	5	0	5	1

Row Offsets	0	1	2	2	4	6	7

commonly used sparse matrix format [26] for graph representation on GPU. The CSR data is managed as a replica of the main graph representation in persistent memory (PMem), although the two are in different formats. Therefore, updates on the main graph representation that are made by transactions have to be propagated to the GPU part to execute the analytics on the most recent version of the graph. However, the CSR format inherently makes updates on the graph difficult because of its highly compact layout.

A CSR is a data structure that stores an *adjacency matrix*. An *adjacency matrix*, $M \in \{0, w\}^{n,n}$, is a matrix representation of a graph topology. Each relationship (or edge) in the graph is represented by an entry w at a coordinate (u, v) in M, where u and v are the source and destination nodes (or vertices) of the relationship, respectively, and w is the relationship *weight*. Entries with weight value 0 denote unconnected nodes. A CSR essentially provides information regarding the non-zero entries in M, linearized in three one-dimensional arrays. The *edge values* array stores the non-zero weight values (i.e., all w for each u in M), the *column indices* array stores the column indices of the values (i.e., all v for each u in M), and the *row offsets* stores the offsets of the values (in the first two arrays) for each row (i.e., u in M). Figure 4.3 shows an example graph along with its CSR representation in Fig. 4.4.

CSR and other static data structures compactly represent graph data, in addition to contiguous storage. These have advantages such as reduced memory consumption, regular memory access, and low interconnect bandwidth consumption when transferring data between the host and the GPU device. However, these data structures are not suitable for updates. Thus, the default way to handle updates is a complete rebuild of the data structures when the graph data changes. In the beginning, the CSR would have to be completely built. However, for subsequent modifications to the graph data, the CSR would have to be repetitively rebuilt. Doing this on an HTAP graph system so that graph analytics run on the most recently committed snapshot of the graph data eventually counterbalances the benefits of using GPU for accelerated analytics in the first place. As a solution to this high cost of CSR rebuild, we adopt a graph-based delta approach, where each delta is associated with an updated node in the graph and it represents the new state of the adjacency list. In addition to committing the updates it made to the main graph,

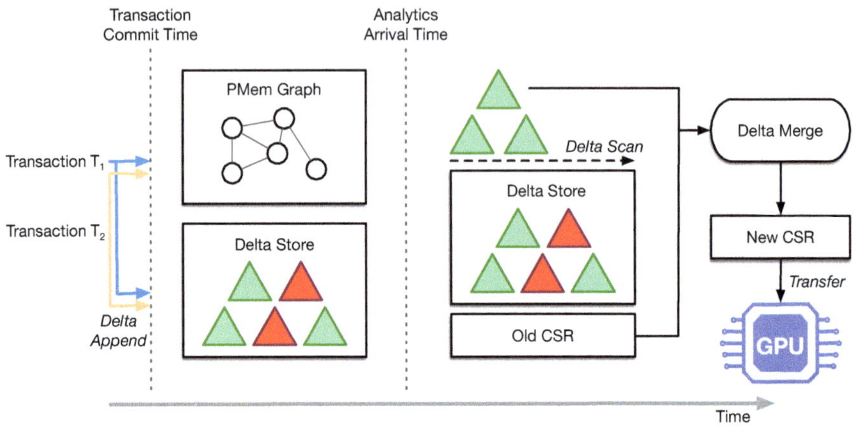

Fig. 4.5 Delta approach

every transaction stores deltas for its updates in a *delta store* at commit time. Before executing analytics, the delta store is first scanned for these deltas, and the deltas are merged to update the CSR so that the analytics execution is on the latest committed snapshot of the graph in a format different from the main graph storage and by the freshness requirements of HTAP. Our solution mainly consists of three steps, (1) Delta Append, (2) Delta Scan, and (3) Delta Merge, , which we describe in the following.

Delta Append Figure 4.5 depicts our delta approach. At commit time, which is denoted by the first vertical dashed line in the figure, each transaction appends deltas into the delta store for the new states of the adjacency lists that changed as a result of the updates it has made to the main graph. This appending of deltas is done in addition to persisting updates to the main graph. At the arrival of analytics, which is denoted by the second vertical dashed line in the figure, the deltas are merged to update the CSR so that the analytics are executed on a CSR representation of the most recently committed snapshot of the main graph. We identify which update operations modify the arrays of a CSR: the creation and deletion of nodes and relationships. To map each delta to a node, we associate each of these operations with the updated node(s). About the addition and deletion of a relationship, we map the delta to only the source node of the relationship (in a directed graph) or both the source and destination nodes of the relationship (in an undirected graph). As for the addition and deletion of a node, we map the delta to the added or deleted node. We also store corresponding deltas for any addition or deletion of relationships that accompany the addition or deletion of a node. At commit time, a transaction stores a delta for each of these mapped nodes, where a delta consists of the ID of the node, its current column indices, and the corresponding edge values. To ensure that the main graph and its CSR representation are consistent under transactional updates, each transaction additionally stores, in each of its deltas, (i) its timestamp and (ii) a flag to indicate whether the delta has been previously used to update the CSR or not (each delta is used only once in a CSR update).

Delta Scan Updating the CSR with the transactional modifications since the last CSR update (or since the initial CSR build) requires scanning the delta store to retrieve the deltas. The delta scan begins with the launching of a special transaction T_s. But while T_s is scanning the delta store, regular update transactions would continue to store their respective deltas in the delta store at their respective commit times. To guarantee data consistency, T_s conducts a *visibility check* on each delta, based on the transaction timestamps stored in the deltas as an extension of the underlying MVTO in Poseidon. The CSR update itself is done transactionally. Therefore, all the deltas (denoted by the green triangles in Fig. 4.5) that are *visible* to the transaction T_s executing the CSR update operation and have not been used in a previous CSR update are merged to update the CSR, thus reflecting the latest committed snapshot of the main PMem graph data. All the deltas (denoted by the red triangles in Fig. 4.5) that have been used in a CSR update are marked using the flag mentioned earlier.

Delta Merge For regular update transactions (not T_s above) T_0, T_1, ... T_n that store deltas after a CSR update, each delta stored by a transaction T_i either overwrites another delta mapped to the same node by an older transaction $T_{j|j<i}$ or is overwritten by another delta mapped to the same node ID by a newer transaction $T_{k|k>i}$ or is the only delta mapped to that node. It follows that overwritten deltas are not valid for a CSR update. Therefore, for a CSR, CSR_0, and transactions T_0, T_1, ... T_n that store deltas, updating CSR_0 to CSR_1 would be as follows:

$$CSR_1 = CSR_0 + \Delta_{T_0}^{dist} \Delta_{T_0}^{owrt} + \Delta_{T_1}^{dist} \Delta_{T_1}^{owrt} + ... + \Delta_{T_n}^{dist} \Delta_{T_n}^{owrt}$$

where $\Delta_{T_i}^{dist}$ is the set of deltas by transaction T_i uniquely mapped to their respective nodes, while $\Delta_{T_i}^{owrt}$ are deltas that were last overwritten by T_i. These deltas ($\Delta_{T_i}^{dist}$ and $\Delta_{T_i}^{owrt}$) that are visible to T_s during the delta store scan described above are used in the delta merge. The algorithm of the delta merge is shown in [33]. The node IDs are first grouped into two sets, L and U, based on the maximum node ID in the old CSR (see Fig. 4.5) before the updates in the deltas, i.e., L are IDs of nodes that existed in the old CSR and U are IDs of newly inserted nodes (Line 1 to 5). For nodes that were not updated since the last CSR update, their corresponding entries in the old CSR are copied to the new CSR (Lines 9 and 14), whereas for newly inserted and updated nodes, the entries are updated with the deltas in the new CSR (Lines 11 and 17). Note that the CSR representation is oversimplified since a CSR has three arrays, not one.

In [35], we also present an adaptive approach that decides at runtime based on a cost model whether a delta update or a complete CSR rebuild is the better option.

4.6 Exploiting the Storage Hierarchy for Time-Travel Queries

In transactional graph DBMSs, the underlying graphs evolve since they are subject to changes. Valuable insights can be obtained when the intermediate states after changes after kept for analysis, which is the purpose of temporal DBMS. To enable effective querying of past data, it is useful to consider (bi-temporal) two distinct time domains: *valid time*, which relates to the real world, and *transaction time*, which relates to system-internal time. However, managing additional states within a DBMS results in increased overhead in data storage and subsequent query processing but also additional constraints in validity and locality challenges.

Most of the approaches are built upon versioning, which decreases query performance (for non-temporal and temporal workloads) due to broken graph locality or a full-snapshot approach, which leads to increased storage costs. We argue that by leveraging the memory and storage hierarchy for modern systems, it is possible to manage both low query processing overhead for non-temporal works and low storage overhead by keeping only relevant data.

To address this, we introduce an approach for storing and processing temporal data in materialized views, taking into account the memory hierarchy of modern systems. We call this approach temporal materialized views (TMV). Further, we demonstrate an effective approach to solving the query containment problem for queries on different time intervals.

4.6.1 Data Model

We extend the labeled property graph model by valid time and transaction time domains under which nodes and relationships are described. The *valid time* is the real-world time, assigned to the data externally, i.e., by the user. Therefore, we store the valid time as additional properties of the nodes and relationships. The *transaction time* is managed by the MVCC protocol, which provides all necessary information like the start and commit of the transaction. Further, we consider a linear order of events, which are inserts, updates, and deletions. Deletions are never executed directly; instead, they will be executed logically by setting the appropriate deleted flag of a record. For validity, we consider that nodes and relationships are only valid if their valid or transaction time periods are contained in a given time period. In graphs, it follows that a relationship is only valid (in the valid time or transaction time) if its source and destination node are valid too.

4.6.2 Temporal Query Processing

We provide several temporal operators, which are described in [10]. These operators are used for navigation through a graph with temporal validation. Valid time or transaction time can be passed as arguments to the operators. We allow the creation of complete snapshots of the graph and an additional temporal operator to add tuples to a specific temporal materialized view. These views can be scanned and accessed with the described operators. Further, we provide validation operators known from the interval algebra as built-in functions in `Filter` operators.

Based on the data model and these operators, we propose an approach to temporal graph processing and temporal materialized views. Query processing can be improved by placing these views in a higher layer of the memory hierarchy.

4.6.3 TMV Model

Materialized Views store typically results of queries. In graphs, MVs are mostly sub-graphs. Calculated results of queries can be recalculated by storing the nodes or relationships to which they belong. This increases the containment of the results of other queries. We define MVs under the valid time and transaction time to temporal materialized views that only store valid tuples in the given time periods.

For creation, the `TMVInsert` operator can be placed in the appropriate position of the query pipeline. Further, a hop argument can be passed to the operator in order to increase the containment for other queries. The n-hop argument indicates the additional hops of nodes subject to insertion into the TMV. A high n-hop argument increases the containment of other queries. Internally, the TMVs use separate tables for nodes and relationships as chunked vectors. At insertion, the tuples are split into nodes and relationships and stored in the TMV tables.

For placement, we store the main graph, which is the recent graph, always on disk or flash. TMVs are placed in a higher layer like DRAM or, if available, PMem. If there is no memory left, the TMVs are evicted to disk and later replaced using an LFU strategy.

For faster access and query containment, we use an interval tree. The interval is a suitable data structure to automatically select suitable TMVs for a query. An interval is a binary search storing intervals ordered by the lower bound. TMVs are stored by their intervals as keys into the tree. By iterating through the tree, overlapping TMVs can be found. The found TMV contains possible results. For uncovered intervals, the main graph has to be scanned again [10].

4.7 Related Work

Related to our work are approaches aiming at leveraging persistent memory for database structures, graph database management in general, as well as temporal data management. In this section, we briefly discuss the relevant work in these areas.

4.7.1 PM-Aware Storage Design

With the commercial availability of Intel Optane DCPMM, researchers have proposed various adaptations of existing data structures to PMem. This includes several variants of the B-Tree [14, 67], hybrid approaches like the FPTree [55] where inner nodes are kept in DRAM and only the leaf nodes are stored in PMem, the BzTree [6], the LB^+-Tree [47], DPTree [71], and HiKV [69], as well as numerous LSM-Tree variations [40] and LSM-based key-value stores such as RStore [46]. In [38] we have proposed an approach for selective caching of the multidimensional persistent index structure Elf.

In addition to such individual data structures, also approaches for PMem-based storage engines have been proposed. SOFORT [54] is a columnar transactional storage engine leveraging PMem by minimizing logging and updating data in place, aiming for mixed OLAP and OLTP workloads. Peloton [57] is another relational DBMS engine already considering PMem by applying write-behind logging [7]. The basic idea is to write and flush all changed entries in place to PMem during the commit.

4.7.2 Graph Database Management

For graph data management, different data models have been proposed in the past. Among these models, RDF for the Semantic Web and property graph models are the most prominent [3]. Based on these, query languages like SPARQL [59] for RDF triple data, diverse SQL dialects, and dedicated languages like Cypher [22], Gremlin [60], and GQL [21] have been developed. Recently, the SQL standardization committee has published SQL/PGQ [16] as part of SQL:2023 Part 16 for integrating graph pattern matching into SQL.

Depending on the supported data model and query language, graph database systems can be classified into:

- Special-purpose systems such as triple stores for RDF data like Virtuoso
- Native stores for property graphs, e.g., Neo4j [52], kuzu [19], Memgraph [50], TigerGraph [65], and Amazon Neptune [2], which supports also RDF and SPARQL
- Relationally backed approaches such as DB2RDF [11] and EmptyHeaded [1]
- Extensions of SQL systems like Grail [18] and SAP HANA [62]

Here, standard DBMS implementation techniques are used for data storage, indexing, transaction management, and query processing. In addition to standard relational features, graph database systems particularly support traversal operations [56], as well as graph analytics [53, 63].

While graph database systems provide the standard features of DBMS including transactional updates, graph processing engines aim at efficient and scalable analytics, often for distributed environments. Examples are [12, 48], and Giraph [4] implementing the bulk-synchronous parallel programming model or extensions for Apache Flink like Gradoop [39] or for Apache Spark like GraphX [23].

4.7.3 Temporal Graph Data Management

In addition to temporal extensions to relational databases that are standardized in SQL:2011 [42], there are also approaches to support temporal data in graph databases.

T-GQL [15] represents temporal connections by introducing additional relationships. Based on GQL and algorithms to capture different path semantics, the temporal graph query language T-GQL is proposed. Clock-G is a temporal graph management system that supports temporal processing [49]. This system introduces the operation-based property graph, suitable for processing temporal data. Additionally, the system supports various temporal queries such as point-based, range-based local queries, and global queries. TGraph is a temporal GDBMS that supports ACID transactions and processing of temporal graph queries [29]. Gradoop extensions for processing and analyzing temporal graph data have been introduced in [61]. It employs the temporal property graph model as the underlying data model and can handle distributed graph workflows. Furthermore, the authors have presented a set of operators for processing bitemporal queries. A similar distributed system is Raphtory [64].

ArangoDB is an open-source graph database that provides additional support for processing time-travel queries [5]. The underlying data model uses techniques known from persistent data structures, also known as non-ephemeral data structures [17]. Another storage engine for temporal graphs is ImmortalGraph [51]. The engine uses snapshot groups to manage historical graphs incrementally. ChronoGraph [13] is an analytical engine for temporal graphs. The underlying data model extends the property graph by events to support point and periodic-based analytics without snapshots. TEA is a temporal engine designed for temporal random walks [28]. The system employs a sampling method to process temporal algorithms.

4.8 Evaluation

We use the Social Media Benchmark (SNB) from the LDBC for our evaluation, especially the interactive short reads. We use different starting points for particular queries to show a variety of executions. These starting points are denoted as `cmt` or `post`. Further, we use the adaptive approach for every execution. The results are given in Fig. 4.6. In general, the higher latency and lower bandwidth of PMem lead to a slower execution for almost all queries. For short-running queries (1–3), the PMem approach shows a similar runtime since latencies can be hidden effectively due to the adaptive approach. This shows that our approach can achieve DRAM-like performances for particular queries. We compare the difference in detail in [8, 9, 34].

For the transactional update propagation for analytics, the microbenchmark is given in Fig. 4.7. The left side shows the update propagation time for updates. The time increases with an increasing number of updating queries. Further, the increase depends on the degree of the underlying graph. On the right, a comparison between PMem and DRAM for the update propagation is given. For both, the query execution runtime is similar, effectively hiding PMem latencies. A detailed evaluation of the analytics is given in [33, 37, 38].

We use the LDBC SNB dataset with synthetical queries adapted from the T-Cypher specification to evaluate the temporal approaches. The results are given in Fig. 4.8. We compare the usual query against the execution of full snapshots and TMVs. The results show that the TMV approach provides a performance between the temporal query execution and optimized full snapshots. TMVs can provide reliable performance while providing less storage overhead, compared to full snapshots. A more detailed evaluation is given in [10].

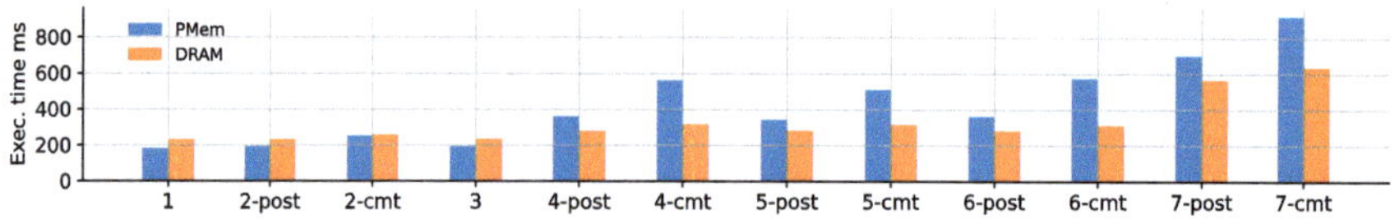

Fig. 4.6 LDBC short reads query execution

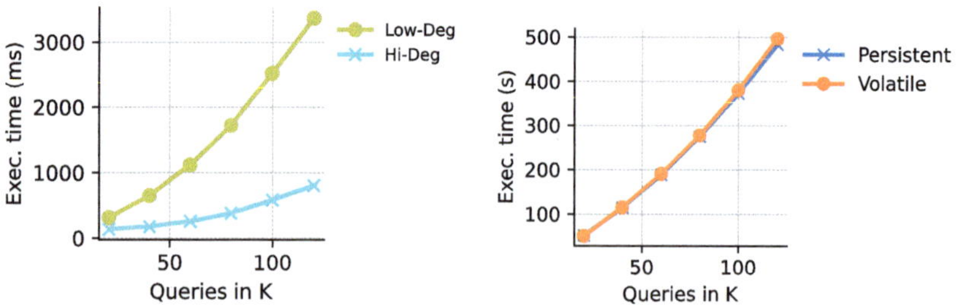

Fig. 4.7 Update propagation time (left) and copy on DRAM and PMem (right) comparison for a mixed workload

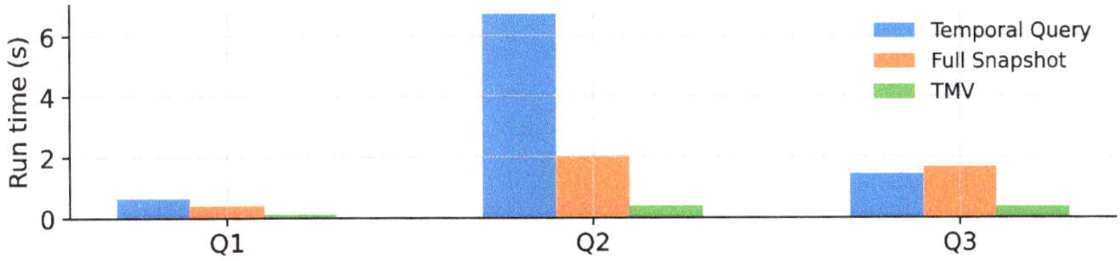

Fig. 4.8 Temporal query execution compared with runtime of full snapshots and TMVs

4.9 Conclusion

In this project, we have explored how persistent memory can be leveraged in modern data management architectures. Though currently commercially not successful, persistent memory represents a promising technology for data management, eliminating the need to move data between disk and memory—at least to some extent. However, the efficient use of PMem requires rethinking data structures and architectures.

Based on an analysis of the specific characteristics of PMem technology regarding latency, bandwidth, and the need for failure atomicity of updates, we have discussed, implemented, and evaluated design choices regarding storage structure, transaction, and query processing in a property graph database. Our implementations and experiments have shown that the higher latency of PMem compared to pure in-memory approaches based on traditional DRAM can be hidden by hybrid data structures and cache-friendly processing, e.g., appropriate data structures and query compilation. The main benefits are, among others, the competitive performance without the need to keep large parts of the data in (volatile) main memory (resulting in constant answer times both for cold and hot data) as well as near-instant recovery guarantees.

However, PMem also provides opportunities for new approaches. As one example, we have presented the idea of query recovery. By inserting materialization steps for intermediate results into the query pipeline and logging the progress level of the query execution, we can recover and continue the query after a system failure. Our evaluation has shown that the materialization overhead is minimal when using PMem while significantly accelerating the failure recovery. The point at which the intermediate results are materialized and the progress level of the query execution before failure play a crucial role in the trade-off between overhead and benefits of recovery.

As a second example, we investigated how the memory hierarchy of modern systems can be better exploited to speed up temporal query processing, as temporal workloads store multiple versions of data, which creates conceivably a large amount of data. Placing relevant sub-graphs, i.e., recent versions of the graph, as a materialized sub-graph in higher layers of the memory hierarchy, e.g., in PMem, improves the performance of future queries.

Although Intel Optane PMem has been discontinued, the findings of this project remain highly relevant to future hardware innovations. CXL (Compute Express Link) stands out as a promising candidate for extending the memory hierarchy of future systems. CXL enables systems to scale beyond the limitations imposed by the DDR interface, providing greater flexibility and capacity. Optimization of DBMS for CXL will focus on latency, as it is expected to be higher than traditional main memory over DDR. Consequently, our findings are expected to be applicable to CXL.

Besides persistent memory, there are more additions to the traditional memory hierarchy of modern systems. Accelerators such as GPUs or FPGAs usually come with their own device memory in the GB range. In our project, we further developed an adaptive update handling approach in a graph HTAP setting where transactional workloads update the main graph on the host while analytics are offloaded to the GPU for accelerated execution. We addressed the problem of update handling by integrating existing GPU-based graph analytics frameworks into HTAP systems, where the transactional updates to the main graph need to be propagated to the CSR replica of the graph on GPU. For this purpose, we adapted the concept of delta store as a faster update handling approach than rebuild immediately.

Acknowledgments This work was funded by the German Research Foundation (DFG) in the context of the projects "Hybrid Transactional/Analytical Graph Processing in Modern Memory Hierarchies (#TAG)" as part of the priority programs "Scalable Data Management for Future Hardware" (SPP 2037) under grant 361498781.

References

1. Aberger, C. R., Tu, S., Olukotun, K., & Ré, C. (2016). Emptyheaded: A relational engine for graph processing. In *Proceedings of the 2016 International Conference on Management of Data, SIGMOD Conference 2016, San Francisco, CA, USA, June 26–July 01, 2016* (pp. 431–446).
2. Amazon. Amazon Neptune: Serverless graph database designed for superior scalability and availability. https://aws.amazon.com/neptune/. Accessed: 14.03.2024.
3. Angles, R., Thakkar, H., & Tomaszuk, D. (2020). Mapping rdf databases to property graph databases. *IEEE Access, 8*, 86091–86110.
4. Apache Giraph. Apache Giraph, an iterative graph processing system built for high scalability. https://giraph.apache.org. Accessed: 14.03.2024.
5. *ArangoDB* (2022). https://www.arangodb.com
6. Arulraj, J., Levandoski, J. J., Minhas, U. F., & Larson, P.-Å. (2018). Bztree: A high-performance latch-free range index for non-volatile memory. *PVLDB, 11*(5), 553–565.
7. Arulraj, J., Perron, M., & Pavlo, A. (2016). Write-behind logging. *PVLDB, 10*(4), 337–348.
8. Baumstark, A., Götze, P., Jibril, M. A., & Sattler, K.-U. (2021). Instant graph query recovery on persistent memory. In *Proceedings of the 17th International Workshop on Data Management on New Hardware* (pp. 1–4).
9. Baumstark, A., Jibril, M. A., & Sattler, K.-U. (2023). Adaptive query compilation in graph databases. In *Distributed and Parallel Databases* (pp. 1–28).
10. Baumstark, A., Jibril, M. A., & Sattler, K.-U. (2023). Temporal graph processing in modern memory hierarchies. In *European Conference on Advances in Databases and Information Systems* (pp. 103–116). Springer.

11. Bornea, M. A., Dolby, J., Kementsietsidis, A., Srinivas, K., Dantressangle, P., Udrea, O., & Bhattacharjee, B. (2013). Building an efficient RDF store over a relational database. In *Proceedings of the ACM SIGMOD International Conference on Management of Data, SIGMOD 2013, New York, NY, USA, June 22-27, 2013* (pp. 121–132).
12. Bu, Y., Borkar, V., Jia, J., Carey, M. J., & Condie, T. (2014). Pregelix: Big (ger) graph analytics on a dataflow engine. *Proceedings of the VLDB Endowment, 8*(2), 161–172.
13. Byun, J., Woo, S., & Kim, D. (2020). Chronograph: Enabling temporal graph traversals for efficient information diffusion analysis over time. In *IEEE 36th International Conference on Data Engineering (ICDE)* (pp. 2026–2027). IEEE COMPUTER SOC.
14. Chen, S. & Jin, Q. (2015). Persistent b+-trees in non-volatile main memory. *PVLDB, 8*(7), 786–797.
15. Debrouvier, A., Parodi, E., Perazzo, M., Soliani, V., & Vaisman, A. (2021). A model and query language for temporal graph databases. *The VLDB Journal, 30*(5), 825–858.
16. Deutsch, A., Francis, N., Green, A., Hare, K., Li, B., Libkin, L., Lindaaker, T., Marsault, V., Martens, W., Michels, J., et al. (2022). Graph pattern matching in gql and sql/pgq. In *Proceedings of the 2022 International Conference on Management of Data* (pp. 2246–2258).
17. Driscoll, J. R., Sarnak, N., Sleator, D. D., & Tarjan, R. E. (1986). Making data structures persistent. In *ACM STOC* (pp. 109–121). ACM.
18. Fan, J., Raj, A. G. S., & Patel, J. M. (2015). The case against specialized graph analytics engines. In *CIDR 2015, Seventh Biennial Conference on Innovative Data Systems Research, Asilomar, CA, USA, January 4–7, 2015, Online Proceedings*. www.cidrdb.org.
19. Feng, X., Jin, G., Chen, Z., Liu, C., & Salihoğlu, S. (2023). Kùzu graph database management system. In *The Conference on Innovative Data Systems Research*.
20. FIO. (2024). Flexible I/O tester documentation. https://fio.readthedocs.io/en/latest/fio_doc.html. Accessed: 26.03.24.
21. Francis, N., Gheerbrant, A., Guagliardo, P., Libkin, L., Marsault, V., Martens, W., Murlak, F., Peterfreund, L., Rogova, A., & Vrgoc, D. (2023). A researcher's digest of GQL. In *The 26th International Conference on Database Theory, 2023* (pp. 1–1). Schloss Dagstuhl-Leibniz-Zentrum für Informatik.
22. Francis, N., Green, A., Guagliardo, P., Libkin, L., Lindaaker, T., Marsault, V., Plantikow, S., Rydberg, M., Selmer, P., & Taylor, A. (2018). Cypher: An evolving query language for property graphs. In *Proceedings of the 2018 International Conference on Management of Data* (pp. 1433–1445).
23. Gonzalez, J. E., Xin, R. S., Dave, A., Crankshaw, D., Franklin, M. J., & Stoica, I. (2014). Graphx: Graph processing in a distributed dataflow framework. In *Proceedings of the 11th USENIX Conference on Operating Systems Design and Implementation*, OSDI'14, pp. 599–613. USENIX Association.
24. Götze, P., Tharanatha, A. K., & Sattler, K.-U. (2020). Data structure primitives on persistent memory: an evaluation. In *16th International Workshop on Data Management on New Hardware, DaMoN 2020, Portland, Oregon, USA, June 15, 2020*, pp. 15:1–15:3.
25. Götze, P., Tharanatha, A. K., & Sattler, K.-U. (2020). Data structure primitives on persistent memory: An evaluation. Technical Report arXiv:2001.02172 [cs.DB], ArXiV.
26. Greathouse, J. L. & Daga, M. (2014). Efficient sparse matrix-vector multiplication on gpus using the CSR storage format. In T. Damkroger, & Dongarra, J. J. (Eds.) *International Conference for High Performance Computing, Networking, Storage and Analysis, SC 2014, New Orleans, LA, USA, November 16–21, 2014* (pp. 769–780). IEEE Computer Society.
27. Hölsch, J., & Grossniklaus, M. (2016). An algebra and equivalences to transform graph patterns in neo4j. In *Proceedings of the Workshops of the EDBT/ICDT 2016 Joint Conference, EDBT/ICDT Workshops 2016, Bordeaux, France, March 15, 2016*.
28. Huan, C., Song, S. L., Pandey, S., Liu, H., Liu, Y., Lepers, B., He, C., Chen, K., Jiang, J., & Wu, Y. (2023). Tea: A general-purpose temporal graph random walk engine. In *Proceedings of the Eighteenth European Conference on Computer Systems*, EuroSys '23 (pp. 182–198). Association for Computing Machinery.

29. Huang, H., Song, J., Lin, X., Ma, S., & Huai, J. (2016). Tgraph: A temporal graph data management system. In *Proceedings of the 25th ACM International on Conference on Information and Knowledge Management*, CIKM '16 (pp. 2469–2472). Association for Computing Machinery.
30. Idreos, S., Zoumpatianos, K., Athanassoulis, M., Dayan, N., Hentschel, B., Kester, M. S., Guo, D., Maas, L. M., Qin, W., Wasay, A., et al. (2018). The periodic table of data structures. *IEEE Data Engineering Bulletin, 43*(3), 64–75.
31. Intel Corporation (2024). Intel memory latency checker (Intel MLC). Accessed: 26.03.24.
32. Intel Corporation (2019). Persistent Memory Development Kit. http://pmem.io/pmdk. Online, accessed April 2020.
33. Jibril, M. A., Al-Sayeh, H., Baumstark, A., & Sattler, K.-U. (2023). Adaptive update handling for graph HTAP. *Distributed Parallel Databases, 41*(3), 331–357.
34. Jibril, M. A., Baumstark, A., Götze, P., & Sattler, K.-U. (2021). JIT happens: Transactional graph processing in persistent memory meets just-in-time compilation. In *Proceedings of the 24th International Conference on Extending Database Technology, EDBT 2021, Nicosia, Cyprus, March 23–26, 2021* (pp. 37–48).
35. Jibril, M. A., Baumstark, A., & Sattler, K.-U. (2023). Adaptive update handling for graph HTAP. In *Distributed and Parallel Databases* (pp. 1–27).
36. Jibril, M. A., Baumstark, A., & Sattler, K.-U. (2023). GTPC: towards a hybrid OLTP-OLAP graph benchmark. In B. König-Ries, S. Scherzinger, W. Lehner, & G. Vossen (Eds.), *Datenbanksysteme für Business, Technologie und Web (BTW 2023), 20. Fachtagung des GI-Fachbereichs, Datenbanken und Informationssysteme" (DBIS), 06.-10, März 2023, Dresden, Germany, Proceedings. LNI* (Vol. P-331, pp. 105–117). Gesellschaft für Informatik e.V.
37. Jibril, M. A., Götze, P., Broneske, D., & Sattler, K.-U. (2020). Selective Caching: A persistent memory approach for multi-dimensional index structures. In *36th IEEE International Conference on Data Engineering Workshops, ICDE Workshops 2020, Dallas, TX, USA, April 20–24, 2020* (pp. 115–120).
38. Jibril, M. A., Götze, P., Broneske, D., & Sattler, K.-U. (2022). Selective caching: a persistent memory approach for multi-dimensional index structures. *Distributed Parallel Databases, 40*(1), 47–66.
39. Junghanns, M., Kießling, M., Teichmann, N., Gómez, K., Petermann, A., & Rahm, E. (2018). Declarative and distributed graph analytics with GRADOOP. *Proceedings of the VLDB Endowment, 11*(12), 2006–2009.
40. Kannan, S., Bhat, N., Gavrilovska, A., Arpaci-Dusseau A., & Arpaci-Dusseau, R. (2018). Redesigning LSMs for nonvolatile memory with novelsm. In *2018 USENIX Annual Technical Conference, USENIX ATC 2018, Boston, MA, USA, July 11–13, 2018* (pp. 993–1005).
41. Kersten, T., Leis, V., Kemper, A., Neumann, T., Pavlo, A., & Boncz, P. A. (2018). Everything you always wanted to know about compiled and vectorized queries but were afraid to ask. *Proceedings of the VLDB Endowment, 11*(13), 2209–2222.
42. Kulkarni, K. & Michels, J.-E. (2012). Temporal features in SQL:2011. *SIGMOD Record, 41*(3), 34–43.
43. Larson, P.-Å., Blanas, S., Diaconu, C., Freedman, C., Patel, J. M., & Zwilling, M. (2011). High-performance concurrency control mechanisms for main-memory databases. *PVLDB, 5*(4), 298–309.
44. Leis, V., Boncz, P. A., Kemper, A., & Neumann, T. (2014). Morsel-driven parallelism: a numa-aware query evaluation framework for the many-core age. In *International Conference on Management of Data, SIGMOD 2014, Snowbird, UT, USA, June 22–27, 2014* (pp. 743–754).
45. Lersch, L., Hao, X., Oukid, I., Wang, T., & Willhalm, T. (2019). Evaluating persistent memory range indexes. *PVLDB, 13*(4), 574–587.
46. Lersch, L., Schreter, I., Oukid, I., & Lehner, W. (2020). Enabling low tail latency on multicore key-value stores. *Proceedings of the VLDB Endowment, 13*(7), 1091–1104.
47. Liu, J., Chen, S., & Wang, L. (2020). LB+-Trees: Optimizing persistent index performance on 3DXPoint memory. *PVLDB, 13*(7), 1078–1090.

48. Malewicz, G., Austern, M. H., Bik, A. J. C., Dehnert, J. C., Horn, I., Leiser, N., & Czajkowski, G. (2010). Pregel: a system for large-scale graph processing. In *Proceedings of the 2010 ACM SIGMOD International Conference on Management of Data*.
49. Massri, M., Miklos, Z., Raipin, P., & Meye, P. (2022). Clock-g: A temporal graph management system with space-efficient storage technique. In *2022 IEEE 38th International Conference on Data Engineering (ICDE)* (pp. 2263–2276).
50. Memgraph—the graph database. https://memgraph.com. Accessed: 14.03.2024.
51. Miao, Y., Han, W., Li, K., Wu, M., Yang, F., Zhou, L., Prabhakaran, V., Chen, E., & Chen, W. (2015). Immortalgraph: A system for storage and analysis of temporal graphs. *ACM Transactions on Storage, 11*(3), 14:1–14:34.
52. Neo4j. Neo4j, the graph data platform. https://neo4j.com. Accessed: 14.03.2024.
53. Nguyen, D., Lenharth, A., & Pingali, K. (2013). A lightweight infrastructure for graph analytics. In *ACM SIGOPS 24th Symposium on Operating Systems Principles, SOSP '13, Farmington, PA, USA, November 3–6, 2013* (pp. 456–471).
54. Oukid, I., Booss, D., Lehner, W., Bumbulis, P., & Willhalm, T. (2014). SOFORT: a hybrid SCM-DRAM storage engine for fast data recovery. In *Tenth International Workshop on Data Management on New Hardware, DaMoN 2014, Snowbird, UT, USA, June 23, 2014* (pp. 8:1–8:7).
55. Oukid, I., Lasperas, J., Nica, A., Willhalm, T., & Lehner, W. (2016). Fptree: A hybrid SCM-DRAM persistent and concurrent b-tree for storage class memory. In *Proceedings of the 2016 International Conference on Management of Data, SIGMOD Conference 2016, San Francisco, CA, USA, June 26–July 01, 2016* (pp. 371–386).
56. Paradies, M., Lehner, W., & Bornhövd, C. (2015). GRAPHITE: An extensible graph traversal framework for relational database management systems. In *Proceedings of the 27th International Conference on Scientific and Statistical Database Management, SSDBM '15, La Jolla, CA, USA, June 29–July 1, 2015* (pp. 29:1–29:12).
57. Pavlo, A., Angulo, G., Arulraj, J., Lin, H., Lin, J., Ma, L., Menon, P., Mowry, T. C., Perron, M., Quah, I., Santurkar, S., Tomasic, A., Toor, S., Aken, D. V., Wang, Z., Wu, Y., Xian, R., & Zhang, T. (2017). Self-driving database management systems. In *CIDR 2017, 8th Biennial Conference on Innovative Data Systems Research, Chaminade, CA, USA, January 8–11, 2017, Online Proceedings*.
58. Pavlo, A. & Aslett, M. (2016). What's really new with newsql? *SIGMOD Record, 45*(2), 45–55.
59. Prud'hommeaux, E., & Seaborne, A. (2008). SPARQL query language for RDF. W3c recommendation, W3C.
60. Rodriguez, M. A. (2015). The gremlin graph traversal machine and language (invited talk). In *Proceedings of the 15th symposium on database programming languages* (pp. 1–10).
61. Rost, C., Gomez, K., Täschner, M., Fritzsche, P., Schons, L., Christ, L., Adameit, T., Junghanns, M., & Rahm, E. (2022). Distributed temporal graph analytics with gradoop. *The VLDB Journal, 31*(2), 375–401.
62. Rudolf, M., Paradies, M., Bornhövd, C., & Lehner, W. (2013). The graph story of the SAP HANA database. In *Datenbanksysteme für Business, Technologie und Web (BTW), 15. Fachtagung des GI-Fachbereichs "Datenbanken und Informationssysteme" (DBIS), 11.-15.3.2013 in Magdeburg, Germany. Proceedings* (pp. 403–420).
63. Satish, N., Sundaram, N., Md. Patwary, M. A., Seo, J., Park, J., Hassaan, M. A., Sengupta, S., Yin, Z., & Dubey, P. (2014). Navigating the maze of graph analytics frameworks using massive graph datasets. In *International Conference on Management of Data, SIGMOD 2014, Snowbird, UT, USA, June 22–27, 2014* (pp. 979–990).
64. Steer, B., Cuadrado, F., & Clegg, R. (2020). Raphtory: Streaming analysis of distributed temporal graphs. *Future Generation Computer Systems, 102*, 453–464.
65. TigerGraph. Tigergraph: The world's fastest and most scalable graph platform. https://www.tigergraph.com. Accessed: 14.03.2024.
66. van Renen, A., Vogel, L., Leis, V., Neumann, T., & Kemper, A. (2019). Persistent memory I/O primitives. In *Proceedings of the 15th International Workshop on Data Management on New Hardware, DaMoN 2019, Amsterdam, The Netherlands, 1 July 2019* (pp. 12:1–12:7).

67. Venkataraman, S., Tolia, N., Ranganathan, P., & Campbell, R. H. (2011). Consistent and durable data structures for non-volatile byte-addressable memory. In *9th USENIX Conference on File and Storage Technologies, San Jose, CA, USA, February 15–17, 2011* (pp. 61–75).
68. Wu, Y., Arulraj, J., Lin, J., Xian, R., & Pavlo, A. (2017). An empirical evaluation of in-memory multi-version concurrency control. *PVLDB, 10*(7), 781–792.
69. Xia, F., Jiang, D., Xiong, J., & Sun, N. (2017). Hikv: A hybrid index key-value store for DRAM-NVM memory systems. In *2017 USENIX Annual Technical Conference, USENIX ATC 2017, Santa Clara, CA, USA, July 12–14, 2017* (pp. 349–362).
70. Yang, J., Kim, J., Hoseinzadeh, M., Izraelevitz, J., & Swanson, S. (2020). An empirical guide to the behavior and use of scalable persistent memory. In *18th USENIX Conference on File and Storage Technologies, FAST 2020, Santa Clara, CA, USA, February 24–27, 2020* (pp. 169–182).
71. Zhou, X., Shou, L., Chen, K., Hu, W., & Chen, G. (2019). DPTree: Differential indexing for persistent memory. *PVLDB, 13*(4), 421–434.

Chapter 5
MxKernel: A Bare-Metal Runtime System for Database Operations on Heterogeneous Many-Core Hardware

Marcel Lütke Dreimann, Jan Mühlig, Michael Müller, Olaf Spinczyk, and Jens Teubner

Abstract Large-scale data processing forms the core of modern online services, such as social media and e-commerce, calling for an ever-increasing performance with predictable service quality. Even though emerging hardware platforms can deliver the required performance, actually harnessing it and guaranteeing a certain service quality is still a challenge for application and system software developers. We argue that the major hindrance for applications and system software alike lies in the design of today's system software architecture. The thread abstraction, for example, hides hardware characteristics, such as the memory topology or accelerators from applications and application behavior from the system software, forcing the latter to base resource management on assumptions while preventing the former from leveraging the potential of modern hardware. We present the `MxKernel` as a novel system software architecture with the requirements of modern data-intensive applications in mind. Instead of threads, the `MxKernel` provides `MxTask`s as control flows, short, closed units of work that can easily be annotated with application-specific hints giving a glimpse into an application's future behavior. These hints are used by the `MxKernel` to provide automatic synchronization and prefetching, as well as efficient dynamic resource partitioning to ensure performance isolation and the observance of quality of service requirements.

M. L. Dreimann · M. Müller · O. Spinczyk (✉)
Osnabrück University, Osnabrück, Germany
e-mail: marcel.luetkedreimann@uni-osnabrueck.de; michael.mueller@uni-osnabrueck.de; olaf.spinczyk@uni-osnabrueck.de

J. Mühlig · J. Teubner
TU Dortmund University, Dortmund, Germany
e-mail: jan.muehlig@tu-dortmund.de; jens.teubner@tu-dortmund.de

K.-U. Sattler et al. (eds.), *Scalable Data Management for Future Hardware*,
https://doi.org/10.1007/978-3-031-74097-8_5

5.1 Introduction

New application classes and software deployment models are putting immense pressure on system software to process data *faster* and at *larger scale* while providing predictable *quality of service* at the same time. For example, "Real-time analytics" on a cloud server demands for high transaction rates even with complex analysis queries running concurrently. Service-level agreements between the cloud service provider and the customer must always be met, as penalties are to be avoided.

Emerging hardware platforms *can* provide the necessary performance. Yet, leveraging it is difficult. It is still unclear how large degrees of *parallelism*, complex *memory hierarchies*, or increasing hardware *heterogeneity* can be adequately supported by systems and application software. While "predictable quality of service" calls for strict resource partitioning, the ability for dynamic resource management is mandatory, because data center servers can host a diverse set of workloads, each potentially exhibiting bursty behavior. Recent research has shown that fast resource migration is crucial for avoiding idle resources and for keeping tail latencies small [16, 20, 43, 48].

All this is a matter of the *whole* system software stack and of how we develop application software for modern hardware. In an ideal world, all affected layers, namely, hypervisor, Operating system (OS), Database management system (DBMS), and application software, would collaborate to handle these cross-layer issues. However, in the real world, their interfaces are narrow and dominated by legacy standards, such as POSIX [2, 3]. Traditionally, each layer aims for full control over all available resources with sub-optimal outcome.

In front of this background, the authors designed a novel and more efficient system software architecture, the `MxKernel`, and evaluated an experimental prototype. This chapter describes the most important concepts and results.

With the `MxKernel` architecture as a blueprint, a system software stack can achieve the following goals:

Tidiness: Each architectural layer has a well-defined redundancy-free purpose.

Efficiency: Applications, DBMS, and OS can *all* fully exploit the parallelism and heterogeneity of modern computer hardware.

Transparency: If needed, physical hardware characteristics are communicated up through all layers even into the application.[1]

Isolation: Concurrent parallel applications are guaranteed a fair share of resources as well as a secure execution environment.

Elasticity: Resources are assigned and revoked at an unprecedented rate to optimize resource usage.

Figure 5.1 provides a high-level overview of the `MxKernel` architecture. Applications and global (system) services "live" inside dynamic resource containers that are

[1] For instance, the OS will never hide crucial information or access paths from the DBMS.

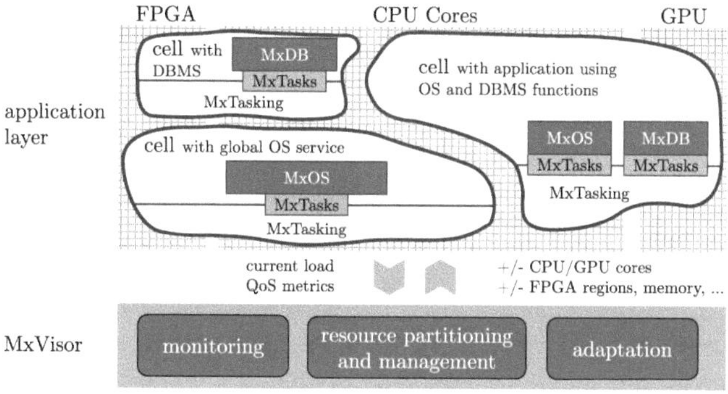

Fig. 5.1 `MxKernel` architecture overview

called *cells*. A cell has full control over its assigned resources, such as CPU cores, GPUs, FPGA regions, or memory. Time-sharing is avoided as long as possible. Cells can make use of `MxTasking`, which is an adaptive user-level tasking framework for heterogeneous many-core systems. `MxTasking` is highly reusable and specialized on handling parallel execution and synchronization of a cell's control flows that are abstracted as so-called `MxTasks`. The resource partitioning and management is performed by the `MxVisor`. It is a thin, privileged software layer that assigns resources to cells on demand and withdraws them when necessary. If a machine is dedicated for a single cell, `MxVisor` would not be used to avoid any resource partitioning overhead. In this case, `MxTasking` would run directly on the bare hardware. OS and DBMS services beyond the functionality provided by `MxVisor` and `MxTasking` are provided as library functions that can either be used within an application cell or as a dedicated system service cell. In any case, OS and DBMS are run as equal peers.

A key enabler for the efficiency of the `MxKernel` architecture is the use of `MxTasks` instead of a classical "thread" model. Section 5.2 therefore explains the advantages of task-based parallelism in modern heterogeneous many-core systems in general and the `MxTask` abstraction of `MxTasking` in particular. Implications of this design for the performance of data processing are addressed in Sect. 5.3. The overall resource management within the `MxVisor` is explained in Sect. 5.4, which also provides an evaluation of the achieved elasticity. Finally, Sect. 5.5 will summarize our insights gained from this experiment.

5.2 Task-Based Parallelism

Today, it is primarily up to the application code to fully exploit modern hardware features such as parallelism and sophisticated memory architectures. However, as hardware becomes more intricate, applications often lack awareness of precise hardware characteristics. A similar situation of partial knowledge, which prohibits efficient use of modern hardware, can also be observed on the level of the execution engine, such as the OS. It is aware of all hardware details but possesses only limited comprehension of the application's intention.

5.2.1 *Background*

We argue that this problem is caused by the limitations of the dominant control flow abstraction: *Threads* serve as the OS-application interface. They abstract computing resources and enable parallel code execution without hardware knowledge. However, threads cannot properly communicate application knowledge to the OS. This leaves a large untapped potential for improving performance. As an example, consider memory accesses: Applications distribute data across several Non-uniform Memory Access (NUMA) regions in modern memory hierarchies. These regions have different access latencies based on the thread's execution location [6]. Without information about future memory accesses, the OS must *guess* the appropriate CPU core to schedule a thread data-local. OSs approach this differently, for example, migrating memory pages between NUMA regions to reduce remote requests by considering a threads' access patterns [14, 35, 47]. However, as the future is unknown, the OS needs to rely on historical data for its scheduling and placement decisions.

5.2.2 *MxTask Abstraction*

In order to address this issue, we present `MxTasking`, a framework designed to facilitate the creation of latch-free and parallel data structures. One of the core principles of `MxTasking` is to replace conventional threads as a control flow abstraction with so-called `MxTasks`. `MxTasks` represent small, self-contained units of work instead of a sequence of straight-line code often represented by threads. An `MxTask` is intentionally designed to access only a limited number of data objects during its execution, making it more fine-grained than threads. The utilization of a thread can be compared to *spawning* multiple tasks, thereby accomplishing a more extensive work package through collaborative efforts. From an application's perspective, `MxTasking` aligns with an event-based design. For computational work, the application spawns one or multiple `MxTasks` received by the `MxTasking` runtime and processed in an asynchronous manner. Once a task has been selected for execution, it is completed in an atomic and non-preemptive manner, allowing tasks to share the stack and minimizing the overhead associated with context switches.

We will use the traversal of a treelike data structure to demonstrate the notion of tasking. Traditionally, tree traversals are implemented by sequentially visiting nodes, following the child pointers from the root to a leaf node. As one node visit leads to the next, this pattern creates a lack of transparency for the thread and the

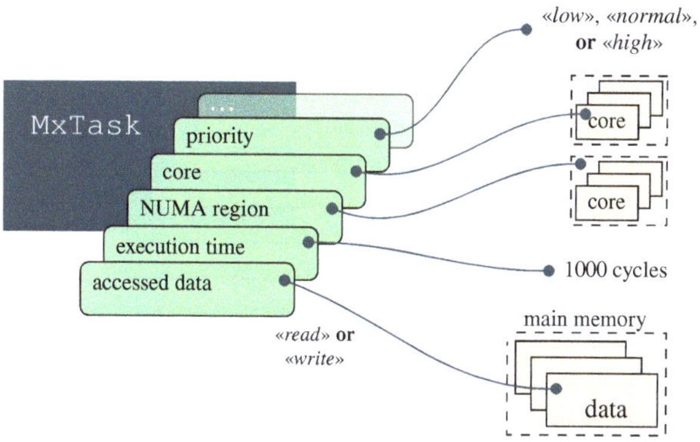

Fig. 5.2 `MxTasks` can be *annotated* with application knowledge to share characteristics and requests with the underlying `MxTasking` framework, such as a task's priority, a specific CPU core or NUMA region, or accessed data objects

underlying system in terms of future memory accesses: The thread knows the next accessed node only within a short timeframe; predicting which nodes the thread will visit is practically impossible. By using `MxTasks`, we break down the traversal process into a sequence of individual steps. One task visits one node and generates a new task to visit the next. As a result, the developer gets an understanding of the specific node an individual processing unit will access during its execution when initiating that task.

In order to make this knowledge also accessible to the system, developers can share their expertise by utilizing *annotations*, which function as an interface between the application and the underlying `MxTasking` framework. The primary objective of annotations is to propagate application-specific knowledge about runtime characteristics to the execution layer and effectively convey a task's demands and requirements. We depict a range of annotations in Fig. 5.2: For instance, the application may request the execution of a task at a designated CPU core or within a specific NUMA domain. The inherent potential of annotations, however, lies in the ability to annotate the *data objects* a given task will interact with. When initiating a task to visit a tree node during traversal, for example, the developer has the opportunity to impart their expertise to the execution layer, thereby enabling the runtime to understand the interaction between code and data.

Annotations will be employed by `MxTasking` in various ways. For instance, the link between tasks and their accessed data objects empowers the runtime to bring data into the cache before the application accesses it, aiming to hide memory latencies behind the execution of preceding tasks. Furthermore, `MxTasking` utilizes the available knowledge to coordinate tasks that concurrently interact with the same data object. Instead of dealing with different synchronization mechanisms, such as latches or optimistic techniques, the developer can delegate this responsibility to the execution layer by requesting synchronization for specific data objects. To achieve this, the developer only needs to annotate tasks with the accessed data object and specify whether the task will read from or write to the data. Finally, the developer can annotate performance hints to task families, which help MxTasking schedule tasks efficiently on heterogeneous computing platforms.

In the following paragraphs, we will dive deeper into annotation-driven prefetching, task synchronization, and annotations for heterogeneous computing.

5.2.3 Annotation-Driven Prefetching

By attaching relevant information about accessed data objects to MxTasks, the developer empowers MxTasking to address a prominent challenge modern data processing systems face: *memory latencies*. Particularly when the data is not cached, the CPU must stall while the memory subsystem transfers data from memory into registers, causing significant delays in data processing. While the hardware already tries to identify access patterns and bring data into the cache ahead of time [13, 45], this is particularly hard for—from the hardware's point of view—random accesses.

The application often possesses a deeper awareness of the data that will be required in the near future. *Software-based prefetching* enables a program to provide hints to the hardware regarding forthcoming data access by executing prefetch instructions. This feature allows the hardware to load data into the cache asynchronously, thereby circumventing the limitations imposed by a stream-based look-ahead mechanism. Treelike data structures represent an excellent example for studying random access patterns that pose challenges to data-stream-based predictions: When traversing a tree structure and transitioning between nodes, the hardware cannot anticipate forthcoming node accesses. But even in the context of software-based prefetching, the *temporal gap* between identifying the subsequent node and accessing it proves inadequate for effectively leveraging a hardware hint. To tackle this problem and ensure a temporal gap between the identification of a node and its access, several approaches reorganize the application code, for example, by grouping access stages [9] or using coroutines [39]. Although these studies have shown promising results, they possess a variety of drawbacks: They necessitate significant reconstruction of data structures and algorithms while offering only little ability to regulate the timing of prefetches. Plus, the optimization is confined to the application level and does not apply across application boundaries.

In contrast, the inherent design of the tasking concept separates the identification of an accessed data object (within one task) from its concrete access (carried out by the follow-up task). This renders prefetching remarkably straightforward for both the developer and the execution engine. Once the developer annotates and spawns MxTasks, the runtime "sees" tasks and their corresponding data objects within the task pools. Based on that information, MxTasking will inject prefetch instructions between the execution of tasks to bring soon-accessed data objects into the cache. Consequently, applications developed using MxTasks do not require any further modifications in order to enable prefetching while offering a higher level of efficacy compared to manually tuned code: In contrast to that, MxTasking has the capability to automatically arrange the execution of prefetch instructions, even when multiple applications operate on the same tasking instance.

5.2.3.1 Managing Prefetch Requests

To effectively implement data prefetching, `MxTasking` must have access to forthcoming tasks and their corresponding annotations. The temporal constraints imposed by the memory subsystem may render it inadequate to prefetch a task's data object right before its execution, thereby requiring the examination of multiple tasks—specifically their accessed data—in succession. For every task-executing *worker*,[2] however, `MxTasking` includes a set of queues that manage tasks like a linked list, connecting tasks through pointers. As a result, to examine the pending tasks for their annotated data objects, the worker is required to sequentially traverse the linked items—leading to costly pointer chasing and implicit cache misses for the task descriptors. To reduce the occurrence of implicit cache misses and optimize the retrieval of a specific impending task, such as the third-closest task, `MxTasking` employs two distinct buffers: one for a limited set of upcoming tasks (extracted from the queues) and one for associated prefetch requests, which are generated based on task annotations. Figure 5.3 outlines this approach.

Whenever the worker is prepared to execute the subsequent task from the *task buffer* ($task_0$ in Fig. 5.3), it initially communicates with the prefetch buffer to start prefetching both a subsequent task descriptor ($task_1$ in the given example) and an annotated data object. Software prefetches are conducted asynchronously by the memory subsystem, allowing the worker to execute the pending task while the system brings data close to the CPU. As a result, the latencies associated with the memory transfer are hidden by the concurrent execution of another task.

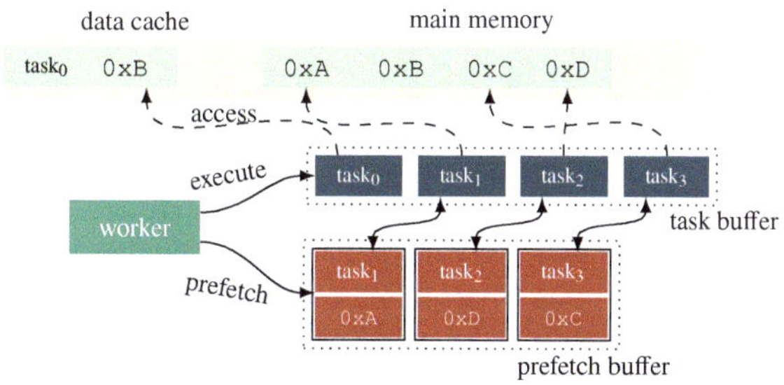

Fig. 5.3 In order to obtain an understanding of the subsequent tasks to be executed and the data objects to be prefetched, `MxTasking` utilizes two separate buffers

[2] `MxTasking` spawns one worker thread per logical CPU core that continuously receives and executes tasks.

5.2.3.2 Prefetch Distance

In the illustrated instance depicted in Fig. 5.3, we assumed that `MxTasking` prefetches the data for the task after the next one, which implies a *prefetch distance* of 1. However, the prefetch distance is of significant importance in ensuring a sufficient temporal interval for the memory subsystem to transfer data into caches. The amount of time needed is contingent upon multiple factors, including hardware-specific parameters like access latencies, as well as software characteristics such as task execution time, while the memory subsystem arranges the transfer of data into the caches. In addition, online characteristics, such as the current memory utilization, can have an influence on the optimal prefetch distance. `MxTasking` offers two strategies to approach this dilemma.

Static Prefetch Distance To assist developers in tuning their applications for a specific prefetch distance, `MxTasking` provides a central parameter for configuration. However, a single parameter can be inadequate, especially when tasks of one application exhibit heterogeneous execution times or multiple applications simultaneously operate on top of one `MxTasking` instance.

Dynamic Prefetch Distance Consequently, the logical improvement is the automatic adjustment of the prefetch distance throughout the execution of a workload. In applications where task durations vary, it is essential to allocate an adequate amount of time between prefetching and execution for every task and its associated data object. This necessitates positioning the prefetch instruction at an optimal point relative to the data access [24]. Nevertheless, the critical factor is not the exact number of instructions but the duration of their execution, which can be attached to every `MxTask` through annotations or monitored automatically by the runtime. With an anticipated execution duration for a task, `MxTasking` aims to allocate an appropriate slot in the prefetch buffer at dispatch time.

5.2.4 Annotation-Driven Synchronization

In addition to facilitating performance optimizations, the comprehension of the interaction between code and data through annotations enables `MxTasking` to ease the implementation of parallel code. We will now focus on how the execution substrate uses annotations to synchronize tasks concurrently accessing the same data object, which can become a bottleneck in parallel-designed applications. Optimizing the software for scalability poses a challenge for developers as they must carefully consider the application's requirements and the underlying hardware's inherent characteristics. Assuming that the developer includes annotations for tasks that access data objects and indicates whether the tasks will read or write, the `MxTasking` framework can effectively manage synchronization. From the developer's point of view, weaving synchronization into application code is no longer seen as necessary—except for annotating appropriately. `MxTasking`, on the other hand, will wrap synchronization around the execution of individual tasks.

5.2.4.1 Integrated Synchronization Primitives

`MxTasking` offers four fundamental synchronization primitives, outlined as follows. The task itself lacks awareness of the primitive `MxTasking` will select, indicating that the synchronization is separate from the tasks' implementation. However, the developer can request a specific primitive through annotations. Based on system state and annotations, `MxTasking` will dynamically choose among its primitives—when not compelled.

Latches Latches,[3] like spinlocks, are a simple way to synchronize concurrent control flows. In `MxTasking`, spinlocks can be employed to synchronize concurrent tasks, just like their usage in thread-based solutions. A rudimentary spinlock mechanism can serialize all accesses, read-only or not, to achieve mutual exclusion. When an application requests parallel reading on a shared object, the engine uses a reader/writer-lock instead.

Optimistic Synchronization Recent research suggests that latch-based techniques struggle with read-heavy workloads [7, 8, 27, 29]. While reader/writer-locks have overhead from cache-coherency protocols, *optimistic mechanisms* avoid writing latch variables by executing read-only operations speculatively. The idea is to check a *version counter* before and after execution to test if the optimistic execution was successful—and try again if the versions do not match. Writing operations continue utilizing other synchronization mechanisms and increment the version counter after the execution to ensure consistent version updates. The `MxTasking` worker manages optimistic versioning for the synchronized task. If the worker finds a version discrepancy, the task is reset and re-executed until it's correct.

Like in other optimistic approaches, physical removals of shared objects need to be handled cautiously. The parallelism enables to execute reads and physical free operations on the same data object concurrently. As a result, one task may mistakenly operate on corrupted data, resulting in errors. To avoid reads to corrupted data, `MxTasking` utilizes Epoch-based memory reclamation (EBMR) [15], similar to Silo [46] and the decentral procedure realized by the open BwTree [52].

Hardware-Assisted Synchronization Besides software-based implementations, synchronization can also be achieved through hardware mechanisms. At first glance, hardware-assisted synchronization, such as Hardware Transactional Memory (HTM), offers a combination of efficiency and user-friendliness [28, 31]. The developer only marks critical sections, e.g., by using compiler built-ins, and explicitly delegates the synchronization to the hardware. However, not all CPUs

[3] In database contexts, in-memory locks are typically called "latches" in order to distinguish them from locking mechanisms on user-level objects (e.g., two-phase locking).

are equipped with built-in synchronization capabilities. And despite its apparent simplicity, the developer must provide a fallback plan that is used when the hardware encounters repeated synchronization failures, leading to intricate application code.

`MxTasking` includes HTM as a potential synchronization mechanism for concurrent tasks. Whenever the application or the framework chooses HTM as a primitive, `MxTasking` injects CPU instructions to wrap hardware transactions around a task's execution. If the transaction fails multiple times, the runtime uses a conventional spinlock as a fallback plan. Consequently, the responsibility of handling the complexities of implementation is shifted to the runtime environment, relieving application developers of this burden. Additionally, `MxTasking` will use a backup synchronization primitive if the underlying hardware does not support HTM.

Synchronization through Dispatching Besides typical synchronization primitives, `MxTasking`'s run-to-completion semantics allows dispatching-driven synchronization. The idea is to assign tasks accessing the same data object to the same worker thread. As all tasks assigned to the same worker run uninterruptedly, their execution follows a sequential order. This way, active waiting for resources and potential contention can be avoided. Furthermore, dispatching-driven synchronization can provide benefits, particularly in NUMA environments, in addition to addressing concerns linked to concurrency. Instead of moving data between NUMA regions, dispatching-based synchronization moves code to data. Previous studies, such as the DORA system [38] and H-Store [22], have shown that employing similar techniques can improve cache locality and transaction throughput.

5.2.4.2 Applying Synchronization

The runtime uses one of the given primitives, automatically or based on annotated requests, to synchronize newly created data objects that seek isolated access. Synchronization affects two framework components. Upon spawning, the *dispatcher* assigns a worker (or logical CPU core) to a task. This allocation is sufficient for dispatching-driven synchronization, since tasks on the same core run atomically and sequentially.

The *worker* is responsible for applying further described mechanisms. If dispatching is not enough, the worker wraps synchronization around task execution depending on the primitive and annotation. Simple latches are acquired before executing the task and released afterward. For optimistic versioning, the worker differentiates between reading and writing tasks. The worker checks the version before and after a read-only action to verify integrity. When versions mismatch, the task is reset and restarted until it succeeds. HTM synchronization requires the worker to start a new transaction before completing the task and commit it afterward. If the transaction fails, it is iteratively replayed until the worker chooses to switch to an alternative synchronization mode.

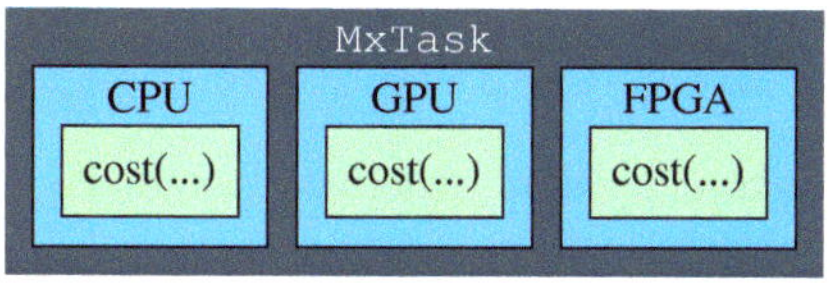

Fig. 5.4 `MxTask` families can implement their operation for CPU, GPU, or FPGAs. The developer annotates a cost function for every implementation

5.2.5 Annotation-Driven Heterogeneity

Modern and heterogeneous hardware enables high performance in today's systems. However, the increased complexity of the architecture also leads to new challenges for scheduling strategies [33]. For example, on the one hand, some accelerators such as integrated GPUs share their memory with CPUs, but on the other hand, dedicated GPUs or FPGAs require a costly data transfer. Moreover, every accelerator has a different execution time for a task. Additionally, a setup phase, and therefore at least one CPU core, is required before a task can be executed. `MxTasking` has to take all these constraints and costs into account and deal with placement of tasks and data objects. To utilize heterogeneous hardware `MxTasking` introduces the concept of task families (see Fig. 5.4). Each member of a family describes the same operation, but implemented for a different accelerator. `MxTasking` is responsible for choosing the best accelerator at runtime. For this kind of decision, a performance prediction model is required. Popular scheduling strategies, such as HEFT, require a task's expected execution time for each accelerator[1]. However, in most cases, the execution time of a task depends on the operation and its parameters. Annotations by the developer can help `MxTasking` with these scheduling decisions for heterogeneous hardware. Instead of a constant value, the developer can define a function for each member of a task family that describes a performance factor. This factor may depend on different parameters such as the size of data objects and is evaluated at runtime. `MxTasking` can use the attached information to select the best performing accelerator at runtime and additionally implement load balancing [37].

5.3 Leveraging Tasks at the DBMS Layer

Using tasks to build data structures and algorithms differs from well-known thread-based programming. Among others, DORA [38], Hyper [26], and Umbra [50] have shown the benefits of task-based approaches for transactional and analytical DBMS engines. However, `MxTasking`'s annotations allow optimizations and a streamlined implementation. This section demonstrates the simplicity of building latch-free, `MxTask`-based data structures by utilizing a B^{link}-tree [25] as an illustrative example.

5.3.1 Building a Task-Based B^{link}-Tree

B-trees [4, 17] serve as crucial index structures in DBMSs and file systems, such as BTRFS [42]. Consequently, B-trees are subject to substantial research and improvement, particularly in relation to their caching behavior (e.g., [18, 40, 44]) and concurrent synchronization (e.g., [25, 27, 30, 34, 52]), leading to numerous variations. Specifically the B^{link}-tree focuses on minimizing simultaneously acquired latches by not immediately introducing newly created nodes to the parent node. Instead, each node includes a reference to its right sibling, making it accessible for parallel traverse operations until a dedicated operation establishes the reference from the parent to the new node—eliminating the necessity for parallel held latches. As a result, each (logical) operation can be transformed into a sequence of discrete steps, with each linked to a single node. This pattern facilitates the alignment of the B^{link}-tree with the task model, wherein each step is executed as an individual task.

5.3.1.1 Operations

Each `MxTask` accesses only a single node and spawns a follow-up task for the successor node, unlike thread-based operations on treelike data structures, which use loops to access each node one after the other.

Insertion Figure 5.5 illustrates a pseudocode implementation of an insert operation for an `MxTask`-based B^{link}-tree, including two segments: one for the traversal

```
INSERT TASK
input: node the task accesses, (key, value) to insert, callback to notify

if node->high_key() ≤ key:                                   // key is out of range of this node
    next = node->right_sibling()
    task = mxtasking::new_task<InsertTask>(next, key, value)
    task->annotate(next, mxtasking::readonly)
    mxtasking::spawn(task)

else if node->type() == inner:                               // continue traversal to the leaf
    next = node->child(key)
    task = mxtasking::new_task<InsertTask>(next, key, value)
    task->annotate(next, mxtasking::readonly)
    mxtasking::spawn(task)

else if node->type() == branch:                              // child is a leaf; next task will insert
    next = node->child(key)
    task = mxtasking::new_task<InsertTask>(next, key, value)
    task->annotate(next, mxtasking::write)
    mxtasking::spawn(task)

else:                                   // found correct leaf, insert value, and notify callback
    node->insert(key, value)
    callback->insertion_finished(key, value)
```

Fig. 5.5 Pseudocode illustrating an `MxTask`-based B^{link}-tree-insert operation (lines 1–15) and one for the actual insert (lines 16–18). While traversing, the task identifies the next node until reaching a leaf node (line 16). How the next node is identified depends on several factors. In the "typical" scenario, the node is examined by employing, for example, binary search (lines 7 and 12). To identify potential concurrently made modifications, each task checks if the accessed node contains the required key-range and, if not, continues the traversal at the right sibling (lines 1–5). In either case, the task spawns a new `MxTask`, annotated accordingly (e.g., lines 8–10).

For simplification, we did not consider node splitting in this implementation. When a node needs to split, the insertion task allocates a new one and moves half the records. The reference to this new node within the parent will be placed by an individual follow-up task.

Lookup and Update Implementing the corresponding *lookup* and *update* tasks is straightforward. `MxTasks` read or update records instead of inserting them on leaf nodes (line 17). The found (or updated) value is sent to the callback function (line 18).

5.3.1.2 Annotation-Based Prefetching

The data object (or node) annotation allows `MxTasking` to bring that data into the cache before the task is executed. Although prefetching can reduce CPU stalls, it intensifies the pressure on memory and instruction bandwidth. Thus, applications must allocate prefetching resources carefully. In treelike data structures, distinguishing important and non-essential prefetches is challenging: While traversing the tree, just a portion of a node's keys is accessed. And only one value (or child pointer) is read. However, when accessing the node, it is unpredictable which keys and payload will be necessary, compelling to prefetch the entire node or speculating on subsets, potentially causing memory stalls if incorrect. Experiments showed that prefetching the first half of a node's keys presents an optimized trade-off between incurred costs and cache misses penalties.

5.3.1.3 Annotation-Based Synchronization

Next, the `MxTask`-based B^{link}-tree uses annotations to pass information about synchronization requirements. Sharing the *access pattern*, i.e., read or write, in combination with accessed data objects enables `MxTasking` to manage the synchronization of concurrent tasks. For this purpose, we annotate the insert task as *read-only* during the traversal (lines 4 and 9 in Fig. 5.5) and as *write* for the leaf level (line 14). To assist the runtime in selecting a matching primitive, we specify two characteristics for new nodes: The anticipated access frequency and the expected read/write ratio. As all queries start at the root, we annotate it as accessed frequently. The number of accesses should decrease as a node's (logical) distance from the root grows. And we assume a reverse reading-to-writing ratio: leaf nodes are written more often than inner nodes. Utilizing this knowledge, `MxTasking` prioritizes optimistic synchronization for nodes logically close to the root.

5.3.2 Experimental Evaluation

To study the potential and limits of `MxTasking` in real-world scenarios, we use the in-memory B^{link}-tree, characterizing the behavior of modern in-memory database engines. We will use both read-heavy and write-heavy workloads based on the YCSB [12]. Before running workloads *A* (read/update, 50/50) and *C* (read-only) with Zipfian distribution and 100 million operations, we insert 100 million records. Each record consists of a 64 b key and a 64 b payload.

All benchmarks are evaluated on a two-socket Intel Xeon Gold 6226 machine, clocked at 2.7 GHz. For all benchmarks showing an ascending number of cores, the logical cores are ordered by NUMA regions, whereas the first 24 logical cores are located in the first region and the next in the second. To be precise, the first 12 cores of each region are only physical cores; from then we add "hyperthreads" (marked as "SMT"). Additionally, we emphasize NUMA borders with a dashed line.

5.3.2.1 Annotation-Based Prefetching

We start with analyzing the impact of prefetching nodes annotated to tasks while traversing the B^{link}-tree. Within this particular scenario, we make a distinction between static and dynamic prefetching and compare the outcomes to an iteration where we deactivated `MxTasking`'s capability to prefetch.

Static Prefetching For static prefetching, we instruct the runtime to initiate the prefetch always p tasks before a task is executed. While the prefetch distance p is tunable, we found that $p = 2$ leads to the best results, reported in Fig. 5.6 (green line). As tree accesses are mostly latency bound, annotation-based prefetching yields a significant improvement, ranging from 24 % more throughput for inserts to 40 % for the read-only workload. Especially the traversal is leveraged by software prefetching, since the CPU—more specifically, the hardware prefetcher—cannot predict the sequence of node accesses. In workloads that include frequent updates, we see that memory prefetching has a rather minor impact ("only" 16 %), which we associate with an elevated level of latch contention.

Dynamic Prefetching However, tuning the central prefetch distance for static prefetching can be cumbersome. And static prefetching may have limitations when it comes to executing tasks with varying execution times. The insert workload, which consists of a combination of short-running traversal tasks and longer-running inserts, offers initial insights into this matter.

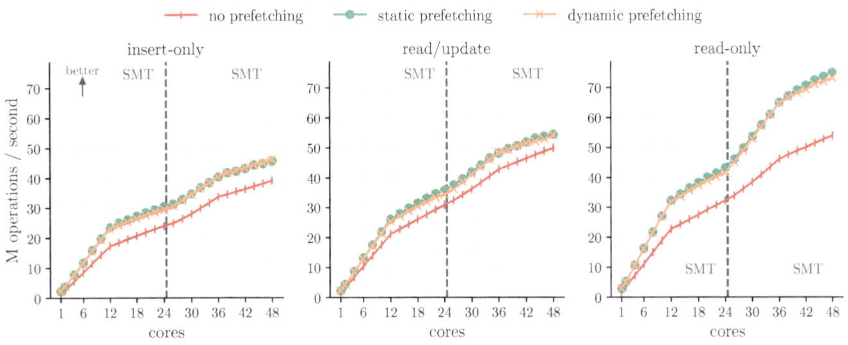

Fig. 5.6 Comparison of annotation-based prefetching for different workloads

To optimize the prefetch distance for every task, `MxTasking` allows to annotate the expected execution time of tasks. Using this knowledge, `MxTasking` calculates the prefetch distance for each task by considering the execution timings of other scheduled tasks, the volume of prefetched cache lines, and the system's memory characteristics. Although this approach increases the complexity of prefetch-scheduling by 400 additional instructions per tree operation, it is worth noting that it decreases the number of memory stalls by 5 % compared to static prefetching for the insert-only workload. The impact is also seen in relation to the throughput. Nevertheless, the higher volume of executed instructions reduces the efficiency for other evaluated workloads. Due to better performance, we will conduct additional benchmarks with a static prefetch distance of 2.

5.3.2.2 Comparison with State-of-the-Art Data Structures

We claim that the `MxTask`-abstraction allows the smooth development of scalable applications on modern and future many-core technology while maintaining great performance.

In order to investigate this theory, we undertake an evaluation of various programming models and state-of-the-art data structures. These include optimistic synchronized B^{link}-tree-implementations on top of conventional threads and Intel's Threading Building Blocks (TBB) [19, 23, 41], as well as the open BwTree [52], Masstree [34], and BtreeOLC [27] (the latter derived from the index-microbench framework [51]). To ensure comparability, we also forced `MxTasking` to use optimistic synchronization primitives for this benchmark. The findings are presented in Fig. 5.7, showing that the `MxTask`-based B^{link}-tree achieves the maximum throughput in the insert-only workload, with 8.5 % more throughput compared to its thread-based implementation and BtreeOLC. The implementation on top of TBB achieves similar results as Masstree while additionally demonstrating scalability beyond NUMA boundaries. In addition, `MxTasking` demonstrates better efficiency

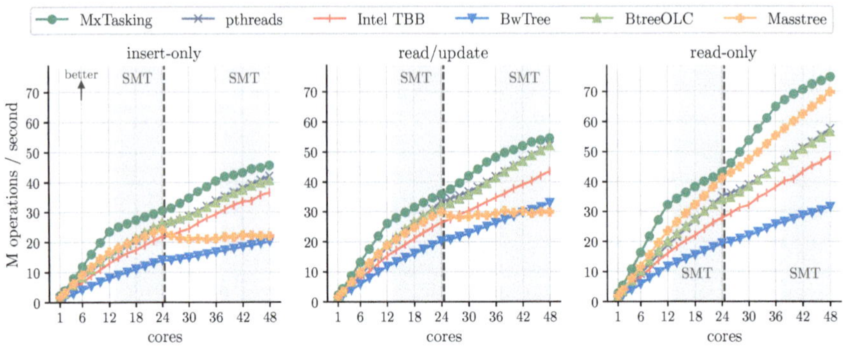

Fig. 5.7 Comparison of various B^{link}-tree implementations (on top of `MxTasking`, threads, and TBB) and state-of-the-art data structures

for mixed read/update workloads with 15 % more throughput than the thread-based variant on average.

The most prominent gaps are evident in the read-only workload. `MxTasks` achieve a lookup rate of 75 million per second, which is 7 % higher than Masstree's rate of 69.8 million. This performance is achieved by leveraging all available processor cores. Notably, both implementations make use of software-based prefetching. Both thread-based variants of the B^{link}-tree and BtreeOLC demonstrate comparable throughput, achieving around 57 million read operations per second. This confirms that our implementation of the B^{link}-tree is on par with latest advancements in the field.

5.4 Dynamic Resource Management with Tasks and Cells

`MxTasks` offer efficient parallelism for real-world applications on modern heterogeneous server hardware, such as key-value stores, while simplifying parallel application development with automatic synchronization and performance improvements through automatic prefetching. However, while `MxTasks` enhance the performance of individual applications, they are not inherently designed to manage multiple applications from different users, necessitating address space and performance isolation. These applications are critical components of interactive, data-intensive services, where minimizing tail latencies is paramount for optimizing performance. However, in data centers around the world, not just application performance matters but also the maximization of resource utilization to avoid wasting expensive resources due to underutilization. Thus, our exploration focused on designing global resource management to efficiently utilize hardware resources while leveraging `MxTasks` advantages to minimize tail latencies.

5.4.1 Background

The design of such a resource manager with the combined goal of maximizing utilization while keeping tail latencies down must solve the following two problems.

Scheduler-Induced Interference Operating systems and hypervisors employ scheduling mechanisms for fairness among processes and virtual machines. However, time-sharing techniques can introduce interference, leading to increased cache misses and execution times, and memory bandwidth contention [5, 10, 32], in turn causing exploding tail latencies [16]. This interference results from the operating system scheduling threads of concurrent applications to the same physical cores or on cores sharing the same last-level cache or memory controller. Hence, simple techniques for performance isolation enforce strict resource partitioning in the form of distinct CPU sets, group limits, and Cache Allocation to address this issue.

Static Resource Partitioning While static resource partitioning ensures performance isolation, especially for CPU cores, it lacks efficiency and flexibility, because it inherently assumes that the resource demand of an application does not change during its runtime. However, this is not the case for data-center applications because the actual resource demand directly depends on its load caused by incoming client requests. Usually, the pattern in which requests arrive changes over time. Often one can recognize stark fluctuations in incoming traffic for an online application depending on the time of the day, day of the week or month, or even the current season. For example, the traffic of a local video-streaming service is higher during the evening than during work hours, leading to the service not needing its resources during work hours but requiring it at evening hours. Thus, static partitioning often results in either performance degradation because partitions are too small to handle the load of an application or resource wastage because partitions are over-dimensioned for a rare worst-case scenario. It may even happen that overloaded partitions and underutilized partitions exist simultaneously. Dynamic resource partitioning offers a solution by allowing the reallocation of unused resources as needed, departing from traditional OS schedulers and static partitioning methods. One way to realize dynamic resource partitioning is *Adaptive Resource Centric Computing*.

Adaptive Resource Centric Computing

Adaptive Resource Centric Computing (ARCC), introduced by Colmenares et al. [11], utilizes elastic resource partitions and proactive monitoring to adjust resource allocation for applications dynamically. In an ARCC system, applications run within elastic resource containers called *cells*, whose sizes are determined at runtime based on performance metrics. A resource monitor periodically evaluates each cell's performance and adjusts resource allocation according to predefined policies. To efficiently handle resource changes, applications communicate their resource demands through an API provided by a runtime system. Several implementations of

ARCC, such as Tessellation [11], have been explored, with recent efforts focusing on enhancing efficiency and performance in data center environments [21, 49].

5.4.2 State of the Art

Figure 5.8 depicts the architecture typical to most systems implementing ARCC on top of Linux. Despite variations in inter-process communication and thread allocation mechanisms, these systems share several key features.

Global Resource and Task Controller First, they feature a centralized controlling and monitoring service in user space (①). This service dynamically adjusts resource allocation based on load and utilization analysis, adhering to configured policies and thresholds, and, thus, functions as a global resource manager.

Preempting and Reassignment in the Kernel Second, the controller leverages Linux mechanisms, such as cgroups and thread pinning, to preempt threads and enforce core allocation (③). Preempting a thread under Linux typically involves sending an inter-processor interrupt (IPI) or instrumenting code with preemption points. Furthermore, changing partition sizes involves system calls to change the respective cgroups' limits.

Informing the Cell's Runtime Third, to prevent performance issues, the controller notifies the runtime environment of each affected cell (②) to ensure proper thread management upon resource allocation changes.

Some systems combine the last two steps by running Linux as a hypervisor and each cell as a virtual machine with the runtime and application as unikernel, such as the IX operating system [5].

Architectural Deficiencies While widespread, this architecture has inherent drawbacks:

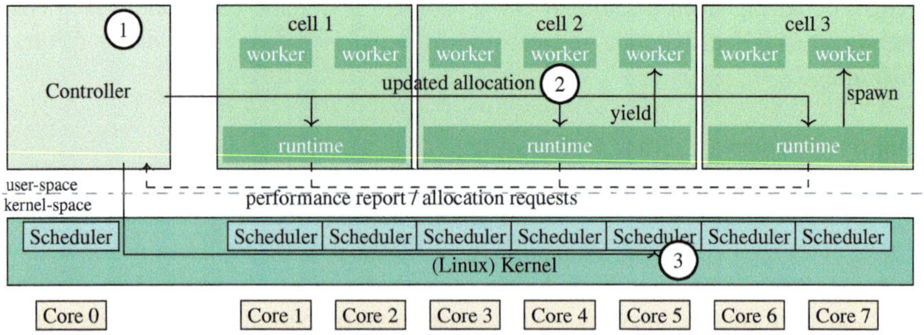

Fig. 5.8 Generic architecture of dynamic partitioners consisting of a central controller in user space

① The user-space controller can become a bottleneck due to its single-threaded maintenance loop, impacting scalability.
② Dependency on existing OS abstractions limits efficient resource allocation, requiring multiple system calls and inducing communication overhead.
③ The runtime environment must be informed of allocation changes, introducing additional overhead and complexity.

Revising this architecture can significantly reduce system overhead and, thus, tail latencies.

5.4.3 Enabling Swift Adaptation with the MxKernel

The `MxKernel` addresses state-of-the-art data center OS deficiencies through a redesigned control and data plane architecture, outlined in Fig. 5.9.

Making Cells Kernel Objects enables the kernel's direct control of worker threads, eliminating communication overhead between the controller and the runtime environment within cells. This eliminates disadvantages ② and ③.

Centralized Cell Creation and Destruction delegates responsibility to the controller. It reads cell configurations, specifying details such as binary, RAM limit, priority, and permission control. The controller calculates CPU core allocations based on priority and creates cell kernel objects via hyper-calls to `MxVisor`. Upon cell destruction, the controller redistributes freed CPU cores to optimize core utilization.

Kernel-Space Core Allocation in `MxKernel` facilitates parallel CPU core allocations without controller requests. Allocation occurs via hyper-calls to the microhypervisor (① in Fig. 5.9), allowing cells to request multiple cores simultaneously. The hypervisor's core allocator uses a pre-calculated core pool to fulfill requests,

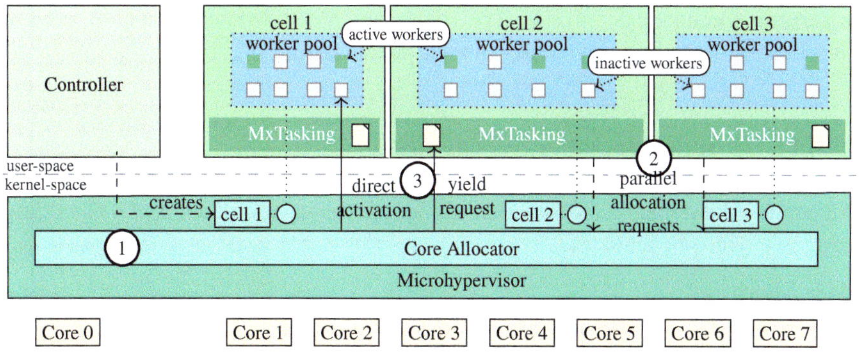

Fig. 5.9 `MxKernel` architecture featuring cells as kernel objects and kernel-space core allocator

ensuring disjoint allocations. Thus, cells can allocate cores in parallel without synchronization, reducing bottlenecks. If a cell exhausts its cores, idle cores from other cells are utilized, necessitating synchronization. The hypervisor can reclaim borrowed cores, ensuring efficient core utilization and overcoming previous bottlenecks (④ in Fig. 5.9).

Pre-created Worker Thread Pools pinned on each physical core enables rapid activation. At cell startup, `MxTasking` creates worker threads for each core, which pause on a per-worker semaphore, except for the main thread. Upon additional CPU core allocation, the hypervisor quickly activates workers by incrementing the corresponding semaphore.

Fast Preemption with Shared Pages and `MxTasks` implements an efficient preemption mechanism for worker threads. Each cell's `MxTasking` runtime creates a shared memory page with the hypervisor, containing preemption flags for each worker. Requesting core yielding involves writing to a cache line (③ in Fig. 5.9), avoiding costly inter-processor interrupts. `MxTasks` enable frequent flag polling between task executions. Upon flag detection, a hypercall blocks the thread on its semaphore, freeing the core without requiring interrupts and reducing core withdrawal costs.

5.4.4 Experimental Evaluation

We conducted experiments to assess our new design's benefits and limitations compared to Caladan, a state-of-the-art data center OS utilizing ARCC. Two micro-benchmarks examined CPU core allocation and withdrawal cost reduction. A benchmark emulated an interactive application with frequent CPU bursts to study the `MxVisor` design's impact on tail latencies.

Experiments ran on a server with two 32-core AMD Epyc 7501 CPUs at 2 GHz, 256 GB RAM, running Debian 11 with Linux kernel 5.10 for Caladan, and an extended Genode OS Framework version 23.11 on a modified NOVA micro-hypervisor for the `MxKernel` prototype. We configure Caladan's controller to perform a maintenance cycle every 10 μs, which is the value Fried et al. used to tune Caladan for minimum latency in their paper [16].

5.4.4.1 Dynamic Adaptation System Cost

We analyze the dynamic CPU resource adaptation cost of Caladan and `MxTasking` using two micro-benchmarks.

Core Allocation
In Caladan, our benchmark triggers CPU core allocation by reporting queuing delays above the threshold, prompting the controller to add a core in each maintenance loop until all cores are allocated. We create threads equal to the desired

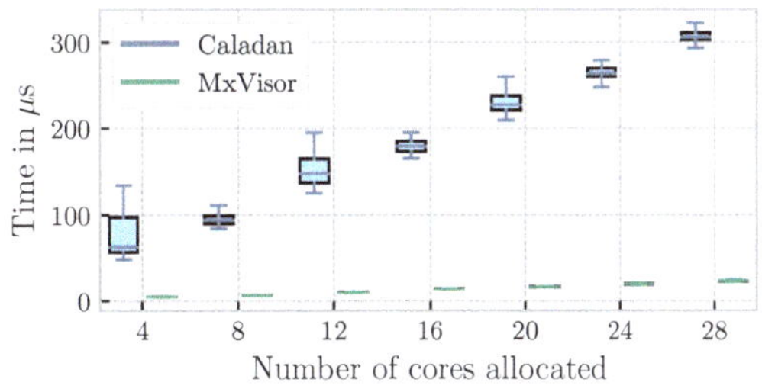

Fig. 5.10 Comparison of allocation cost for varying amount of CPU cores allocated

core count to ensure specified core allocation. Initially, only one thread runs, but Caladan repeatedly adds a core after the first 10 μs maintenance period until all threads start, with a core allocated for each. Costs increase with requested cores, with about 55 μs for 4 cores and nearly 100 μs for 8 cores, reaching over 300 μs for 28 cores. Caladan adds one core per maintenance cycle, incurring 1 μs to 2 μs overhead per core due to required IPIs.

For the `MxKernel`, our micro-benchmark periodically requests CPU cores every 20 μs, sleeping between periods. Utilizing our design, we allocate all cores simultaneously. We measured the time from allocation requests to all worker threads waking up. Figure 5.10 displays the results, showing `MxVisor` significantly outperforming Caladan with a core allocation cost reduction of 77 % to 86 %. This improvement stems from several factors: our design allows core allocation anytime, eliminates Caladan's costly maintenance period, and enables adding multiple cores per request. Additionally, leveraging x86's `monitor` and `mwait` instructions allows us to let a CPU wait while monitoring a cache line in the C1 state until it wakes up when the cache line is written to by another CPU core. Hence, we can avoid using `hlt` to let idle CPU cores sleep and requiring an IPI to wake them up again.

Core Withdrawal

We utilized the allocation micro-benchmark as a measurement cell to assess the costs of withdrawing and redistributing CPU cores, expanding the experiment by adding two additional cells to create a constant load. Each background cell executed tasks with a length of 1.3 μs, simulating `MxTasks` responsiveness in the B^{link}-tree benchmark. With 30 CPU cores, the maximum for Caladan, and 3 cells, we ensured each cell received 10 CPU cores when the measurement cell and background cells were active simultaneously and 15 CPU cores per background cell when the benchmark slept. Both systems withdrew ten CPU cores from the background cells and allocated them to the measurement cell each time it woke up. Figure 5.11a illustrates `MxVisor` significantly outperforming Caladan, with core redistribution in `MxVisor` costing only 4

In Caladan, the high cost of redistributing 10 CPU cores stems from two factors. Firstly, Caladan can only redistribute one CPU core per maintenance period, adding 10 μs for each core. Secondly, Caladan relies on inter-processor interrupts (IPIs) to trigger preemption at the target core. However, Caladan's IPI handler cannot directly perform preemption as it employs user-space threads invisible to the Linux kernel.

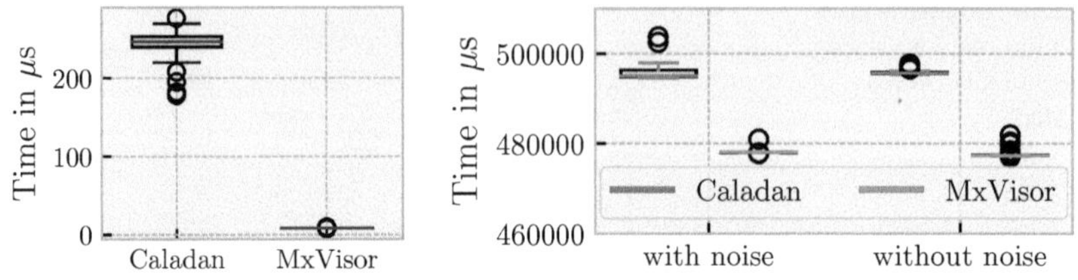

(a) Comparison of cost of redistributing 10 CPU cores among three cells

(b) Execution time oflatency benchmark for 128 CPU cores, with background cell (N) and without

Fig. 5.11 Evaluation results for core withdrawal and latency. (**a**) Comparison of cost of redistributing 10 CPU cores among three cells. (**b**) Execution time of latency benchmark for 128 CPU cores, with background cell (N) and without

Consequently, Caladan signals the target core's runtime environment to pause the worker thread, necessitating a switch between user and kernel space for each core. Activating the worker thread of the core's new owner requires additional traversals between user space and kernel, resulting in four transitions on the target core alone to redistribute one core.

In contrast, the `MxVisor` requires only two traversals: one for entering the hypervisor via the yield hyper-call and another for returning to user space to execute the new worker thread. The pausing of the yielding worker thread and activation of the new worker thread are performed entirely in kernel mode within the hypervisor. Additionally, our yielding mechanism (described in Sect. 5.4.3) eliminates the need for sending an inter-processor interrupt by polling a shared cache line to inform the worker thread to yield directly. Furthermore, the `MxVisor` can request preemption at any time, not just during maintenance periods, further reducing adaptation costs.

5.4.4.2 Impact on Tail Latencies

With its low system overhead, the design of the `MxVisor` can also reduce tail latencies. To demonstrate this, we evaluated the perceived tail latency of a simple interactive benchmark application. The benchmark simulates interactive behavior by periodically sleeping and then executing CPU bursts. These bursts consist of executing an extensive series of `NOP` instructions. We measured the time to perform 128 bursts as the perceived tail latency. We performed 100 iterations of these measurements in two configurations: one without concurrent cells running and one with one background cell continuously creating a high load on each CPU. Figure 5.11b shows the results.

We observed that the benchmark execution time on Caladan takes about 20 ms longer than on the `MxVisor`, with average times of 495 ms for Caladan and 478 ms for the `MxVisor`. Comparing the tail latencies, Caladan has a tail latency of 504 ms compared to 481 ms for the `MxVisor`, yielding a reduction in tail latency of about 5 %. Additionally, we determined that the `MxVisor`'s overhead is about 20 ms smaller on average than Caladan's, with a maximum difference of 23 ms. Hence, the MxVisor reduces system overhead by 80 % compared to Caladan, consistent with our micro-benchmark results.

5.5 Conclusion and Future Work

The aim of this work was to improve both the implementation effort and efficiency of data processing on modern hardware by using fine-grained and metadata-annotated MxTasks as execution units. Traditional models, such as threads, face significant challenges in exchanging knowledge with the hardware, obscuring characteristics across abstraction layers. In contrast, MxTasks enhance communication with the execution engine through annotations. This interaction between the application and execution layers enables optimizations based on actual knowledge, such as preloading data objects into the CPU cache based on anticipated task data access. Additionally, annotated tasks streamline the implementation of highly parallel data structures and algorithms by managing concurrent tasks at the execution logic level, thereby eliminating the burden of complex synchronization protocols at the application level. MxTasks have also been proven to simplify the implementation of database operators, such as partitioned hash joins, while simultaneously enhancing performance through more cache-friendly access patterns [36]. However, this exploration of annotations within MxTasks is just the starting point, promising a range of potential applications where annotations could further enhance performance and streamline implementations. Notable examples include using asynchronous, task-driven I/O to hide disk latency and leveraging optimized task scheduling to minimize contention among CPU cores during transaction processing.

Moreover, we assessed the impact of the design on system overhead in typical data center resource managers and proposed modifications to reduce overhead and tail latencies. Implementing these adjustments, including in our prototype MxVisor, demonstrates a tangible reduction in resource management costs and tail latencies. However, the current MxVisor design has limitations.

First, the cooperative mechanism for withdrawing CPU cores relies on the speed of the worker thread's reaction to the preemption flag, assuming uninterrupted thread execution. While MxTasks typically execute quickly, preemptive core withdrawal methods are under consideration for future improvement. Second, monitoring to prevent interferences among cells, similar to Caladan, is not employed currently, potentially leading to increased costs for the MxKernel when implemented. Integration and evaluation of proactive performance monitoring into the MxTasking runtime environment are ongoing, however.

Regardless of future improvements, this research has already shown that rethinking the system software stack for modern heterogeneous many-core systems leads to better resource utilization and cleaner interfaces for application and system software developers.

Acknowledgments This work has been funded by the Deutsche Forschungsgemeinschaft (DFG, German Research Foundation)—361498541.

References

1. Alebrahim, S. & Ahmad, I. (2017). Task scheduling for heterogeneous computing systems. *The Journal of Supercomputing, 73*(6), 2313–2338.
2. Atlidakis, V., Andrus, J., Geambasu, R., Mitropoulos, D., & Nieh, J. (2016). Posix abstractions in modern operating systems: The old, the new, and the missing. In *Proceedings of the Eleventh European Conference on Computer Systems*, EuroSys '16 (pp. 1–17), New York: Association for Computing Machinery.
3. Baumann, A., Appavoo, J., Krieger, O., & Roscoe, T. (2019). A fork() in the road. In *Proceedings of the workshop on hot topics in operating systems*, HotOS '19 (pp. 14–22). New York: Association for Computing Machinery.
4. Bayer, R. & McCreight, E. M. (1970). Organization and maintenance of large ordered indexes. In *Record of the 1970 ACM SIGFIDET workshop on data description and access* (pp. 107–141). New York: ACM.
5. Belay, A., Prekas, G., Primorac, M., Klimovic, A., Grossman, S., Kozyrakis, C., & Bugnion, E. (2016). The IX Operating System: combining low latency, high throughput, and efficiency in a protected dataplane. *ACM Transactions on Computer Systems, 34*(4), 1–39.
6. Bergstrom, L. (2011). Measuring NUMA effects with the STREAM benchmark. *CoRR*, abs/1103.3225.
7. Böttcher, J., Leis, V., Giceva, J., Neumann, T., & Kemper, A. (2020). Scalable and robust latches for database systems. In *16th International Workshop on Data Management on New Hardware, DaMoN 2020* (pp. 2:1–2:8). New York: ACM.
8. Cha, S. K., Hwang, S., Kim, K., & Kwon, K. (2001). Cache-conscious concurrency control of main-memory indexes on shared-memory multiprocessor systems. In *Proceedings of 27th International Conference on Very Large Data Bases* (pp. 181–190).
9. Chen, S., Ailamaki, A., Gibbons, P. B., & Mowry, T. C. (2004). Improving hash join performance through prefetching. In *Proceedings of the 20th International Conference on Data Engineering, ICDE* (pp. 116–127).
10. Chen, S., Delimitrou, C., & Martínez, J. F. (2019). PARTIES: QoS-Aware resource partitioning for multiple interactive services. In *Proceedings of the twenty-fourth international conference on architectural support for programming languages and operating systems*, ASPLOS '19. ACM.
11. Colmenares, J. A., Eads, G., Hofmeyr, S., Bird, S., Moretó, M., Chou, D., Gluzman, B., Roman, E., Bartolini, D. B., Mor, N., Asanović, K., & Kubiatowicz, J. D. (2013). Tessellation: Refactoring the OS around explicit resource containers with continuous adaptation. In *Proceedings of the 50th Annual Design Automation Conference* (pp. 1–10). Association for Computing Machinery.
12. Cooper, B. F., Silberstein, A., Tam, E., Ramakrishnan, R., & Sears, R. (2010). Benchmarking cloud serving systems with YCSB. In *Proceedings of the 1st ACM symposium on cloud computing, SoCC* (pp. 143–154). ACM.
13. Dahlgren, F., & Stenström, P. (1996). Evaluation of Hardware-Based Stride and Sequential Prefetching in Shared-Memory Multiprocessors. *IEEE Transactions on Parallel and Distributed Systems, 7*(4):385–398.
14. Diener, M., da Cruz, E. H. M., & Navaux, P. O. A. (2015). Locality vs. Balance: Exploring Data Mapping Policies on NUMA Systems. In *23rd Euromicro International Conference on Parallel, Distributed, and Network-Based Processing, PDP* (pp. 9–16). IEEE Computer Society.
15. Fraser, K. (2004). *Practical lock-freedom*. PhD thesis, UK: University of Cambridge.

16. Fried, J., Ruan, Z., Ousterhout, A., & Belay, A. (2020). Caladan: Mitigating interference at microsecond timescales. In *Proceedings of the 14th USENIX conference on operating systems design and implementation* (pp. 281–297).
17. Graefe, G. (2011). Modern b-tree techniques. *Foundations and Trends in Databases, 3*(4):203–402.
18. Hankins, R. A. & Patel, J. M. (2003). Effect of node size on the performance of cache-conscious B^+-trees. In *Proceedings of the international conference on measurements and modeling of computer systems, SIGMETRICS* (pp. 283–294). ACM.
19. Intel (2023). Intel oneTBB. https://github.com/oneapi-src/oneTBB. [Online; accessed March 2023].
20. Iorgulescu, C., Azimi, R., Kwon, Y., Elnikety, S., Syamala, M., Narasayya, V., Herodotou, H., Tomita, P., Chen, A., Zhang, J. & Wang, J. (2018). PerfIso: Performance isolation for commercial Latency-Sensitive services. (pp. 519–532).
21. Iorgulescu, C., Azimi, R., Kwon, Y., Elnikety, S., Syamala, M., Narasayya, V., Herodotou, H., Tomita, P., Chen, A., Zhang, J., & Wang, J. (2018). PerfIso: Performance isolation for commercial Latency-Sensitive services. In H. S. Gunawi, & B. C. Reed (Eds.), *2018 USENIX Annual Technical Conference, USENIX ATC 2018, Boston, MA, USA, July 11–13, 2018* (pp. 519–532). USENIX Association.
22. Kallman, R., Kimura, H., Natkins, J., Pavlo, A., Rasin, A., Zdonik, S. B., Jones, E. P. C., Madden, S., Stonebraker, M., Zhang, Y., Hugg, J., & Abadi, D. J. (2008). H-store: a high-performance, distributed main memory transaction processing system. *Proceedings of the VLDB Endowment, 1*(2), 1496–1499.
23. Kukanov, A. & Voss, M. J. (2007). The foundations for scalable multi-core software in intel threading building blocks. *Intel Technology Journal, 11*(4), 309–322.
24. Lee, J., Kim, H., & Vuduc, R. W. (2012). When Prefetching Works, When It Doesn't, and Why. *ACM Transactions on Architecture and Code Optimization, 9*, 2:1–2:29.
25. Lehman, P. L. & Yao, S. B. (1981). Efficient locking for concurrent operations on b-trees. *ACM Transactions on Database Systems, 6*(4), 650–670.
26. Leis, V., Boncz, P. A., Kemper, A., & Neumann, T. (2014). Morsel-driven parallelism: a numa-aware query evaluation framework for the many-core age. In *Proceedings of the 2014 International Conference on Management of Data, SIGMOD* (pp. 743–754). ACM.
27. Leis, V., Haubenschild, M., & Neumann, T. (2019). Optimistic lock coupling: A scalable and efficient general-purpose synchronization method. *IEEE Data Engineering Bulletin, 42*(1), 73–84.
28. Leis, V., Kemper, A., & Neumann, T. (2014). Exploiting hardware transactional memory in main-memory databases. In *IEEE 30th International Conference on Data Engineering* (pp. 580–591). IEEE Computer Society.
29. Leis, V., Scheibner, F., Kemper, A., & Neumann, T. (2016). The ART of practical synchronization. In *Proceedings of the 12th International Workshop on Data Management on New Hardware, DaMoN* (pp. 3:1–3:8). ACM.
30. Levandoski, J. J., Lomet, D. B., & Sengupta, S. (2013). The bw-tree: A b-tree for new hardware platforms. In *29th IEEE International Conference on Data Engineering, ICDE* (pp. 302–313). IEEE Computer Society.
31. Li, C., Ding, C., & Shen, K. (2007). Quantifying the cost of context switch. In *Proceedings of the Workshop on Experimental Computer Science, Part of ACM FCRC* (p. 2). ACM.
32. Lo, D., Cheng, L., Govindaraju, R., Ranganathan, P., & Kozyrakis, C. (2015). Heracles: improving resource efficiency at scale. In *Proceedings of the 42nd Annual International Symposium on Computer Architecture*, ISCA '15. ACM.
33. Lütke Dreimann, M., Friesel, B., & Spinczyk, O. (2024). HetSim: A Simulator for Task-based Scheduling on Heterogeneous Hardware. In *Companion of the 15th ACM/SPEC International Conference on Performance Engineering*, ICPE '24 Companion (pp. 261–268). Association for Computing Machinery.
34. Mao, Y., Kohler, E., & Morris, R. T. (2012). Cache craftiness for fast multicore key-value storage. In *Proceedings of the Seventh EuroSys Conference* (pp. 183–196). ACM.

35. Marathe, J., Thakkar, V., & Mueller, F. (2010). Feedback-directed page placement for ccnuma via hardware-generated memory traces. *Journal of Parallel and Distributed Computing, 70*(12), 1204–1219.
36. Mühlig, J., & Teubner, J. (2023). Micro Partitioning: Friendly to the hardware and the developer. In *Proceedings of the 19th International Workshop on Data Management on New Hardware, DaMoN* (pp. 27–34). ACM.
37. Müller, M., Leich, T., Pionteck, T., Saake, G., Teubner, J., & Spinczyk, O. (2020). He..ro db: A concept for parallel data processing on heterogeneous hardware. In A. Brinkmann, W. Karl, S. Lankes, S. Tomforde, T. Pionteck, & C. Trinitis (Eds.), *Architecture of Computing Systems—ARCS 2020* (pp. 82–96). Springer International Publishing.
38. Pandis, I., Johnson, R., Hardavellas, N., & Ailamaki, A. (2010). Data-oriented transaction execution. *Proceedings of the VLDB Endowment, 3*(1), 928–939.
39. Psaropoulos, G., Legler, T., May, N., & Ailamaki, A. (2017). Interleaving with Coroutines: A practical approach for robust index joins. *Proceedings of the VLDB Endowment, 11*(2), 230–242.
40. Rao, J. & Ross, K. A. (2000). Making B^+-trees cache conscious in main memory. In *Proceedings of the 2000 international conference on management of data, SIGMOD* (pp. 475–486). ACM.
41. Reinders, J. (2007). *Intel threading building blocks—outfitting C++ for multi-core processor parallelism*. O'Reilly.
42. Rodeh, O., Bacik, J., & Mason, C. (2013). BTRFS: The Linux B-Tree Filesystem. *ACM Transactions on Storage, 9*(3), 9.
43. Roy, R. B., Patel, T., & Tiwari, D. (2021). Satori: Efficient and fair resource partitioning by sacrificing short-term benefits for long-term gains. In *2021 ACM/IEEE 48th annual international symposium on computer architecture (ISCA)* (pp. 292–305).
44. Samuel, M. L., Pedersen, A. U., & Bonnet, P. (2005). Making csb+-tree processor conscious. In *Workshop on data management on new hardware, DaMoN*.
45. Srinath, S., Mutlu, O., Kim, H., & Patt, Y. N. (2007). Feedback directed prefetching: improving the performance and bandwidth-efficiency of hardware prefetchers. In *13st International conference on high-performance computer architecture* (pp. 63–74). IEEE Computer Society.
46. Tu, S., Zheng, W., Kohler, E., Liskov, B., & Madden, S. (2013). Speedy transactions in multicore in-memory databases. In *ACM SIGOPS 24th Symposium on Operating Systems Principles, SOSP* (pp. 18–32). ACM.
47. Verghese, B., Devine, S., Gupta, A., & Rosenblum, M. (1996). Operating system support for improving data locality on CC-NUMA compute servers. In *ASPLOS-VII proceedings—seventh international conference on architectural support for programming languages & operating systems* (pp. 279–289). ACM Press.
48. Verma, A., Pedrosa, L., Korupolu, M., Oppenheimer, D., Tune, E., & Wilkes, J. (2015). Large-scale cluster management at google with borg. In *Proceedings of the tenth European conference on computer systems*, EuroSys '15 (pp. 1–17) Association for Computing Machinery.
49. Verma, A., Pedrosa, L., Korupolu, M., Oppenheimer, D., Tune, E., & Wilkes, J. (2015). Large-scale cluster management at google with borg. In *Proceedings of the tenth European conference on computer systems*, EuroSys '15. ACM.
50. Wagner, B., Kohn, A., & Neumann, T. (2021). Self-tuning query scheduling for analytical workloads. In *Proceedings of the 2021 international conference on management of data, SIGMOD* (pp. 1879–1891). ACM.
51. Wang, Z. (2018). index-microbench. https://github.com/wangziqi2016/index-microbench. [Online; accessed April 2023]
52. Wang, Z., Pavlo, A., Lim, H., Leis, V., Zhang, H., Kaminsky, M., & Andersen, D. G. (2018). Building a bw-tree takes more than just buzz words. In *Proceedings of the 2018 International conference on management of data, SIGMOD* (pp. 473–488). ACM.

Chapter 6
Scaling Beyond DRAM Without Compromising Performance

Lukas Vogel, Christoph Anneser, Ferdinand Gruber, Thomas Neumann, Jana Giceva, and Alfons Kemper

Abstract In the past, the common assumption was that main memory would become cheap and abundant enough to power database systems solely. This assumption did not hold. This chapter presents approaches on how modern database systems can scale beyond a single server's main memory capacity by utilizing trends in modern hardware without sacrificing performance. To this end, we present four systems: Mosaic, a storage engine for analytical workloads; Plush, a PMem-optimized storage structure for transactional workloads; PMFDS, a novel programming model for fully disaggregated systems; and finally, FireArm, a just-in-time compilation framework for rising ARM systems in the server space.

6.1 Introduction

Ten years ago, the common assumption in the database system community was that main memory (i.e., dynamic random access memory, DRAM) would become cheap enough and available in a large enough capacity to make it feasible to develop database management systems (DBMS) purely residing in main memory. In this predicted future, main memory DBMS could have made use of multiple advantages:

Fast DRAM Compared to a slow spinning disk drive (HDD) with $\approx$100 MB/s throughput and $\approx$10 ms latency, DRAM is blazingly fast, achieving $\approx$100 GB/s (1000$\times$ more) throughput and $\approx$10 ns ($10^6\times$ less) latency. Main-memory DBMSs, thus, do not have to concern themselves with the disk bottleneck, provided the datasets they work on fit into DRAM.

Simpler Architecture Since all data is stored on DRAM, no data must be written back to disk except for logs and periodic system backups. Thus, no buffer manager is required, freeing the system from keeping the state consistent between

L. Vogel · C. Anneser · F. Gruber (✉) · T. Neumann · J. Giceva · A. Kemper
Technische Universität München, München, Germany
e-mail: lukas.vogel@in.tum.de; anneser@in.tum.de; gruberfe@in.tum.de; neumann@in.tum.de; jana.giceva@in.tum.de; kemper@in.tum.de

K.-U. Sattler et al. (eds.), *Scalable Data Management for Future Hardware*,
https://doi.org/10.1007/978-3-031-74097-8_6

multiple storage locations. Forgoing a buffer manager allows for a comparatively uncomplicated system architecture with one less bottleneck.

Many-Core Age As frequency scaling of CPUs hit a wall, chip manufacturers have put increasing numbers of cores onto a single chip: A modern single socket server may have as many as 128 cores (256 threads). Thanks to the high throughput of DRAM, database systems can employ massively parallel algorithms without being too bottlenecked by slow data access (i.e., reading data from disk), thus profiting from advanced multi-core chips.

6.1.1 The Tough Reality

Unfortunately, the assumption that a typical server's DRAM capacity grows while price drops did not hold. Even worse, DRAM capacity did not keep up with the world's increasing dataset sizes, making it impossible to analyze terabyte-sized datasets without employing cheap but slow background storage [36].

Some developments have tried to escape this issue by scaling *out*, i.e., distributing data and computing between multiple servers in a cluster. Distributed processing, however, incurs a high communication overhead. Instead, we looked at multiple hardware advancements of the last years, which help us scale *up* (i.e., keeping data and computing on a single server) beyond DRAM capacities. The following lists some promising advancements and the challenges in exploiting them.

SSDs Got Fast A modern SSD can have a throughput of multiple gigabytes per second, handle random reads, and write reasonably well, narrowing the gap (in throughput at least) to DRAM. A traditional HDD has a throughput of $\approx$100 MiB/s and seek times of $\approx$10 ms, making random access prohibitively expensive. Fast SSDs thus enable memory-first database systems that gracefully decline to (still quite fast) SSD speeds when running out of memory. Such a system, however, has to be built with SSDs in mind from the ground up, as existing systems are built around the shortcomings of HDDs and have many bottlenecks when directly ported to SSDs.

The "Storage Zoo" Nowadays, one can buy many different device classes at different price/performance points, as visualized by Fig. 6.1 first published in [50]. Each device class has its niche and complements the shortcomings of others well: While HDDs are much slower than SSDs, they are also far cheaper per gigabyte and thus predestined for cold data. On the other hand, Intel's Optane Persistent Memory technology has exceptionally low latency and higher throughput, making it a good fit for hot data at a price premium. While all these device classes expose the same well-known interface for storing and retrieving data, it is already challenging for

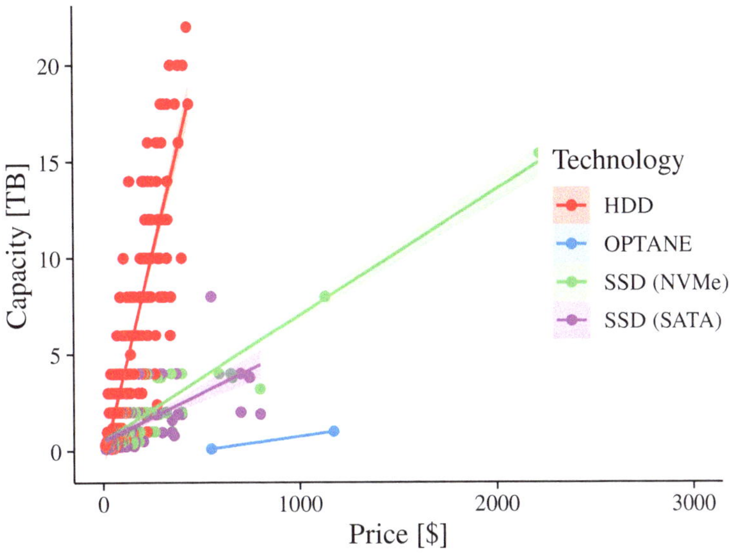

Fig. 6.1 Price of different storage media in relation to capacity

database systems to exploit the unique benefits of a *single* device class.[1] Preferably, a database system should use *multiple* device classes to maximize performance for a given budget, which is especially relevant in a cloud setting where one pays by the hour.

New Storage Technologies Technological advancements have introduced device classes that blur the line between storage and memory. Intel's Persistent Memory (PMem), for example, offers throughput and latency in the same order of magnitude as DRAM while storing data persistently, i.e., it retains stored data on power loss, unlike DRAM. While PMem's low write latency and high throughput have immediately apparent performance benefits for existing database systems, unlocking its full potential requires careful rearchitecting of existing systems: Since it is byte-addressable like traditional DRAM, writes can theoretically be persisted atomically and thus do not have the issues of traditional block-based interfaces like those used by SSDs or HDDs, whose larger block sizes mean applications have to account for torn writes or buffered data that is lost on a crash. This allows new database design approaches to eschew write-ahead logs if designed carefully.

[1] Intel's Optane Persistent Memory has two modes of operation: *Memory Mode* and the *App Direct Mode* (*ADM*). The ADM offers byte-addressable access to persistent memory using regular file systems supporting *DAX*, making persistent memory share a common interface with common storage devices.

Disaggregated Memory DRAM has become an important cost factor in data centers (e.g., DRAM accounts for 50% of Azure's servers [16] and 40% of Meta's rack costs [33]). At the same time, applications are overprovisioned fixed with memory resources to accommodate peak workloads, leading to significant underutilization of memory resources on average of only 50–65% [32, 47]. To mitigate the limits on DRAM capacity per socket and to improve utilization, data centers have started to disaggregate the memory resources by connecting multiple machines over high-speed interconnects. While memory disaggregation improves utilization, it significantly impacts application performance and requires careful data placement.

Arrival of ARM The x86-64 architecture has dominated the server and desktop market over the last decades. It is the main platform for compute-intensive workloads like database systems, high-performance computing, or data analytics. Following Moore's Law, the performance x86-64 increased constantly over the years. However, there was a slowdown in growth similar to stagnating DRAM capacities. At the same time, the ARM architecture (formerly only used for mobile and embedded applications) started to push in the x86-64-dominated markets, offering an energy-efficient alternative for computation with high performance. In addition, ARM processors offer new flexibility for accessing memory: i.e., ARM provides instructions reflecting the increased control within a weak memory ordering model. That combination of high-performance computation, the integration in all stacks of modern data centers, and flexible memory management makes ARM an integral part of addressing the challenges of modern data-intensive applications.

6.1.2 Our Contributions

This chapter explores taking advantage of the abovementioned opportunities while mitigating the challenges. To this end, we propose four different systems.

Mosaic is a storage engine designed to accelerate *analytical* workloads [52]. To make the most use of the modern storage zoo and fast SSDs, it manages devices in a tierless pool and provides purchase recommendations for a specified workload and budget. Consequently, Mosaic enables system administrators to utilize the many available storage device types with varying throughput and costs for analytical workloads. With Mosaic, we show that higher query throughputs at the same budget as state-of-the-art approaches are possible, or the user can choose similar query throughputs at a lower storage cost than existing solutions.

Plush is a storage structure optimized for *transactional* workloads and exploits PMem's low write latency, demonstrating how software can be designed to adapt to breakthroughs in storage technology [51]. It is a write-optimized hybrid hash table for PMem with support for variable-length records and complete crash consistency, able to replace the storage engine in a key-value store. Plush plays to PMem's strengths of DRAM-like performance, byte addressability, and the persistency guarantees of conventional block storage.

PMFDS is an envisioned programming model that would facilitate the sustainable development and optimization of data-intensive applications for fully disaggregated systems and modern hardware [4]. To achieve sustainable development and to become more independent of future development of memory device types, PMFDS adopts a memory-centric approach based on memory regions to abstract from hardware details. A runtime system co-optimizes data and task placement and maps the memory regions to the most suitable devices at execution time and assigns tasks to computational devices.

FireARM is a just-in-time compilation framework for database systems that puts a strong emphasis on low-latency compilation and high code quality [23]. FireARM translates the domain-specific intermediate representation *Umbra IR* orders of magnitude faster to ARM machine code than existing compilers like GCC and LLVM. At the same time, the performance of code generated by FireARM is nearly on par with compiler optimized code and can compete with the performance of x86-64. Since FireARM has a small resource overhead compared to larger compiler frameworks, it is not only suitable for high-end ARM servers but also for smaller edge-like devices.

6.2 Mosaic

As explained earlier, storing all data on DRAM is prohibitively expensive for medium-sized datasets and impossible for large datasets. Storing all data on fast storage devices (i.e., NVMe SSDs) works, as one can easily attach hundreds of TiB of such storage to a single server via PCIe, but this also becomes expensive quickly and needlessly wasteful: Most data is usually seldom accessed (i.e., cold) and could thus *in theory* be stored on much cheaper, larger, but also slower HDDs without impacting performance while saving money.

In practice, traditional DBMS are unsuitable for this task as they have been built with a specific device class in mind (e.g., HDDs for PostgreSQL, SSDs for Umbra [36], or SAP HANA for DRAM [21]). At best, they allow users to choose a storage location per table (i.e., at table granularity) via crutches such as table spaces. This coarse granularity, however, is far too coarse-grained for modern analytical workloads: Some columns of a table are usually accessed disproportionally more often than others, resulting either in bad performance—if the whole table, including frequently accessed columns, is stored on a slow device—or high costs, if the whole table, including seldom-accessed columns, is stored on a fast but expensive device. Furthermore, even if the user *could* place columns independently, it is not apparent how to make the best placement decisions: If even just one column accessed by an often-run query is stored on a slow device, all other data scanned by this query wastes valuable storage space of a faster device. Since different queries scan

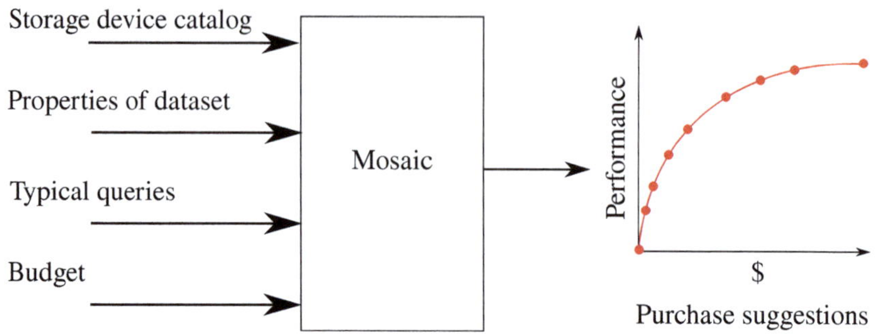

Fig. 6.2 Overview over the Mosaic recommendation system

different subsets of the data, one has to keep track of a lot of *interdependencies* when choosing an optimal data placement for a given workload and cannot rely on a simple hot-cold classification. Mosaic fixes this problem by offering help during all stages of the deployment process [52].

Before Hardware Is Purchased Mosaic acts as a storage device purchase recommendation system, as shown in Fig. 6.2: Given a list of devices available for purchase, a description of the dataset's properties, and a set of queries assumed to be representative of the later workload, Mosaic gives purchase recommendations for arbitrary budgets. Each recommendation is guaranteed to be Pareto optimal, i.e., no other configuration is faster while also being cheaper.

After Purchase Given the trace of a typical set of queries and storage devices, Mosaic places data optimally to maximize throughput. Mosaic can work with any set of storage devices, not only those bought based on its recommendations. Data can also be re-distributed should workload patterns change.

During Operation Mosaic acts as a pluggable storage engine component for any columnar relational database system.

6.2.1 *Placement Mechanism*

To place data optimally, Mosaic makes use of one simple observation shown in Fig. 6.3. Under the assumption that queries are bottlenecked by I/O, the runtime is always determined by the throughput of the storage device taking the longest to read all columns required for the given query. To minimize the runtime of an (I/O dominated) workload, Mosaic thus has to find a data placement that minimizes the time devices are idling. Instead of imperfect heuristics, Mosaic uses a mathematical model to predict database performance for a given data placement. It then employs a constraint solver using linear programming to optimize for the best placement

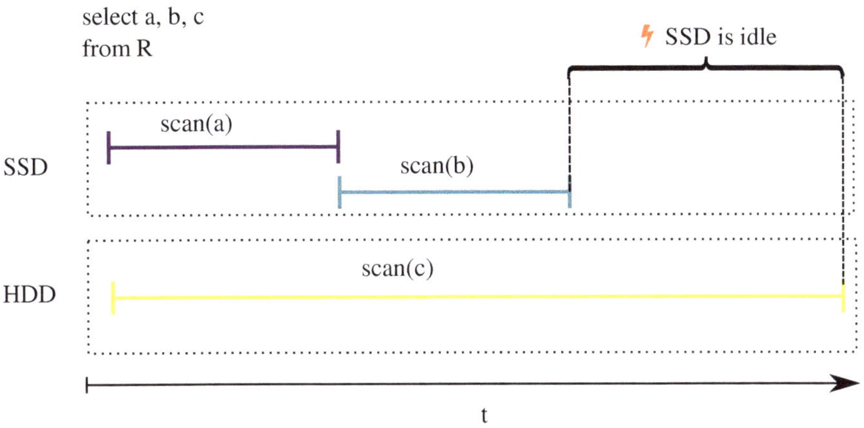

Fig. 6.3 Query runtime is determined by the slow HDD, assuming columns a and b are stored on a fast SSD and column c is stored on the slower HDD

decision while fulfilling the constraints the user has provided. This model is shown in Eq. 6.1 and predicts how long a single table scan will take. Since we assume the workload is I/O dominated, summing all table scans within a workload will give us the overall workload runtime.

$$t_{\mathrm{TScan}} = \max \left\{ \sum_{c \in \mathrm{cols}(\mathrm{TScan})} I(d, c) \cdot \frac{\mathrm{size}(c)}{\mathrm{tpt}(d)} \;\middle|\; d \in \mathrm{Devices} \right\} \tag{6.1}$$

In this equation, $I(d, c)$ is an indicator function evaluating to 1 if the column c is on device d and to 0 otherwise.

This model is just a more rigorously formalized version of the observations of Fig. 6.3: For each device, we calculate how long it takes to scan all the requested columns (i.e., the columns for which I tells us that they are on the given device). We then return the time of the device taking the longest.

With this formalization, we can now instruct a constraint solver to define the indicator function I so that it assigns each column to exactly one device while minimizing t_{TScan}. To ensure that Mosaic observes our budget constraints and does not just place all data on an array of really fast but expensive storage devices, we add the constraint shown in Eq. 6.2 that ensures that the total device budget stays below the budget $\mathrm{cost}_{\max}$ the user is willing to pay.

$$\mathrm{cost}_{\max} \geq \left(\sum_{d \in \mathrm{Devices}} \sum_{c \in \mathrm{Cols}} I(d, c) \cdot \mathrm{cost}(d) \cdot \mathrm{size}(c) \right) \tag{6.2}$$

By re-running the constraint solver at different budgets, Mosaic can generate a Pareto-optimal curve of hardware to buy. If the user has already purchased hardware,

Mosaic drops the cost constraint but adds additional constraints that ensure no device is overfilled.

6.2.2 *Evaluation*

To evaluate Mosaic, we have built an evaluation system comprised of three different device classes (see Table 6.1). We then import a trace of the TPC-H benchmark executing queries 1 to 22 once in sequence. Afterward, we let Mosaic place the dataset strategy for different budgets. After data placement, we measure the runtime of the benchmark. As a baseline, we benchmark all possible options when placing data at table granularity. Figure 6.4 shows the results. Each triangle represents a configuration a user could have achieved manually by placing data at table granularity. We highlight the three configurations where all tables are completely on HDD, SATA SSD, or NVMe SSD. Some configurations are strictly better than others. The dashed line indicates the Pareto optimal front, i.e., all configurations for which no cheaper *and* faster alternative exists. This line thus indicates the *best* an experienced system administrator could have done with legacy database systems.

Conversely, Mosaic can find much more fine granular data placements, as indicated by the dotted line. It provides far superior performance at the same budget or allows the user to save considerable costs without impacting performance.

Table 6.1 Storage devices of the evaluation system

Device	Price per GB	Throughput
NVMe PCIe SSD	125 ct	2.10 GB/s
SATA SSD	60 ct	0.41 GB/s
RAID 5 of HDDs	45 ct	0.32 GB/s

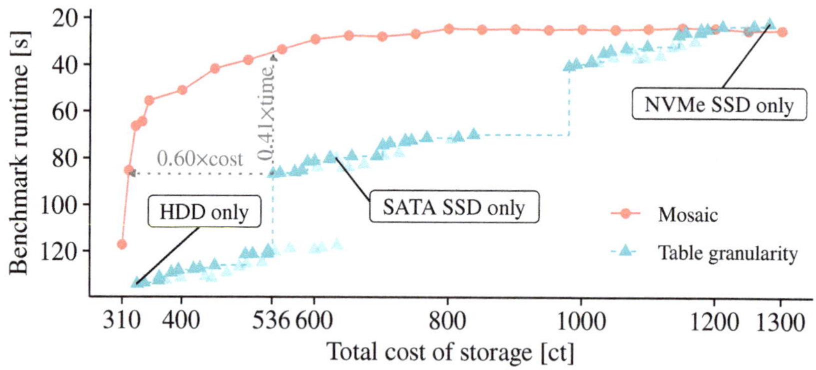

Fig. 6.4 Performance of Mosaic compared to manual data placement

6.3 Plush

While Mosaic can efficiently utilize many different storage device types, one technology is suspiciously missing: Persistent Memory (PMem). It promised to combine DRAM-like throughput, latency, and byte addressability with storage-like persistency. However, some issues became apparent when it finally became generally available, as demonstrated by Table 6.2. While PMem's latency is within reach of DRAM, its throughput is closer to that of a reasonably fast SSD. Even though this low throughput provides some challenges (as one can outmatch it by writing to multiple SSDs in parallel for far cheaper), it is offset by its amazingly low write latency, which existing storage hardware cannot achieve. The unparalleled write latency makes PMem especially attractive to workloads that repeatedly persist small amounts of data (i.e., latency-bound workloads), as is common with key-value stores.

6.3.1 The Problem with Persistent Memory

However, even for those workloads, PMem has a problem to overcome, pictured in Fig. 6.5: Write amplification. To ensure that PMem has safely persisted newly written data, the data has to be evicted from the volatile CPU cache to the physical PMem medium. The CPU cache is internally organized into cache lines sized 64 bytes. Data thus can only ever be updated in 16-byte increments. When a smaller range of data is written (i.e., a 16-byte record consisting of an 8-byte key and an 8-byte value), it thus takes the same time as if a contiguous 64-byte record was written,

Table 6.2 Write access characteristics for different media

Medium	Latency	Bandwidth	Price	Access unit
DRAM	90 ns	80 GB/s	7.2 $/GB	cache line (64 B)
PMem	130 ns	6.5 GB/s	4.0 $/GB	block (256 B)
SSD	≥1,000,000 ns	3.4 GB/s	0.3 $/GB	page (4KiB)

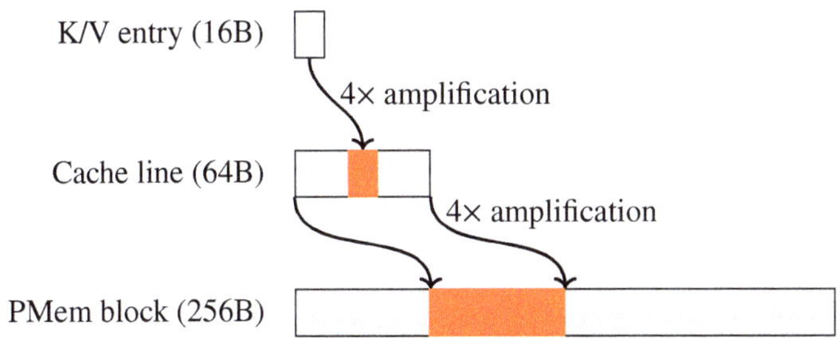

Fig. 6.5 Writing records to PMem: Up to 16× write amplification

resulting in a write amplification of 4× (i.e., four times as much data as the payload was actually written). PMem is internally organized in 256-byte blocks, so each block consists of 4 cache lines, leading to another 4× write amplification. Persisting a single record to PMem thus incurs a write amplification of up to 16× if we assume random accesses. Even though PMem has that attractively low write latency, which should make it predestined for small random writes, its low bandwidth is quickly eaten up by high write amplification. To investigate this effect and find solutions, we build Plush, a Persistent Log-StrUred haSH table that minimizes write amplification while exploiting PMem's low write latency.

6.3.2 Architecture

We built Plush [51] on the central observation that to minimize write amplification, one must write to PMem in 256-byte blocks. This need for block size optimization conceptually differs from the traditional approach for storage, where writing large, contiguous sequential chunks is optimal. For example, HDD- and SSD-optimized log-structured merge (LSM) trees put up with a lot of CPU overhead to sort data into runs, which pays off when multiple such sorted runs are merged and written back to disk with a sequential write pattern, reducing write amplification.

Since PMem already reaches its full throughput with 256 byte writes, Plush forgoes the traditional sorting approach of LSM trees and employs a hashtable approach, as shown in Fig. 6.6 instead. Plush consists of multiple hash tables of growing size, with the smallest one residing on DRAM. Plush uses the key's hash when inserting to determine which DRAM bucket the record is to be inserted (②). To minimize write amplification, Plush employs 256 bytes large buckets. Whenever

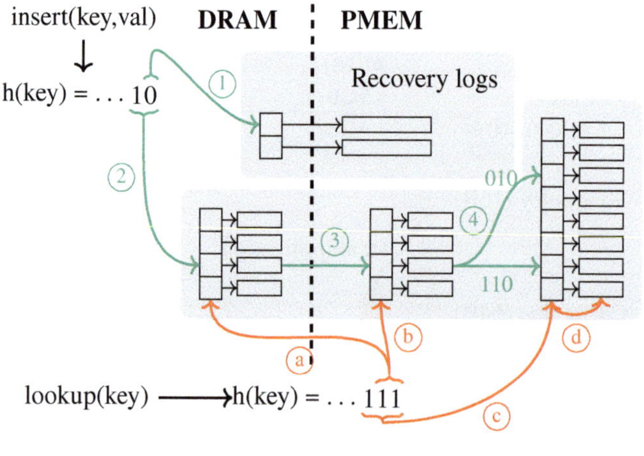

Fig. 6.6 Plush's architecture with illustrated insert (①–⑤) and lookup algorithms (ⓐ–ⓓ). The colored lines represent steps in the algorithms, and the black lines are pointers of the data structure

a bucket is full, Plush appends it to a chain of buckets in a PMem hash table of the same size (③), guaranteeing no write amplification is happening. All buckets are re-hashed once this chain is full and inserted into the next larger hash table on PMem (④). Plush ensures that the chain length is a multiple of the number of bins the buckets are re-hashed into. This ratio ensures that for each bin on the next level, an approximate multiple of 256 bytes is written, keeping write amplification low.

This approach has a huge drawback: Records that Plush has written to DRAM but not yet migrated to PMem will be lost upon a system crash. To ensure all data is persisted instantly, Plush thus first writes the record to a recovery log (①). Keeping a recovery log in PMem seems counterintuitive as this results in many writes smaller than 256 bytes, increasing write amplification. However, since Plush populates these logs *sequentially*, it can employ the PMem medium's small but fast write combining buffer, which holds data until a whole block is complete. The PMem memory controller then writes the whole block to the medium. Plush truncates the log when it can guarantee that it has flushed all records stored within to PMem.

For lookups, Plush has to subsequently look into each level (ⓐ–ⓒ) until it has either found the key or has exhausted all levels. Since most keys are expected to be on the last level, Plush employs bloom filters in each hash table's index to speed up negative lookups (ⓓ).

6.3.3 Evaluation

Our evaluation system uses a 24-core Xeon Gold 6212U CPU (48 logical cores). It has access to 192 GB (6 × 32 GB) DRAM and 768 GB (6 × 128 GB) of Intel's first-generation PMem DIMMs. We compare Plush against nine indexes listed, four of which are *hash tables* (Dash [8], PmemKV [40], Viper [9], FASTER [13]), while the other five are *treelike data structures* (μTree [14], FPTree [38], FAST+FAIR [26], DPTree [53], RocksDB [39]). Plush combines aspects of both approaches, allowing us to compare different trade-offs made by each approach.

In the first experiment, we preload 100 million 16-byte records consisting of 8-byte keys and values. Keys are uniformly distributed. We then execute 100 million operations for varying thread counts. Figure 6.7 shows the results. For lookups (Fig. 6.7a), Plush is in the middle of the pack. Since it behaves somewhat treelike (i.e., a lookup has to search each level with most records statistically residing on the last level), it has a considerable disadvantage over the hash table implementations but keeps up with the other trees. However, Plush shines when inserting or updating records (see Fig. 6.7b). Thanks to its lower write amplification, it can utilize PMem's low bandwidth far better than other data structures.

Another critical aspect of PMem-optimized data structures is their space consumption. One of PMem's selling points was that one can install significantly more PMem capacity per CPU socket than DRAM capacity since each PMem DIMM can hold up to 512 GiB of data. However, almost all data structures *also* use DRAM

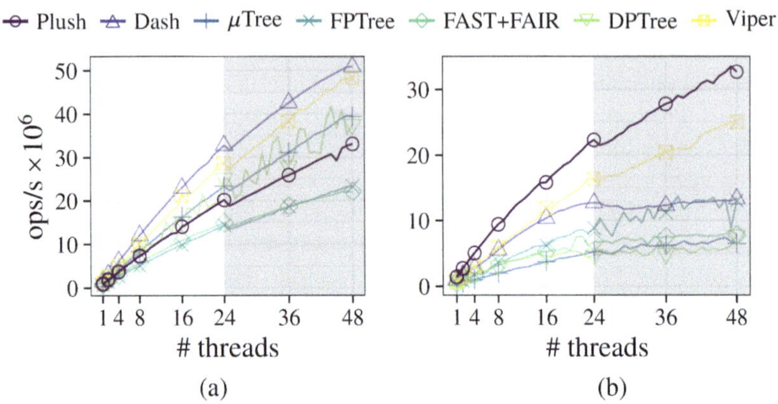

Fig. 6.7 Plush's performance for inserts and lookups, compared to other PMem-optimized data structures. (**a**) 100% lookup. (**b**) 100% insert

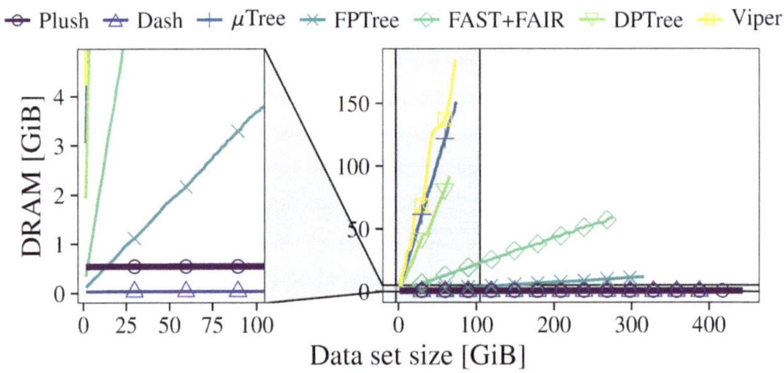

Fig. 6.8 Plush's DRAM consumption compared to the size of the dataset

for data that they can reconstruct if a crash happens. FPTree, for example, stores its inner nodes on volatile DRAM and rebuilds them after a system crash.

Figure 6.8 shows the DRAM consumption of the data structure plotted against the dataset size (i.e., the useful payload supposed to be stored on PMem). Here, most data structures' DRAM consumption scales linearly or even superlinearly with the payload size. Especially Viper, μTree, and DPTree store most of their data in DRAM. They thus cannot scale with the amount of installed PMem, obsoleting one of its advantages. Plush, however, only uses a *static* amount of DRAM, taking the second spot in DRAM consumption after Dash, a PMem-only data structure. Plush is, therefore, able to profit from DRAM but is not limited by the amount of installed DRAM and can thus scale to arbitrary amounts of installed PMem.

Overall, Plush demonstrates that there is a lot to gain by optimizing for low write amplification on PMem. It is competitive with other PMem-optimized data structures for lookups while significantly outclassing them for inserts. It enables users to perform millions of operations per second in a crash-consistent manner, which was previously impossible.

6.4 Programming Fully Disaggregated Systems

The modern hardware landscape for large-scale data processing has become highly complex over the last few years, which makes it challenging for developers to fully exploit their potential. In the following, we elaborate on six trends that were previously described in more detail [5]. These trends contribute to the hardware landscape's complexity and then discuss the key design principles for a new programming model that would facilitate the implementation of data-intensive applications and their optimization for modern hardware.

6.4.1 *Trends in Large-Scale Data Processing*

Trend 1: Hardware Specialization For decades, Moore's law, Dennard's, and Amdahl's scaling have effectively predicted and modeled the exponential growth in computational power. This increase in processing capabilities has facilitated the rapid analysis of vast datasets. However, as modern processors are currently approaching their physical limits, we observe a push toward specialized compute devices [25], like GPUs and TPUs, which offers a pathway for developers to create more energy-efficient data-processing pipelines with higher performance. These advantages, however, come at the expense of increased complexity in software development.

Furthermore, it becomes impractical to store large datasets entirely in DRAM. In response, emerging memory technologies like Persistent Memory (PMEM) are being integrated into today's processor-centric architecture, further complicating the landscape of modern memory architectures, as depicted in Fig. 6.9a.

Trend 2: Data Explosion Concurrently, stagnating DRAM prices coupled with the explosive growth in data volume—projected to exceed 175 zettabytes by the year 2025 [44]—put significant pressure on data-processing systems. To achieve high-performance data processing on rapidly growing data volumes, an increasing number of users are moving to cloud computing solutions, which offer highly flexible spot instances and provide high-performance data-processing capabilities that can scale dynamically with the increasing data volumes.

Trend 3: Cloud Computing Dynamic random access memory (DRAM) is an important cost factor in data centers (50% of Azure's servers [16] and 40% of Meta's rack costs come from memory [33]). However, as more data systems move to the cloud, where they run in containers with fixed memory and compute

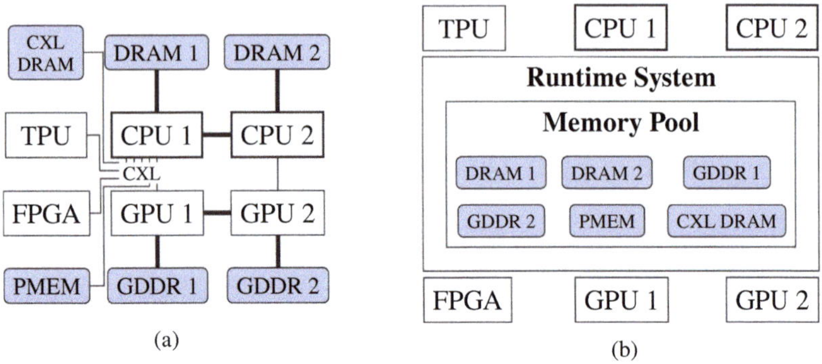

Fig. 6.9 Moving from a compute-centric to a memory-centric architecture [4]. (**a**) Processor-centric architecture. (**b**) Memory-centric model

resources, the average memory utilization is reported to be only between 50 and 65% on average [32, 47]. This is because of the containers' "over-provisioning" with memory and compute resources to reliably serve peak workloads.

Trend 4: Disaggregated Memory Therefore, disaggregated memory has emerged as a promising solution to enhance resource utilization. Disaggregated architectures use fast networks [7, 41] to interconnect computing [6, 10–12, 18, 27, 28, 43] and memory resources [2, 15, 20, 49] of different machines, thereby creating larger and more flexible resource pools.

Trend 5: Data Movement While disaggregated memory architectures address the problems of underutilized memory resources, they also introduce new complexities and problems concerning data placement. Poorly placed data within the disaggregated memory pool can lead to substantial latencies and might require expensive data movement to transfer data closer to the computational device [29, 41].

Trend 6: Cache-Coherent Interconnects The complexity within the computing landscape is further increased by recent advancements in data center processors, like Intel's 4th Generation Xeon® Scalable Processors [1] and AMD's 4th Generation Epyc processors [3].

They adopt Compute Express Link™ (CXL™) [15], a new cache-coherency protocol based on PCIe 5.0. CXL™ has been adopted by many industry-leading companies and will potentially facilitate the development of PCIe-attached memory expansion cards. The first cards have already been announced by Micron [34] and Samsung [45], contributing to a more diverse and complex memory device landscape. Table 6.3 shows attributes like bandwidth, latency, and access granularity for different memory types as seen from a CPU. Developer must know these properties to optimize their software applications.

Table 6.3 Selected properties of memory devices as perceived from a CPU [4]

Name	Bandwidth	Latency	Access granularity	Sync	Persist
HBM	++	+	64 B	✓	✗
DRAM	+	+	64 B	✓	✗
PMem	∘	∘	256 B	✓	✓
CXL-DRAM	∘	∘	64 B	✓ / ✗	✓ / ✗
SSD	−	−	4 KiB	✗	✓
HDD	−−	−−	4 KiB	✗	✓

A New Memory-Centric Programming Model It is unclear how developers can sustainably leverage the potential that modern hardware offers. Furthermore, the available hardware accelerators and memory types are often known only at execution and not yet during development and compile time. These trends collectively motivate a new programming model that abstracts from the hardware advancements and facilitates the sustainable development and optimization of data-intensive applications. Trends 4 and 5 have highlighted that memory-related costs are the primary concern in developing data-intensive applications at data center scale. To minimize data movement, we envision a memory-centric programming model as shown in Fig. 6.9b. In the following, we discuss the key design principles of the new programming model.

6.4.2 Design Principles

We propose several key design principles for a new programming model for fully disaggregated systems (PMFDS). To make the programming model applicable to a broader range of applications, we generalize and represent them as dataflow graphs. Dataflow graphs are directed acyclic graphs whose nodes are computational tasks and arrows denote the data flow between tasks. This generalization works well for various application types, including database query plans and AI/ML pipelines. Figure 6.10 shows an example of a dataflow graph.

Abstracting from Physical Memory Devices Through Memory Regions As shown in Table 6.3, the hardware landscape comprises various memory device types. Furthermore, CXL™ facilitates the development of new device types and enables new data- and compute placement options, thereby increasing the optimization space and complexity. However, at development time, it is often unknown what memory devices are available at execution time. Rather than assigning data to particular memory devices in advance for a given task t, we argue to select the memory device based on the specific requirements, such as bandwidth or latency, needed by t.

Therefore, we propose a memory-centric design based on memory regions ① that abstract from memory devices. As depicted in Fig. 6.11, every memory region

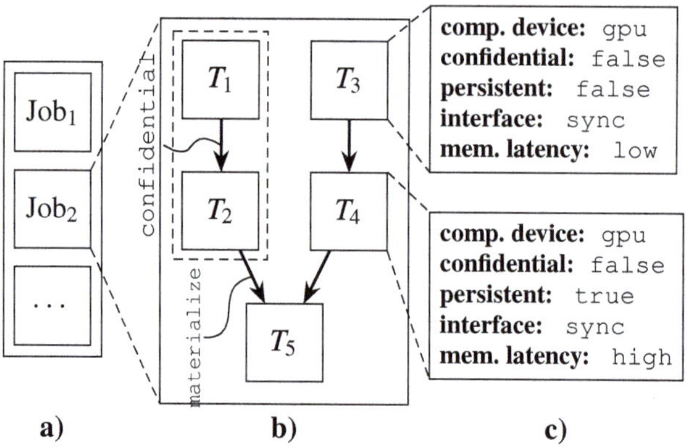

Fig. 6.10 Representing dataflow graphs as directed acyclic graphs (DAG) [4]. (**a**) Jobs. (**b**) Tasks. (**c**) Declarative progr.

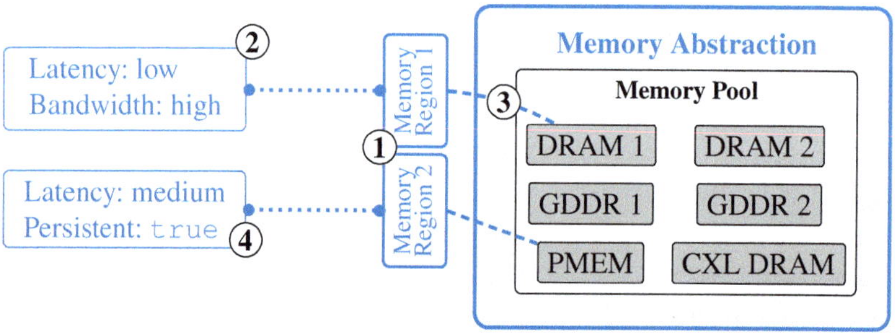

Fig. 6.11 Memory regions are defined with declarative properties and abstract from physical memory devices. The runtime system maps the regions to physical devices at execution time

can be assigned declarative properties like bandwidth or latency requirements ((2) and (4)). At runtime, more information about the available memory devices and their utilization is known to better map memory regions to hardware devices (3). Also, other frequently required functionalities, such as the encryption of sensitive data, can be declared by attaching properties to the memory region. This approach simplifies the application development by abstracting away much of the complexity.

Typed Memory Regions In most data-intensive applications, memory is primarily used for synchronizing threads, exchanging data, and enabling fast thread-local computations. Our programming model introduces *typed memory regions*, which are predefined first-class entities to facilitate these tasks and ease adoption:

- **Global State:** coherent and synchronous memory, for synchronizing tasks
- **Global Scratch:** coherent and asynchronous memory, for data exchange
- **Private Scratch:** non-coherent and synchronous memory, for thread-local computations

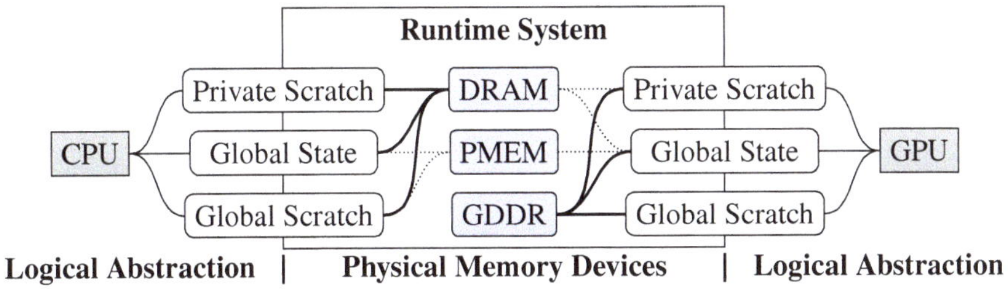

Fig. 6.12 The runtime system co-optimizes data and compute placement and maps the memory regions to actual memory devices [4]

Memory Region Ownership Memory regions can hide hardware complexity but also introduce questions of ownership and cleanup responsibility for regions that are no longer used. These issues can be efficiently addressed by adopting principles from modern languages like Rust and C++11, specifically smart pointers. The cleanup responsibility falls to the last task holding ownership. Furthermore, memory region ownership can provide valuable information to the runtime system's optimizer to improve data placement.

Runtime System The proposed programming model necessitates a runtime system (RTS) to implement the concepts of memory regions and ownership. Additionally, the RTS optimizes task and data placement. Placement decisions are deferred to runtime to leverage detailed information on hardware availability and utilization, which is crucial in cloud environments where resources are dynamically allocated. The interdependence of task and data placement is illustrated in Fig. 6.12, highlighting how the processing devices influence the choice of optimal memory devices for data. For example, if a task runs on the CPU, binding the memory regions to the socket-local DRAM results in lower access latency and higher bandwidth. Conversely, when the task runs on the GPU, execution time benefits from mapping the memory regions to the GPU's local GDDR memory.

Future Work There is much potential for future work in cost-based optimization of memory mapping in heterogeneous systems. This could involve examining the hardware topology and its effects on access latency and bandwidth, as well as the handover of memory regions between tasks. Furthermore, recent work showed that query execution could benefit from heterogeneous device-parallel executions [31]. For example, they found that scheduling tasks should not be a binary decision between CPU and GPU.

6.5 ARM: Code Generation for High-End and Edge Devices

Since Hyper [35], query compilation has emerged as the key technology for substantial performance improvements in data processing, and many database systems [19, 22, 24, 30, 37] and data-processing systems [17] shifted toward machine code compilation. Most systems focused on the x86-64 architecture due to its dominance in the server segment and because powerful ARM processors were not broadly available. The *ArmV8* architecture, which drives most modern ARM-based processors, was announced in 2011, and the first core designs (e.g., the *Cortex-A53* also used for the Raspberry Pi) were shown in 2012. However, powerful ARM processors started pushing into the desktop and server market, starting with Apple's M series and Amazon's Graviton line. Modern ARM processors achieve performance comparable to the established x86-64 competitors or surpass them, making ARM now a valid choice for query compiling systems.

6.5.1 Query Compilation

In the last decade, various compilation approaches that satisfy different requirements regarding compilation latency, performance, and portability emerged. Some database systems compile SQL queries by translating them to C or C++ programs that are then compiled with GCC or LLVM [19]. In contrast, others directly translate query plans to intermediate representations (IRs) [35]. With the Umbra database system, we developed a system with a strong focus on low compilation overhead and maximum tuple throughput for in-memory workloads [37]. Since existing compiler infrastructure like GCC or LLVM did not meet our requirements, we implemented a new ARM-specific compilation backend called *FireARM* [23]. FireARM generates ARM machine code a magnitude faster than non-optimizing LLVM-JIT while achieving similar or better code quality, as we showed in our previous publication [23]. FireARM thus has a minimal resource overhead, making it suitable for high-end processors and less-powerful, *edge-like* processors.

6.5.1.1 Architectural Challenges

Changing the target architecture for code generation using GCC or LLVM is straightforward because the compilers do all necessary tasks like lowering or instruction selection. However, that requires high-level languages like C or C++ to express queries or internal compiler IRs like GCC Gimple or LLVM IR. With a focus on low-latency compilation, such approaches are suboptimal, so a custom query program abstraction like *Umbra IR* and an IR-specific code generator are used. Umbra IR is a *domain-specific* IR designed for low-latency code generation in database systems inspired by LLVM IR. However, Umbra IR implements database-specific IR optimizations to simplify the expression of database operators, making code generation less complex than LLVM IR. While that technology was already designed and implemented for x86-64 systems in the Umbra, support for the ARM architecture required a new code-generation layer called FireARM. Unfortunately, our internal IR was optimized for efficient code generation for x86-64, implementing constructs that make code generation for other architectures more complex. That earlier focus on x86-64 and the architectural differences between x86-64 and ARM made the implementation of FireARM non-trivial.

While ARM uses a *weak-ordering* consistency model [42], x86-64 features a *processor-ordering* consistency [46]. Except for explicit atomic store operations that require sequential consistency, the ordering of reads and writes does not concern developers on x86-64. Load and store operations with relaxed or acquire-release semantics have the same ordering on x86-64. In contrast, ARM offers fine-graded control over the ordering of memory operations. That flexibility allows multiple optimizations but must be handled carefully because wrong ordering semantics can degrade the performance on ARM. Furthermore, it affects the correctness of database pipelines by implementing wrong or insufficient barrier semantics on ARM.

While memory ordering is more flexible, the ARM instruction set is more restricted than the instruction set of x86-64. Most memory accesses (e.g., operand loads or operand stores) must be done in explicit operations and cannot be fused into arithmetic instructions, as is the case on x86-64. Since ARM has a fixed instruction encoding length of 32 bits, the encoding of immediate operands is also limited, leading to bloated machine code for immediate-heavy workloads.

Like our code generator for x86-64, FireARM does not optimize for specific processor models. Such an approach is sufficient on x86-64 because the vendor differences in processor behavior between AMD and Intel are marginal. However, various ARM core designs from different vendors have individual performance characteristics. While such optimizations can increase performance significantly, the implementation complexity of the code generator grows proportionally, making custom code generators like FireARM not maintainable anymore.

Those and other challenges (e.g., the limited operand bit width or strict memory alignment requirements) make the just-in-time generation of high-performant machine code on ARM more complex than on x86-64. Nonetheless, FireARM shows that it is possible to tackle those challenges while satisfying the requirements regarding compilation and code quality.

6.5.1.2 Code Generation Evaluation

To evaluate the performance characteristics of different compilation strategies in terms of compilation time and tuple throughput (i.e., quality of generated machine code) on ARM, we used the TPC-H benchmark and the Umbra database system. Since all code-generation backends start with the same Umbra IR programs (e.g.,

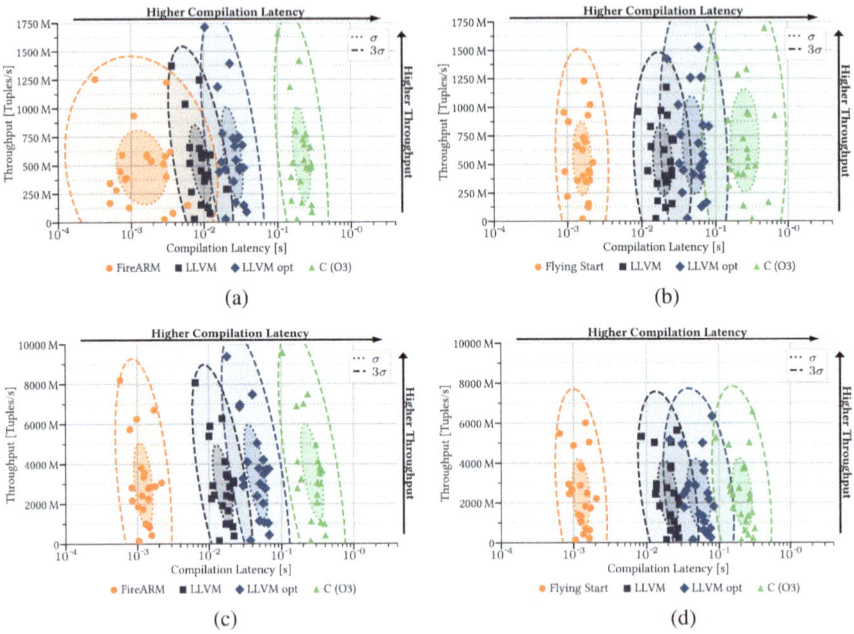

Fig. 6.13 The tuple throughput and the compilation time of different query compilation approaches in the Umbra database system using the TPC-H benchmark. Compilers like GCC and LLVM produce slightly better code (offering better performance), but compilation takes orders of magnitude longer. (**a**) Apple M1 (8 Cores, 16 GB, sf = 10). (**b**) AMD Ryzen 7 4750U (8 Cores, 32 GB, sf = 10). (**c**) Graviton 3 (64 Cores, 128 GB, sf = 30). (**d**) AMD Epyc 7713 (64 Cores, 1 TB, sf = 30)

same query and execution plans) to generate ARM machine code, the performance results are comparable.

Figure 6.13 shows an excerpt of our extensive benchmark evaluation that was previously published in [23]. We analyzed the performance of the different compilation strategies on consumer hardware (e.g., Apple M1 and Ryzen 4750U) and state-of-the-art server hardware (e.g., Amazon Graviton 3 and Epyc 7713) on ARM and x86-64. Our results show similar patterns for compilation time and dimensions for tuple throughput on both architectures, showing the potential of modern ARM processors.

Compilation Time The query compilation time of LLVM and GCC is slightly faster on ARM than on x86-64. We argue that the implementation of the architecture-specific machine code generation pass for ARM is newer and better structured than the old code base for the x86-64 architecture, so code generation for ARM is slightly faster. However, on the Apple M1, FireARM shows a larger variety for the compilation time than other code-generation strategies and processors. That is due to the *efficiency cores* of the Apple M1, as query compilation done on the less-powerful efficiency cores is slow. We expect that with the increasing number of processors implementing a combination of *performance* and *efficiency* cores, other ARM and x86-64 processors will show similar performance patterns.

Tuple Throughput All code-generation strategies achieve multiple orders of magnitude higher tuple throughput than virtual machine-based interpretation. However, optimized GCC and LLVM code still performs slightly better than FireARM. The difference between a limited set of optimizations (LLVM opt) and the application of all available optimizations (GCC O3) is marginal. We argue that the better instruction selection between optimized and unoptimized GCC and LLVM compilation is the reason for achieving better code quality than FireARM.

6.5.2 Embedded ARM Processors

While ARM pushes in the desktop and server market, most ARM-based processors are designed for mobile or embedded applications. Computational storage devices like the Catalina SSD [48] integrate energy-efficient ARM coprocessors not comparable to Apple's M-series or Amazon's Graviton line. However, those embedded ARM processors still allow systems to offload work to devices, so memory and compute resources on the host can be saved. A Catalina SSD uses four *Cortex A53* processors with 8 GB of device main memory and runs an independent Linux-based operating system. Those specifications are similar to the *Raspberry Pi 4* we evaluated for query compilation in Umbra [23]. Figure 6.14 shows the compilation time and the tuple throughput for the TPC-H benchmark with scale factor 5 in a best-case scenario (e.g., all data in memory). While benchmarks show that code generation enables impressive data processing on edge-like devices, performance is orders of magnitude worse than entry-level consumer hardware (e.g., Fig. 6.13b).

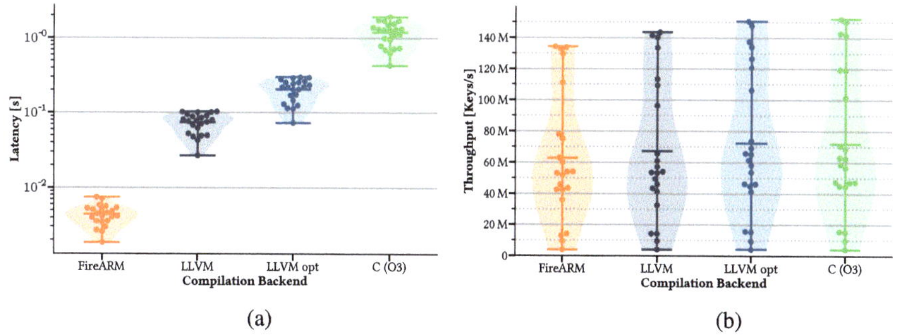

Fig. 6.14 The compilation time and the tuple throughput of different compilation strategies in Umbra on a Raspberry Pi 4 with 8 GB main memory using the TPC-H benchmark with scale factor 5. (**a**) Compilation latency. (**b**) Tuple throughput

Offloading operations like table scans and filtering to computational storage seem reasonable for compiling in-memory systems to save host resources. However, the performance of the embedded processor becomes the bottleneck. While the embedded ARM processor can access the SSD flash storage with full speed and the lowest possible latency, the memory for intermediate results is limited, and the TCP/IP-based data exchange with the host system introduces additional overhead. While the direct access to the SSD device from the host is limited to the bandwidth of *PCIe Gen3*, the performance without the offloading of filter operations to the ARM processor was still better.

Future smart storage devices may integrate more efficient processors and a higher amount of device memory, tackling the limitations of the Catalina SSD. Furthermore, new interconnect technologies like *CXL.mem* could allow low-overhead data exchange between device and host memory. Tackling those limitations for accelerators makes offloading computation to ARM processors a valuable option for compiling database systems.

6.6 Conclusions

This chapter introduced four innovative concepts designed to enable data-intensive systems to scale beyond DRAM without compromising performance. Mosaic is a storage engine that manages a tierless pool of memory and storage devices. Given specified workloads and budget constraints, it recommends what database tables and columns should be placed on what devices. We have shown that Mosaic can effectively improve the overall system performance on modern heterogeneous storage setups. Plush is a new write-optimized hybrid hash table for persistent memory that optimizes transactional workloads and supports variable-length records and crash consistency, showing how novel memory technologies can overcome limited DRAM capacities. We introduced PMFDS, a new programming model that facilitates the implementation and optimization of data-intensive systems for today's increasingly heterogeneous and disaggregated hardware landscape. Given the shift toward heterogeneity not only in storage but also in processing devices, like ARM, we examined how established data-processing methods like just-in-time compilation can be adapted to new processor architectures.

Acknowledgments This work was funded by the German Research Foundation (DFG) within the SPP 2037 under grant no. 361477420.

References

1. 4th Generation Intel® Xeon® Scalable Processors (2023). Last Accessed: September 18, 2024.
2. Aguilera, M. K., Amit, N., Calciu, I., Deguillard, X., Gandhi, J., Novakovic, S., Ramanathan, A., Subrahmanyam, P., Suresh, L., Tati, K., Venkatasubramanian, R., & Wei, M. (2018). Remote regions: A simple abstraction for remote memory. In *USENIX Annual Technical Conference* (pp. 775–787). USENIX Association.
3. AMD. (2023) 4th Generation amd Epyc® Processors (2023). Last Accessed: February 28, 2024.
4. Anneser, C., Vogel, L., Gruber, F., Bandle, M., & Giceva, J. (2023). Programming fully disaggregated systems. In *HotOS* (pp. 188–195). ACM.
5. Anneser, C. M. (2024). *Adaptive Optimizations for Databases*. PhD Thesis, Technische Universität München.
6. Armenatzoglou, N., Basu, S., Bhanoori, N., Cai, M., Chainani, N., Chinta, K., Govindaraju, V., Green, T. J., Gupta, M., Hillig, S., et al. (2022). Amazon redshift re-invented. In *Proceedings of the 2022 International Conference on Management of Data* (pp. 2205–2217).
7. Ballani, H., Costa, P., Behrendt, R., Cletheroe, D., Haller, I., Jozwik, K., Karinou, F., Lange, S., Shi, K., Thomsen, B., & Williams, H. (2020). Sirius: A flat datacenter network with nanosecond optical switching. In *SIGCOMM* (pp. 782–797). ACM.
8. Baotong, L., Hao, X., Wang, T., & Lo, E. (2020). Dash: Scalable hashing on persistent memory. *PVLDB, 13*(8), 1147–1161.
9. Benson, L., Makait, H., & Rabl, T. (2021). Viper: An efficient hybrid PMem-DRAM key-value store. *PVLDB, 14*(9), 1544–1556.
10. Bosshart, P., Daly, D., Gibb, G., Izzard, M., McKeown, N., Rexford, J., et al. (2014). P4: Programming protocol-independent packet processors. *ACM SIGCOMM Computer Communication Review, 44*(3), 87–95.
11. Cao, W., Liu, Y., Cheng, Z., Zheng, N., Li, W., Wu, W., Ouyang, L., Wang, P., Wang, Y., Kuan, R., Liu, Z., Zhu, F., & Zhang, T. (2020). POLARDB meets computational storage: Efficiently support analytical workloads in cloud-native relational database. In *FAST*, (pp. 29–41). USENIX Association.
12. Caulfield, A. M., Chung, E. S., Putnam, A., Angepat, H., Fowers, J., Haselman, M., Heil, S., Humphrey, M., Kaur, P., Kim, J.-Y., Lo, D., Massengill, T., Ovtcharov, K., Papamichael, M., Woods, L., Lanka, S., Chiou, D., & Burger, D. (2016). A cloud-scale acceleration architecture. In *MICRO* (pp. 7:1–7:13). IEEE Computer Society.
13. Chandramouli, B., Prasaad, G., Kossmann, D., Levandoski, J. J., Hunter, J., & Barnett, M. (2018). FASTER: A concurrent key-value store with in-place updates. In *SIGMOD Conference* (pp. 275–290). ACM.
14. Chen, Y., Youyou, L., Fang, K., Wang, Q., & Shu, J. (2020). uTree: A persistent B+-tree with low tail latency. *PVLDB, 13*(11), 2634–2648.
15. Compute Express Link (2023). Last Accessed: February 28, 2024.
16. CXL and Gen-Z Iron Out a Coherent Interconnect Strategy (2020). Last Accessed: September 18, 2024.
17. Damme, P., Birkenbach, M., Bitsakos, C., Boehm, M., Bonnet, P., Ciorba, F. M., Dokter, M., Dowgiallo, P., Eleliemy, A., Faerber, C., Goumas, G. I., Habich, D., Hedam, N., Hofer, M., Huang, W., Innerebner, K., Karakostas, V., Kern, R. , Kosar, T., Krause, A., Krems, D., Laber, A., Lehner, W., Mier, E., Paradies, M., Peischl, B., Poerwawinata, G., Psomadakis, S., Rabl, T., Ratuszniak, P., Silva, P., Skuppin, N., Starzacher, A., Steinwender, B., Tolovski, I., Tözün, P., Ulatowski, W., Wang, Y., Wrosz, I. P., Zamuda, A., Zhang, C., & Zhu, X. (2022). DAPHNE: An open and extensible system infrastructure for integrated data analysis pipelines. In *CIDR*. www.cidrdb.org
18. Data Processing Units (2020). Last Accessed: September 18, 2024.
19. Diaconu, C., Freedman, C., Ismert, E., Larson, P.-Å., Mittal, P., Stonecipher, R., Verma, N., & Zwilling, M. (2013). Hekaton: SQL server's memory-optimized OLTP engine. In *SIGMOD Conference* (pp. 1243–1254). ACM.

20. Dragojevic, A., Narayanan, D., Castro, M., & Hodson, O. (2014). Farm: Fast remote memory. In *NSDI* (pp. 401–414). USENIX Association.
21. Färber, F., Cha, S. K., Primsch, J., Bornhövd, C., Sigg, S., & Lehner, W. (2011). SAP HANA database: Data management for modern business applications. *ACM Sigmod Record, 40*(4), 45–51.
22. Funke, H., Mühlig, J., & Teubner, J. (2020). Efficient generation of machine code for query compilers. In *DaMoN* (pp. 6:1–6:7). ACM.
23. Gruber, F., Bandle, M., Engelke, A., Neumann, T., & Giceva, J. (2023). Bringing compiling databases to RISC architectures. *Proceedings of the VLDB Endowment, 16*(6), 1222–1234.
24. Gubner, T., & Boncz, P. A. (2021). Charting the design space of query execution using VOILA. *Proceedings of the VLDB Endowment, 14*(6), 1067–1079.
25. Hennessy, J., & Patterson, D. (2018). *ACM Turing Lecture*.
26. Hwang, D., Kim, W.-H., Won, Y., & Nam, B. (2018). Endurable transient inconsistency in byte-addressable persistent B+-tree. In *FAST* (pp. 187–200). USENIX Association.
27. Jouppi, N. P., Young, C., Patil, N., Patterson, D. A., Agrawal, G., Bajwa, R., Bates, S., Bhatia, S., Boden, N., et al. (2017) In-datacenter performance analysis of a tensor processing unit. In *ISCA* (pp. 1–12). ACM.
28. Kim, J., Jang, I., Reda, W., Im, J., Canini, M., Kostic, D., Kwon, Y., Peter, S., & Witchel, E. (2021). Linefs: Efficient smartnic offload of a distributed file system with pipeline parallelism. In *SOSP* (pp. 756–771). ACM.
29. Kogge, P. M., & Shalf, J. (2013). Exascale computing trends: Adjusting to the "new normal" for computer architecture. *Computing in Science & Engineering, 15*(6), 16–26.
30. Kornacker, M., Behm, A., Bittorf, V., Bobrovytsky, T., Ching, C., Choi, A., Erickson, J., Grund, M., Hecht, D., Jacobs, M., Joshi, I., Kuff, L., Kumar, D., Leblang, A., Li, N., Pandis, I., Robinson, H., Rorke, D., Rus, S., Russell, J., Tsirogiannis, D., Wanderman-Milne, S., & Yoder, M. (2015). Impala: A modern, open-source SQL engine for hadoop. In *CIDR*. www.cidrdb.org
31. Kroviakov, A., Kurapov, P., Anneser, C., & Giceva, J. (2024). Heterogeneous intra-pipeline device-parallel aggregations. In *DaMoN* (pp. 3:1–3:10). ACM.
32. Li, H., Berger, D. S., Novakovic, S., Hsu, L., Ernst, D., Zardoshti, P., Shah, M., Rajadnya, S., Lee, S., Agarwal, I., et al. (2023). Pond: CXL-based memory pooling systems for cloud platforms. In *ASPLOS*.
33. Maruf, H. A., Wang, H., Dhanotia, A., Weiner, J., Agarwal, N., Bhattacharya, P., Petersen, C., Chowdhury, M., Kanaujia, S. O., & Chauhan, P. (2023). TPP: Transparent page placement for CXL-enabled tiered-memory. In *ASPLOS (2023)* (pp. 742–755). ACM.
34. Micron Memory Expansion Module. Last Accessed: February 28, 2024.
35. Neumann, T. (2011). Efficiently compiling efficient query plans for modern hardware. *Proceedings of the VLDB Endowment, 4*(9), 539–550.
36. Neumann, T., & Freitag, M. J. (2020). Umbra: A disk-based system with in-memory performance. In *CIDR*. www.cidrdb.org.
37. Neumann, T., & Freitag, M. J. (2020). Umbra: A disk-based system with in-memory performance. In *CIDR*. www.cidrdb.org.
38. Oukid, I., Lasperas, J., Nica, A., Willhalm, T., & Lehner, W. (2016). Fptree: A hybrid SCM-DRAM persistent and concurrent b-tree for storage class memory. In *SIGMOD Conference* (pp. 371–386). ACM.
39. Pmem-Rocksdb. https://github.com/pmem/pmem-rocksdb. Accessed June 09, 2023.
40. Pmemkv. https://pmem.io/pmemkv/. Last Accessed: February 28, 2024.
41. Poutievski, L., Mashayekhi, O., Ong, J., Singh, A., Tariq, M. M. B., Wang, R., Zhang, J., Beauregard, V., Conner, P., Gribble, S. D., Kapoor, R., Kratzer, S., Li, N., Liu, H., Nagaraj, K., Ornstein, J., Sawhney, S., Urata, R., Vicisano, L., Yasumura, K., Zhang, S., Zhou, J., & Vahdat, A. (2022). Jupiter evolving: Transforming Google's datacenter network via optical circuit switches and software-defined networking. In *SIGCOMM* (pp. 66–85). ACM.
42. Pulte, C., Flur, S., Deacon, W., French, J., Sarkar, S., & Sewell, P. (2018). Simplifying ARM concurrency: Multicopy-atomic axiomatic and operational models for ARMV8. *Proceedings of the ACM on Programming Languages, 2*(POPL), 19:1–19:29.

43. Putnam, A., Caulfield, A. M., Chung, E. S., Chiou, D., Constantinides, K., Demme, J., Esmaeilzadeh, H., Fowers, J., Gopal, G. P., Gray, J., Haselman, M., Hauck, S., Heil, S., Hormati, A., Kim, J.-Y., Lanka, S., Larus, J. R. , Peterson, E., Pope, S., Smith, A., Thong, J., Xiao, P. Y., & Burger, D. (2014). A reconfigurable fabric for accelerating large-scale datacenter services. In *ISCA* (pp. 13–24). IEEE Computer Society.
44. Rydning, D. R. J. G. J., Reinsel, J., & Gantz, J. (2018). The digitization of the world from edge to core. *Framingham: International Data Corporation, 16*, 1–28.
45. Samsung CXL Memory Module. Last Accessed: February 28, 2024.
46. Sewell, P., Sarkar, S., Owens, S., Nardelli, F. Z., & Myreen, M. O. (2010). x86-TSO: A rigorous and usable programmer's model for x86 multiprocessors. *Communications of the ACM, 53*(7), 89–97.
47. Tirmazi, M., Barker, A., Deng, N., Haque, M. E., Qin, Z. G., Hand, S., Harchol-Balter, M., & Wilkes, J. (2020). Borg: The next generation. In *EuroSys* (pp. 30:1–30:14). ACM.
48. Torabzadehkashi, M., Rezaei, S., Heydarigorji, A., Bobarshad, H., Alves, V. C., & Bagherzadeh, N. (2019). Catalina: In-storage processing acceleration for scalable big data analytics. In *PDP* (pp. 430–437). IEEE.
49. van Renen, A., Vogel, L., Leis, V., Neumann, T., & Kemper, A. (2020). Building blocks for persistent memory. *The VLDB Journal, 29*(6), 1223–1241.
50. Vogel, L. (2023). *Adaptive Storage Structures*. PhD thesis, Technische Universität München.
51. Vogel, L., van Renen, A., Imamura, S., Giceva, J., Neumann, T., & Kemper, A. (2022). Plush: A write-optimized persistent log-structured hash-table. *PVLDB, 15*(11), 2895–2907.
52. Vogel, L., van Renen, A., Imamura, S., Leis, V., Neumann, T., & Kemper, A. (2020). Mosaic: A budget-conscious storage engine for relational database systems. *Proceedings of the VLDB Endowment, 13*(11), 2662–2675.
53. Zhou, X., Shou, L., Chen, K., Wei, H., & Chen, G. (2019). Dptree: Differential indexing for persistent memory. *PVLDB, 13*(4), 421–434.

Chapter 7
ReProVide: Query Optimization and Near-Data Processing on Reconfigurable SoCs for Big Data Analysis

Tobias Hahn, Maximilian Langohr, Andreas Becher, Lekshmi Beena Gopalakrishnan Nair, Klaus Meyer-Wegener, Jürgen Teich, and Stefan Wildermann

Abstract The available parallelism and heterogeneity of emerging computer systems must be exploited for being able to process the huge amounts of data produced every day. As a consequence, we observe an increasing research interest in accelerating database query processing on multi-cores and attached co-processors like Graphics Processing Units (GPUs) and Field-Programmable Gate Arrays (FPGAs). This chapter presents ReProVide, an approach combining near-data processing and FPGA-based acceleration. The System-on-Chip (SoC) architecture of ReProVide including a flexibly reconfigurable FPGA can load and execute hardware accelerators for various operators on relational and streaming data. Moreover, we present novel DBMS techniques for partitioning query-execution plans between a host and Reconfigurable data-Provider Units (RPUs) and for mapping operators onto RPUs by means of hardware reconfiguration.

7.1 Introduction

The exponential growth in the volume, velocity, and variety of data gathered on servers all around the world poses immense challenges. Analyzing petabytes of data with an affordable amount of time and energy requires a massively parallel processing of data at their source. Active research is therefore directed toward emerging hardware architectures to reduce data volume early and toward sound query analysis and optimization techniques to exploit such novel architectures.

T. Hahn · M. Langohr · L. B. G. Nair · K. Meyer-Wegener · J. Teich · S. Wildermann (✉)
Friedrich-Alexander-Universität Erlangen-Nürnberg (FAU), Erlangen, Germany
e-mail: tobias.hahn@fau.de; maximilian.langohr@fau.de; lekshmi.bgnair@york.ac.uk; klaus.meyer-wegener@fau.de; juergen.teich@fau.de; stefan.wildermann@fau.de

A. Becher
TU Ilmenau, Ilmenau, Germany
e-mail: andreas.becher@tu-ilmenau.de

K.-U. Sattler et al. (eds.), *Scalable Data Management for Future Hardware*,
https://doi.org/10.1007/978-3-031-74097-8_7

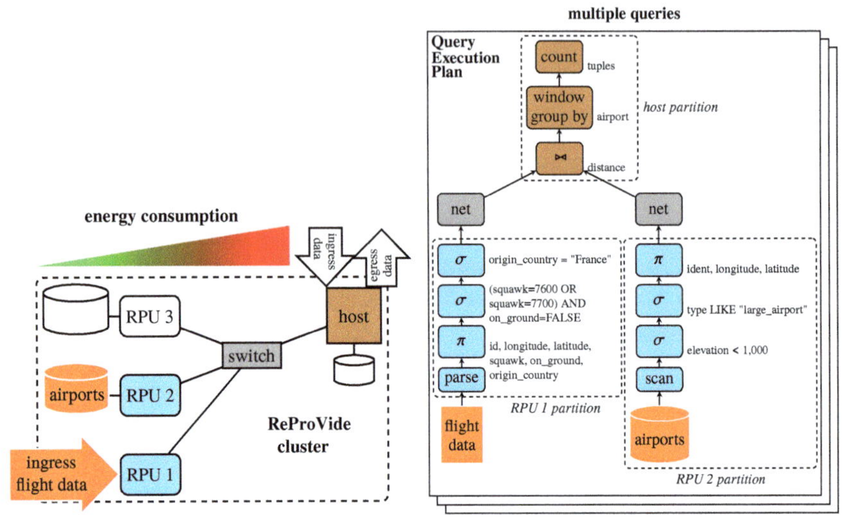

Fig. 7.1 Overview of a ReProVide cluster (left) where multiple RPUs are connected to a host, which schedules multiple applications (as shown by example right) on the cluster. RPUs can process relational data originating from local storage devices as well as ingress streaming data from external sources

The goal of ReProVide (**Re**configurable Data **ProVide**r) as illustrated in Fig. 7.1 is to investigate FPGA-based solutions for smart storage and near-data processing together with novel query-optimization techniques that exploit the speed and reconfigurability of FPGA hardware for a scalable and powerful (pre-)filtering of Big Data.

ReProVide is based on clusters of FPGA-based Programmable System-on-Chip (PSoC) architectures called Reconfigurable data-Provider Units (RPUs) (see Fig. 7.1, left). RPUs can serve as storage-attached devices, with direct interfaces to a multitude of memory and storage types (e.g., SSDs), but also network-attached devices to process ingress streaming data from external sources. For data processing and filtering, an RPU exploits the capabilities of dynamic (runtime) hardware reconfiguration of modern FPGAs to load pre-designed hardware accelerators on the fly. ReProVide is able to process user-defined queries or parts thereof in hardware in combination with CPU cores also available on the PSoC. Query-specific filtering provided by RPUs establishes the basis for drastically shrinking the huge amount of data already at its source, thus reducing the dominant factor of energy consumption in data-center networks: data transport.

For the integration of RPUs into a DBMS and exploiting their potential, we present novel optimization techniques for multiple objectives including end-to-end latency, throughput, and energy consumption of query processing. These determine which operations are worthwhile to be assigned to an RPU (see Fig. 7.1, right) by applying adequate cost models that take the capabilities and characteristics of an RPU into account. Moreover, the optimizer decides how to deploy and execute the assigned (sub-)queries or database operators on hardware accelerators, which are then mapped onto RPUs by means of hardware reconfiguration.

This chapter gives an overview of the underlying concepts of ReProVide. After presenting the related work in Sect. 7.2, Sect. 7.3 summarizes the hardware architecture of RPUs and how to use them for query-specific operation. Section 7.4 gives details of near-data processing of streaming data on RPUs. Section 7.5 then introduces the developed optimization techniques for managing queries in clusters consisting of multiple RPUs. Finally, Sect. 7.6 evaluates a hardware setup for near-data processing before the summary in Sect. 7.7.

7.2 Related Work

FPGAs are promising target architectures for modern query processing (see, e.g., [24]). This is facilitated by being able to implement parallel and deeply pipelined hardware circuits that are highly optimized for specific operations. At the same time, it is possible to exchange hardware modules at runtime to adapt the FPGA to changing queries and accelerate various query operators. There exist different approaches to using FPGA as accelerators for query processing (see also [24]). They can be directly attached to CPUs as *co-processors*, as, e.g., proposed in [38, 42, 57], and [21]. The CPU is responsible to transfer the data to the local memory of the FPGA, which can then process this input. However, as the size of the local memory is limited, multiple transfers may be required for calculating final results. This design choice is therefore inefficient for processing high volumes of data generated at high velocity. In *shared memory systems* (also called *IO-attached accelerators*; see [24]) as, e.g., proposed in [53–55] and [43], CPU and FPGA can both access the same main memory. While this helps avoid additional memory transfers, CPU and FPGA not only share the same memory but also memory buses. The bandwidth required by the accelerator can thus limit the processing speed of the CPU. *Near-data processing* systems such as [45, 58], and [56] differ significantly. Here, the FPGA is placed between the data source and the CPU (such deployed FPGAs are also called *bandwidth amplifiers*; see [24]). Even then it might not be possible to fully process a query on the FPGA, but it can significantly accelerate certain tasks such as filtering data. ReProVide follows the near-data-processing design principle.

Approaches for deploying FPGA accelerators in compute clusters and data centers often rely on existing frameworks for Big Data like Apache Spark [22, 37, 44] and Apache Storm [59]. These frameworks are tailored to batch or micro-batch processing. All of them assume a compute cluster where a global master node gathers the data, partitions them, and distributes the data partitions to worker nodes, which contain (PCIe-connected) FPGA co-processors (see, e.g., [31, 59]). Such approaches thus are based on *moving the data to the accelerators*. Yet, the main idea of near-data processing is to *move the accelerators to the data*. With the sheer amount of data stored in data centers and the speed at which data are arriving (data streams), moving data in data centers has become a performance bottleneck.

Reduction of data along the path from its source to its destination is therefore a viable means to improve performance and latency and can moreover lead to drastic energy savings, as shown in [4].

Exploiting the full potential of FPGA-based computing requires specialized techniques for integrating them into DBMS. With the introduction of high-performance processor units and new accelerators, database architecture has changed from centralized computing to multiple homogeneous and then to heterogeneous systems. This has made query optimization much more complex, addressing topics such as enhanced data and operator placement algorithms [34, 36], adaptive query-execution models [20, 35, 39], novel co-processing methodologies [13, 15–17], query optimizers that take hardware heterogeneity into account [5, 14, 18, 20, 36], and operator programming models to minimize development overheads [19]. While some approaches opt for hardware-oblivious algorithm design [2, 18, 30, 60], we decided to be hardware-conscious in order to achieve the best possible results, taking into account all hardware-specific characteristics while optimizing a query.

Karnagel et al. suggest the *HOP (Heterogeneity-conscious Operator Placement)* model to determine the best query-operator assignment to heterogeneous GPU processors [34, 36]. Their cost model measures the runtime per operator and computing unit, using their operator-execution model, which involves latency, data transfer, and execution prediction, as well as placement heuristics. However, it is limited to GPU. Similarly, Breß et al. look at a co-processor environment for operator placement and query chopping to prevent cache thrashing and heap contention [17]. However, their studies are also focused on GPU-based processing environments. The *HAPE (Heterogeneity-conscious Analytical queryProcessing Engine)* is proposed by Chrysogelos et al. [23] for effective and concurrent multi-CPU, multi-GPU query execution. It can achieve up to an 8x performance benefit over commercial CPU-GPU-based DBMS.

While current hardware-conscious query-processing methods have shown that the performance improvement and possibility of incorporating hardware knowledge into query processing is quite exciting, expanding these findings to an FPGA-based environment, especially in a near-data-processing system, remains a topic of active investigation. Hence in our work, we try to fill this gap by proposing a hardware-conscious optimizer for FPGA-based near-data processing. We focus on providing accurate hardware information to this optimizer and on implementing new optimization rules and cost models. We use this information to offload SQL queries/query operators to our near-data processing hardware according to its capabilities and dynamic state.

7.3 Heterogeneous Partially Reconfigurable Architecture for Near-Data Processing

Reconfigurable data-Provider Units (RPUs) form the basis of ReProVide clusters. In this section, we give an overview of the underlying hardware architecture that can be flexibly adapted by loading different accelerator modules via hardware reconfiguration. We moreover provide a summary of fundamental operations that can be accelerated on RPUs and how to cover various database operators with these accelerators.

7.3.1 Reconfigurable Data-Provider Unit (RPU) Architecture

ReProVide builds upon the synergies of a heterogeneous processing architecture consisting of CPU and reconfigurable hardware, which combines the flexibility and ease of software implementations with the energy efficiency and performance of specialized hardware implementations (see Fig. 7.1 (left)). Figure 7.2a[1] illustrates the concept and design of an RPU more closely (see also [5]). The RPU architecture contains a tightly-coupled *Processing System (PS)* and *Programmable Logic (PL)*. The RPU management has been implemented as part of the firmware and is running on one core of the processing system. While the PS could execute the full set of query operators, the performance might be inferior. Thus, data processing is mostly performed within the PL, i.e., the FPGA logic. The PL is divided into a *static* part, which contains all components that remain fixed, like hardware controllers and interfaces, and one or multiple *Partially Reconfigurable Areas (PRs)*. Hardware

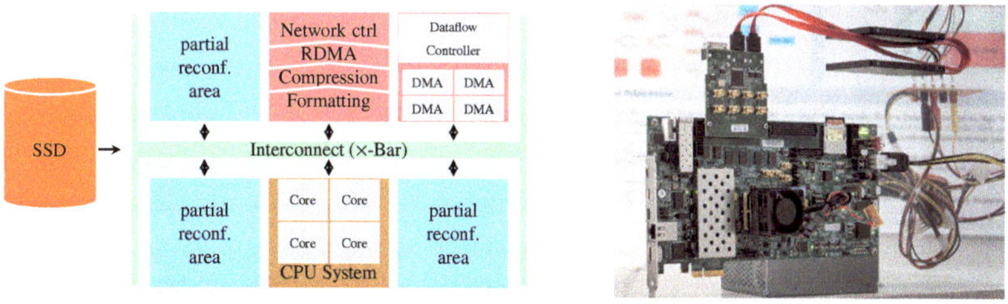

(a) RPU architecture (b) RPU prototype

Fig. 7.2 (**a**) ReProVide platform architecture that encompasses statically implemented hardware modules like a Network Controller, a Scan Controller, and diverse memory resources, as well as partially reconfigurable areas PR_i for hardware accelerator modules. (**b**) RPU prototype implemented on a Xilinx Zynq All Programmable SoC

[1] https://doi.org/10.1007/s13222-020-00363-7, CC BY 4.0.

accelerators can be dynamically loaded into these PRs and configured to process operations on data streams. The accelerators can be exchanged dynamically via hardware reconfiguration. The number and area of the PRs are decided during the design phase and constrained by the overall amount of reconfigurable resources available on the chosen FPGA as well as the resource requirements of the static system components. The system-management software runs on the CPU system for controlling the platform for query processing, e.g., reconfiguration of partial regions, setting configuration registers of accelerators and memory addresses of Direct Memory Access (DMA) controllers, as well as configuring the network interface. This RPU design has been implemented using existing FPGA technology like the Xilinx Zynq All Programmable SoC (see Fig. 7.2b), which contains programmable (FPGA) logic, multi-core CPUs, and peripherals.

7.3.2 Determining a Query-Specific Configuration for RPUs

ReProVide builds upon partially reconfigurable hardware-accelerator modules. Various hardware designs to accelerate a wide range of fundamental operations of query processing have been developed as part of ReProVide. Table 7.1 provides an overview of operations covered by ReProVide, the supported data types, and the references describing details about their implementation. One or multiple of these designs can be synthesized, instantiated, and loaded into one of the partially reconfigurable areas (PRs).

The fundamental question is now which of such pre-synthesized accelerators to select and how to configure the PR of the RPU platform for being able to process a query. First, the given query is formally described by a Query Execution Plan (QEP) that specifies the order in which operations have to be applied on input

Table 7.1 Operations for which hardware designs have been developed in ReProVide

Operation	Supported data type	Publication
Scan operator	*all*	[3, 5, 8]
Avro parsing	Avro records	[26, 27]
JSON parsing	JSON records	[29]
Raw filtering	JSON records	[25, 28]
Arithmetic $+, -, *, /$	INTEGER, UNSIGNED, FLOAT	[3]
Comparison $<, \leq, =, \neq, \geq, >$	INTEGER, UNSIGNED, FLOAT	[3, 25, 26, 28, 29]
Comparison $=, \neq$	VARCHAR	[3, 25, 26, 28, 29]
Boolean function evaluation	BOOLEAN	[3, 25, 26, 28, 29]
Regular expression matching	VARCHAR	[3, 9]
Hash join	INTEGER, UNSIGNED, FLOAT	[3, 10]
MIN, MAX, SUM, COUNT	INTEGER, UNSIGNED, FLOAT	[3, 7]
Histograms	INTEGER, UNSIGNED, FLOAT	[3]

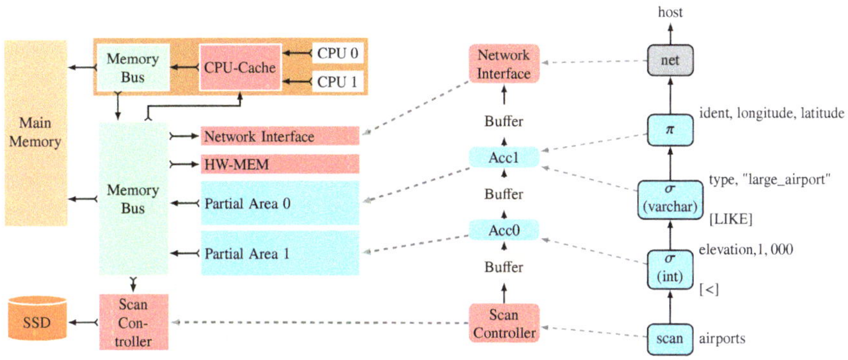

Fig. 7.3 Left: Architecture of an RPU [5]. Middle: Buffer and accelerator allocation. Right: Example query plan (RPU 2 partition from Fig. 7.1). The query-placement problem includes allocating buffers and accelerators for operators of a given query plan and subsequently mapping these onto the PRs, CPUs, and memory of the RPU

data. Figure 7.1 (right) illustrates such a plan and also highlights two partitions that should be mapped onto two RPUs. For determining the query-specific configuration of an RPU, we assume that the set of pre-synthesized hardware modules is available in an accelerator library denoted by L. Moreover, the query is represented by a QEP containing a set of operators O. As illustrated in Fig. 7.3, the first step for generating the query-specific configuration is to allocate a set of accelerator instances A from L. Then, each operator node $o \in O$ of the query plan has to be mapped to an accelerator that supports the operations that are required to implement the respective operator (Sect. 7.3.3 gives more details which set of query operators is supported and thus can be implemented via the developed hardware designs summarized in Table 7.1). As exemplified by accelerator $Acc1$ in Fig. 7.3, accelerators may be synthesized such that they can be dynamically configured to support multiple operators. Furthermore, buffers have to be allocated between the selected accelerators for enabling data exchange between subsequent operations. The problem of determining a query-specific configuration on the reconfigurable target platform can then again be formalized as a mapping problem for deciding how to assign the allocated accelerators to PR and buffers to the memories available on RPUs. Details of solving this query-placement problem are discussed in [5].

7.3.3 RPU-Supported Operators and Operations

The RPU architecture is designed to process data streams stemming from locally connected storage devices (like SDDs) as well as for processing data obtained from network streaming sources such as IoT devices. Operations performed on such data streams can be divided into pipelined (non-blocking) operations and pipeline-breaking (blocking) operations (see, e.g., [6]). Examples of the latter category are sorting and joining data as well as machine-learning algorithms such as clustering. They require the complete data or at least a huge amount of data tuples to be available for processing and also have random data-access patterns. Implementing such operators in hardware on FPGAs is often inefficient or even not feasible due to the restricted local memory and hardware resources and relatively low clock frequencies of FPGAs. As even large data paths containing multiple accelerators may not be able to cover complete queries, the aim of near-data processing on RPUs is therefore to load accelerators that allow to reduce the amount of data that a DBMS subsequently has to process as much as possible. *A key prerequisite of ReProVide is that each operation can execute at I/O rate so that no processing step introduces any throughput penalty.* Next, we give a brief summary of supported operators and which RPU operations are available to implement these (see Table 7.1). The discussed operators are also part of the example query in Fig. 7.1 (right).

Scan Operator (Scan) The RPU provides a dedicated and parameterizable hardware component called *Scan Controller* [5] to perform the *scan* operator. It is based on ReOrder units as presented first in [8]. The controller can be programmed to gather data from multiple locations (i.e., attached storage devices) and then provide them in the expected order. A DBMS using an RPU for near-data processing may request data using a specified schema (row-store or column-store layout), while the data source (e.g., the locally connected storage of the RPU) might store the data in another schema.

Parsing Operator (Parse) In many Big-Data applications, in particular data-stream processing, the data originates from external sources. The incoming data is usually encoded in an exchange format, such as JSON or Avro, to provide a standardized interface. Also, with the popularity of NoSQL databases, more and more data is stored in such formats. RPUs therefore provide hardware acceleration for parsing, as detailed in Sect. 7.4.2.

Selection Operator (σ) Separating relevant data tuples from irrelevant data is fundamental in query processing. ReProVide supports filtering on arithmetic expressions and comparisons on INTEGER, UNSIGNED, and FLOAT data types. Moreover, filtering based on string matching is supported. Although regular-expression matching is a complex operation, it is supported as discussed in Sect. 7.3.4. Multiple of such comparisons can be concatenated by means of Boolean functions to form complex filtering conditions.

Projection Operator (π) Only picking those attributes that are relevant for subsequent queries, the application, or the user is another fundamental operator of query processing. This can be easily implemented in hardware, by only writing or reading the relevant attributes in registers. Particularly, the Scan Controller (see above) can be programmed to only selectively read those data from the data source that are actually required.

Join Operator ($\bowtie$) Joining data from multiple data sources is another fundamental database operator. Joins are blocking operators. Nonetheless, ReProVide provides support for hash joins, as discussed in Sect. 7.3.4.

Aggregation Operators Such operators calculate values by iterating over multiple tuples, for example, counting tuples (COUNT), accumulating values of attributes (SUM), or determining their average, maximum (MAX), or minimum (MIN). ReProVide provides hardware designs for most of these. Aggregating over virtually infinite data streams requires windows. This is discussed in Sect. 7.4.2.

Statistics Calculation Statistics about the data are relevant for DBMS particularly for query optimization (see [48, 49]). It has been shown in [32] that accelerators to generate statistics can be implemented with basically no execution-time overheads by using additional hardware resources. However, in [7], we presented a technique on how they can be generated even without having to reserve additional FPGA resources. We achieve this in ReProVide by making use of dynamic partial reconfiguration to exchange hardware accelerators at runtime according to the query to execute. These accelerators are loaded into PRs. Locations and sizes of these regions on the FPGA are fixed at design time. However, accelerators for query processing do often not allocate all available resources in such regions. In [7], we presented modules for gathering statistical information that can be added to accelerator designs using such free FPGA resources. These include counters as well as maximum, minimum, average, and histograms over attribute values (see [7] and [3]). So, besides implementing the previously enumerated operators, the accelerator can produce statistical information as a by-product.

7.3.4 Optimistic Filtering to Support Complex and Blocking Operators

One challenge is developing reconfigurable hardware accelerators for complex and/or blocking operators. Some operators might not satisfy the limited memory or resource constraints on an FPGA, while some may be inefficient when blocking. Thus, in order to support as much data filtering/reduction as possible on an RPU without blocking, we have introduced the concept of *optimistic filtering* for complex and/or blocking operators such as regular-expression matching [9] and hash joins [10]. An *optimistic filtering operator* is an operator delivering an over-approximation of the result data, driven by the goal to reduce the amount of result data as much as possible. In effect, the resulting data stream of an optimistic filtering operator may still contain false-positive tuples that do not match the original operator's condition (e.g., tuples with no matching key in the case of hash joins [10], or text documents that do not match a regular expression [9]). To deliver exact results, the operator still has to be performed again, e.g., in software on the host, but on a typically much smaller set of data. One prerequisite of ReProVide remains: *Optimistic operators should process the data at I/O rate*. Only in this case it is guaranteed that throughput is not penalized. So, with the significantly reduced amount of data, not only the overall execution time but also the energy consumption has been shown to be reduceable (see [10]).

7.4 Near-Data Processing of Streaming Data

In many Big-Data applications like the Internet of Things (IoT) and Industry 4.0, the data originates from external sources. Stream processing has emerged as a crucial approach to continuously process and analyze data as it is generated or received.

The query plan in Fig. 7.1 (right) illustrates a typical stream-processing query on a *flight data* stream. The incoming data is usually encoded in an exchange format, such as JSON [12] or Avro [1], to provide a programmer-friendly and extensible application interface. The first step in the stream-processing pipeline has then to be parsing the input data into a format that is easier for the machine to use. A projection is often applied directly during parsing to extract only the wanted attributes. Subsequently, filter expressions are analyzed to filter out entire tuples. Next, the data may be joined with other data. Here, two fundamental types of joins can be distinguished. A *static join* joins the elements of the data stream with tuples of a relational table, as is the case with the join ($\bowtie$) of *flight data* and *airports data* in Fig. 7.1. On the other hand, two streams can also be joined against each other. However, as streams are usually unbound, this must be performed via a bounded window, which can then be joined like a traditional relation. In the same way, windows are used to apply aggregate functions in stream processing. Such windows can be bounded by a fixed number of tuples, e.g., the last 100 tuples. Alternatively, a time-based boundary can be used, e.g., all tuples in the last 10 seconds.

Parsing is essential for processing of data streams. However, parsing can pose a severe bottleneck: [41] reports that Big-Data applications can spend between 80 and 90% of their execution time on parsing.

In the following, we present near-data-processing techniques to avoid this bottleneck, discussing a concept of optimistic filtering in Sect. 7.4.1 as well as concepts for hardware-based parsing in Sect. 7.4.2.

7.4.1 Raw Filtering for Optimistic Data-Stream Processing

JSON data is a byte stream of ASCII-encoded data. So-called Raw Filters were introduced in [25, 51] for applying filter expressions directly to a raw JSON byte stream, e.g., inserted between the *flight data* source and the parse operator in Fig. 7.1. The most basic Raw Filters are string comparisons that check whether a string occurs anywhere in a given JSON record. For example, one of the selection operators (σ) from the exemplary query in Fig. 7.1 checks whether the attribute *origin_country* is equal to the value "France." A respective Raw Filter might check only whether the string "France" occurs anywhere in the record and passes on records with a match. By doing so, even if no false negatives are generated, false positives might occur through this optimistic filtering (see Sect. 7.3.4). Such false positives would then be filtered out later in the stream-processing pipeline they have been parsed, and the filter condition has been checked.

As raw filtering follows the paradigm of optimistic filtering, the approach can be further simplified by performing even the string search itself optimistically. To do this, a given search string of size N characters can be broken down into smaller n-grams of $n \leq N$ characters, each of which is to be searched for. For example, for the search string "France" and $n = 2$, this would be "Fr," "ra," "an," "nc," and "ce." If at least $N - n + 1$ n-grams match (in the example, $6 - 2 + 1 = 5$ n-grams), the entire search string is considered to match. We describe this concept called *block partitioning* in [25] including an FPGA hardware implementation with a minimized resource cost.

In addition to string comparisons, filter expressions frequently involve number comparisons, which can be used to further increase the selectivity. As JSON encodes numerical values in ASCII format, filtering for specific numbers can be mapped to a string search. To also support numerical comparisons including $<$, $\leq$, $>$, and $\geq$, we introduced a raw-filtering technique in [25] for mapping any such comparison to a regular expression, which can then be implemented in hardware by a Finite State Machine (FSM).

Usually, filter expressions contain multiple comparisons combined via logical operators (*and*, *or*, *xor*, *not*). To cover these cases, individual Raw Filters can also be combined using Boolean expressions. Note that in case of an *or* or *xor* expression in the filter operation, all operands must be evaluated, whereas in case of an *and* expression, one or multiple operands may be omitted even in optimistic filtering at the expense of an increased number of false positives.

For the correct processing of stream-processing pipelines, parsing becomes indispensable. Only then can operators such as projection and filtering be carried out accurately. Nevertheless, it may still be worthwhile to use Raw Filters before parsing, as these can significantly reduce the effective data volume to be processed by the subsequent operators.

7.4.2 *Parse-Filter-Project: Selective Data-Stream Parsing*

In general, the complexity of parsing is highly dependent on the data format used. Here, one important characteristic of the data format is whether it is *schema-based* or *schema-free* since schema-free formats require the parser to reconstruct the schema itself. Another distinction, particularly interesting for hardware processing, is whether the data is binary or ASCII-encoded. ASCII-encoded formats tend to be very sparse. However, the conversion of data types such as numerical values into binary format becomes more complex. In the following, the parsing of two semi-structured formats, strongly differing in the above characteristics while being also widely used in stream-processing systems, will be discussed. These are *JSON* [12], an ASCII-encoded schema-free format, and *Avro* [1], a binary-encoded schema-based format.

In both cases, two fundamental tasks have to be carried out during parsing. One is *schema tracing*, where the current position of the input data in the given schema needs to be identified in schema-based formats. In schema-free formats, a schema reconstruction must be performed instead. The other fundamental task is *data conversion*, for example, the conversion of numerical values into binary format. Here, it is advantageous to perform the projection directly during parsing, as then only the relevant attributes required by subsequent operators need to be converted. In addition, we show in [29] for JSON that the integration of the projection into the parser may greatly simplify schema tracing, since irrelevant parts of the schema only need to be checked for their structural correctness.

7.4.2.1 Avro Parsing

The sequence of attributes in Avro is pre-determined by a given schema. For tracing the schema, we propose in [26] to map it to a nested FSM, with each state representing an attribute. The state of the current attribute remains active until the respective attribute has been completely parsed. States for complex data types such as records or arrays again contain a nested FSM that traces their respective sequence. A peculiarity of Avro is the encoding of integers, which follows a variable-length format. Numbers with a small absolute value therefore require fewer bytes than numbers with a larger absolute value. Each byte of an encoded integer contains a continuation bit that indicates whether a subsequent byte follows. A straightforward approach for hardware acceleration of Avro data parsing [26] needs to process only one byte at a time. For being able to reach a parsing throughput that matches the I/O rate, independent records are simultaneously processed on multiple parallel parser modules. It is also possible to apply simple filter expressions on the parsed attributes. Moreover, projections are realized by only connecting the registers of required attributes to the accelerator output.

In [27], we present an alternative solution to Avro parsing in the form of an application-specific instruction set processor (ASIP) architecture design. An instruction program controls the ASIP to parse a specific schema. Any schema change therefore only requires the loading of a new instruction sequence into an instruction memory, thus requiring neither resynthesis nor reconfiguration.

7.4.2.2 JSON Parsing

An advantage when parsing JSON data is its sparsity, which can be exploited to derive resource-efficient implementations, e.g., as shown in [29] for FPGAs. This sparsity is illustrated in the example depicted in Fig. 7.4, where three attributes, *id*,

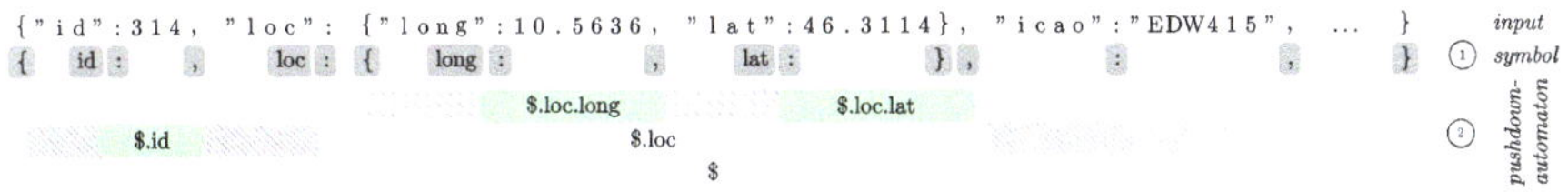

Fig. 7.4 JSON parser flow example for projecting attributes *id*, *loc.long*, and *loc.lat* from a flight record

lat (latitude), and *long* (longitude), are projected, where the *lat* and *long* attributes are part of the nested attribute *loc* (location).

Only structural characters (i.e., { , } , [,] , : , ,) and key strings (i.e., id , loc , long , lat) are relevant to track the current projection paths within a JSON record. This information is first extracted from the stream ① and encoded in symbols. The number of data to be processed is thus significantly reduced (in the example, the overall 71 ASCII input characters is reduced to 17 symbols, corresponding to a reduction down to 23.9%). The symbols are then passed to a pushdown automaton ② that keeps track of the current position in the JSON record. Since pushdown automatons are difficult to parallelize in hardware, a decent symbol reduction is necessary in the extraction step ① to achieve line rate. Whenever a new hierarchy level is reached in the stream, an uninitialized state is pushed onto the automaton's stack (areas filled with hashed patterns in the figure). Whenever a relevant key symbol is observed in the correct state according to the given projection path, the state is initialized correspondingly (areas filled without pattern). Furthermore, if this state represents the end of a path of the projected attribute (green areas in the figure), the extraction of the respective attribute is triggered.

The extracted data must then be converted into the desired data type. In JSON, this conversion is particularly complex for integers and floats but can be easily parallelized as extracted attributes can be processed independently of each other. The number of type-conversion units can then be matched to the throughput requirements of the numbers to be processed, so that the I/O rate is sustained with a minimum of resources.

7.5 Query Optimization for Heterogeneous ReProVide Clusters

Connecting an RPU, as introduced, to a database and/or data-stream management system on a host—to make its power usable in query processing—leads to a *heterogeneous* system. This can be seen in Fig. 7.1 on page 172. A network must be used in establishing the connection, which must be fast enough in order not to thwart the benefits. This is a simple version of a *distributed* system, with all the challenges coming with those systems. And the two types of processors on both sides—the CPUs on each RPU and the standard CPU on the host—require very different ways of optimizing the query processing. The first specific architectural problem of the ReProVide project is that the data in the current version only flows from the RPU to the host, and this only happens when a query is being processed. So the host has no knowledge of the data (except for the schema). This must be overcome.

The second problem is that we want to support line-rate data processing, because that is the most appropriate way of using an FPGA (see Sect. 7.2). However, the set of operators used in query processing is large, and not every operator can be implemented efficiently on an FPGA (Sect. 7.3.3). So the set of operators suitable for execution on the RPU is smaller—which makes the two systems even more heterogeneous.

The third problem is the near-data processing w.r.t. the storage device (an SSD in our prototype) or the ingress data stream. This should take substantial load from the following processing units downstream, i.e., the RPU itself, the network, and the host. It is in competition with many proposals for smart devices, e.g., [33, 52].

And finally we have to accept that resources on an FPGA even today are limited. The reconfigurable regions allow for adaptation to a large set of queries (a starting point for the whole project years ago). However, such a region is only capable of being loaded with a module that has been specifically synthesized for it. All of this must be taken into account when planning query execution. Still, we have built a prototype that successfully demonstrated the execution of queries at the EDBT conference 2020 [48].

7.5.1 Holistic Query Optimization

Confronting the multifaceted challenges outlined in the preceding paragraphs, we have devised the following methodologies to manage the intricacies involved in query optimization.

Based on an initial distinction between a *global* and a *local optimizer* in [47], we propose a unified holistic optimization framework. A fundamental principle of this revised methodology is encapsulated in the concept of "one fact, one place." This paradigm mandates the consolidation of all optimization-relevant information, such as statistical data, schema details, and data placement, into a singular, centralized *query repository* (Sect. 7.5.3.3). This streamlining of information flow not only enhances efficiency but also contributes to a more cohesive and effective optimization process. By centralizing data, our system gains the ability to more accurately allocate resources, leading to more predictable outcomes when executing queries. The required information for optimizing our system is acquired through a combination of probe queries (Sect. 7.5.3.2) and continuous monitoring of data streams as they traverse our query-execution engine. Additionally, maintaining a historical record of executed queries in the query repository provides valuable insights on possible query sequences. These sequences, typically characterized by a consistent series of queries with varying parameters, are common in certain applications. In our previous research, detailed in [47], we explored the potential of exploiting such patterns to optimize the placement of accelerators on our RPU. By recognizing these query sequences, we can strategically position accelerators on the RPU to maximize performance, thereby enhancing the overall efficiency of query execution within our system. This integration of historical data and predictive analytics into our holistic approach represents a significant advancement in our ability to fine-tune our system for optimal performance.

7.5.2 *Optimizing Relational and Stream-Based Queries for Heterogeneous Systems*

In this section, we present our innovative query optimizer, KR@KEN. Figure 7.5 illustrates the core components of our system on the left and outlines the comprehensive optimization process on the right. KR@KEN enables the optimization of both relational and stream-based queries across heterogeneous and distributed environments. Central to our system is the cost model (see Sect. 7.5.2.2), which facilitates the integration of various hardware platforms (such as x86 and FPGA) and supports query optimization over multiple platforms. Taking into account the hardware resources available and the user's expectations (see Sect. 7.5.2.4), we determine the most suitable accelerator for executing the query.

7.5.2.1 Plan Enumeration and Selection

The formulation of alternative QEP and the subsequent selection of the most cost-effective approach present complex challenges, fraught with potential pitfalls. A consistent element within our system has been the incorporation of Apache Calcite [11]. This open-source framework is instrumental in constructing database and streaming systems, distinguished by its sophisticated optimization capacities, its compatibility with diverse data sources, and its support for stream-data processing. For our hierarchical optimizer COPRAO [50], we modified and extended Apache Calcite using our own optimization rules. We also implemented algorithms to predict the execution of certain queries based on query sequences [49]. For our new holistic optimizer KR@KEN, Calcite's role is confined to functioning as an SQL parser, which translates SQL statements into preliminary logical query execution plans (QEP). These plans undergo further refinement through KR@KEN, which employs dynamic programming coupled with a suite of predefined transformation rules to modify and optimize segments of our execution plan. A novel cost model, specifically designed to address the nuances of distributed systems and to leverage modern hardware advancements like our RPU, is utilized to ascertain the most economical execution plan. This cost model, in conjunction with our resource model, enables the generation of execution plans that are not only optimized for

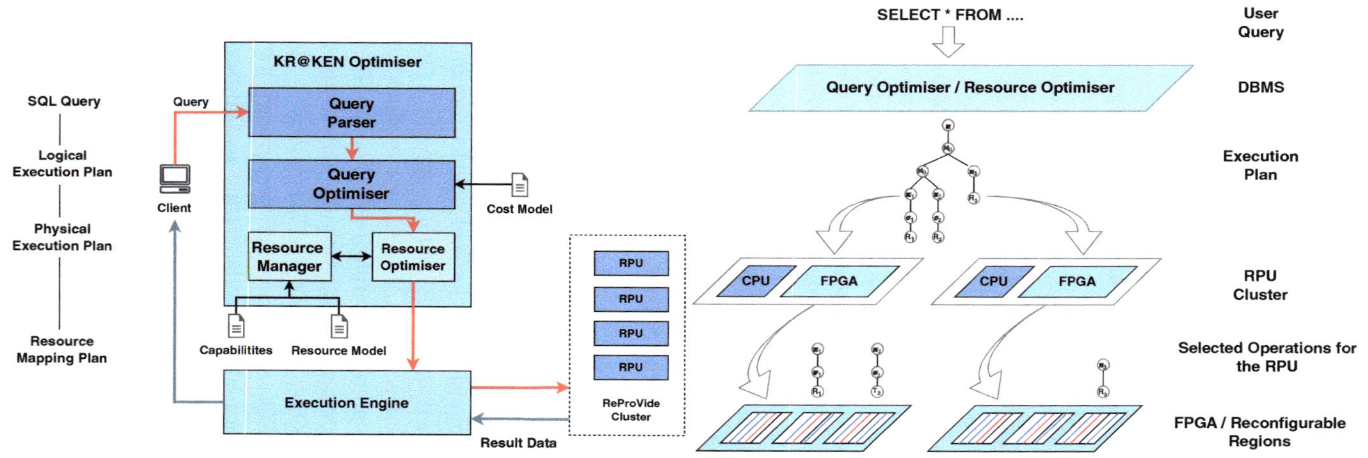

Fig. 7.5 Overview of the KR@KEN optimizer (left) and the optimization process from query to accelerator placement (right)

performance but also meticulously tailored to the limited processing resources available on our FPGAs.

7.5.2.2 A Cost Model for Heterogeneous Query Processing

Modelling costs for heterogeneous systems, which encompass not only standard x86 CPUs but also network components and FPGAs, pose significant challenges. Traditional cost models in the realm of database query optimization have predominantly focused on factors such as CPU usage, I/O operations, and cardinality estimations. These factors are critical for the host query-execution engine, yet they do not comprehensively address the complexities and unique characteristics of a system that integrates diverse hardware components like FPGAs. Acknowledging this gap, we developed a hardware-independent cost model tailored to evaluate costs pertinent to the end-to-end performance of queries in such a heterogeneous environment. This model diverges from traditional approaches by considering a broader spectrum of performance indicators. The key components of our model are:

End-to-End Latency (t)**:** Our model takes into account the total time a tuple takes from the input (storage or receiving from the network) to the user or application that has issued the query. This end-to-end latency measurement is crucial in heterogeneous systems where data might traverse through various processing units (like CPUs, FPGAs, and network routers) each contributing to the total processing time.

Throughput (r)**:** The model also evaluates throughput, which is the amount of data (rows) processed in a given time frame. In a system combining CPUs, FPGAs, and network components, throughput becomes a critical measure, as each component can have varying data-processing capabilities and speeds.

Energy Consumption (e)**:** Given the varied power requirements of different components in a heterogeneous system, our model assesses the energy consumption relative to the tasks performed. This approach ensures a more sustainable and cost-effective utilization of resources, especially important in systems where FPGAs and network components may have different power profiles compared to standard CPUs.

In addition to the aforementioned components, there is also auxiliary information used in the cost model. This auxiliary information is not included in the comparison of two execution plans, but it is required to calculate the cost components. Depending on the type of query—relational or stream-based—different sets of auxiliary information are incorporated.

Number of tuples (n_{tuples})**:** An estimation of the number of tuples the operator will produce (relational queries only).

Tuple size (s_{tuple})**:** The number of bytes of each tuple the operator produces, determined using the execution plan.

Output rate (r_{out})**:** An estimation of the number of tuples per (nano)second the operator will output (streaming queries only).

Maximum throughput ($r_{\max}$): The theoretically possible maximum throughput the operator can achieve.

By integrating cost components with the auxiliary information, we can now define the cost tuple for any given operator as follows:

$$C_{rel}(op) = [t(op), r(op), e(op)] \quad \text{with} \quad Aux_{rel}(op) = [n_{tuples}, s_{tuple}, r_{\max}]$$

$$C_{stream}(op) = [t(op), r(op), e(op)] \quad \text{with} \quad Aux_{stream}(op) = [r_{out}, s_{tuple}, r_{\max}]$$

The values for the whole QEP are those of the last operator in the plan. Cardinality estimations and statistics are used to determine these values. In order to compare two QEP with each other, we use a function mapping the three costs to a scalar value. To do this, we use a weighted function, where w_t, w_r, and w_e represent a weight we multiply with the associated cost. The weights provided in our system can be adjusted by the user to place greater emphasis on certain cost components, depending on their specific expectations for hardware usage.

$$Cost(plan) = t(plan) \times w_t + (r_{\max}(plan) - r(plan)) \times w_r + e(plan) \times w_e$$

Since the goal is to minimize the cost, and while the throughput should be maximized, the cost calculation uses the maximum achievable throughput (over all operators) and subtracts the actual throughput.
To optimize queries effectively, it is crucial to estimate cardinalities. Cardinalities (n_{tuples}, r_{out}) are just one aspect we need to consider for our cost model. It also relies on a variety of other hardware and implementation-depending parameters, e.g., number of instructions per second, block-read time, and many more. We developed a micro-benchmark suite to measure these values, enabling us to tailor our model to the specific characteristics of the underlying hardware. The benchmark uses our own execution engine to run multiple tests with varying filter expressions and projections. For estimating cardinalities, we currently employ a sample-based approach, which is updated periodically. We also include statistics collected using our query repositories. This includes statistics we create using, for example, probe queries (see Sect. 7.5.3.2).

7.5.2.3 Example Query and Execution Plans

In order to illustrate the capabilities of our cost model, we will look at a small example demonstrating how it helps us optimize queries. The execution plan we want to be optimized can be seen in Fig. 7.6 (left). It performs a series of operators (parsing, selection σ, projection π) on a stream S. Moreover, Fig. 7.6 displays four possible QEPs (plan A to D) the optimizer could create during query optimization. Plan A represents a configuration in which all data is processed on the host. This is of course possible but highly inefficient as we have to parse the incoming JSON data, which requires a lot of processing power. Our goal is now to offload as many

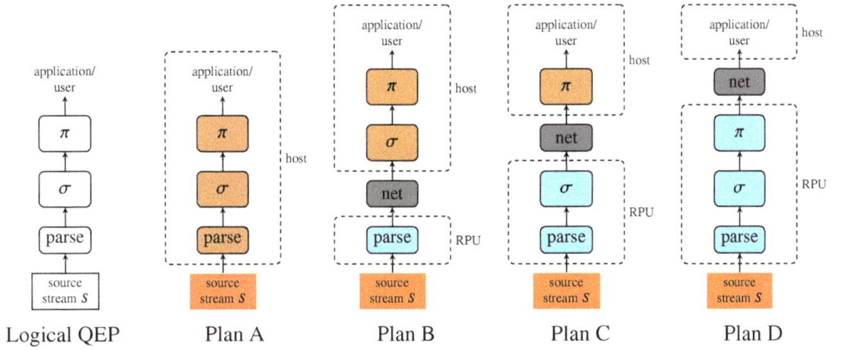

Fig. 7.6 Example of a logical query execution plan (left) and four possible execution plans for partitioning operators (parsing, selection σ, projection π) between RPU and host

Table 7.2 List of exemplary execution plans shown in Fig. 7.6 together with their estimated cost

Plan	Execution order	Latency	Throughput	Energy	Cost
A	$\pi_{host}(\sigma_{host}(scan_{host(S)}))$	54.079	0.016	3	89.17
B	$\pi_{host}(\sigma_{host}(net(scan_{rpu}(S))))$	62.70	0.020	3	97.40
C	$\pi_{host}(net(\sigma_{rpu}(scan_{rpu}(S))))$	60.12	0.012	2	84.71
D	$net(\pi_{rpu}(\sigma_{rpu}(scan_{rpu}(S))))$	48.74	0.020	1	65.51

scan includes parsing, π = projection, σ = filter, *net* = network transmission

operations as possible to the RPU. Table 7.2 shows the cost of the plans A to D according to Fig. 7.6. As we can see, plan D has the lowest cost. This QEP would push down all operations to the RPU and would only require the network transfer to the host in order to send the data to the user. The calculations used in the table cannot be listed here explicitly due to lack of space.

7.5.2.4 Managing Limited Hardware Resources and Accelerators

In managing the limited processing resources of/on RPUs, it is essential to strategize the resource allocation for each query based on user expectations and system capabilities. Figure 7.5 (right) shows this last step, where the KR@KEN optimizer has to choose the right accelerator based on these requirements. We offer multiple strategies to utilize the available resources on the RPU.

Event Monitoring: Event-monitoring queries, typically employed for monitoring production lines or sensor networks, are designed to run for extended periods, often spanning weeks or months. Due to their long-running nature, the latency between initiating the query and beginning the processing of tuples is less critical compared to other use cases. For optimizing these long-running queries, we can provide users with the option to synthesize accelerators tailored specifically to their query. These custom accelerators are designed to occupy a minimal amount of resources on the FPGA, making them an efficient choice for prolonged operations where space efficiency and sustained performance are key considerations.

Regular Reporting: Queries of this type, typically executed on a daily, weekly, or monthly basis, often differ only in a few parameters, such as dates or business unit IDs. For these scenarios, we provide pre-synthesized accelerators designed with the flexibility to modify specific values. This approach allows for efficient reuse of the accelerators while accommodating the minor variations in query parameters.

Realtime BI: For this highly dynamic use case, where a rapid response time between issuing the query and receiving results is crucial, we cannot afford the time required to synthesize accelerators. Instead, we need to deploy programmable accelerators. These programmable accelerators, while consuming more space on the FPGA, offer greater processing flexibility. This trade-off is essential to meet the demand for quick query-turnaround times, making them a suitable choice for scenarios where speed is a priority.

7.5.3 Learning from the Past: Offline Optimization to Improve Query Optimization

We will now finally look at offline optimization, which has the important task to prepare everything for online optimization. This includes data from history and statistics. A very important decision concerns the *placement of data*: Which table should be stored in the RPU and not on the host itself? And which stream should be received by the RPU and not by the host? If we have more than one RPU in operation, these questions must be answered for each of them. A substantial characterization of the expected workload is a prerequisite of such a decision.

7.5.3.1 Detecting Query Sequences

As we presented in Sect. 7.5, query sequences are very helpful in optimizing the reconfiguration and placement of accelerators in the RPU. This requires, however, that we have identified such query sequences first. Database query logs are a good source for that, and our own query executor also logs any query it has seen. Still it is not easy to identify repeated query sequences in such a log because each repetition varies at least a bit. This of course refers to the constants used in the queries, often in comparisons of filter expressions. But even the number of queries can vary, while you would still consider it to be the same query sequence. This is because of loops in the application programs that issue the queries. How a detection of sequences can still be automated is discussed in Beena Gopalakrishnan Nair's PhD thesis [46].

7.5.3.2 Probe Queries

While the RPU can send many messages to inform the host about the data it stores, this traffic tends to disturb the operation of the system. An alternative are the so-called probe queries, which are sent to the RPU in spare times. The host can generate them tailored to its information needs, and they are executed just as any other query, yielding a whole set of useful information for the optimizer, e.g., real cardinalities, execution times, and throughput values. They might particularly make use of statistics calculations as presented in Sect. 7.3.3.

7.5.3.3 Query Repository

To efficiently store and manage the wealth of information discussed in the preceding sections, we developed a query repository. This repository archives all queries executed on our system, along with comprehensive statistics related to our sources, including relations and streams. Furthermore, it accommodates our cost models and execution plans. Such consolidation of data within the repository facilitates the identification of query sequences, as highlighted in Sect. 7.5.3.1, enabling us to glean insights from historical data. Through the application of statistical methods, we can now more accurately characterize the workload encountered by our system. This enhanced understanding allows us to refine our cost and resource models (as part of offline optimization), ensuring they are optimally aligned with our operational requirements and objectives.

7.6 Experimental Evaluation

This section presents an experimental evaluation of ReProVide by means of a case study on processing real-world data. This case study is based on SKYSHARK.[2] We developed SKYSHARK [40] as a comprehensive benchmark tailored for evaluating heterogeneous stream-processing systems like ReProVide clusters. The benchmark is derived from a combination of real-world, publicly accessible air-traffic surveillance data (ADS-B) and relational data, such as information on airports and aircrafts. The benchmark leverages a rich dataset amassed from a broad network of receivers contributing to the OpenSky Network,[3] a collaborative open-source project dedicated to the collection and storage of ADS-B messages. This dataset is characterized by its complexity and breadth, encompassing detailed information on aircraft movements, flight paths, and airport operations. To enhance its applicability for benchmarking, the dataset has been thoughtfully augmented

[2] https://skyshark.org

[3] https://opensky-network.org/

with additional details about the aircrafts and airports, enriching its utility for performance evaluation while preserving the original data's integrity. The SKYSHARK benchmark also includes a set of diverse queries, which are designed to rigorously test a system's performance across various operational scenarios, ranging from simple data retrieval to intricate analytical tasks. Accompanied by a specialized benchmarking tool, SKYSHARK facilitates the measurement of system latency and throughput, offering researchers a robust framework for assessing stream-processing capabilities.

For the following experiments, we selected two queries on the dataset provided by SKYSHARK to evaluate the near-data processing capabilities of ReProVide.

Query 7.1 Searches for flight data tuples with specific transponder codes (squawk):

```
SELECT id,icao24,callsign,longitude,latitude,
    baro_altitude
FROM states
WHERE squawk = 1000 OR squawk = 7120 OR squawk = 7637
```

Query 7.2 Searches for flight data tuples with a more complex filtering condition based on altitude, vertical velocity, and transponder code:

```
SELECT id,icao24,callsign,longitude,latitude,
    baro_altitude
FROM states
WHERE baro_altitude > 10668 AND
  (vertical_rate < -0.33 OR
  ((squawk = 8600 OR squawk = 1000) AND vertical_rate <
      -4.88)
  )
```

The QEPs of both queries thus are a sequence of parse, selection, and projection operators and consequently follow the form as also depicted in Fig. 7.6 (left).

A dataset consisting of 100,000 flight data JSON records with an overall size of 38 MB is stored in the main memory of an RPU as representative for both the scenarios where data comes from an attached SSD or from an external data source via Ethernet. In both cases, the data would be buffered in main memory to be subsequently processed by the RPU. For each query, we have evaluated four query execution plans that follow the structure of the plans illustrated in Fig. 7.6: In *Plan A*, the JSON data is transmitted to the host which is in charge of parsing and processing the data. In *Plan B*, each JSON record is parsed by a hardware accelerator. Tuples only containing the attributes required for further processing are transmitted to the host. In *Plan C*, the selection operator and, in *Plan D*, all operators are hardware accelerated on the RPU before transmission.

The basic idea of near-data processing is to reduce the data volume and velocity close to the source at the rate of data generation (i.e., at I/O rate). For our analysis, we therefore measured the input rate (RPU reading from the main memory) and output rate (RPU sending over the network) in both MB/s and tuples/s. The results

Table 7.3 Results measured on an RPU implemented on a Xilinx ZCU106 Zynq SoC for executing queries 1 and 2 according to the four different plans A to D, giving the average over 100 runs per query and plan. For plan A, a tuple corresponds to a JSON record. For all other plans, a tuple is an ordered list of attributes

	Size of sent data [MB]	Time [ms]	Input rate [MB/s]	Output rate [MB/s]	Input tuple rate [tuple/s]	Output tuple rate [tuple/s]
Query 1						
Plan A	38.023	77.03	493.7	493.7	1,298,373	1,298,373
Plan B	4.012	59.50	631.5	67.5	1,681,749	1,681,749
Plan C	0.860	35.99	1043.9	23.9	2,779,779	595,596
Plan D	0.856	35.92	1045.9	23.9	2,785092	596,734
Query 2						
Plan A	38.022	77.52	490.6	490.6	1,290,234	1,290,234
Plan B	4.814	65.86	570.4	73.1	1,518,970	1,518,970
Plan C	0.079	30.09	1248.5	2.6	3,324,640	712,337
Plan D	0.066	30.15	1246.1	2.2	3,318,337	710,987

for executing both queries according to plans A to D are shown in Table 7.3. It displays the input and output rates as well as the execution time for processing the query including the reconfiguration time for loading the respective accelerator. Both the size of sent data and the output rate, but also the overall execution time for processing a query, are significantly reduced by near-data processing on the RPU, without degrading the input rate. The reduction becomes even greater the more operations are outsourced to the RPU (plans C and D). Also the input rates increase here. This is because the ARM CPU on the RPU has to set memory addresses and to control the network transfers. If the amount and rate of data is reduced, this also relieves the CPU on the RPU so that the overall system performance increases. This case study assumes that accelerators for the query are already synthesized and can be loaded on the platform when processing a query. If they had to be generated first, an additional overhead would be incurred for the synthesis. For the accelerators used in the above experiments, the synthesis time was around 20 minutes.

7.7 Summary

The core of the ReProVide methodology is to use reconfigurable near-data query-processing systems called RPUs for processing data at its source. RPUs can be configured to apply various operations on relational as well as streaming data to filter out relevant data tuples before pushing them further to a DBMS. Only transmitting this information-rich subset of data to the host system has the potential of significantly reducing the dominant factor of power consumption in data-center networks: data transport. An explicit focus in the design of RPUs was laid on the I/O-rate processing capability and the coverage of a wide range of queries. For optimally utilizing RPUs for query processing, novel optimization techniques are required that take into account which operators can be accelerated in hardware and the overhead for loading the respective accelerator module. We have particularly identified optimization strategies that can be used to implement heuristics for query partitioning and discussed how statistical information, e.g., about query sequences, can furthermore help design these systems in terms of synthesizing hardware accelerators and partitioning the data.

Acknowledgments This work has been funded by the Deutsche Forschungsgemeinschaft (DFG, German Research Foundation)—361498444.

References

1. Apache Software Foundation. *Apache Avro 1.11.0 Specification.*
2. Balkesen, Ç., Teubner, J., Alonso, G., & Özsu, M. T. (2015). Main-memory hash joins on modern processor architectures. *IEEE Transactions on Knowledge and Data Engineering, 27*(7), 1754–1766.
3. Becher, A. (2022). *Near-Data Query Processing on Heterogeneous FPGA-based Systems.* PhD Thesis, Friedrich-Alexander-Universität Erlangen-Nürnberg.
4. Becher, A., Bauer, F., Ziener, D., & Teich, J. (2014). Energy-aware SQL query acceleration through FPGA-based dynamic partial reconfiguration. In *: 2014 24th International Conference on Field Programmable Logic and Applications, FPL 2014, Munich, 2–4 September* (pp. 1–8)
5. Becher, A., Herrmann, A., Wildermann, S., & Teich, J. (2019). ReProVide: Towards utilizing heterogeneous partially reconfigurable architectures for near-memory data processing. In *1st Workshop on Novel Data Management Ideas on Heterogeneous (Co-)Processors (NoDMC)* (pp. 51–70).
6. Becher, A., Lekshmi, B. G., Broneske, D., Drewes, T., Gurumurthy, B., Meyer-Wegener, K., et al. (2018). Integration of FPGAs in database management systems: Challenges and opportunities. *Datenbank-Spektrum, 18*(3), 145–156.
7. Becher, A., & Teich, J. (2019). In situ statistics generation within partially reconfigurable hardware accelerators for query processing. In *15th International Workshop on Data Management on New Hardware (DaMoN)* (pp. 20:1–20:3).
8. Becher, A., Wildermann, S., Mühlenthaler, M., & Teich, J. (2016). ReOrder: Runtime datapath generation for high-throughput multi-stream processing. In *International Conference on Reconfigurable Computing and FPGAs (ReConFig)* (pp. 1–8).
9. Becher, A., Wildermann, S., & Teich, J. (2018). Optimistic regular expression matching on FPGAs for near-data processing. In *14th International Workshop on Data Management on New Hardware (DaMoN)* (pp. 4:1–4:3). ACM.
10. Becher, A., Ziener, D., Meyer-Wegener, K., & Teich, J. (2015). A co-design approach for accelerated SQL query processing via FPGA-based data filtering. In *International Conference on Field Programmable Technology (FPT), Queenstown, December 7–9* (pp. 192–195).
11. Begoli, E., Camacho-Rodríguez, J., Hyde, J., Mior, M. J. , & Lemire, D. (2018). Apache Calcite: A foundational framework for optimized query processing over heterogeneous data sources. In *SIGMOD* (pp. 221–230). ACM.
12. Bray, T. (2017). *The JavaScript Object Notation (JSON) Data Interchange Format.* RFC 8259.
13. Breß, S. (2013). Why it is time for a HyPE: A hybrid query processing engine for efficient GPU coprocessing in DBMS. *PVLDB, 6*(12), 1398–1403.
14. Breß, S. (2014). The design and implementation of CoGaDB: A column-oriented GPU-accelerated DBMS. *Datenbank-Spektrum, 14*(3), 199–209.

15. Breß, S., Beier, F., Rauhe, H., Sattler, K.-U., Schallehn, E., & Saake, G. (2013). Efficient co-processor utilization in database query processing. *Information Systems, 38*(8), 1084–1096.
16. Breß, S., Beier, F., Rauhe, H., Schallehn, E., Sattler, K.-U., & Saake, G. (2012). Automatic selection of processing units for coprocessing in databases. In *ADBIS* (pp. 57–70).
17. Breß, S., Funke, H., & Teubner, J. (2016). Robust query processing in co-processor-accelerated databases. In *SIGMOD* (pp. 1891–1906).
18. Breß, S., Heimel, M., Saecker, M., Kocher, B., Markl, V., & Saake, G. (2014). Ocelot/HyPE: Optimized data processing on heterogeneous hardware. *PVLDB, 7*(13), 1609–1612.
19. Breß, S., Köcher, B., Funke, H., Zeuch, S., Rabl, T., & Markl, V. (2018). Generating custom code for efficient query execution on heterogeneous processors. *The VLDB Journal, 27*(6), 797–822.
20. Breß, S., Schallehn, E., & Geist, I. (2012). Towards optimization of hybrid CPU/GPU query plans in database systems. In *New Trends in Databases and Information Systems, Workshop ADBIS* (pp. 27–35).
21. Casper, J., & Olukotun, K. (2014). Hardware acceleration of database operations. In *The 2014 ACM/SIGDA International Symposium on Field-Programmable Gate Arrays, FPGA '14, Monterey, CA- February 26–28, 2014* (pp. 151–160). ACM.
22. Chen, Y.-T., Cong, J., Fang, Z., Lei, J., & Wei, P. (2016). When spark meets FPGAs: A case study for next-generation DNA sequencing acceleration. In *8th USENIX Workshop on Hot Topics in Cloud Computing (HotCloud 16)*, Denver, CO. USENIX Association.
23. Chrysogelos, P., Sioulas, P., & Ailamaki, A. (2019). Hardware-conscious query processing in GPU-accelerated analytical engines. In *CIDR*.
24. Fang, J., Mulder, Y. T. B., Hidders, J., Lee, J., & Hofstee, H. P. (2020). In-memory database acceleration on FPGAs: A survey. *The VLDB Journal, 29*(1), 33–59.
25. Hahn, T., Becher, A., Wildermann, S., & Teich, J. (2022). Raw filtering of JSON data on FPGAs. In *Conference & Exhibition on Design, Automation & Test in Europe*.
26. Hahn, T., Schüll, D., Wildermann, S., & Teich, J. (2023). An FPGA Avro parser generator for accelerated data stream processing. In *2nd Workshop on Novel Data Management Ideas on Heterogeneous (Co-)Processors (NoDMC)*.
27. Hahn, T., Schüll, D., Wildermann, S., & Teich, J. (2024). ABACUS: ASIP-based Avro schema-customizable parser acceleration on FPGAs. In *IEEE Proceedings of the 27th International Symposium on Design and Diagnostics of Electronic Circuits & Systems*.
28. Hahn, T., Wildermann, S., & Teich, J. (2022). Auto-tuning of raw filters for FPGAs. In *32nd International Conference on Field Programmable Logic and Applications*.
29. Hahn, T., Wildermann, S., & Teich, J. (2023). SPEAR-JSON: Selective parsing of JSON to enable accelerated stream processing on FPGAs. In *33rd International Conference on Field Programmable Logic and Applications*.
30. Heimel, M., Saecker, M., Pirk, H., Manegold, S., & Markl, V. (2013). Hardware-oblivious parallelism for in-memory column-stores. *PVLDB, 6*(9), 709–720.
31. Huang, M., Wu, D., Yu, C. H., Fang, Z., Interlandi, M., Condie, T., & Cong, J. (2016). Programming and runtime support to blaze FPGA accelerator deployment at datacenter scale. In *7th ACM Symposium on Cloud Computing, SoCC '16* (pp. 456–469). ACM.
32. Istvan, Z., Woods, L., & Alonso, G. (2014). Histograms as a side effect of data movement for big data. In *SIGMOD* (pp. 1567–1578). ACM.
33. Jo, I., Bae, D.-H., Yoon, A. S., Kang, J.-U., Cho, S., Lee, D. D. G., & Jeong, J. (2016). YourSQL: A high-performance database system leveraging in-storage computing. *PVLDB, 9*(12), 924–935.
34. Karnagel, T., Habich, D., & Lehner, W. (2015). Local vs. global optimization: Operator placement strategies in heterogeneous environments. In *Workshops EDBT/ICDT* of *CEUR Workshop Proceedings* (Vol. 1330, pp. 48–55).
35. Karnagel, T., Habich, D., & Lehner, W. (2017). Adaptive work placement for query processing on heterogeneous computing resources. *PVLDB, 10*(7), 733–744.
36. Karnagel, T., Habich, D., Schlegel, B., & Lehner, W. (2014). Heterogeneity-aware operator placement in column-store DBMS. *Datenbank-Spektrum, 14*(3), 211–221.

37. Kim, H., Myung, R., Hong, B., Yu, H., Suh, T., Xu, L., & Shi, W. (2019). SafeDB: Spark acceleration on FPGA clouds with enclaved data processing and bitstream protection. In *12th International Conferences on Cloud Computing (CLOUD)* (pp. 107–114).
38. Koch, D., & Torresen, J. (2011). FPGASort: A high performance sorting architecture exploiting run-time reconfiguration on FPGAs for large problem sorting. In *Proceedings of the 19th ACM/SIGDA International Symposium on Field Programmable Gate Arrays*, FPGA '11 (pp. 45–54). Association for Computing Machinery.
39. Kohn, A., Leis, V., & Neumann, T. (2018). Adaptive execution of compiled queries. In *ICDE* (pp. 197–208).
40. Langohr, M., Vogler, T., & Meyer-Wegener, K. (2023). SKYSHARK: A benchmark with real-world data for line-rate stream processing with FPGAs. In *LWDA, CEUR Workshop Proceedings* (Vol. 3630, pp. 12).
41. Li, Y., Katsipoulakis, N. R., Chandramouli, B., Goldstein, J., & Kossmann, D. (2017). Mison: A fast JSON parser for data analytics. *PVLDB, 10*(10), 1118–1129.
42. Manev, K., Vaishnav, A., Kritikakis, C., & Koch, D. (2019). Scalable filtering modules for database acceleration on FPGAs. In *10th International Symposium on Highly-Efficient Accelerators and Reconfigurable Technologies, HEART 2019, Nagasaki, June 6–7, 2019* (pp. 4:1–4:6). ACM.
43. Moghaddamfar, M. (2023). *Database System Acceleration on FPGAs*. PhD Thesis, Technische Universität Dresden.
44. Morcel, R., Ezzeddine, M., & Akkary, H. (2016). FPGA-based accelerator for deep convolutional neural networks for the SPARK environment. In *International Conference on Smart Cloud (SmartCloud)* (pp. 126–133).
45. Müller, R., Teubner, J., & Alonso, G. (2010). Glacier: A query-to-hardware compiler. In *SIGMOD* (pp. 1159–1162). ACM.
46. Nair, L. B. G. (2021). *Capability Aware Query Optimizer For An FPGA-Based Near-Data Processor*. PhD thesis, Friedrich-Alexander-Universität Erlangen-Nürnberg.
47. Nair, L. B. G., Becher, A., & Meyer-Wegener, K. (2020). The ReProVide query-sequence optimization in a hardware-accelerated DBMS. In *16th International Workshop on Data Management on New Hardware (DaMoN)* (pp. 17:1–17:3). ACM.
48. Nair, L. B. G., Becher, A., Meyer-Wegener, K., Wildermann, S., & Teich, J. (2020). SQL query processing using an integrated FPGA-based near-data accelerator in ReProVide. In *Extending Database Technology* (pp. 639–642).
49. Nair, L. B. G., Becher, A., Wildermann, S., Meyer-Wegener, K., & Teich, J. (2021). Speculative dynamic reconfiguration and table prefetching using query look-ahead in the ReProVide near-data-processing system. *Datenbank-Spektrum, 21*(1), 55–64.
50. Nair, L. B. G., & Meyer-Wegener, K. (2021). COPRAO: A capability aware query optimizer for reconfigurable near data processors. In *IEEE 37th International Conference on Data Engineering Workshops (ICDEW)* (pp. 54–59).
51. Palkar, S., Abuzaid, F., Bailis, P., & Zaharia, M. (2018). Filter before you parse: Faster analytics on raw data with sparser. *PVLDB, 11*(11), 1576–1589.
52. Salamat, S., Aboutalebi, A. H., Khaleghi, B., Lee, J. H., Ki, Y.-S., & Rosing, T. (2021). NASCENT: Near-storage acceleration of database sort on SmartSSD. In *FPGA* (pp. 262–272). ACM.
53. Sidler, D., István, Z., Owaida, M., & Alonso, G. (2017). Accelerating pattern matching queries in hybrid CPU-FPGA architectures. In *SIGMOD* (pp. 403–415). ACM.
54. Sidler, D., Owaida, M., István, Z., Kara, K., & Alonso, G. (2017). doppioDB: A hardware accelerated database. In *27th International Conference on Field Programmable Logic and Applications, FPL 2017, Ghent, September 4–8* (p. 1). IEEE.
55. Stuecheli, J., Blaner, B., Johns, C. R., & Siegel, M. S. (2015). CAPI: A coherent accelerator processor interface. *IBM Journal of Research and Development, 59*(1), 7:1–7:7.
56. Teubner, J., Woods, L., & Nie, C. (2013). XLynx—an FPGA-based XML filter for hybrid XQuery processing. *ACM Transactions on Database Systems, 38*(4), 1–39.

57. Wang, Z.-k., Paul, J., Cheah, H. Y., He, B., & Zhang, W. (2016). Relational query processing on OpenCL-based FPGAs. In *26th International Conference on Field Programmable Logic and Applications, FPL, Lausanne, August 29–September 2* (pp. 1–10). IEEE.
58. Woods, L., István, Z., & Alonso, G. (2014). Ibex: An intelligent storage engine with support for advanced SQL offloading. *PVLDB, 7*(11), 963–974.
59. Wu, S., Hu, D., Ibrahim, S., Jin, H., Xiao, J., Chen, F., & Liu, H. (2019). When FPGA-accelerator meets stream data processing in the edge. In *39th International Conference on Distributed Computing Systems (ICDCS)* (pp. 1818–1829).
60. Zhang, S., He, J., He, B., & Mian, L. (2013). OmniDB: Towards portable and efficient query processing on parallel CPU/GPU architectures. *PVLDB, 6*(12), 1374–1377.

Chapter 8
Scalable Data Management on Next-Generation Data Center Networks

Matthias Jasny, Tobias Ziegler, and Carsten Binnig

Abstract The landscape of distributed Database Management Systems (DBMSs) has been fundamentally transformed by advancements in data center network technologies. Traditionally, these systems were designed to minimize network communication, which was perceived as a significant bottleneck. However, with the advent of high-speed networks and technologies such as Remote Direct Memory Access (RDMA), this perception is changing. RDMA allows direct memory access to remote machines at speeds comparable to local memory access, challenging the long-standing belief that network communication is inherently slow. This chapter explores how the evolution of data center networks, mainly through RDMA, has enabled new designs for disaggregated databases. Moreover, the chapter delves into programmable networks as a solution beyond RDMA. In particular, this chapter provides an overview of RDMA and programmable networks and introduces novel ideas for optimizing databases in disaggregated setups using RDMA. Furthermore, two approaches are highlighted that leverage programmable networks in addition to RDMA to improve the efficiency of disaggregated databases even further: P4DB, which leverages programmable data planes for in-network OLTP processing, and zero-sided RDMA, a network-driven data shuffling method that enhances communication efficiency between heterogeneous accelerators. By showcasing these advancements, we demonstrate how database systems can utilize specialized networking hardware to achieve unprecedented performance levels. The chapter concludes with a summary and discussion of future research directions in the field of data center network technologies and their impact on distributed DBMSs.

M. Jasny (✉) · T. Ziegler · C. Binnig
Technische Universität Darmstadt, Darmstadt, Germany
e-mail: matthias.jasny@cs.tu-darmstadt.de; tobias.ziegler@cs.tu-darmstadt.de; carsten.binnig@cs.tu-darmstadt.de

K.-U. Sattler et al. (eds.), *Scalable Data Management for Future Hardware*,
https://doi.org/10.1007/978-3-031-74097-8_8

8.1 Introduction

Evolution of Data-Center Networks Advancements in data center networks have dramatically transformed the landscape of distributed Database Management Systems (DBMSs). Historically, these systems implemented complex strategies to minimize or bypass network communication, operating under the assumption that the network was a significant bottleneck.

This traditional view is now being challenged by the advent of high-speed networks and new technologies such as Remote Direct Memory Access (RDMA). RDMA revolutionizes data access across networks by enabling direct memory access to a remote machine's memory nearly as fast as accessing local memory. This development invalidates the long-standing belief that network communication is inherently a significant bottleneck.

Given these advancements, a major change has occurred in how we build database systems for the cloud.

Disaggregation Using Fast Interconnects The trends in data center networks have enabled new designs for distributed databases. With the performance improvement of networks, there has been a shift toward disaggregation, separating compute and storage or even accelerator pools from traditional compute [7, 12, 26, 38]. Nowadays, most cloud-native systems are disaggregated since they offer improved resource utilization, as each resource can be scaled independently based on demand. However, since all data is accessed over the network, considerable attention has been paid to developing fast network solutions. Major cloud vendors deploy Remote Direct Memory Access (RDMA) to enable efficient resource disaggregation [2, 4, 52]. In database use cases, RDMA has successfully improved the performance for distributed join operators [6, 34], reduced the cost of concurrency control [12], and made storage access [50] possible at unprecedented speeds.

Programmable Networks: Beyond RDMA RDMA has undeniably revolutionized efficient networking by optimizing the network stack with dedicated DMA engines in the NIC and a more streamlined protocol. However, as bandwidth and message rates continue to increase, RDMA alone is no longer sufficient. To illustrate, a 400G network stack can deliver a new packet every 3 nanoseconds, while an L3 cache access typically takes around 10 nanoseconds.

Furthermore, when examining Fig. 8.1a, we observe that CPU frequencies have plateaued with the end of Moore's Law, indicating that CPUs are not increasing in speed. This means we cannot rely on increasing frequencies to improve our networking performance. In contrast, Fig. 8.1b shows that network bandwidth continues to rise; this year, 400G Ethernet was standardized, and 1TB is expected soon. We argue that this mismatch between CPU speed and network bandwidth development underscores the need for further specialization in network technology—we need to look beyond RDMA.

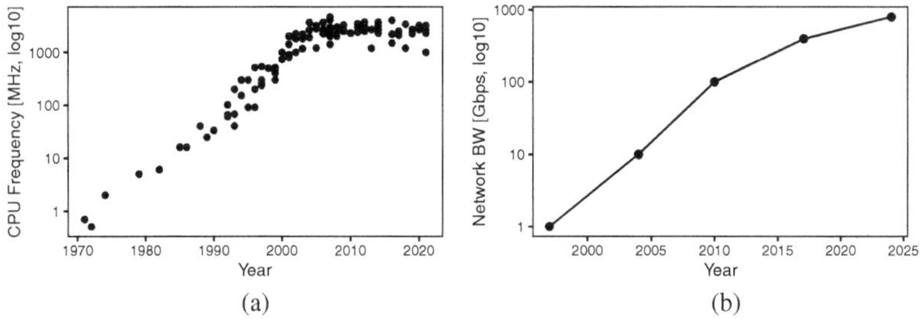

Fig. 8.1 CPU frequency and network bandwidth development over the last years. (**a**) CPU frequency. (**b**) Network bandwidth

Outline In the remainder of the chapter, in Sect. 8.2, we will first provide the necessary background on RDMA and programmable networks. Afterward, we will then provide an overview of novel ideas we have developed to adjust databases in disaggregated setup to make efficient use of RDMA . Furthermore, we will then do a deep dive into two approaches that leverage programmable networks and demonstrate how database systems can utilize specialized networking hardware: (1) Sect. 8.4 is dedicated to P4DB and its use of programmable data planes for in-network OLTP processing. (2) Sect. 8.5 explores the concept of network-driven data transfers and its role in efficient RDMA-based communication between heterogeneous accelerators. Finally, we will conclude with a summary and discuss interesting future avenues.

8.2 Background

8.2.1 Remote Direct Memory Access (RDMA)

RDMA has become the state-of-the-art communication method for distributed data-processing systems over high-speed networks [7, 40, 43, 44, 54]. Its main benefit is that it removes the overhead of traditional kernel-space network stacks such as TCP/IP. Major cloud vendors have already adopted RDMA in their pursuit of faster networking with little CPU overhead. An example of this is Microsoft Azure, which reports that already around 70% of internal ToR traffic is RDMA [4].

Communication schemes in RDMA can be categorized as one-sided (READ-/WRITE) or two-sided (SEND/RECEIVE) operations, which refer to the involvement of the sender and receiver in the communication. For one-sided operations, only the sender is actively involved and thus has to decide where the data should be placed on the remote node; see Fig. 8.2. With two-sided operations, the receiver is also actively involved in the communication and decides where to place data by issuing RECEIVE requests before SEND requests can be issued on the sender side.

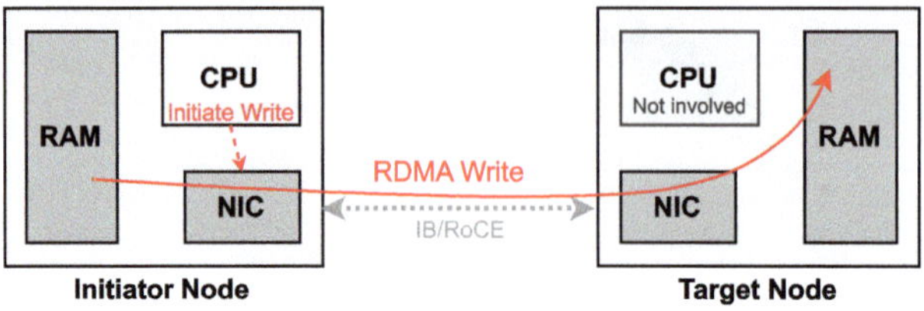

Fig. 8.2 One-sided RDMA allows access to remote memory directly without involving the remote CPU. Read, Write, and Atomic operations are executed by the remote NIC

This scheme simplifies remote memory management and resembles message-based data exchanges.

Especially the one-sided RDMA operations have seen high adoption in distributed data-processing systems since they allow sender nodes to write into remote memory directly, fully bypassing CPU cores of the receiving nodes [6, 51]. This led to the crystalization of new computing architectures that use network-attached memory to allow systems to scale memory independent from compute [7].

RDMA communication can run over different transport types, such as Reliable Connection or Unreliable Datagram. The most commonly used transport is the Reliable Connection, which requires stateful connections between any end-points. The reliability is provided through acknowledgments and re-transmissions. While Unreliable Datagram has the lowest complexity and overhead, most systems require reliable data transfers and need to implement it manually in the application with added CPU overhead [20, 21]. In addition, Unreliable Datagram only supports two-sided operations. Thus, for the following contributions, we exclusively use Reliable RDMA Connections, as one-sided operations are essential to achieving network-initiated communication, and reliability is vital for most systems.

8.2.2 Programmable Switches

Programmable switches have gained widespread adoption in data centers, offering a significant advantage to traditional fixed-function switches by enabling flexible, high-speed packet-processing capabilities. These capabilities allow for processing rates of several billion packets per second, attributed to the programmable packet-processing pipeline. In networking, the control plane, typically running on the network device's CPU, makes routing decisions, while the data plane handles the actual packet processing and routing, directing traffic to its destinations.

The programmability of the data plane is achieved through a reconfigurable architecture utilizing match-action tables, enabling not just data routing but also the offloading of application-specific logic via custom match-action rules. The P4 language, designed for creating these rules, facilitates packet-processing definition within the data plane with a C-like syntax but disallows features like pointers and

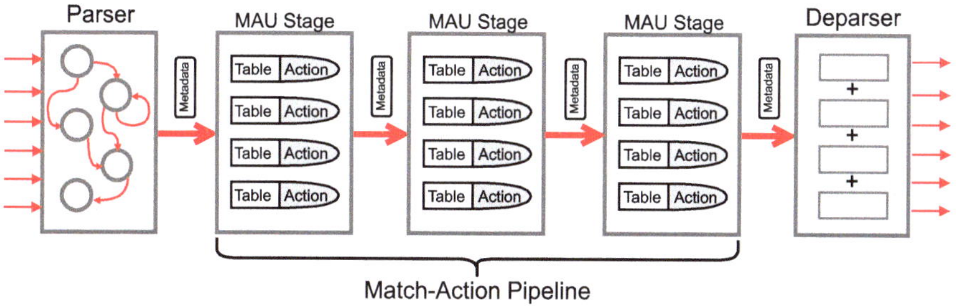

Fig. 8.3 The Protocol Independent Switch Architecture (PISA): all stages (Parser, MAU Stages, and Deparser) are programmable and allow flexible packet processing in the data plane based on packet headers and metadata

loops to ensure efficiency. This approach has broadened P4's application beyond network switches to devices like SmartNICs and FPGAs, enabling the efficient implementation of performance-sensitive applications directly on the switch.

A key implementation of this concept is the Protocol Independent Switch Architecture (PISA), widely used in commercially available programmable switches to run P4 programs (Fig. 8.3). PISA promotes protocol independence, allowing for flexible packet processing based on packet headers and metadata through declarative match-action tables. In the P4DB project, for instance, we leverage this architecture to integrate a transaction processing engine into the switch, employing customized match-action rules for this purpose.

PISA-based switches handle specialized match-action rules starting with the parsing of a network packet's header in the ingress phase, which may include both routing data and metadata to trigger specific match-action rules in the switch's Match-Action Units (MAUs). These MAUs, organized in a pipeline, process packets in parallel, ensuring that each stage handles one packet at a time. For optimal processing, interdependent match-action rules are sequenced in successive MAU stages, allowing a packet to be processed sequentially through the pipeline before being sent to its destination.

While PISA provides an abstract model for switch architecture, it still offers vendors the flexibility to introduce specific implementations, such as additional parsers for tunnel processing or specialized components for checksum computation or executing stateful operations within the MAUs.

8.3 Scalable Data Management with RDMA

RDMA has arguably had a significant impact on database design [12, 13, 20, 50, 51, 53, 54, 54], though it presents distinct challenges due to its complexity and different communication paradigm. To provide more context, we will provide a concise overview of our research and discuss how RDMA is reshaping modern database

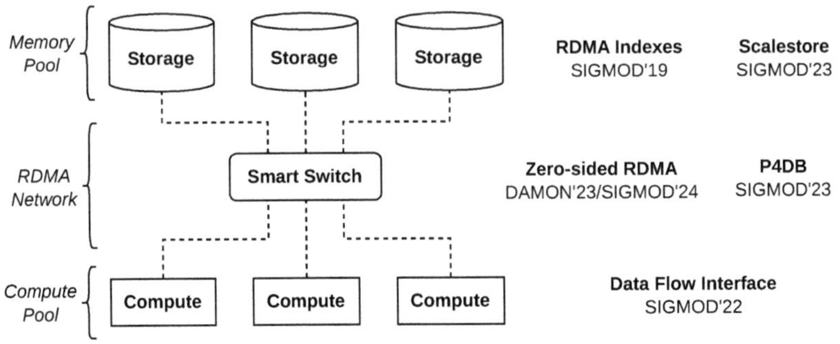

Fig. 8.4 Overview of the relevant topics related to Scalable Data Management with RDMA

systems in the following. In particular, we discuss challenges and opportunities in distributed DBMSs that have emerged from advancements in modern data center networks using RDMA. An overview of the topics we will discuss is shown in Fig. 8.4

Programming Abstractions: The Data Flow Interface

RDMA, as discussed above, has become an indispensable tool for building disaggregated database systems [12, 13, 24, 29, 32, 43, 45]. Unfortunately, RDMA is also complicated since it provides only low-level abstractions (RDMA verbs) for data processing [12]. Thus, adapting database systems for RDMA demands substantial effort to manage various low-level details, including remote memory and connection management, and selecting the most suited RDMA verb (cf. Sect. 8.2) for specific workloads.

In this chapter, we introduce the Data Flow Interface (DFI), an abstraction layer designed to simplify the utilization of high-speed networks for data-processing systems. DFI offers simple interfaces that are well suited for a wide range of data-intensive applications, ensuring predictable performance with minimal overhead compared to customized, ad hoc solutions. Like the high-performance computing abstraction MPI, we designed DFI to provide an efficient and effective way to leverage high-speed data-processing networks. However, unlike MPI, which was tailored for computation-intensive tasks like large-scale simulations, DFI is optimal for data-intensive workloads [23]. As a result, DFI revises many design choices in MPI that are not well suited for data-intensive workloads, leading to its very limited adoption for data-processing systems [5].

The main idea of DFI is that data movements are represented as *flows*. DFI flows are abstractions that provide primitives for efficient network communication. These primitives are intended to be a foundation for building data-intensive systems and provide many benefits over MPI (e.g., thread-centricity, pipelined communication). DFI flows are higher-level abstractions than existing ones, such as [12, 14]. By lifting the level of abstraction, DFI flows not only hide much of the low-level complexity of network communication but also allow developers to declaratively express how data should be efficiently routed to accomplish a given distributed data-processing task. Moreover, DFI flows allow developers to specify *optimization hints*, e.g., to maximize bandwidth utilization or minimize network latency of transfers. By using flows as the main abstraction, DFI supports a wide variety of data-centric applications ranging from bandwidth-sensitive distributed OLAP to more latency-sensitive workloads such as distributed OLTP or replication with consensus protocols. The full paper can be found in [34], and the code is published here [33].

Disaggregated Storage: RDMA-Enabled Tree-Based Indexes
Disaggregated RDMA-enabled DBMSs like NAM-DB [43] demonstrate considerable flexibility, allowing independent scaling of compute and storage resources. Nevertheless, this decoupling introduces a unique challenge: the need for efficient data retrieval via the network from remote storage. Although RDMA primitives enable direct access to remote memory for data retrieval, the specific memory location must be known, which is frequently not met in advance and requires distributed indexes. Thus, many papers have proposed RDMA-enabled hashtables as a solution to find tuples efficiently [19, 31, 39, 40, 43]. Those hashtables exploit one-sided RDMA to access a remote hashtable first to find the required location for the tuple.

While RDMA-enabled hashtables are an excellent fit for primary key lookups, they are not ideally suited to all database operations. For instance, scanning and filtering operations are common in OLTP workloads and require other index structures, so-called secondary indexes. For these scenarios, B-Tree indexes are the better choice. Due to their capability to support point lookups, inserts, deletions, and range scans, B-Trees have become ubiquitous in general-purpose OLTP databases [9, 15]. In this publication [53, 54], we investigated how to design a scalable RDMA-optimized tree-based index structure for disaggregated databases. In particular, we investigated two design questions: (1) which RDMA verb to use for efficiently traversing the index and (2) how data should be distributed across storage servers to optimize RDMA-based access.

Caching for Disaggregated Storage: A Fast and Cost-Efficient Storage Engine
Most disaggregated RDMA-enabled database systems are in-memory only. While these in-memory systems are very efficient, memory prices have started to plateau, reducing their economic feasibility. Concurrently, flash storage costs have decreased by 30x over the past decade, starting a transition from in-memory to flash-based databases. However, flash storage's access latency of approximately 70 microseconds significantly exceeds RDMA's latency of just a few microseconds. Therefore, leveraging the combined in-memory resources of all compute nodes to access "hot" data on remote nodes through RDMA is more efficient while reserving cost-efficient flash storage for "cold" data that is accessed less frequently.

An interesting direction to tackle this is ScaleStore [49, 50], which is a distributed storage engine that exploits RDMA, NVMe, and DRAM across multiple nodes. Like a traditional single-node buffer manager, our buffer manager organizes data into units termed *pages* and transparently loads and evicts pages to and from the SSD. All data, including tables and indexes, are stored on these fixed-size pages, allowing them to be managed transparently. However, unlike traditional buffer managers, ours leverages low-latency RDMA to enable a transparent memory abstraction that accesses the collective DRAM and NVMe storage across multiple nodes. The core of our buffer manager is a distributed caching strategy that dynamically decides which data to keep in memory (and which on SSDs) based on the workload.

Thus, ScaleStore is a building block for building future distributed systems. It provides efficient and transparent data access across a cluster, dynamically adjusts to workload changes, and hides all this complexity behind a simple interface. ScaleStore's code is published here [48].

8.4 P4DB: The Case for In-Network OLTP

In recent years, we have seen increased use of in-network processing (INP) capabilities for database applications. Offloading computational tasks to the network spans various domains. This includes key-value stores and distributed OLAP and ML applications [8, 18, 25, 27, 28, 30, 35, 42]. However, the exploration of INP for OLTP workloads remains nascent, with limited work focusing on specific components such as lock management or replication protocols [18, 42, 47]. OLTP transactions, which typically access only a few tuples and greatly benefit from reduced latencies, are particularly well-suited to exploit these network advancements. The unique architecture of programmable switches, coupled with the opportunity to halve round-trip times (RTT), positions OLTP as an ideal candidate for leveraging the full potential of faster and programmable networks.

8.4.1 Overview of P4DB

To demonstrate the efficiency of programmable switches as transaction engines, we introduce our prototype, P4DB, in this chapter. P4DB optimizes the execution of OLTP in distributed DBMSs by combining two recent trends in networking, namely, fast and smart networks. The main idea is to use a programmable switch that offers both of these properties as an additional database node inside the network and executes transactions directly on it (cf: Fig. 8.5). Since the memory is limited, only hot and frequently accessed tuples are stored on the switch. This, as our evaluation shows, is already sufficient to speed up various OLTP workloads significantly. Executing transactions on the switch yields two main benefits: First, transactions can be executed pipelined and in a lock-free manner. The packet-processing pipeline of such a switch inherently offers these properties, which can potentially scale up to a billion transactions per second. Second, the network latency for such transactions is cut in half because network packets only need half of the round-trip time as normal packets between nodes because the switch sits in the middle.

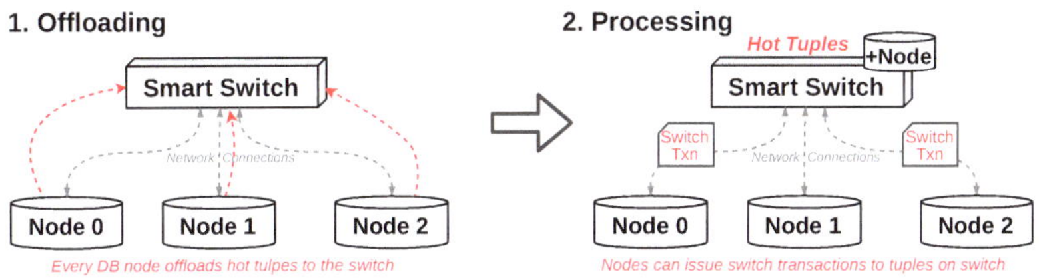

Fig. 8.5 In P4DB, the programmable switch functions as an additional database node for hot data. The switch can execute transactions at a packet-switching speed of up to a billion transactions per second

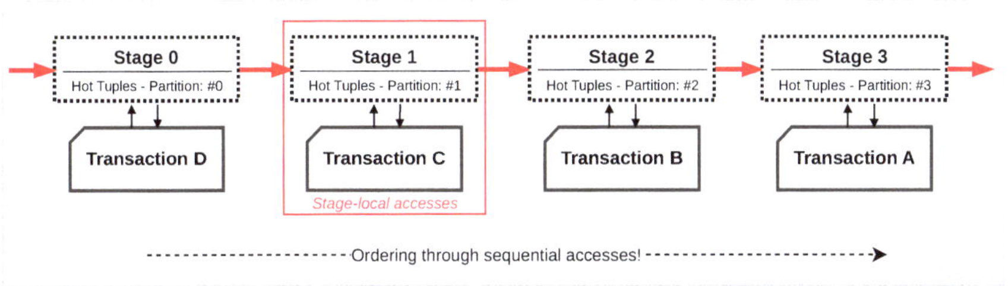

Fig. 8.6 Transaction flowing in a fixed order through the switch pipeline. Each transaction corresponds to a packet and advances in the pipeline each clock cycle. A transaction can only make stage-local accesses

8.4.1.1 Declustered Storage Model

Since programmable switches need to handle line rates of up to a billion packets per second, their packet-processing pipeline poses some constraints on how network packets can access its resources. As a first step we intuitively map the entity of a transaction to a network packet. This network packet contains all the necessary information like the transaction type and user-supplied parameters in its payload. Now, when a switch-transaction arrives, the switch is able to parse the contents and execute the transactions. But before it can do that, tuples need to be first stored in the different MAU-stages within the switch's dataplane. Each transaction can only access stage-local resources when the transactions flow through the switch pipeline, as depicted in Fig. 8.6. Packets only flow from start to end through the pipeline and cannot take over each other. In each clock cycle, all packets move one stage further. This property allows us to define transactional properties as we do in the following section (Sect. 8.4.1.2).

Additionally, the sequence in which transactions access tuples influences their assignment to MAU stages. For instance, if a transaction reads tuple A and then writes to tuple B, tuple A must be positioned in an earlier stage than tuple B. This necessitates aligning tuple storage within the register arrays of MAU stages to the transaction access sequence. In more detail, each MAU stage processes a subset of operations of single transaction per cycle, with transactions moving sequentially through the pipeline stages. Additional concurrency control is not necessary because there is maximally one transaction within a stage. A good data layout aims to allocate tuples across different MAU stages in such a way that a transaction only necessitates a single pass through the pipeline.

We use a graph-based approach to determine the optimal data layout of tuples across MAU stages. In this method, tuples are represented as nodes, and access patterns are depicted as directed edges between the nodes. After using a max-cut algorithm to partition the graph into as many partitions as we have stages, the partitions are topologically sorted to get the optimal order and optimize for single-pass transaction execution on the switch.

Despite these optimizations, certain transactions cannot be executed in a single pass and necessitate multiple passes through the pipeline. This can happen due to the switch's memory model constraints, especially when multiple operations on the same tuple are needed.

To support isolation for multi-pass transactions, we thus provide a lock-based execution scheme in P4DB. This is done by a so-called pipeline-lock to prevent the concurrent execution of multiple transactions in the same pipeline. The locking logic is located in the first MAU stage of a pipeline and can also be limited to a subset of tuples instead of the whole pipeline. When a new transaction arrives while another multi-pass transaction is currently in the pipeline, its execution is prevented by scheduling it for another pass through the switch using a recirculation port. Normal transactions resume directly after the multi-pass transaction unlocks the pipeline lock at the start of its last pipeline pass. Nonetheless, such multi-pass transactions are relatively rare, and a locking mechanism at the pipeline's outset ensures consistency for these transactions.

8.4.1.2 Transactional Properties

Overall, the switch's pipeline provides guarantees for *Atomicity*, *Isolation*, and *Consistency* for the execution of hot transactions, as we discuss next, while *Durability* is guaranteed by logging on the host DBMS.

In P4DB, as discussed in Sect. 8.4.1.1, a switch-transaction is equivalent to a single network packet. The pipelined execution of transactions is shown in Fig. 8.6. The properties of the PISA architecture dictate that the order of transactions is fixed and that a single MAU stage contains at most one transaction. Moreover, operations executed in one MAU stage by one transaction happen atomically within a single clock cycle and are immediately visible to the next transaction in the pipeline. Hence, the pipelined execution of transactions on the switch is equivalent to a serial execution order of transactions that results from the order as they are routed through the pipeline. For example, in Fig. 8.6, the execution is equivalent to the serial order: *A*, *B*, *C*, and then *D*.

Switch transactions also inherit the properties that the order of packets in a pipeline is fixed, and each packet traverses the whole pipeline. This, in addition to the switch's memory model, which only allows access to stage-local resources, provides the necessary guarantees for Atomicity of transactions. However, constraint checks to enable consistency could potentially still lead to aborts and thus would require additional efforts on the switch to roll back a transaction in case constraints are violated. To avoid these additional overheads for single-pass transactions, we use so-called constrained-writes of P4 to implement constraint checks as a single MAU memory access. The main idea of a constrained-write in P4 is that a write is only executed if a predicate is satisfied. This allows us to support simple constraint checks on individual tuples within single-pass transactions, such as executing a banking transaction only if the account balance's value is larger than zero. However, to support more complex constraint checks, one needs to fall back to a multi-pass execution scheme.

The database nodes handle durability and recovery for switch transactions. Before a switch-transaction is sent out to the switch, its operations are appended to the local write-ahead log. To enable correct recovery of the switch state from different local logs of database nodes (in case of a switch failure), the switch adds a unique transaction ID to each switch transaction that it executes. This represents the (serial) execution order of transactions on the switch. This ID is sent back together with the results of the read and write operations of a switch transaction to the database node in the response packet. The information is then appended to the write-ahead log of the database node.

When the switch fails, the information from all write-head logs combined can be used to reconstruct the execution order of switch transactions using the global ID, and with that the most recent switch-state. Only the unique transaction ID is missing in the database logs for transactions that were in flight during a switch failure. The missing transaction ID can be restored from dependencies in the read/write-set stored in the log. If no such dependency exists, any order of switch transaction can be used during recovery for log replay.

8.4.1.3 Warm Transactions

Until now, we have two different kinds of transactions: Hot transactions that only access hot tuples on the switch and cold transactions that only access tuples on the nodes. However, warm transactions that access both hot tuples on the switch and cold tuples on the nodes can appear.

Since hot transactions do not support rollback on the switch, the host DBMS needs to ensure that all operations on cold items cannot abort after the hot sub-transaction is sent out to the switch. Therefore, in the first step, P4DB acquires the locks on all cold items on the database nodes. Once all locks on cold items are acquired, P4DB then executes operations on the cold items and checks all constraints using a sub-transaction that runs only on the database nodes. Once the sub-transaction on the cold items is ready to commit, P4DB sends out a network packet to the switch to trigger a sub-transaction, which then executes the operations on the hot items. After receiving the executed switch transaction, the updates on the hosts on cold items are committed, as we discuss below (see 2PC).

For cases where warm transactions need to access cold tuples after warm tuples (e.g., a write to a cold tuple that depends on a read of a hot tuple), P4DB moves those cold tuples additionally to the switch's memory during the offload phase. These previously warm transactions can then be processed using the same scheme as for hot switch-only transactions. Durability and recovery of warm transactions are guaranteed using the same techniques as with hot transactions. Since the cold-part of a warm transaction is considered as committed and written to the WAL before the hot part is sent out to the switch, P4DB only needs to reconstruct the switch state in case of failure.

8.4.2 Experimental Evaluation

We present two highlights from the experimental evaluation of P4DB. Our testbed consists of eight nodes that are directly connected via 10G links to an Intel Tofino 1 switch [3]. For a detailed description of the experimental setup, please refer to the original paper [17].

Workloads
The YCSB benchmark [10] resembles a key-value store, where a transaction comprises eight read/write operations, which is a common practice [41, 46]. The SmallBank benchmark [1, 11, 22], simulates a banking application where transactions contain read-dependent-writes between accounts. As the third benchmark, we use TPC-C [37], which, despite its design for high partitionability, includes critical contention points, such as the "NewOrder" and "Payment" transactions.

Performance of P4DB
In this experiment, we evaluate the performance enhancements achieved by P4DB in distributed DBMSs across the three aforementioned workloads. The results depicted in Fig. 8.7 show that P4DB significantly accelerates different types of workloads by executing hot transactions on the switch. Specifically, YCSB achieves

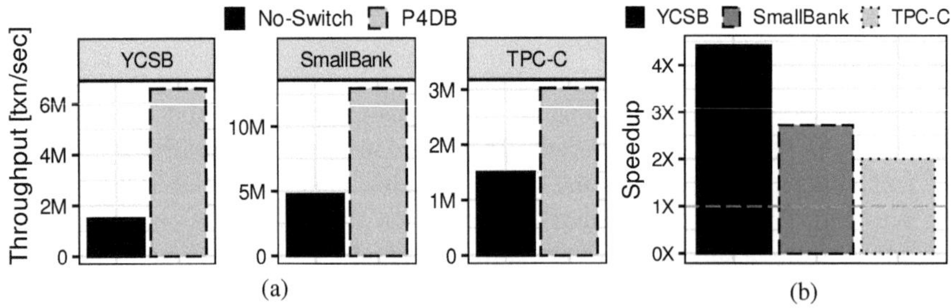

Fig. 8.7 Throughput of P4DB for YCSB, SmallBank, and TPC-C compared to a traditional DBMS. P4DB provides significant speedups for all workloads. (**a**) Throughput. (**b**) Speedup

substantial speedups with its simple transactions. Due to the switch's architecture, read and write tuple accesses take exactly the same amount of time. SmallBank, with its slightly more complex transactions, also sees considerable performance improvements. TPC-C, despite its complexity and the use of warm-transactions that necessitate some processing on the nodes, still benefits from the switch-based acceleration, albeit to a lesser extent.

8.4.3 Growing Hot-Sets Beyond Switch's Capacity

In this experiment, we aim to investigate the scalability and efficiency of P4DB when handling hot sets of varying sizes, particularly focusing on scenarios where the hot set size exceeds the switch's inherent storage capacity. For that, we use the YCSB workload and incrementally increase the hot-set sizes by varying the tuple widths to simulate different switch storage capacities. In the following, we explore not only how P4DB manages larger hot-sets by utilizing standard nodes for overflow but also to observe the impact on throughput as the hot-set grows beyond the switch's capacity.

The results, depicted in Fig. 8.8, illustrate the throughput trends as the hot-set size expands beyond four predetermined switch capacities, with the highest being 650,000 rows. Notably, the throughput demonstrates a graceful degradation across all scenarios as the hot-set size exceeds the switch's capacity. For instance, even with a hot-set size of 2 million tuples, significantly beyond the switch's highest capacity, P4DB maintains a throughput of approximately 3 million transactions per second, with a hot-set more than twice as large as the switch. Looking further, this shows that P4DB does not have a negative impact on overall system throughput when the access patterns do not produce a hot-set that can fit on the switch's memory.

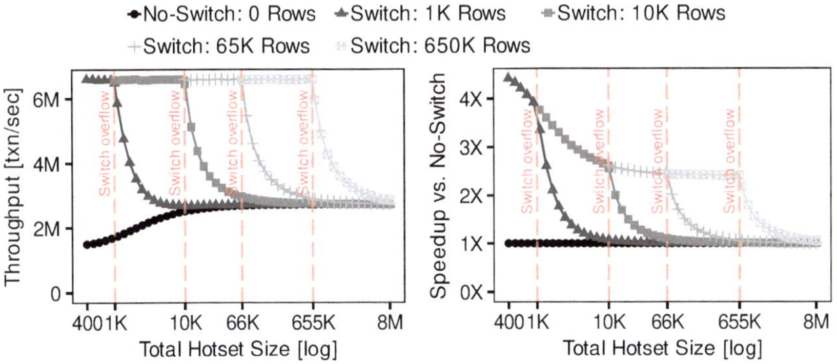

Fig. 8.8 Throughput of YCSB-A for when hot-sets grow beyond various switch capacities. If the hot-set is too big, the throughput degrades gracefully to that of a traditional DBMS

8.4.4 *Summary*

In this section, we introduced P4DB, a novel approach that utilizes a programmable switch to enhance highly contented OLTP workloads by offloading transaction processing to the switch. By treating the switch as an additional database node, P4DB stores hot tuples on it and performs transaction processing with ACID guarantees within the network's data plane. This design offers two key advantages: reduced latency and increased processing bandwidth from all connected nodes. P4DB also remains effective even if the workload size exceeds switch capacity, with fallbacks for transactions that are too complex for the switch. Our evaluation demonstrates that P4DB effectively mitigates contention on hot tuples, resulting in a significant throughput improvement.

8.5 Zero-Sided RDMA

Heterogeneous computing, featuring accelerators like GPUs and FPGAs, is emerging as a critical solution to the performance limitations of CPUs in cloud data centers. These accelerators, however, are typically bottlenecked by their dependency on host CPUs for control and data transfer. We advocate for a new communication scheme to bypass these bottlenecks by eliminating the CPU from the control and data path, enabling direct accelerator-to-accelerator communication via smart switches.

Current RDMA practices involve the CPU, either through two-sided operations requiring both sender and receiver CPUs or one-sided operations that still need the sender's CPU. This CPU involvement limits the full potential of accelerators in cloud environments due to overheads and bottlenecks in coordinating data transfers. See Fig. 8.9.

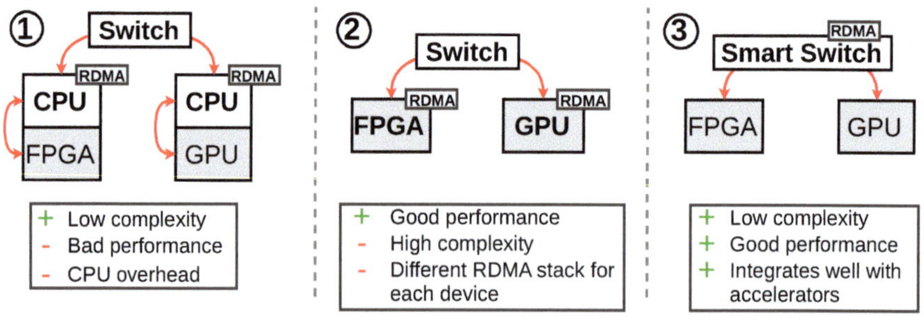

Fig. 8.9 Network-driven communication with zero-sided RDMA vs. alternative communication schemes. In a CPU-driven scheme ①, the CPU is responsible for carrying out the communication. In the accelerator-driven scheme ②, the RDMA stack is realized directly on the accelerator. With zero-sided RDMA ③, the RDMA stack and communication scheme are fully offloaded into the network, removing the need for CPUs, while only one RDMA stack (e.g., on the switch) is needed

An alternative, accelerator-driven RDMA, faces challenges like the absence of RDMA primitives for all accelerators and the high cost of implementing communication logic on each accelerator, consuming valuable compute resources. However, even with one-sided RDMA, achieving direct accelerator-to-accelerator communication is often not possible or infeasible. As such, the communication control flow must be relayed over the CPU [36].

With this contribution, we shift toward network-driven RDMA, offloading the RDMA stack and communication logic to the network, particularly to programmable switches. This approach, termed zero-sided RDMA, leverages the switch's central network position to manage data transfers without involving CPUs or requiring accelerators to support RDMA natively. Programmable switches are ideal for implementing zero-sided RDMA due to their ability to handle complex data operations and efficiently coordinate transfers, supporting diverse communication flows and distributed data management tasks while ensuring scalability at line-rate speeds.

8.5.1 *Overview of Zero-Sided RDMA*

Our approach to zero-sided RDMA leverages the centralized programmable switch's capability to manage data traffic directly, enabling seamless communication between processing units (PUs) without their active involvement. To realize zero-sided RDMA, we have to enable a switch-driven data transfer scheme that transfers data from producers to consumers without their active involvement. This section outlines the mechanism and hardware requirements for implementing zero-sided RDMA.

8.5.1.1 Core Challenges of Realizing Zero-Sided RDMA

A core challenge of realizing zero-sided RDMA is to map the data transfer logic to the pipelined execution model of a switch, which provides a limited set of instructions and memory per stage. In addition, since all connected PUs are not directly connected to each other but are connected to the switch, the switch must adhere to the exact protocol to be compliant with off-the-shelf RDMA NICs. This includes managing stateful RDMA connections with reliability and correctly propagating congestion- and flow-control information from consumers to producers within the switch's data-plane to guarantee execution at line-rate.

8.5.1.2 Communication Abstractions

At the heart of our approach is a circular buffer abstraction for each PU, simplifying the interface between the network and PUs in zero-sided RDMA. This buffer allows

PUs to push and pop data items using straightforward local memory operations while the switch handles data transfer asynchronously. Coordination is maintained through head and tail pointers in the buffer, indicating where data items can be written and read, respectively.

8.5.1.3 Flow of Data Transfers

The process of data transfer involves the switch mirroring the state of producer and consumer buffers to identify when to initiate transfers. The steps are visually shown in Fig. 8.10.

The process of transferring data involves several critical steps that update circular queue pointers and write the data into the designated slot, ensuring efficient movement of data without requiring direct communication between processing units (PUs). Initially, the switch initiates the transfer by issuing an RDMA READ command to access data within the producer's buffer. Once the switch receives the data from the READ operation, it transforms this data into an RDMA WRITE request, which is then directed to insert the data into the consumer's buffer. Following the successful acknowledgment of the RDMA WRITE operation, the consumer's head pointer is updated to indicate the addition of the new item. After that, the producer's tail pointer is adjusted to mark the space that the transferred data occupies as available for future use. This sequence of actions ensures that data is moved efficiently between producers and consumers without necessitating direct interactions between their respective processing units.

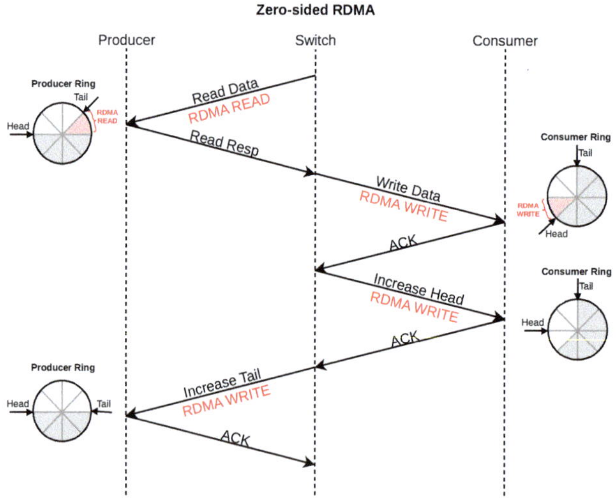

Fig. 8.10 Sequence of network packets for a switch-driven 1:1 data flow. The switch transfers data by reading from the producer and converting the READ response into a WRITE to persist the data in the consumer memory

8.5.1.4 Hardware Requirements

To support zero-sided RDMA, devices must have suitable memory to host the circular buffer structure, including enough space for head and tail pointers and the data items themselves. This memory should also be accessible by a standard RDMA-enabled NIC. Furthermore, the device's memory consistency model must ensure the orderly execution of writing to an item and subsequently updating the head pointer; devices with weaker consistency models may require memory fences to enforce this sequence.

8.5.2 Switch vs. SmartNICs

Network communication offloading can be centralized or decentralized. Decentralized approaches use SmartNICs, like Nvidia BlueField or Mellanox Innova, for RDMA operations, allowing direct accelerator or GPU communication without CPU intervention. Despite enabling specialized compute units to manage communications, they face challenges with complex one-sided RDMA schemes and high costs due to the necessity for a SmartNIC per server, with costs significantly higher than standard RDMA NICs. Conversely, centralized approaches that use programmable switches for direct accelerator communication offer line-rate processing without performance bottlenecks and avoid the complexities of distributed coordination, resulting in lower hardware costs for scale-out solutions. In data center deployments, single-rack setups with Top-of-the-Rack switches enhance job processing locality and bandwidth for distributed operations. While zero-sided RDMA supports cross-rack communication, this setup also opens up areas for future investigation, such as latency, bandwidth, congestion control, and failover mechanisms in multi-switch scenarios. Encrypted data streams in data centers, a challenge for in-network processing, do not affect zero-sided RDMA, as it only requires header modification and packet forwarding.

8.5.3 Advanced Communication Flows in Zero-Sided RDMA

Zero-sided RDMA introduces several advanced communication flows and features, which are discussed below, to address the complexities and performance bottlenecks in distributed Database Management Systems (DBMSs).

N:M Shuffle and Load Balancing
For distributed joins and other tasks requiring data shuffling, zero-sided RDMA simplifies the N:M communication flow. By centralizing connections to the switch, it facilitates efficient coordination between multiple producers and consumers within the switch's data-plane, requiring only one connection at the consumer side

for all incoming data. This model not only reduces memory overhead but also simplifies data polling for PUs. Similarly, for load balancing, zero-sided RDMA automates the distribution of workloads across PUs without the need for intricate coordination mechanisms, thanks to the switch's independent management of data transfers for each consumer.

N:M Replication with Global Order
The multicast communication flow with ordering is another key feature, ensuring globally ordered data distribution from producers to all consumers. This is especially beneficial for replicated joins or state replication tasks, where conventional RDMA multicast methods are inadequate due to their dependency on unreliable transport and two-sided communication, which increases CPU overhead.

Fine-grained Quality of Service (QoS)
Addressing the demand for fine-grained QoS in DBMSs, zero-sided RDMA allows for critical job prioritization over less crucial tasks without the complexity of network reconfiguration required by Priority-based Flow Control (PFC). By utilizing congestion control primitives native to RoCE, it supports dynamic bandwidth allocation and flow prioritization at a granular level, enhancing the overall efficiency of data exchanges.

8.5.4 Experimental Evaluation

We present two highlights from the evaluation of zero-sided RDMA. For a detailed description of the experimental setup, please refer to the original paper [16].

8.5.4.1 Efficiency of Network-Driven Transfers

In this experiment, we compare traditional CPU-driven RDMA against zero-sided RDMA for direct accelerator-to-accelerator communication between two nodes. All data transfers occur directly between GPUs without intermediate main memory copies. Both approaches use identical persistent GPU kernels and buffer abstractions for processing data items. In the CPU-driven model, the co-located CPU is responsible for detecting new items in the buffer and initiating RDMA transfers on behalf of the GPU. The results, shown in Fig. 8.11, highlight the bandwidth differences between CPU-driven and network-driven communication for four concurrent flows using 4KiB items. Achieving comparable performance to zero-sided RDMA requires multiple CPU cores, because in the basic setup with a single CPU thread transfers are CPU-bound. On the other hand, the zero-sided approach shows good scalability while also eliminating the need for dedicated CPU resources per flow. Additionally, the application does not need to re-implement the communication on the accelerator and only uses the memory-based abstraction, as discussed above.

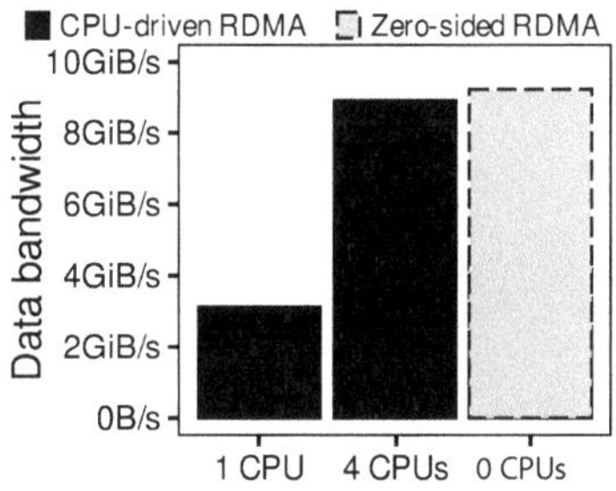

Fig. 8.11 GPU-to-GPU shuffle. Zero-sided RDMA outperforms traditional CPU-based schemes without the need to co-locate a CPU per accelerator

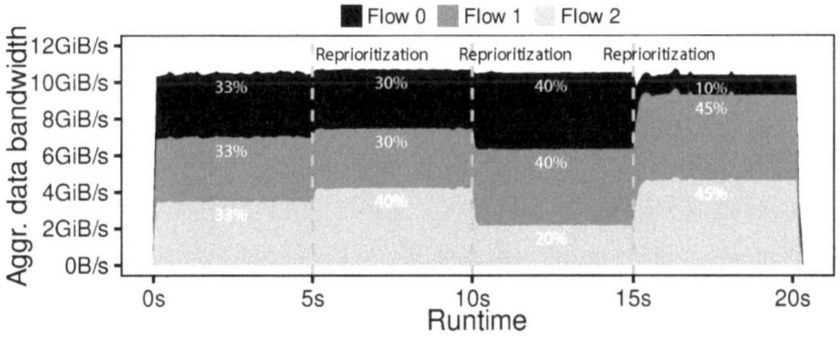

Fig. 8.12 QoS flow prioritization between two PUs with 3 concurrent flows. Prioritization changes every 5 seconds

8.5.4.2 Fine-Grained Flow Prioritization

In this experiment, we investigate the fine-grained (per flow) prioritization capabilities provided by our zero-sided communication scheme. Figure 8.12 shows the individual data bandwidth for three active concurrent flows between two nodes over 20 seconds, with the ratio altered every 5 seconds. Our system demonstrates a swift and efficient response to changes in the prioritization of different flows, with the processing units remaining oblivious to the adjustments. Centralized initiated data transfers allow fine-grained prioritization of different flows, which is not supported natively within RDMA.

8.5.5 Summary

In this chapter, we introduced zero-sided RDMA, a new communication scheme that enables direct RDMA-based communication between accelerators without requiring CPU coordination. All communication and data transfers are fully managed by the network using a programmable switch that can access the PUs memory directly. Additionally, zero-sided RDMA facilitates efficient data shuffling between heterogeneous hardware devices without needing a full RDMA stack on each device. Our evaluation demonstrated that zero-sided RDMA outperforms traditional

CPU-driven one-sided RDMA schemes for accelerators and offers efficient communication flows tailored for disaggregated cloud DBMSs.

8.6 Conclusion and Future Directions

As discussed in the introduction, RDMA represents just the initial step toward future-ready disaggregated database systems. To fully leverage the rapid advancements in networking bandwidth, database systems must specialize their networking stack even more. In this chapter, we have explored programmable switches, which offer a compelling programming and execution model. When fully utilized, these switches can lead to significant performance improvements.

However, this exploration is only the beginning. Future work could include SmartNICs and SmartSSDs and adopt a comprehensive approach to integrating all programmable accelerators within a complete database system. This holistic view is essential for unlocking the full potential of modern networking technologies in databases.

Acknowledgments This work was partially funded by the German Research Foundation (DFG) under the grant 361478211 (DFG priority program SPP 2037) and the DFG Collaborative Research Center 1053 (MAKI). We also thank hessian.AI, 3AI, DFKI, as well as Intel for their support.

References

1. Alomari, M., Cahill, M., Fekete, A., & Uwe Rohm. (2008). The cost of serializability on platforms that use snapshot isolation. In *2008 IEEE 24th International Conference on Data Engineering* (pp. 576–585). IEEE.
2. Amazon Web Services. (2023). *Elastic fabric adapter*. https://aws.amazon.com/hpc/efa/
3. APS Networks. (2021). *Intel Tofino APS Networks BF2556X-1T-A1F*. https://www.aps-networks.com/wp-content/uploads/2021/07/210712_APS_BF2556X-1T_V04.pdf
4. Bai, W., Abdeen, S. S., Agrawal, A., Attre, K. K., Bahl, P., Bhagat, A., Bhaskara, G., Brokhman, T., Cao, L., Cheema, A., Chow, R., Cohen, J., Elhaddad, M., Ette, V., Figlin, I., Firestone, D., George, M., German, I., Ghai, L., Green, E., Greenberg, A. G., Gupta, M., Haagens, R., Hendel, M., Howlader, R., John, N., Johnstone, J., Jolly, T., Kramer, G., Kruse, D., Kumar, A., Lan, E., Lee, I., Levy, A., Lipshteyn, M., Liu, X., Liu, C., Lu, G., Lu, Y., Lu, X., Makhervaks, V., Malashanka, U., Maltz, D. A., Marinos, I., Mehta, R., Murthi, S., Namdhari, A., Ogus, A., Padhye, J., Pandya, M., Phillips, D., Power, A., Puri, S., Raindel, S., Rhee, J., Russo, A., Sah, M., Sheriff, A., Sparacino, C., Srivastava, A., Sun, W., Swanson, N., Tian, F., Tomczyk, L., Vadlamuri, V., Wolman, A., Xie, Y., Yom, J., Yuan, L., Zhang, Y., & Zill, B. (2023). Empowering azure storage with RDMA. In M. Balakrishnan & M. Ghobadi (Eds.), *20th USENIX Symposium on Networked Systems Design and Implementation, NSDI 2023, Boston, MA, April 17–19, 2023* (pp. 49–67). USENIX Association.
5. Barthels, C., Alonso, G., Hoefler, T., Schneider, T., & Müller, I. (2017). Distributed join algorithms on thousands of cores. *Proceedings of the VLDB Endowment, 10*(5), 517–528.
6. Barthels, C., Loesing, S., Alonso, G., & Kossmann, D. (2015). Rack-scale in-memory join processing using RDMA. In T. K. Sellis, S. B. Davidson, & Z. G. Ives (Eds.), *Proceedings*

of the 2015 ACM SIGMOD International Conference on Management of Data, Melbourne, Victoria, May 31– June 4, 2015 (pp. 1463–1475). ACM.
7. Binnig, C., Crotty, A., Galakatos, A., Kraska, T. & Zamanian, E. (2016). The end of slow networks: It's time for a redesign. *Proceedings of the VLDB Endowment, 9*(7), 528–539.
8. Blöcher, M., Ziegler, T., Binnig, C., & Eugster, P. (2018). Boosting scalable data analytics with modern programmable networks. In *Proceedings of the 14th International Workshop on Data Management on New Hardware* (pp. 1–3).
9. Comer, D. (1979). The Ubiquitous B-tree. *ACM Computing Surveys (CSUR), 11*(2), 121–137.
10. Cooper, B. F., Silberstein, A., Tam, E., Ramakrishnan, R., & Sears, R. (2010). Benchmarking cloud serving systems with ycsb. In *Proceedings of the 1st ACM symposium on Cloud computing* (pp. 143–154).
11. Difallah, D. E., Pavlo, A., Curino, C., & Cudre-Mauroux, P. (2013). Oltp-bench: An extensible testbed for benchmarking relational databases. *Proceedings of the VLDB Endowment, 7*(4), 277–288.
12. Dragojevic, A., Narayanan, D., Castro, M., & Hodson, O. (2014). Farm: Fast remote memory. In R. Mahajan & I. Stoica (Eds.), *Proceedings of the 11th USENIX Symposium on Networked Systems Design and Implementation, NSDI 2014, Seattle, WA, April 2–4, 2014* (pp. 401–414). USENIX Association.
13. Dragojevic, A., Narayanan, D., Nightingale, E. B., Renzelmann, M., Shamis, A., Badam, A., & Castro, M. (2015). No compromises: Distributed transactions with consistency, availability, and performance. In *SOSP*.
14. Fent, P., van Renen, A., Kipf, A., Leis, V., Neumann, T., & Kemper, A. (2020). Low-latency communication for fast DBMS using RDMA and shared memory. In *ICDE*.
15. Graefe, G. (2011). *Modern B-Tree Techniques. Found. Trends Databases, 3*(4), 203–402.
16. Jasny, M., Thostrup, L., & Binnig, C. (2023). Zero-sided RDMA: Network-driven data shuffling. In N. May & N. Tatbul (Eds.), *Proceedings of the 19th International Workshop on Data Management on New Hardware, DaMoN 2023, Seattle, WA, June 18–23, 2023* (pp. 82–85). ACM.
17. Jasny, M., Thostrup, L., Ziegler, T., & Binnig, C. (2022). P4DB—The case for in-network OLTP. In Z. G. Ives, A. Bonifati, & A. E. Abbadi (Eds.), *SIGMOD '22: International Conference on Management of Data, Philadelphia, PA, June 12–17, 2022* (pp. 1375–1389). ACM.
18. Jin, X., Li, X., Zhang, H., Foster, N., Lee, J., Soulé, R., Kim, C., & Stoica, I. (2018). Netchain: Scale-free sub-RTT coordination. In *15th {USENIX} Symposium on Networked Systems Design and Implementation ({NSDI} 18)* (pp. 35–49).
19. Kalia, A., Kaminsky, M., & Andersen, D. G. (2014). Using RDMA efficiently for key-value services. In *SIGCOMM*.
20. Kalia, A., Kaminsky, M., & Andersen, D. G. (2016). Fasst: Fast, scalable and simple distributed transactions with two-sided (RDMA) datagram RPCS. In K. Keeton & T. Roscoe (Eds.), *12th USENIX Symposium on Operating Systems Design and Implementation, OSDI 2016, Savannah, GA, November 2–4, 2016* (pp. 185–201). USENIX Association.
21. Kalia, A., Kaminsky, M., & Andersen, D. G. (2019). Datacenter RPCS can be general and fast. In J. R. Lorch & M. Yu (Eds.), *16th USENIX Symposium on Networked Systems Design and Implementation, NSDI 2019, Boston, MA, February 26–28, 2019* (pp. 1–16). USENIX Association.
22. Kallman, R., Kimura, H., Natkins, J., Pavlo, A., Rasin, A., Zdonik, S., Jones, E. P. C., Madden, S., Stonebraker, M., Zhang, Y., et al. (2008). H-store: A high-performance, distributed main memory transaction processing system. *Proceedings of the VLDB Endowment, 1*(2), 1496–1499.
23. Kang, S. J., Lee, S.-H., & Lee, K.-M. (2015). Performance comparison of OpenMP, MPI, and MapReduce in practical problems. *Advances in Multimedia, 2015*, 575687:1–575687:9.
24. Korolija, D., Koutsoukos, D., Keeton, K., Taranov, K., Milojicic, D. S., & Alonso, G. (2022). Farview: Disaggregated memory with operator off-loading for database engines. In *12th Conference on Innovative Data Systems Research, CIDR 2022, Chaminade, CA, January 9–12, 2022*. www.cidrdb.org

25. Lerner, A., Hussein, R., Cudre-Mauroux, P., & eXascale Infolab, U. (2019). The case for network accelerated query processing. In *CIDR*.
26. Li, F., Das, S., Syamala, M., & Narasayya, V. R. (2016). Accelerating relational databases by leveraging remote memory and RDMA. In F. Özcan, G. Koutrika, & S. Madden (Eds.), *Proceedings of the 2016 International Conference on Management of Data, SIGMOD Conference 2016, San Francisco, CA, June 26–July 01, 2016* (pp. 355–370). ACM.
27. Li, X., Sethi, R., Kaminsky, M., Andersen, D. G., & Freedman, M. J. (2016). Be fast, cheap and in control with switchkv. In *13th {USENIX}* Symposium on Networked Systems Design and Implementation (*{NSDI} 16)* (pp. 31–44).
28. Li, Y., Liu, I.-J., Yuan, Y., Chen, D., Schwing, A., & Huang, J. (2019). Accelerating distributed reinforcement learning with in-switch computing. In *2019 ACM/IEEE 46th Annual International Symposium on Computer Architecture (ISCA)* (pp. 279–291). IEEE.
29. Loesing, S., Pilman, M., Etter, T., & Kossmann, D. (2015). On the design and scalability of distributed shared-data databases. In *SIGMOD*.
30. Sapio, A., Canini, M., Ho, C.-Y., Nelson, J., Kalnis, P., Kim, C., Krishnamurthy, A., Moshref, M., Ports, D., & Richtarik, P. (2021). Scaling distributed machine learning with in-network aggregation. In *18th {USENIX}* Symposium on Networked Systems Design and Implementation *({NSDI}* 21*)* (pp. 785–808).
31. Szepesi, T., Wong, B., Cassell, B., & Brecht, T. (2014). Designing a low-latency cuckoo hash table for write-intensive workloads using rdma. In *First International Workshop on Rack-scale Computing*.
32. Taranov, K., Girolamo, S. D., & Hoefler, T. (2021). Corm: Compactable remote memory over RDMA. In *SIGMOD '21: International Conference on Management of Data, Virtual Event, June 20–25, 2021* (pp. 1811–1824).
33. Thostrup, L. (2021). *DFI: The Data Flow Interface for High-Speed Networks Code*. https://github.com/DataManagementLab/DFI-public.
34. Thostrup, L., Skrzypczak, J., Jasny, M., Ziegler, T., & Binnig, C. (2022). DFI: The data flow interface for high-speed networks. *SIGMOD Record, 51*(1), 15–22.
35. Tirmazi, M., Basat, R. B., Gao, J., & Yu, M. (2020). Cheetah: Accelerating database queries with switch pruning. In *Proceedings of the 2020 ACM SIGMOD International Conference on Management of Data* (pp. 2407–2422).
36. Tork, M., Maudlej, L., & Silberstein, M. (2020). Lynx: A smartnic-driven accelerator-centric architecture for network servers. In J. R. Larus, L. Ceze, & K. Strauss (Eds.), *ASPLOS '20: Architectural Support for Programming Languages and Operating Systems, Lausanne, March 16–20, 2020* (pp. 117–131). ACM.
37. TPC-C Specification (2021). http://www.tpc.org/tpc_documents_current_versions/pdf/tpc-c_v5.11.0.pdf
38. Vilanova, L., Maudlej, L., Bergman, S., Miemietz, T., Hille, M., Asmussen, N., Roitzsch, M., Härtig, H., & Silberstein, M. (2022). Slashing the disaggregation tax in heterogeneous data centers with fractos. In Y.-D. Bromberg, A.-M. Kermarrec, & C. Kozyrakis (Eds.), *EuroSys '22: Seventeenth European Conference on Computer Systems, Rennes, April 5–8, 2022* (pp. 352–367). ACM.
39. Wang, T., Yang, S., Kimura, H., Swart, G., & Blanas, S. (2020). Efficient usage of one-sided RDMA for linear probing. In R. Bordawekar & T. Lahiri (Eds.), *International Workshop on Accelerating Analytics and Data Management Systems Using Modern Processor and Storage Architectures, ADMS@VLDB 2020, Tokyo, August 31, 2020* (pp. 1–13).
40. Wei, X., Shi, J., Chen, Y., Chen, R., & Chen, H. (2015). Fast in-memory transaction processing using RDMA and HTM. In E. L. Miller & S. Hand (Eds.), *Proceedings of the 25th Symposium on Operating Systems Principles, SOSP 2015, Monterey, CA, October 4–7, 2015* (pp. 87–104). ACM.
41. Xiangyao, Y., Bezerra, G., Pavlo, A., Devadas, S., & Stonebraker, M. (2014). Staring into the abyss: An evaluation of concurrency control with one thousand cores. *Proceedings of the VLDB Endowment, 8*(3): 209–220.

42. Yu, Z., Zhang, Y., Braverman, V., Chowdhury, M., & Jin, X. (2020). Netlock: Fast, centralized lock management using programmable switches. In *Proceedings of the Annual Conference of the ACM Special Interest Group on Data Communication on the Applications, Technologies, Architectures, and Protocols for Computer Communication* (pp. 126–138).
43. Zamanian, E., Binnig, C., Kraska, T., & Harris, T. (2017). The end of a myth: Distributed transaction can scale. *Proceedings of the VLDB Endowment, 10*(6), 685–696.
44. Zamanian, E., Shun, J., Binnig, C., & Kraska, T. (2020). Chiller: Contention-centric transaction execution and data partitioning for modern networks. In D. Maier, R. Pottinger, A. Doan, W.-C. Tan, A. Alawini, & H. Q. Ngo (Eds.), *Proceedings of the 2020 International Conference on Management of Data, SIGMOD Conference 2020, Online Conference [Portland, OR], June 14–19, 2020*, SIGMOD '20 (pp. 511–526). ACM.
45. Zamanian, E., Shun, J., Binnig, C., & Kraska, T. (2021). Chiller: Contention-centric transaction execution and data partitioning for modern networks. *ACM SIGMOD Record, 50*(1), 14.
46. Zamanian, E., Xiangyao, Y., Stonebraker, M., & Kraska, T. (2019). Rethinking database high availability with rdma networks. *Proceedings of the VLDB Endowment, 12*(11), 1637–1650.
47. Zhu, H., Bai, Z., Li, J., Michael, E., Ports, D. R. K., Stoica, I., & Jin, X. (2019). Harmonia: Near-linear scalability for replicated storage with in-network conflict detection. *Proceedings of the VLDB Endowment, 13*(3), 376–389.
48. Ziegler, T. (2022). *ScaleStore Code*. https://github.com/DataManagementLab/ScaleStore.
49. Ziegler, T., Bernstein, P. A., Leis, V., & Binnig, C. (2023). Is scalable OLTP in the cloud a solved problem? In *13th Annual Conference on Innovative Data Systems Research, CIDR 2023, Amsterdam, January 8–11, 2023, Online Proceedings*. www.cidrdb.org.
50. Ziegler, T., Binnig, C., & Leis, V. (2022). Scalestore: A fast and cost-efficient storage engine using dram, NVME, and RDMA. In Z. Ives, A. Bonifati, & A. E. Abbadi (Eds.), *SIGMOD '22: International Conference on Management of Data, Philadelphia, PA June 12–17, 2022* (pp. 685–699). ACM.
51. Ziegler, T., Leis, V., & Binnig, C. (2020). RDMA communication patterns. *Datenbank-Spektrum, 20*(3), 199–210.
52. Ziegler, T., Mohan, D. B., Leis, V., & Binnig, C. (2022). EFA: A viable alternative to RDMA over infiniband for dbmss? In S. Blanas & N. May (Eds.), *International Conference on Management of Data, DaMoN 2022, Philadelphia, PA, 13 June 2022* (pp. 10:1–10:5). ACM.
53. Ziegler, T., Nelson-Slivon, J., Leis, V., & Binnig, C. (2023). Design guidelines for correct, efficient, and scalable synchronization using one-sided rdma. In *SIGMOD '23: International Conference on Management of Data, Seattle, WA, June 18–23, 2023*. ACM.
54. Ziegler, T., Vani, S. T., Binnig, C., Fonseca, R., & Kraska, T. (2019). Designing distributed tree-based index structures for fast RDMA-capable networks. In P.A. Boncz, S. Manegold, A. Ailamaki, A. Deshpande, & T. Kraska (Eds.), *Proceedings of the 2019 International Conference on Management of Data, SIGMOD Conference 2019, Amsterdam, June 30– July 5, 2019* (pp. 741–758). ACM.

Chapter 9
Managing Very Large Datasets on Directly Attached NVMe Arrays

Gabriel Haas, Adnan Alhomssi, and Viktor Leis

Abstract High-performance solid-state drives based on flash memory have replaced hard disks as the primary storage medium. Modern servers can host ten or more NVMe SSDs, and the aggregate bandwidth is approaching main memory bandwidth. In response to this evolution, this project evaluates the performance trade-offs posed by the abstraction layers and interfaces involved in I/O management. We experimentally slice through the software stack, exploring the limits of how efficient I/O can be done, and provide a discussion about durability. Finally, we discuss the implications of fast storage devices on the architecture and implementation of database storage engines. Overall, our work shows that exploiting the full potential of modern NVMe storage arrays is achievable but requires substantial engineering effort.

9.1 Introduction

Handling storage I/O has always been a key task for database systems. Historically, storage devices were slow, making disk accesses the performance bottleneck for traditional database systems. Hence, disk-based database systems spend a lot of effort in minimizing the number of disk accesses, especially random accesses.

The emergence of much faster flash-based solid-state drives (SSDs) around 2010 changed this, initially generating enthusiasm for the technology. Much of this pioneering research focused on using flash SSDs as accelerators [7, 9, 12, 24, 31, 32, 44, 45] and on building specialized storage hardware for database systems [25]. However, at that time, flash was expensive, and much of the research focus in the database community shifted toward main-memory database systems [13, 27, 47].

G. Haas (✉) · V. Leis
Technische Universität München, München, Germany
e-mail: gabriel.haas@tum.de; leis@in.tum.de

A. Alhomssi
RelationalAI, Friedrich-Alexander-Universität Erlangen-Nürnberg, Erlangen, Germany

K.-U. Sattler et al. (eds.), *Scalable Data Management for Future Hardware*,
https://doi.org/10.1007/978-3-031-74097-8_9

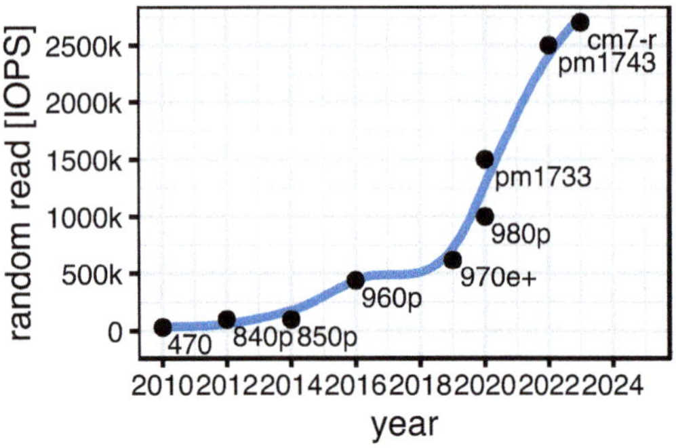

Fig. 9.1 Exponential growth in SSD bandwidth. Bandwidth in terms of I/O operations per second (IOPS) has doubled with every update in PCIe generation for 4 KiB random reads

In more recent years, the focus remained on specialized storage hardware [11, 35, 43] and new interfaces for SSDs, like Open Channel SSDs [8, 40]. The interest in *commodity SSDs* for database systems was limited. Much research in the storage field went into Optane Persistent Memory [15–17, 30, 33, 48, 49], high bandwidth memory [41, 42], near and in-memory processing [5, 6, 14, 22, 28], heterogeneous memory architectures, and exploiting fast networks for distributed storage [29, 52]. We concluded that research on flash storage would be valuable for the DFG Priority Program 2037 and the database system community as a whole.

In early 2020, we looked at the state of storage I/O using multiple directly attached NVMe SSDs [18]. Even then, it was difficult to fully exploit the performance of multiple SSDs. Since then, NVMe SSDs have become mainstream, and their bandwidth has quadrupled. Figure 9.1 illustrates this exponential bandwidth growth over the past half decade.

During that time frame, other promising storage technologies such as the aforementioned persistent memory have not achieved anticipated success and DRAM prices have stagnated. Against this backdrop, flash-based NVMe storage has emerged as the most economically viable solution for large datasets. There have also been notable advancements in software that play a critical role in enhancing I/O performance for NVMe storage. A key example is the Linux Kernel's I/O interface, io_uring, which has attracted significant interest and seen substantial progress. These hardware and software changes have significant implications on the performance of modern NVMe storage and how we perceive and manage I/O.

Research on the impact of the NVMe I/O stack on performance is sparse. Many papers focus on how storage engines and key value stores can be built for modern storage hardware [10, 19, 38, 51]. These papers focus on the system side, while this chapter provides a comprehensive analysis that includes the operating system I/O stack, the hardware, and the application itself. Section 9.2 presents microbenchmarks that evaluate the performance impact of all I/O layers, including the I/O interface, page cache, and file system. Section 9.3 discusses common pitfalls when working and benchmarking SSDs that we have encountered in the last years. Section 9.4 shows how we engineered our storage engine LeanStore to exploit NVMe-era storage performance.

9.2 Slicing Through the I/O Stack Abstraction Layers

In 2019, we investigated how fast NVMe arrays can be exploited by database systems [18]. This work aims to reassess the experiments utilizing the newer-generation hardware and incorporating knowledge accumulated in the last years. Since then, two subsequent generations of PCIe have emerged, resulting in a quadrupling of bandwidth. At first glance, the I/O stack seems similar to how it was before, but there has been substantial development on the software side as well.

9.2.1 Experimental Setup

All experiments were carried out on Linux 6.7, which is the latest kernel version available at the time of writing. Our server is equipped with an AMD EPYC 9654P Genoa processor with 96 cores (192 hardware threads) and has 384 GB of DRAM using 12 DDR5 channels, achieving over 300 GB/s of memory bandwidth. The system has 128 PCIe 5.0 lanes and 8 Kioxia CM7-R PCIe 5.0 SSDs with 3.8 TB capacity per SSD. Each SSD is specified to achieve 2.7 M random 4 KB I/O operations per second (IOPS), 14.000 MB/s sequential read bandwidth, and 6.750 MB/s sequential write bandwidth. When all 8 SSDs are used in parallel, this amounts to over 100 GB/s of I/O bandwidth, which is comparable to the main memory bandwidth of many servers.

We compare two simple workloads: random reads and a mix of 75% random reads and 25% random writes. All experiments use 4 KB pages, which maximizes the achievable number of I/O operations. Unless otherwise mentioned, we rely on the fio benchmarking tool.

9.2.2 Slicing Through the I/O Stack

Baseline: Synchronous IO We disable features of the I/O stack step by step, with Table 9.1 showing the resulting performance for our read-only and mixed workloads. The baseline is accessing a file on a mounted file system through the POSIX interface. Using pread and pwrite, we submit read and write operations synchronously, in a blocking fashion, to the kernel. Each I/O operation goes through several layers: the file system, the page cache, the block layer, the NVMe driver, and, finally, the SSD. Each of these abstraction layers contributes to considerable CPU overhead, resulting in relatively low performance, achieving only 810k read IOPS. This is less than 4% of what the hardware can do when compared to its specification of 2.7*8 = 21.6 M IOPS.

fsync The fsync system call guarantees that dirty pages are written to non-volatile storage. It will flush dirty pages from the page cache to storage; if necessary, it

Table 9.1 Slicing through the layers of abstraction: comparison of I/O operations and cycles in different setups under read-only and mixed workloads. Max IOPS and cycles/operation, for read-only and a 75%/25% read/write workload using fio [4]. Maximum achievable IOPS was measured using optimal number of threads for the specific setup. Efficiency in terms of cycles/io was done with 64 threads for pread/write setups and 8 threads for the asynchronous interfaces (io_uring and SPDK)

	100% read		75% read, 25% write	
	read M IOPS	cycles [k] per IO	total M IOPS	cycles [k] per IO
pread/pwrite/fsync	0.81	87.2	0.09	332.2
– fsync	0.81	87.2	0.05	163.5
– page cache (O_DIRECT)	6.07	48.1	2.28	56.4
io_uring	6.73	28.4	1.77	32.9
– file system (XFS)	21.60	22.4	13.19	22.7
– RAID 0 (md)	23.30	19.0	13.20	18.2
+ uring opt. (polling, passthru)	23.30	9.7	13.27	9.9
SPDK	23.27	1.6	13.18	2.3

also moves data from volatile caches on the SSD to flash memory. Surprisingly, the mixed workload actually gets worse after removing the fsync system call. One theory for this is that Linux's page cache eviction algorithm is too slow to keep up. When using the fsync call, the page cache is forced to evict pages on a different code path. We discuss flushing and durability in more detail in Sect. 9.2.5.

Page Cache The next step is to remove the page cache from the I/O path. Most database systems implement their own buffer pool, which makes the page cache unnecessary and redundant. Using O_DIRECT results in a large performance improvement, with read IOPS increasing by an order of magnitude and the efficiency in terms of cycles/IO halving. By removing the page cache, we can unlock the potential of NVMe-era performance, achieving over 6 million read operations per second (which corresponds to 25 GB/s). However, this performance is still far from reaching the hardware's full potential, especially for mixed workloads, which only achieve around 2 million IOPS (MIOPS).

Asynchronous IO: io_uring Achieving millions of IOPS using a synchronous model requires hundreds of threads, resulting in extreme thread oversubscription. The next obvious optimization is therefore to switch from hundreds of blocking threads to a non-blocking I/O library such as io_uring. When only eight threads are used (same for all following efficiency experiments), the CPU efficiency increases substantially. However, the maximum throughput increases only slightly.

File System We next investigate the file system, which provides useful features at the cost of additional OS-level CPU overhead. Removing the file system and directly accessing the underlying Linux software RAID 0 block device (i.e., /dev/mdX) gives a large increase in overall throughput. The results indicate that file systems are the main bottleneck on fast NVMe arrays. Without a file system, it is possible to get the specified bandwidth of our system: 21 million read IOPS, or almost 90 GB/s. Note, however, that achieving these results requires microbenchmarks that consume the entire server CPU for I/O submission and polling. This leaves few resources for actual data processing.

RAID Instead of using software RAID provided by the operating system, RAID can also be implemented directly by the application to bypass another layer of abstraction. Interestingly, without RAID, it is possible to achieve higher read throughput than SSDs are specified for. However, this still does not solve the CPU efficiency problem: 19k cycles are required per I/O operation. Using 19k CPU cycles for 23.3 M IOPS implies that our high-end 96-core CPU is completely occupied doing I/O.

Polling io_uring comes with a broad palette of optimization settings, which we investigate in 9.2.3. By using polling-based I/O and the new I/O Passthru interface [23], it is possible to halve the number of cycles required. Passthru saves CPU cycles by bypassing the file system and block abstraction. However, we argue that 10k cycles per I/O operation is still very high, leaving little room for data processing.

User-Space IO: SPDK A radical approach for doing I/O is to bypass the kernel altogether. With the SPDK NVMe driver [46], an application can directly issue I/O requests in user space. As shown in the table, using the SPDK NVMe driver increases efficiency substantially, achieving a rate of 1600 cycles per I/O. It should be noted that for the SPDK result, we used our own benchmarking tool to avoid fio bottlenecks. With our own tool, the io_uring (with polling and passthru enabled) overhead is around 5.5k cycles

9.2.3 Secret Flags in the Kernel Universe

io_uring Linux Kernel Team [36] comes with several settings for tuning its performance, which we investigate in the following. For comparison, we also include its predecessor for asynchronous I/O: libaio. As Fig. 9.2 shows, it is, in principle, possible to achieve the full I/O bandwidth with both interfaces and all measured settings. However, the number of threads required to reach maximum performance varies considerably. Libaio requires 14.2k cycles per I/O operation even with a single thread; higher thread counts would incur additional CPU overhead for synchronization.

Polling-based I/O Compared to libaio, io_uring showcases greater efficiency even in its default setting, requiring 10.6k cycles per I/O in the single-threaded setting. The first optimization is to switch from the interrupt-driven model to polling-based I/O completion (IOPOLL). This requires adjusting the NVMe driver poll_queues setting.

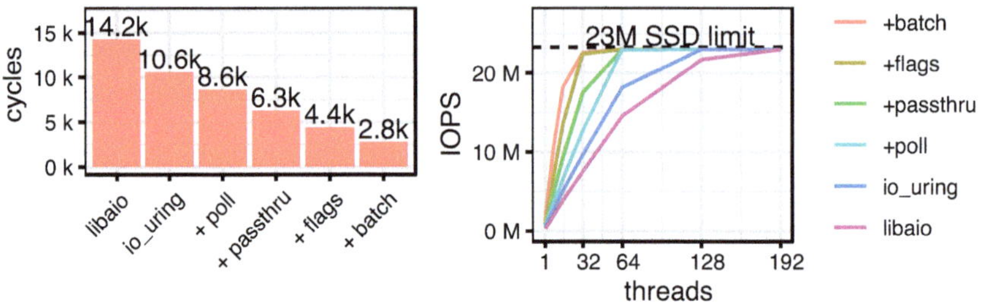

Fig. 9.2 Read-only throughput scalability with varying number of threads for libaio and different io_uring settings. Corresponding cycles per I/O-operation when using a single thread. Measured with t/io_uring tool from the fio repository [4]

I/O Passthru Joshi et al. [23] is an extension to io_uring that allows for the submission of arbitrary NVMe commands through the kernel to NVMe devices. The change in io_uring was necessary, as it requires larger entries in the submission and completion queues. This will allow the quick adoption of new NVMe commands without necessitating changes to the kernel. The new I/O path is also more lightweight and leads to better scalability since it does not go through all the abstraction layers. This improvement can be seen in the figure, where cycles have been reduced by almost 30%, from 8.6k to 6.3k.

Other Flags The kernel pins data buffers to prevent eviction or relocation during an I/O operation. Instead of pinning the buffer for every operation, buffers used for I/O can be registered with the kernel and only pinned once. Additional flags (REGISTER_RING_FDS and REGISTER_FILES) can further enhance io_uring efficiency. This leads to a cycle reduction of approximately another 30% when using all three flags.

Batching Next, we consider the effects of batching I/O requests. Batching operations together reduce the overhead otherwise required for individual requests. This reduces the number of context switches and kernel overhead, as well as required Memory-Mapped I/O (MMIO) calls in the NVMe driver. In the model we proposed for LeanStore [19]—where every database thread communicates with every SSD—batching is difficult. In this model, the benefits from batching would be limited due to the small number of subsequent requests that could be batched. Nonetheless, we want to show the significant impact of batching in micro benchmarks, as can be seen in the figure with io_uring and even more so with SPDK. Note that SPDK only benefits from the reduction of MMIO calls to the SSD, while with io_uring batching also reduces the number of system calls.

SQPOLL For similar architectural reasons, we omit the SQPOLL flag. SQPOLL is used to eliminate system calls. When SQPOLL is enabled, the kernel spawns threads that poll on the io_uring submission queue to check for incoming requests and to handle polling on the NVMe completion queues. While it removes context switching, it essentially just shifts work from user threads to kernel workers. In our architecture, this is undesirable since it introduces unpredictability and necessitates tuning of the number of kernel threads.

9.2.4 A Lower Bound for I/O Handling

In Sect. 9.2, we discussed that the number of cycles necessary for I/O can be as low as 1.6k when using SPDK (without batching). It raises the question why a simple I/O request needs to consume over a thousand CPU cycles and what the true lower bound is.

The NVMe protocol is simple and efficient once everything is set up: An I/O submission is in essence setting up the request parameters, i.e., request type, data pointer, SSD offset, and size on the submission queue, and a memory-mapped I/O (MMIO) call to notify the SSD of the new request. When interrupts are disabled, the application can check (poll) for updates on the completion queue. Transferring the data to and from the SSD is handled by the Direct Memory Access (DMA) engine and does not require additional CPU cycles.

As Fig. 9.3 shows, with SPDK, the lowest number we could achieve is 733 cycles/IO when enabling batching (with delay_cmd_submit). This was measured using a single thread with about 5.4 M IOPS in our I/O benchmarking tool. The benchmarking tool uses the same I/O backend used in LeanStore that supports all I/O interfaces. Though less than other benchmarking tools, the tool itself and the I/O backend incur some overhead. Employing a minimal benchmarking tool that uses SPDK without any indirection results in about 12.7 M IOPS or 292 cycles (696 instructions). These results closely align with figures reported on the SPDK blog [26].

However, efficiency can be increased further. Even when using SPDK directly, it itself is not necessarily a lightweight library. As described, submitting an I/O request to an NVMe queue is a very simple operation that should not take hundreds of instructions. The SPDK NVMe driver implements features like queueing, splitting requests, handling admin commands, creating tracking objects, and more. Hence, we went one step further and optimized the remaining I/O path to do the bare minimum to submit requests on the NVMe queues.

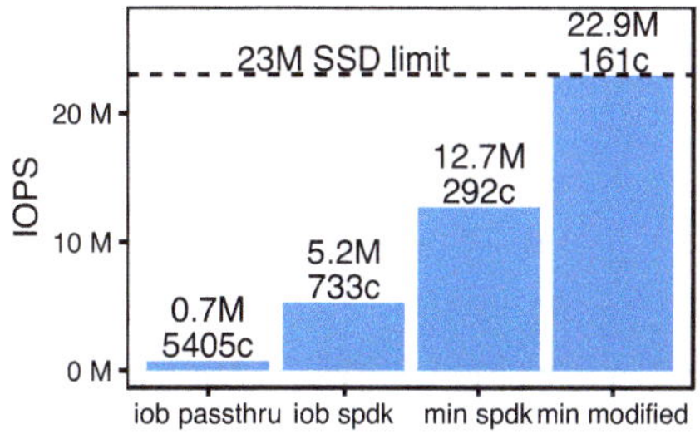

Fig. 9.3 Maximum I/O bandwidth achievable in a single thread. Values denoted with "c" are the corresponding cycles/IO. "iob" is the I/O backend used by LeanStore. "min" uses SPDK and NVMe without the "iob" overhead

These optimizations allow us to achieve the full SSD bandwidth of 23 M IOPS on a single thread ("modified" in Fig. 9.3). A request is now handled in 161 cycles (276 instructions). This is the lower bound in this microbenchmark, where we are now limited by SSD bandwidth. Further optimizations would merely reallocate saved cycles to additional polling on the completion queue. A real system, on the other hand, could benefit from this and use the additional saved cycles for other useful processing.

It should be noted that all SPDK runs here use the delay_cmd_submit flag, which delays the MMIO call until the next poll call. The "modified" version explained below does not use this flag but similarly issues one MMIO call for multiple I/O requests. Not limiting the number of MMIO calls results in an upper limit of 5.75 MIOPS.

9.2.5 Thank God It's Fsynced: Durability

In our first paper on NVMe using consumer SSDs [18], we reported a significant performance degradation when using the fsync/fdatasync system call. The fdatasync system call is used to let the operating system know that dirty pages should be flushed to the storage device. This is relevant for pages that are cached in the Linux page cache (i.e., when O_DIRECT is not used). The operating system then writes dirty buffer pool pages to storage. The system call also affects the file system to ensure that the necessary metadata, journal entries, and modified pages are made durable.

The operating system will also issue a flush command to the SSDs. This is necessary if the SSD has volatile write back caches (e.g., DRAM), which then have to be written to flash. On consumer SSDs, the said flush command incurs high latency. We have observed latency of 1.7 ms, which is comparable to flash write latency.

Enterprise SSDs are not constrained by the small M.2 form factor. Therefore, they can contain capacitors that guarantee a short time of backup power in case of power loss. This is enough time to bridge power until all dirty data from the cache is flushed to flash memory. Therefore, enterprise SSDs report via NVMe that they do not utilize write-back caching, ensuring completed I/Os are durable. Linux exploits this by not issuing a flush command when fsync/fdatasync is called. When using O_DIRECT, the fdatasync call becomes a no-op.

9.3 Benchmarking and Hardware Pitfalls

It is challenging to run SSD benchmarks correctly. Many results found are inaccurate, not representative, or plainly incorrect. This includes incorrect throughput numbers, unrealistic latency values, or the use of benchmark tools that cannot fully exploit NVMe performance. Errors can also arise from running benchmarks on unsuitable abstraction layers, such as evaluating an SSD's performance using results from buffered I/O, bottlenecked RAID configurations, or file systems. We know this because we have made many such mistakes ourselves and have learned from them the hard way. Hence, in this section, we describe below how to avoid common pitfalls.

9.3.1 Don't Trust a Benchmark You Did Not Do Yourself

Initialization A common reason for misleading performance numbers is failing to correctly initialize the SSD. Reading data from SSD that has never been written before (i.e., deallocated or unwritten blocks) is defined semantically in the NVM Command Set Specification [39] but leads to unpredictable performance. This also applies to reading data beyond the SSD's logical block range. According to the NVMe specification, the SSD can either return all-zeros or all-0xFF, depending on the configuration. In terms of performance, depending on the SSD model, we have observed three cases for uninitialized reads: Uninitialized reads can be faster, slower, or equally fast compared to reading initialized data. Benchmarks that read uninitialized data are therefore not meaningful.

SSD State Another reason for obtaining incorrect or inconsistent performance numbers involves disregarding the current state of the SSD. Significant differences in write speed are observable when comparing an empty SSD (best case) with an SSD filled to 100% capacity by small random writes (worst case). In the case of a full SSD, the garbage collector has to do a lot of internal copying to free up empty blocks, which can result in a lower write speed by an order of magnitude. For write-intensive benchmarks, it is therefore crucial to ensure that the SSD state is comparable.

Reproducibility and Representativeness To achieve reproducible benchmark results, the SSD should be erased after every experiment, which involves writing a substantial amount of data. Erasing can be done using the blkdiscard or sanitize commands. Blkdiscard deallocates logical blocks, meaning the mapping in the FTL from logical to physical blocks is deleted. The sanitize command further erases all flash blocks. This means that performance is reproducible, but it is not necessarily representative of all states an SSD can be in. Researchers should also perform prolonged experiments where the entire SSD is overwritten multiple times to reach the steady state and examine performance at various fill levels. Another reason for non-reproducible I/O results can be the OS scheduler moving threads to different CPU cores, which can lead to performance variations. Furthermore, peculiar effects can arise in multi-threaded benchmarks, if all thread-local random number generators share an identical seeding value.[1]

9.3.2 The Strange Case of the IOMMU and Its Root-Complex

IOMMU Overhead The I/O Memory Management Unit (IOMMU) manages direct and secure connection between I/O devices and system memory. It is responsible for remapping physical memory addresses to virtual ones for I/O devices. This enables the system to benefit from hardware-based I/O virtualization. By controlling and restricting access to main memory, the IOMMU can mitigate unauthorized and malicious accesses to memory from other processes or virtual machines through the I/O device.

Much as the previous section noted with software, hardware abstraction also carries a cost. Table 9.2 demonstrates the difference in terms of latency for single read operations is quite small with a difference of only 0.81 µs. However, the number of cycles that is necessary per I/O request takes more than 2k additional cycles, which is 46% more. In our system that can reach 23 MIOPS, this is a substantial number of threads that must be added. Further, we have noticed that our SSDs do not work with SPDK when using the vfio-pci driver, which is required when the IOMMU is enabled.[2]

Root-Complex Limitations In an EPYC Milan (PCIe 4.0) server with 128 PCIe lanes, we encountered a limitation where the PCIe root-complex began to pose a bottleneck at 10 M IOPS. The server contains four PCIe root-complexes, and if more than four SSDs were attached to one complex, performance was limited. In such cases, it is beneficial to increase performance by physically spreading the SSDs across the root-complexes.

Table 9.2 IOMMU latency overhead (at iodepth=1) and cycles per I/O (iodepth=256) on a single thread with 4 KiB reads. Measured with 8 SSD using fio (io_uring with poll + passthrough)

	read latency [us]	cycles / io [k]
IOMMU off	63.96	4.39
IOMMU on	64.76	6.47

[1] Unfortunately, this is the default setting in fio when used together with the numjobs flag.

[2] https://spdk.io/doc/system_configuration.html.

Fig. 9.4 Where is the bug?

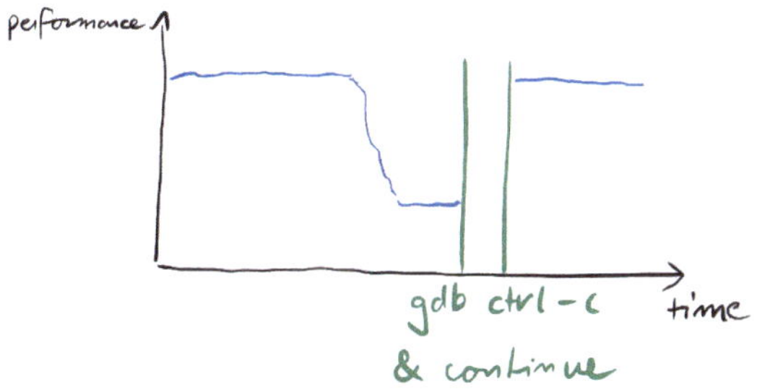

9.3.3 *Too Hot to Handle*

In Fig. 9.4, we visualize a scenario where overall system and I/O performance is initially stable but drops after some time. To investigate, we interrupted the program using the gdb debugger to inspect its internal state, finding no obvious issues. Surprisingly, after continuing execution in the debugger, performance temporarily returned to its original high level. The behavior is reproducible; after a certain period of time, performance plummets once again, only to be rectified by pausing the application in the debugger.

Utilizing the smart commands incorporated in the NVMe protocol for device temperature monitoring, we eventually found out that the root cause is SSD overheating. Consumer-grade SSDs (M.2) do not have active cooling systems, and often not have a heat sink mounted. Enterprise SSDs, in contrast, have a larger form factor and can use the casing as a heat sink, and we have never observed such behavior. This can be verified on SSDs that support the OCP (Open Compute Project) NVM extension, which includes counters for thermal throttling events.

9.3.4 *The Shark*

Another peculiar performance bug emerged during tests of LeanStore with TPC-C workloads. The transaction rate would be stable for a while and then suddenly collapse at seemingly random times. It would then recover over a period of 20–30 seconds and return to full speed. In terms of transaction rate and consequently I/O bandwidth, it would resemble an upside down shark fin, as seen in Fig. 9.5.

Notably, this unusual behavior did not manifest in any other benchmark that used SSDs, such as random read/write micro benchmarks or YCSB-like read/write setups in LeanStore. Also, no such performance decrease was observed when the TPC-C transaction rate was limited or fewer threads were used, which made debugging even harder and seemed to indicate that this was a locking issue. One clue emerged when stopping the execution in the slow part: many threads/tasks were queued to get a single lock. This observation indicated it could be a synchronization issue in the I/O stack of LeanStore. We spent several days reevaluating locking

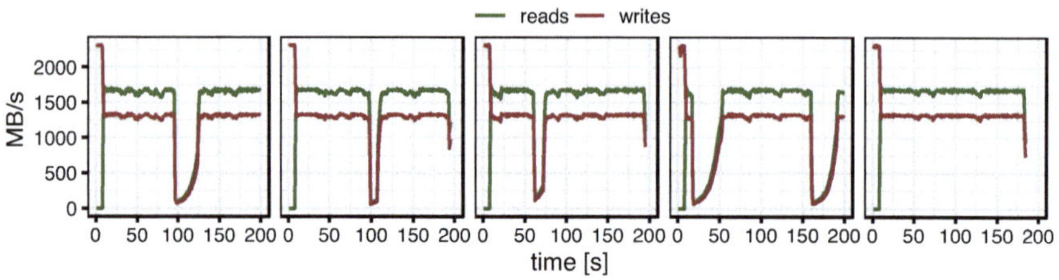

Fig. 9.5 Read and write bandwidth for multiple replays of a TPC-C I/O trace

interactions that could possibly lead to such behavior. However, these observations were symptomatic rather than causal.

To isolate the problem and rule out potential LeanStore issues, we recorded the I/O trace and wrote a program to replay it. To our surprise, when replaying the I/O trace in a minimal, single-threaded application, the issue persisted. Therefore, it was clear that our performance problem had to be due to an SSD issue. Even more surprisingly, after updating the SSD firmware, the previously mentioned "shark fin" performance pattern disappeared, resulting in consistently stable performance.

9.4 I/O in High-Performance Storage Engines

This section outlines the implementation of a high-performance storage engine that can capitalize on the I/O performance detailed in preceding sections. Initially, we will conduct a back of the envelope estimation of the available CPU budget per operation when the SSDs are saturated. With our 96-core AMD Genoa CPU system and eight SSDs, this gives a result of 11.2k cycles/IO (2.7 GHz * 96cores / 23M).

Using io_uring with polling (without passthru, optimization flags, or batching), this would mean 8.6k cycles (or 79 cores) are required just for I/O handling. This leaves us with only 2.6k cycles for all the other database components. This is not a lot, considering we have query processing, index traversal, concurrency control, logging, and page eviction. Given these cycle constraints, it is critical to ensure all components of the database system are well optimized and streamlined.

9.4.1 Visible Without Looking Glass

To build a storage engine that can exploit the high performance of modern NVMe arrays, a fast in-memory system is required. That means spending 93.2% of CPU instructions on *non-useful* work as observed in the Shore system [20] is infeasible. We have solved this with our storage engine LeanStore [1–3, 21, 34, 50], which can handle transactions using an order of magnitude fewer instructions than those used

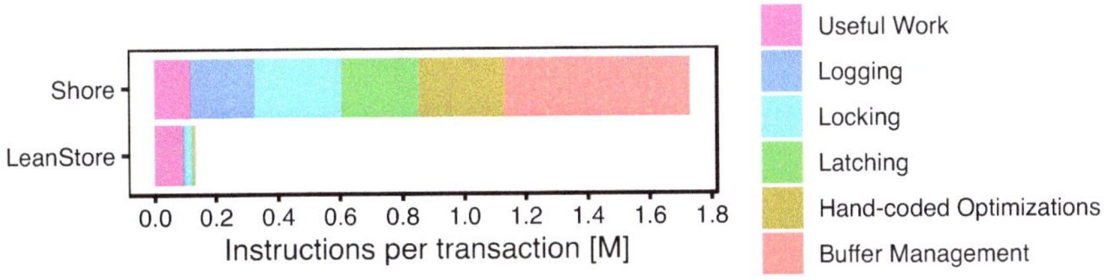

Fig. 9.6 Revisiting OLTP through the looking glass [20], comparing Shore and LeanStore for the in-memory TPC-C neworder transaction

by Shore. In LeanStore, more than 70% of instructions are used for useful work and less than 3% is used for buffer management (Fig. 9.6). The challenge that has to be solved next is to keep the overhead of the non-useful work as small as possible even when data size exceeds the buffer pool.

9.4.2 NVMe-Enabled Performance in Storage Engines

In order to achieve fast performance in out-of-memory workloads with minimal cycles, the following optimizations to the original version of LeanStore were necessary [19]:

- The original LeanStore implementation [34] used a global lock for I/O management. With multiple SSDs, this immediately became the bottleneck. We addressed this issue by introducing a partitioned lock for the whole eviction and I/O path.
- While 16 KiB pages were a suitable size for in-memory workloads, we demonstrated that one should use 4 KiB pages for optimal performance with current SSDs. Although this should theoretically quadruple throughput, it did not significantly increase performance due to subsequent bottlenecks that needed to be addressed as well.
- We implemented numerous CPU optimizations, such as application-level RAID and streamlining the eviction and I/O path, by removing memory allocations and locks.
- We implemented user-space threading to address high thread-oversubscription. This eliminated the need for difficult-to-tune background threads and resulted in a more symmetric and robust system.
- We introduced optional kernel bypassing I/O to maximize CPU efficiency.

Figure 9.7 shows the results for running TPC-C and random lookups on LeanStore on our 92-core PCIe 5.0 platform. When compared to our previous system that utilized eight PCIe 4.0 SSDs and a 64-core CPU, TPC-C performance

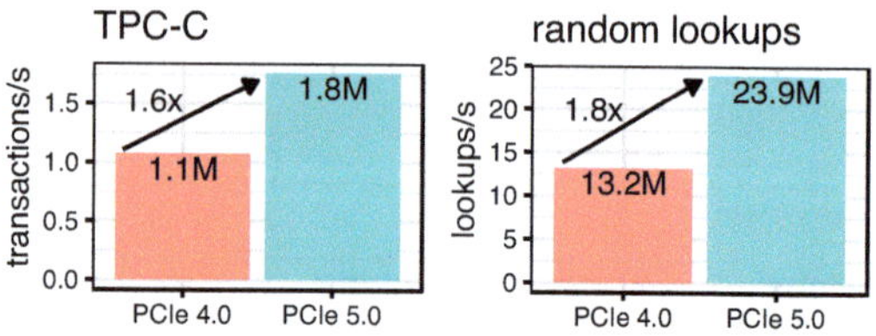

Fig. 9.7 LeanStore performance on 64-core PCIe 5.0 [19] and new 96-core PCIe 5.0 system (16 GB buffer pool, 160 GB data, using SPDK)

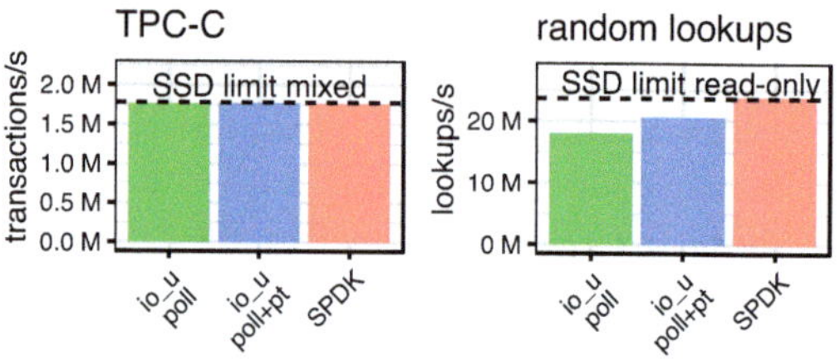

Fig. 9.8 LeanStore maximum performance with optimal number of threads (128 for SPDK, 192 for io_uring backend). pt: io_uring with passthru mode (16 GB buffer pool, 160 GB data)

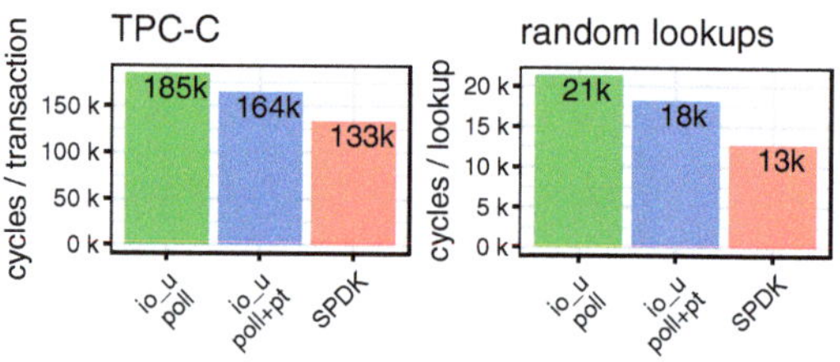

Fig. 9.9 LeanStore cycles per transaction or lookup when using 8 threads. pt: io_uring passthru mode (16 GB buffer pool, 160 GB data)

increased by 1.6x, and random lookups improved by 1.8x. This performance increase exactly matches the increase in single SSD read bandwidth from 1.5M to 2.7M IOPS (1.8x) for the two systems. These results show that with continuing hardware advancements, LeanStore maintains its ability to attain unparalleled out-of-memory performance.

9.4.3 *Exploiting New Kernel Features*

Having implemented these optimizations, we now take a look at recent changes and the new knowledge we have gathered since then. First of all is the new feature provided by io_uring: the passthru mode [23]. In terms of maximum performance, seen in Fig. 9.8, its impact is minimal, as the maximum bandwidth can also be reached without it. The efficiency, as measured by cycles per transaction, does increase when running LeanStore with 8 threads (Fig. 9.9).

The next step would be to use the register buffer flag, discussed in Sect. 9.2.3. This flag is not applicable to the use case of a buffer pool that contains millions of pages. All of these millions of pages would have to be registered with io_uring, which is currently not possible. There appears to be a limit of 16k buffers that can currently be registered. Another approach could be to register a limited number of data buffers that are only used for I/O and then copy the data to the eventual location inside the buffer pool. However, this defeats the purpose and due to the additional memory copy, it would likely perform worse. In situations where the data has to be copied anyway, like when using compression, the flag would be beneficial.

LeanStore employs a symmetric design [19] in which each thread is responsible for all database system tasks, including I/O. This design offers numerous benefits; for I/O, it means that every thread can manage its own requests without any synchronization. It aligns remarkably well with SPDK or, to be more precise, the NVMe protocol. The NVMe protocol allows the creation of multiple queues that can be used independently. io_uring also shares this approach with its queue-pair architecture. In Sect. 9.2.3, we discussed that io_uring profits a lot from submit batching, but batching in such a design is difficult. Assuming 128 threads and a required IO depth of 256 requests to saturate an SSD, on average, only 2 simultaneous requests are required per thread per SSD. There is a difference between SPDK and io_uring. SPDK only profits from batching per SSD, as it reduces aforementioned MMIO calls (see Sect. 9.2.4). io_uring, on the other hand, can handle multiple devices on a single ring instance, which does save system call overhead, but internally also does not help with reducing MMIO calls. However, the system call overhead when using eight SSDs makes batching practically irrelevant.

9.5 Conclusion

Software Can Exploit NVMe Hardware configurations that support tens of millions of I/O operations per second are a reality. These hardware advancements put I/O on the hot path, and the entire system stack must be properly designed to utilize it. The software and the operating system abstraction layers, like page cache and increasingly the file system, become the liming factor, as we have shown in Sect. 9.2. With our storage engine LeanStore, we have shown that it is possible to use the full potential of modern NVMe storage arrays. As a prerequisite to achieve this, a highly efficient buffer manager is needed. We have seen that LeanStore has almost no overhead in in-memory workloads. Optimizing the out-of-memory paths as well has enabled us to saturate even a PCIe 5.0-based system with 23 M IOPS.

Linux is Catching Up While the operating system I/O stack is often the bottleneck, kernel developers are working on catching up and making NVMe performance more widely accessible to system developers. For example, with the introduction of new features like I/O passthru, the gap between kernel interfaces and user space drivers is shrinking.

Novel I/O Abstractions The most efficient way of doing I/O is by removing all abstractions and using user-space NVMe drivers like SPDK. However, this also comes with well-known disadvantages. It is crucial to evaluate for every application if this trade-off is justified, especially with the recent improvements in the kernel. A possible solution is to use an I/O backend like xNVMe [37] that abstracts the specifics of interfaces away and instead allows the usage of all of them.

Acknowledgments This work was funded by the Deutsche Forschungsgemeinschaft (DFG, German Research Foundation) under grant 447457559.

References

1. Alhomssi, A., Haubenschild, M., & Leis, V. (2023). The evolution of leanstore. In *BTW* (Vol. P-331, pp. 259–281).
2. Alhomssi, A., & Leis, V. (2021). Contention and space management in b-trees. In *CIDR*. www.cidrdb.org.
3. Alhomssi, A., & Leis, V. (2023). Scalable and robust snapshot isolation for high-performance storage engines. *Proceedings of the VLDB Endowment, 16*(6), 1426–1438.
4. Axboe, J. (2023). fio - flexible i/o tester.
5. Baumstark, A., Jibril, M. A., & Sattler, K.-U. (2023). Accelerating large table scan using processing-in-memory technology. In *BTW. LNI* (Vol. P-331, pp. 797–814). Gesellschaft für Informatik e.V.
6. Becher, A., Herrmann, A., Wildermann, S., & Teich, J. (2019). Reprovide: Towards utilizing heterogeneous partially reconfigurable architectures for near-memory data processing. In *BTW (Workshops). LNI* (Vol. P-290, pp. 51–70). Gesellschaft für Informatik, Bonn.
7. Bhattacharjee, B., Ross, K. A., Lang, C. A., Mihaila, G. A., & Banikazemi, M. (2011). Enhancing recovery using an SSD buffer pool extension. In *DaMoN* (pp. 10–16).
8. Bjørling, M., Gonzalez, J., & Bonnet, P. (2017). Lightnvm: The linux open-channel SSD subsystem. In *FAST* (pp. 359–374).
9. Canim, M., Mihaila, G. A., Bhattacharjee, B., Ross, K. A., & Lang, C. A. (2010). SSD bufferpool extensions for database systems. *Proceedings of the VLDB Endowment, 3*(2), 1435–1446.
10. Conway, A., Gupta, A., Chidambaram, V., Farach-Colton, M., Spillane, R. P., Tai, A., & Johnson, R. (2020). Splinterdb: Closing the bandwidth gap for nvme key-value stores. In *USENIX Annual Technical Conference* (pp. 49–63).
11. Do, J., Picoli, I. L., Lomet, D. B., & Bonnet, P. (2021). Better database cost/performance via batched I/O on programmable SSD. *The VLDB Journal, 30*(3), 403–424.
12. Du, M., Zhao, Y., & Le, J. (2009). Using flash memory as storage for read-intensive database. In *DBTA* (pp. 472–475).
13. Färber, F., May, N., Lehner, W., Große, P., Müller, I., Rauhe, H., & Dees, J. (2012). The SAP HANA database—an architecture overview. *IEEE Data Engineering Bulletin, 35*(1), 28–33.
14. Lekshmi B. G., Becher, A., Meyer-Wegener, K., Wildermann, S., & Teich, J. (2020). SQL query processing using an integrated fpga-based near-data accelerator in reprovide. In *EDBT* (pp. 639–642). OpenProceedings.org.
15. Götze, P., Baumann, S., & Sattler, K.-U. (2018). An nvm-aware storage layout for analytical workloads. In *ICDE Workshops* (pp. 110–115). New York: IEEE Computer Society.
16. Götze, P., Tharanatha, A. K., & Sattler, K.-U. (2020). Data structure primitives on persistent memory: An evaluation. *CoRR*, abs/2001.02172.
17. Götze, P., van Renen, A., Lersch, L., Leis, V., & Oukid, I. (2018). Data management on non-volatile memory: A perspective. *Datenbank-Spektrum, 18*(3), 171–182.
18. Haas, G., Haubenschild, M., & Leis, V. (2020). Exploiting directly-attached nvme arrays in DBMS. In *CIDR*.
19. Haas, G., & Leis, V. (2023). What modern nvme storage can do, and how to exploit it: High-performance I/O for high-performance storage engines. *Proceedings of the VLDB Endowment, 16*(9), 2090–2102.
20. Harizopoulos, S., Abadi, D. J., Madden, S., & Stonebraker, M. (2008). OLTP through the looking glass, and what we found there. In *SIGMOD Conference* (pp. 981–992). New York: ACM.

21. Haubenschild, M., Sauer, C., Neumann, T., & Leis, V. (2020). Rethinking logging, checkpoints, and recovery for high-performance storage engines. In *SIGMOD Conference* (pp. 877–892). New York: ACM.
22. Jasny, M., Ziegler, T., Kraska, T., Röhm, U., & Binnig, C. (2020). DB4ML—an in-memory database kernel with machine learning support. In *SIGMOD Conference* (pp. 159–173). New York: ACM.
23. Joshi, K., Gupta, A., González, J., Kumar, A., Reddy, K. K., George, A., Lund, S. A. F., & Axboe, J. (2024). I/O passthru: Upstreaming a flexible and efficient I/O path in linux. In *FAST* (pp. 107–121). California: USENIX Association.
24. Kang, W.-H., Lee, S.-W., Moon, B., Kee, Y.-S., & Oh, M. (2014). Durable write cache in flash memory SSD for relational and nosql databases. In *SIGMOD Conference* (pp. 529–540).
25. Kang, W.-H., Lee, S.-W., Moon, B., Oh, G.-H., & Min, C. (2014). Supporting transactional atomicity in flash storage devices. IEEE Data Engineering Bulletin, 37(2), 27–34.
26. Kariuki, J. (2021). What? 80 million I/O per second with a standard 2U Intel®Xeon®system!.
27. Kemper, A., Neumann, T., Funke, F., Leis, V., & Mühe, H. (2012). Hyper: Adapting columnar main-memory data management for transactional AND query processing. *IEEE Data Engineering Bulletin, 35*(1), 46–51.
28. Kumaigorodski, A., Lutz, C., & Markl, V. (2021). Fast CSV loading using gpus and RDMA for in-memory data processing. In *BTW. LNI* (Vol. P-311, pp. 19–38). Bonn: Gesellschaft für Informatik.
29. Lasch, R., Legler, T., May, N., Scheirle, B., & Sattler, K.-U. (2022). Cost modelling for optimal data placement in heterogeneous main memory. *Proceedings of the VLDB Endowment, 15*(11), 2867–2880.
30. Lasch, R., Schulze, R., Legler, T., & Sattler, K.-U. (2021). Workload-driven placement of column-store data structures on DRAM and NVM. In *DaMoN* (pp. 5:1–5:8). New York: ACM.
31. Lee, S.-W., Moon, B., & Park, C. (2009). Advances in flash memory SSD technology for enterprise database applications. In *SIGMOD Conference* (pp. 863–870).
32. Lee, S.-W., Moon, B., Park, C., Kim, J.-M., & Kim, S.-W. (2008). A case for flash memory ssd in enterprise database applications. In *SIGMOD Conference* (pp. 1075–1086).
33. Lee, S., Lerner, A., Ryser, A., Park, K., Jeon, C., Park, J., Song, Y. H., & Cudré-Mauroux, P. (2022). X-SSD: A storage system with native support for database logging and replication. In *SIGMOD Conference* (pp. 988–1002).
34. Leis, V., Haubenschild, M., Kemper, A., & Neumann, T. (2018). Leanstore: In-memory data management beyond main memory. In *ICDE* (pp. 185–196).
35. Lerner, A., & Bonnet, P. (2021). Not your grandpa's SSD: the era of co-designed storage devices. In *SIGMOD Conference* (pp. 2852–2858).
36. Linux Kernel Team. Efficient io with io_uring (2019).
37. Lund, S. A. F., Bonnet, P., Jensen, K. B. A., & González, J. (2022). I/O interface independence with xNVMe. In *SYSTOR* (pp. 108–119). New York: ACM.
38. Neumann, T., Freitag, M. J. (2020). Umbra: A disk-based system with in-memory performance. In *CIDR*.
39. NVM Express Workgroup. (2023). *NVM Command Set Specification*, 1.0 d.
40. Picoli, I. L., Hedam, N., Bonnet, P., & Tözün, P. (2020). Open-channel SSD (what is it good for). In *CIDR*.
41. Pohl, C., & Sattler, K.-U. (2018). Joins in a heterogeneous memory hierarchy: Exploiting high-bandwidth memory. In *DaMoN* (pp. 8:1–8:10). New York: ACM.
42. Pohl, C., Sattler, K.-U., & Graefe, G. (2020). Joins on high-bandwidth memory: a new level in the memory hierarchy. *The VLDB Journal, 29*(2–3), 797–817.
43. Purandare, D. R., Wilcox, P., Litz, H., & Finkelstein, S. (2022). Append is near: Log-based data management on ZNS SSDs. In *CIDR*.
44. Sadoghi, M., Ross, K. A., Canim, M., & Bhattacharjee, B. (2013). Making updates disk-I/O friendly using SSDs. *Proceedings of the VLDB Endowment, 6*(11), 997–1008.
45. Sadoghi, M., Ross, K. A., Canim, M., & Bhattacharjee, B. (2016). Exploiting SSDs in operational multiversion databases. *The VLDB Journal, 25*(5), 651–672.

46. SPDK Team (2023). Storage performance development kit (SPDK).
47. Tu, S., Zheng, W., Kohler, E., Liskov, B., & Madden, S. (2013). Speedy transactions in multicore in-memory databases. In *SOSP*, pp. 18–32. New York: ACM.
48. van Renen, A., Vogel, L., Leis, V., Neumann, T., & Kemper, A. (2020). Building blocks for persistent memory. *The VLDB Journal, 29*(6), 1223–1241.
49. Vogel, L., van Renen, A., Imamura, S., Giceva, J., Neumann, T., & Kemper, A. (2022). Plush: A write-optimized persistent log-structured hash-table. *Proceedings of the VLDB Endowment, 15*(11), 2895–2907.
50. Vöhringer, D. E., & Leis, V. (2023). Write-aware timestamp tracking: Effective and efficient page replacement for modern hardware. *Proceedings of the VLDB Endowment, 16*(11), 3323–3334.
51. Yu, G. X., Markakis, M., Kipf, A., Larson, P.-Å., Minhas, U. F., & Kraska, T. (2022). Treeline: An update-in-place key-value store for modern storage. *Proceedings of the VLDB Endowment, 16*(1), 99–112.
52. Ziegler, T., Binnig, C., & Leis, V. (2022). Scalestore: A fast and cost-efficient storage engine using DRAM, NVMe, and RDMA. In *SIGMOD Conference* (pp. 685–699). New York: ACM.

MIX
Papier aus verantwortungsvollen Quellen
Paper from responsible sources
FSC® C105338

If you have any concerns about our products,
you can contact us on
ProductSafety@springernature.com

In case Publisher is established outside the EU,
the EU authorized representative is:
Springer Nature Customer Service Center GmbH
Europaplatz 3, 69115 Heidelberg, Germany

Printed by Libri Plureos GmbH
in Hamburg, Germany